# HOW TO WRITE A MI££ION

# How to Write a Million

PLOT *by Ansen Dibell*
CHARACTERS & VIEWPOINT *by Orson Scott Card*
DIALOGUE *by Lewis Turco*

**ROBINSON**

**London**

Robinson Publishing Ltd
7, Kensington Church Court
London W8 4SP

*Plot* and *Characters & Viewpoint* first published in the UK
by Robinson Publishing 1990;
*Dialogue* first published in the UK by Robinson Publishing 1991.

This collected edition first published in the UK
by Robinson Publishing Ltd 1995

*Plot* copyright © Ansen Dibell 1988
*Characters & Viewpoint* copyright © Orson Scott Card 1988;
illustrations by Janice Card
*Dialogue* copyright © Lewis Turco 1989
Cover photo of Michael Ridpath by Trevor Leighton

The Authors assert the moral right
to be identified as the authors of these works.

All rights reserved. No part of this publication may be reproduced,
stored in a retrieval system, or transmitted in any form or by any means,
electronic, mechanical, photocopying, recording or otherwise,
without the prior written permission of the publisher.

This book is sold subject to the condition that it shall not,
by way of trade or otherwise, be lent, re-sold, hired out
or otherwise circulated without the publisher's prior consent
in any form of binding or cover other than that in which it is published
and without a similar condition including this condition
being imposed on the subsequent purchaser.

A copy of the British Library Cataloguing in Publication Data
for this title is available from the British Library.

ISBN 1-85487-367-9

Printed and bound in the EC

10   9   8   7   6   5

# *FOREWORD*

## by Michael Ridpath

In the summer of 1990 I decided that I wanted to start writing. I had the means (a computer), I had a little time, and I had the desire to do something a little more creative than watching TV. So, being that sort of chap, I bought half a dozen books on the subject. The first few I read gave some thoughts on the wonders of being a writer, ran over some basic techniques, discussed Hemingway and Faulkner, and suggested some exercises which ranged from the interesting to the inane. They gave me some ideas to while away a few hours whilst making it perfectly clear that someone like me would never actually be able to complete a book, let alone get it published.

Then I turned to the two Writer's Workshop books, *Characters & Viewpoint* and *Plot*. Suddenly my interest was quickened. These books were about writing real books and stories, the sort which are all around us, which people read every day. They discussed the practicalities of making characters come to life, of planning and then controlling a plot. And, what was most important, they made me think that writing a book could be fun, something that even I could do, and something I would enjoy. Somehow the nitty gritty of how to put a book together seemed to make the whole activity much more exciting than inspirational thoughts on the trials and tribulations of being an author.

I couldn't wait to get started. But, I thought, I had better pace myself, write a few scenes, a short story or two. My first exercise was to write the opening scene of a novel. I wrote about the most exciting thing I could think of that had happened to me (coping with a large bond trade that went wrong), and then exaggerated it a bit.

After half an hour of clumsy tapping, I was hooked. Bugger the exercises, I wanted to write a whole book! So, I started to plan, much of it whilst munching a sandwich in a quiet courtyard just behind the Bank of England. Planning was difficult. I spent several weeks worrying over character and plot, and practical tips eked from the pages of my two Writer's Workshop books were invaluable.

Eventually, I began writing. Much to my surprise, a year later I actually completed a draft. I showed it to my wife and friends. The criticisms came flooding back: characters too superficial, no sense of place, too many clichés in character as well as metaphor, not enough twists in the plot, the ending was no good, and many more. Depressed, I put the writing to one side.

But I missed it. Several months later, I dug my manuscript out and reread it. It wasn't all bad, and I could see what my circle of critics meant – I even agreed with them on most things. So, I set out to solve the problems. Once again the Writer's Workshop books were useful. How could I make my hero more sympathetic? How could I pace the plot better? The existing ending had to go entirely, what would work as a replacement? I found hints and clues which eventually led to answers.

To work again. Another draft, more criticism, yet another draft, and by the autumn of 1993 I had a book which was about as good as it was going to get. I wrote a synopsis and sent it off to some agents together with a couple of chapters.

I was fully prepared for a rejection. I knew the odds were against finding a publisher for a first novel, however good, but I was willing to persevere, working my way down a long list of agents. But even if the book were never published the three years of hard work were well worthwhile. I had enjoyed writing it, and my wife and friends had, eventually, enjoyed reading it.

I was lucky. The second agent on my list, Carole Blake of Blake Friedmann, liked my book. She sent it to a number of publishers with an enthusiastic note. Five of them began bidding against each other, and within a month I had sold *Free to Trade* * to Heinemann for an advance which exceeded all my expectations. Carole subsequently sold the rights to thirteen countries. I can now afford to write during the day rather than in odd corners of the evening or weekend.

It would be wrong to pretend that publication isn't important; of course we all want to see our books in bookshops. But there is so

---

* *Free to Trade* is published by Heinemann, January 1995, price £10.00.

much more about the process of writing a book that is interesting, rewarding and just plain fun, which I believe is more important. I am convinced that it is the enjoyment of the writing process, rather than a desire for publication or an attempt to write what sells, which leads in the end to the creation of a good book.

These books helped me understand something of this process, and made me realize it was something I wanted to do. I have subsequently read *Dialogue, Setting* and *Revision*,* all of which have an equally down to earth approach to the problems every writer faces. Read these books. Enjoy them. And start writing. It's fun!

* *Revision* is also available from Robinson Publishing Ltd

# PLOT

BY

*ANSEN DIBELL*

Ansen Dibell is the pen name of a teacher, writer and editor whose five-novel science fiction series *The Rule of One* has been published internationally. She began her career delivering phone books door to door.

She now calls herself a writing *coach*: "Many people contend that creativity can't be taught. Maybe not. But, like any other sophisticated performance skill – like playing the violin or bowling for dollars – it certainly can be *coached*."

# CONTENTS

| Introduction | COMING TO PLOT THE HARD WAY | 1 |
|---|---|---|
| Chapter 1 | WHAT IS PLOT? | 5 |
| Chapter 2 | GRAND OPENINGS | 19 |
| Chapter 3 | WOULD YOU TRUST A VIEWPOINT WITH SHIFTY EYES? | 30 |
| Chapter 4 | "SHUT UP!" HE EXPLAINED—HANDLING EXPOSITION | 43 |
| Chapter 5 | EARLY MIDDLES: NEW DIRECTIONS AND SUBPLOTS | 58 |
| Chapter 6 | BUILDING THE BIG SCENES: SET-PIECES | 69 |
| Chapter 7 | HARNESSING MELODRAMA | 81 |

Chapter 8    **PATTERNS, MIRRORS,
             AND ECHOES**              94

Chapter 9    **PACING, TRANSITIONS,
             FLASHES, AND FRAMES**     111

Chapter 10   **WHEN YOU COME TO
             THE END, STOP**           120

Chapter 11   **BEYOND PLOT**          144

             **INDEX**                 164

# INTRODUCTION

# COMING TO PLOT THE HARD WAY

If you're like me and most of the writers I've known over the years in writers' groups, at conferences and in classes, you're coming to plot the hard way. A scene, a bit of dialogue, a character sets you happily scribbling or keyboarding away. And then, too often, something happens. The story starts to slow and go sour, dead ending in frustrated scraps of revision. It's eventually tossed with the rest of the might-have-beens—in the bottom of your sock drawer or even in the wastebasket.

Or maybe you want to write a story based on real life and real incidents. That should be a cinch, right? All the events really happened; the characters are people you know. Nothing easier than writing it all down, you think confidently. Just change the names and locale, and you're set.

But then the events, so compelling when they happened and when you thought about them, bog down in detail and explanations. The familiar people you felt certain would be enthralling characters turn into jabbering trolls.

You feel the silent inner thud that tells you that truth—or, more accurately, fact-based fiction—is no more a guarantee against writing dull, unconvincing tales than is inventing the whole thing from the start.

Begin to sound familiar yet?

Have you ever had what seemed like a vivid story idea that fizzled out as soon as you got your first words on paper? Or have you written a story you thought was great and had it come back with a rejection slip commenting that it "seemed distant and uninvolving"? What's *distant*, for heaven's sake? What do you do now?

Or you're starting your second novel while the first one is in the mail, and somewhere about page 90 you find one of your subplots is becoming a lot more interesting than your main plot. It seems to want to take over the whole book. You get bored whenever you have to return to the main character's problems, which now seem to you about as dramatic as watching ice cream melt.

Or you've written and sold some fiction by good gut instinct. And now the problem arises: how did you do it before? And how can you do it again? You want to bring your unconscious craft under greater conscious control, so that you can make choices, not just blunder through until something goes wrong, or right.

Are you one of the writers whose instincts are better than their knowledge, who write merrily along when inspiration strikes and bog down in despair when inspiration inevitably fails?

If this list of woes sounds at all familiar, you're in good company.

Melville wrote a large chunk of *Moby Dick* thinking that the pivotal figure was going to be a man named (I'm not kidding) Bulkington. Read the first couple of chapters and notice all the build-up about Bulkington, who's then abruptly washed overboard the first day the *Pequod* leaves harbor and is never heard of again. What happened? Melville had discovered a character named Ahab. Melville wasn't a tidy writer: the original beginning is still there. Alas, poor Bulkington.

Similarly, J. R. R. Tolkien has confessed that about a third of the way through *The Fellowship of the Ring*, some ruffian named Strider confronted the hobbits in an inn, and Tolkien was in despair. He didn't know who Strider was, where the book was going, or what to write next. Strider turns out to be no lesser person than Aragorn, the unrecognized and uncrowned king of all the forces of good, whose restoration to rule is, along with the destruction of the evil ring, the engine that moves the plot of the whole massive trilogy, *The Lord of the Rings*.

Neither Melville nor Tolkien knew what he was getting into,

going in. And neither was, at that point, a beginner.

It happens, one time or another, to everybody. Fiction is so nearly like life that a good fiction nearly always changes under your hands, takes on an atmosphere, a feel, a will of its own. Your subconscious is sending you smoke signals: ideas seem to come out of nowhere and flash onto the page. Sometimes, as with Ahab and Strider, that's for the good, and a wise, experienced writer recognizes that what was imagined along the way is stronger than what was originally intended. But sometimes, the turning of the material into its own shape can be destructive, and the story collapses into mismatched fragments.

The subconscious sends up, not only smoke signals, but smoke screens that can obscure, distort, and sometimes destroy your vision of what you're trying to create.

You can make outlines and try to lock out that kind of change. But you know, and I know, that writing is as much a process of discovery as it is one of invention, and the more serious you are about your writing and the more complex the story you're trying to tell, the more likely it is to start creating itself in unexpected ways.

Unfortunately, the inevitable flip side is that the story is also much more likely to take a quick dive into the sock drawer, unless you can identify what's going wrong and choose an effective strategy for coping with it.

There are really two problems, then: creating plot, and controlling plot. In your first tries at fiction, whether short stories or novels, you're apt to be coping more with the creating part of the problem. The more experienced you are, the more apt you are to be dealing with the difficulties of controlling plot—which sometimes involves simply getting out of the plot's way and discovering your Strider, your Ahab, your own special story.

Whatever stage you're at now, it's important to recognize that all the false starts, the fizzled conclusions, the saggy, random middles, the corners you paint your characters into, and all the rest of the trolls that pop up from under what seemed safe bridges are a normal part of fiction writing. One of the writers' corollaries to Murphy's Law should read: *Every Plot Starts to Go Wrong Just After the First Big Scene*. The exceptions to this rule, in a writing life, you could fold into an average-size paper airplane.

Expect it, accept it. Any story worth writing is going to bring problems, for you as well as for your characters. As in fiction, the interesting part will be how those problems get solved.

Meeting a problem only means you're smart enough to know one when you see one: it's not a short-cut to the sock drawer. Don't give up. When initial inspiration and enthusiasm sag, that's when craft and experience can get you rolling again. Whatever doesn't kill your story dead in its tracks is likely to make it, and you, stronger.

There's life after the sock drawer—and maybe life *in* it for stories you gave up on too soon. There are ways to create, fix, steer, and discover plots—ways which, over a writing life, you'd eventually puzzle out for yourself. They aren't laws. They're an array of choices, things to try, once you've put a name to the particular problem your story is facing *now*.

That's what this book is about: learning to put a name to the problem and then deciding which, of the whole array of possible choices, is the one that's appropriate for *your* story, whether short fiction or long.

Whether you're writing fact-based fiction or spinning the whole thing out of your head, you have the responsibility of creating a satisfying, self-consistent, independent world and making it all come alive on the page.

Other writers have evolved methods of making worlds out of words. You can use them too.

# CHAPTER 1

# WHAT IS PLOT?

THE COMMON DEFINITION OF PLOT is that it's whatever happens in a story. That's useful when talking about completed stories, but when we're considering stories being written, it's about as useful as saying that a birthday cake is a large baked confection with frosting and candles. It doesn't tell you how to make one.

Plot is built of significant events in a given story—significant because they have important consequences. Taking a shower isn't necessarily plot, or braiding one's hair, or opening a door. Let's call them incidents. They happen, but they don't lead to anything much. No important consequences.

But if the character is Rapunzel, and the hair is what's going to let the prince climb to her window, braiding her hair is a crucial action. If the character is Bluebeard's newest wife, opening the forbidden door which reveals the corpses of her predecessors is a pivotal point. Taking a shower is, in *Psycho*, considerably more dramatic and shocking than the theft of a large sum of money, both in itself and in terms of its later repercussions. By the way they're weighted and presented, by what they lead to, these events are transformed from incident to plot.

A grammar school play in which a little girl dresses up in a frame of chickenwire and canvas to portray a ham, representing Pork, could be trivial, a mere incident; but in Harper Lee's *To Kill a Mockingbird*, the chickenwire costume is what prevents Scout Finch from being stabbed by a man with a murderous grudge against her lawyer father.

The wearing of the costume has important consequences and makes a meaningful difference in the story's fictional world.

It's a cause that has significant effects. Cause and effect: that's what makes plot.

## The Border of Actuality

Plot is the things characters do, feel, think, or say, that make a difference to what comes afterward.

If you once thought about dying your hair pink but never acted on the thought, that tells something about your psychology, but it's not a potential story plot. If you really went ahead and *did* it, that not only tells about your psychology but creates repercussions, like a stone tossed in a pond. *That* might become the basis for a story like Fitzgerald's "Bernice Bobs Her Hair."

Thought or emotion crosses the line into plot when it becomes action and causes reactions. Until then, attitudes, however interesting in themselves, are just potential, just cloudy possibilities. They're static. They're not going anywhere. Nothing comes of them.

No thought, in and of itself, is plot. No action, however dramatic, is plot if the story would have been about the same if it hadn't happened at all. Any action, however seemingly trivial, can be vital and memorable if it has significant consequences and changes the story's outcome.

Plotting is a way of looking at things. It's a way of deciding what's important and then *showing* it to be important through the way you construct and connect the major events of your story. It's the way you show things mattering.

## What's at Stake?

For a reader to care about your story, there has to be something at stake—something of value to gain, something of value to be lost. Paul Boles, in his book *Storycrafting*, called it "wrestling," and I like that image because, unlike "theme" or "message," it doesn't imply something that could be painted on a billboard or winkled out of a fortune cookie. Wrestling is something specific happening: two strong forces are meeting, one of them triumphing over the other—for better or for worse.

One of the forces may be external to the main character (protagonist): a villain, an opponent, a set of circumstances, a feature of the environment or of the landscape. Or both forces may be within the protagonist: the fear of doing something wrestling with the need to do it; a sense of injury wrestling with love or admiration, as with a person of any age trying to come to terms with a demanding parent.

Bringing out the importance of seemingly small things leads to subtlety, drama; showing large things grappling and clashing is melodrama, of which more in Chapter 7.

You have to convince the reader not only that something is happening, but that what's happening matters intensely—not just to the writer, but to the characters involved.

In Golding's *Lord of the Flies*, what's at stake is survival itself. A group of boys are trying to stay alive, solely by their own efforts, on an otherwise uninhabited tropical island. At least, that's the external form of their struggle. Internally, it's the battle between fear and courage, distrust of the unknown and the will to find out, as played out within individual characters like the protagonist, Ralph; visionary Simon; and Jack, leader of the hunters. It's not only survival at stake, but a particular, civilized kind of survival.

In other words, there can be an outer plot and an inner one which in some sense mirrors and reinforces it, or conflicts and contrasts with it. Or either outer plot or inner plot may stand alone as the main focus of the necessary struggle played out in actions, through scenes.

## MAKING A SCENE

If you've been to a writer's conference or a creative writing class, or if you've read any books on fiction writing, you've already heard the major principle that older writers are always telling younger writers: SHOW, DON'T TELL. As I hope I've *shown* (and maybe told, a little: but this isn't fiction), it's an important concept that's *very* risky not to take very seriously indeed.

Showing, in fiction, means creating scenes. You have to be able to cast your ideas in terms of something happening, people talking and doing, an event going on while the reader reads. If you're not writing scenes, you may be writing fine essays, or speeches, or sermons—but you're not writing fiction.

A definition: A *scene* is one connected and sequential action, together with its embedded description and background material. It seems to happen just as if a reader were watching and listening to it happen. It's built on talk and action. It's dramatized, *shown*, rather than being summarized or talked about. In some ways, it's like a little independent story; some short stories, in fact, are all one single scene.

A scene isn't a random stretch of action. It arises for a reason, and it's going somewhere. It has meaning. It has a point: at least one thing that needs to be shown or established at that spot in a story. That can be something as basic as the fact that your main character wants, this once, to walk his dog in peace without being pestered by an amorous neighbor or something as subtle as your main character's realization that the tolerance she has prided herself on is really just a mask for indifference. Attitudes turning into motives, meeting resistance, creating conflict, and leading to consequences—becoming plot.

A scene can convey many things: moods, attitudes, a sense of place and time, an anticipation of what's to come, a reflection of what's past. But first and foremost, a scene must advance the plot and demonstrate the characters. You may not fully know what a given scene's job is, whether simple or complex, until you've written it. You may need to go back then and cut away the things that would mislead a reader, and add things to support, lead into, and highlight that scene's special chores in the context of the whole story. But when the story is finished, no matter how many rewrites it takes, you ought to be able to name to yourself what each scene brought out, how it developed the characters, how it showed action or led toward consequences.

Scenes can be long or short—just a paragraph, or a dozen

pages or more. Creating scenes means finding ways for your story to show itself, rather than ways for you to *tell* it.

## IS IT A FAIR FIGHT?

Your story's scenes are going to be the specific stages by which your main character's motivations are enacted against opposition, internal or external or both. A motivation against no opposition is boring. How somebody always got everything he wanted, succeeded in every task, won every girl in sight, and never met a comeuppance, wouldn't have any drama. A chronicle of Don Juan's amorous exploits would be dull (even if pornographically dull) without the avenging paternal statue to send the don gibbering off to a well-deserved damnation.

Likewise, opposition without determined contrary motivation, pure victimization, is not only dull, but depressing. This is true even when, as with Oedipus and with Romeo and Juliet, the protagonist's motivation ultimately ends in tragedy or unsuccess. The protagonist of Lovecraft's "The Shadow Over Innsmouth" may end up becoming a part of the horror he tried to escape; Ahab may be the victim of the White Whale he so desired to destroy; but each fought all the way through the shadows into the eventual dark.

A narrative of Dracula's slaughters during the centuries before he met his determined and ultimately successful adversaries, Van Helsing and the thoroughly modern Mina, would be about as engrossing as feeding time at the zoo. Dracula is pure appetite, and his victims merely food, if there is no involving battle between predator and prey. Incidentally, Ann Rice's effective reinventions of the vampire legends (the series *The Vampire Chronicles*) concentrate on the aspirations of the vampires themselves as individuals, and dwell very little on the neck-biting or on their victims. The resulting stories, because the vampires are the protagonists, tend to be surprisingly upbeat in spite of the implied body count.

# Bambi Meets Godzilla: *a Cautionary Tale*

Some of you may have seen or heard about a short satirical film called *Bambi Meets Godzilla*. While the opening credits are rolling, we see the terminally cute little fawn nibbling and gamboling in a leafy clearing. Then a big reptilian foot comes down and squashes him. Splat. End of movie. It's startling and funny, in a gruesome sort of way, the first time. But a whole hour of build-up, followed by that expressive splat? A whole novel, even? It would be dreadful.

Anytime you're tempted to write a pure-victim story, in which the protagonist doesn't have a chance, think about *Bambi Meets Godzilla* and try something else.

# *An Even Battle Is More Fun to Watch*

Whether the ending is happy or unhappy in the traditional sense, any story needs to be founded on an effective and strongly-felt conflict, in which the opposing forces—whether people, ideas, attitudes, or a mix—are at least fairly evenly matched, enough so that the final outcome is in doubt. If anything, the forces opposing the protagonist ought to seem the stronger, to create drama and suspense. But not an utter mismatch.

Oedipus was doomed from the beginning; but he didn't know it, and he was fighting all the way. The emphasis was on the fighting, not on the doom. That's what makes the fighting, the wrestling, become engrossing narrative.

It's been said that happy families don't make good stories. Only unhappy families, or people who for whatever reason are discontented with their current circumstances, give rise to good fiction. If Scarlett O'Hara had easily forgotten Ashley and been rapturously married to an easily domesticated Rhett Butler early in the novel, if the Civil War hadn't intruded to complicate their unvarying domestic bliss, if their child had grown happily into adolescence and beyond, who would want to read *Gone With the Wind*?

Struggle, conflict, dissatisfaction, aspiration, choice: these are the basis of effective plots.

# HOW TO TEST A STORY IDEA

If you're like most of the writers I've run into, you have more story ideas than you know what to do with. They're popping into your mind faster than you can jot them down in your handy bedside notebook.

And how could it be otherwise? Things have been happening to you, and to everybody you know, all your life. You've been reading, and absorbing stories, almost that long. The newspapers and the evening news offer conflicts galore, and memorable people, events of apparent importance. Once you've been writing awhile, people will start forcing stories on you, claiming that they were always going to write them themselves but somehow never got the time. They'll insist the stories are just the thing for your next fiction, and you may even agree with them.

There is no shortage of story ideas that might even *become* stories in the right hands.

Truman Capote took a news account of a brutal and apparently senseless multiple murder and developed it into the nonfiction novel, *In Cold Blood*. Mary Shelley's *Frankenstein* was reportedly based on an alarmingly vivid dream. I took a speculation on the nature of emotion, combined it with some unpleasant childhood memories, and found in the mix the basis for a five-book science fiction series.

Story ideas are everywhere. Finding ideas isn't the problem.

Your problem is every writer's problem: figuring out which, of this barrage of fragmentary ideas, is a potential story; and, even more difficult, a story *you* care about and can tell well.

There are four basic questions you should ask of any new story idea you come up with to decide whether or not it's ready to be developed, or whether it needs to mature awhile longer in your notebook.

## 1. Is It Your Story to Tell?

All ideas can't become stories *for you*. I could no more write a story about magic than I could sprout wings, or roots. I've realized that, on some fundamental level, I don't believe in magic. Although I heartily enjoy reading stories about witches and occult happenings, I can't really imagine magic and don't take it seriously, not with the fundamental seriousness needed to write convincingly.

I'm interested, I'm willing to play that game with another writer for awhile; but I don't *really care*. Not about magic, anyway.

And most of the ideas that come to you, from whatever source, are going to be like that. They won't be things of profound importance to *you*. And if they're not, how are you going to persuade a reader to care about them? It will all be forced, mechanical, intellectualized, unconvincing. That's even more true if they are things you uncomfortably think you *ought* to care about, like cruel parents, faithless lovers, The Bomb, World Hunger, or the Heartbreak of Psoriasis.

I think that's what the traditional advice to "write what you know" really means: to choose things that matter enormously to you, things you have a stake in settling, at least on paper.

I've never been aboard a spaceship, but I've lived in cramped quarters, and I can project an experience I've known on one I've only imagined. So I can honestly say that I know what it *could* be like to be the sole crew of a one-man scout ship traveling on a long haul between the stars. And I care how it would feel: it seems worth trying to imagine myself into. I've never been a serious sculptor, but I know something of the way any artist can get lost in his work—perfectly normal, experienced from the inside, but often laughably odd, observed from the outside. So I was able to write, with conviction, a story about a sculptor who carves bas-relief horses out of botched tombstones she calls "meat" and who loses track of the hours and even the days.

I'm not saying that these were the most wonderful story ideas ever concocted, just that they were *my* stories to tell. They had a special resonance. I could imagine my way into them, from things I've known about, first-hand. And they had a dynamic: they seemed to be going somewhere from the first moment they came into my head. They felt as if they had little hooks built in that refused to let go until I had the whole puzzle solved, the thing written in the form it seemed to want to go into.

Most often these valid, dynamic story ideas won't be things

that you already know and have settled. Settled things make for explanations, not for absorbing fiction. Instead, they'll be situations or people or memories that are troubling you, things you want, for yourself, to work out and understand. Explorations, not explanations.

That's the first criterion: *Is this something I really care about, something I partly understand, something that seems to want working out?*

## 2. Is It Too Personal for Readers to Become Involved With?

The second criterion has to do with the purpose of writing. Partly, it's self-expression. But partly—and increasingly, the more and the longer you write—it's communication. You want what you say to reach, and move, a reader. You want to share the exploration. You want to have fun writing your story so that readers can have fun reading it. Maybe you even want it to sell, and to help you become famous. Those are valid reasons too, provided they're not the main or the only ones. (If the results are more important to you than the process, if you don't want to write but only *to have written*, you're in trouble.)

So the second thing you need to ask yourself, about any story idea, is whether it's something that's *too* personal, something that's very important to you but would justifiably bore a stranger sitting next to you on a cross-country bus.

Some experience is too close to us. We feel deep emotion about it, but haven't digested it yet and aren't able to put it in perspective for somebody else to view. Or maybe it's too exotic, like a specialist on the intimate habits of the Amazonian tree snail assuming the subject is going to be fascinating to vast numbers of people.

Personal blind spots.

It's understandable, if mildly tedious, from people waving around pictures of their kids or wanting us to pore through snapshots from their vacations or sit through their home movies of the family washing the dog. From a writer, it's unforgivable— and probably unpublishable.

For such highly personal subjects, the context that would make them meaningful would just take too much explaining for somebody else to understand.

That's a particular problem, by the way, with autobiographical or fact-based fiction. You have to be able to distance it. You not only have to care about it but care just the right way, ruthlessly cutting this incident, changing this character, altering this reaction in the interests of good fiction, regardless of what *really* happened. You have to be, in some meaningful sense, *free* of it before you're ready to write about it. You have to be willing to look at it through a stranger's eyes—the eyes of your potential readers.

But don't underestimate your own experiences as a source of story ideas, either. Tiny, vivid impressions—the feel of new sneakers, sunlight through a colored window, getting up in the middle of the night when it's dark and scary, being the only pedestrian on an empty street—have been the basis of wonderful, imaginative short stories by Ray Bradbury. Coveting an overcoat was the basis of a classic story by Gogol. A chickenwire costume can be life-saving armor. Small things can have immense impact, if you give them a context that brings out their importance.

Your own experience is an inexhaustible mine of fiction ideas, provided only that you can make readers see the experience as important and applicable to their own lives.

You can never know this for sure. You can only recognize the problem and do your best to strike a balance between the personal and the universal. After that, the story has to take its chances, as all stories must.

And always bring, to whatever you write, everything you've known, felt, experienced, imagined. Like Tolkien's Elves of Lorien, put something of what you love in everything you make. If you're cynical or want to escape sentimentality, put in something that you loathe, too. Such first-hand direct experience is the main and invaluable source of the kind of immediately convincing, personal, vivid details that flesh out a plot and make it seem real to a reader.

Dickens, in particular, was a master of this. Joseph Heller's

*Catch-22* is another good source for precisely observed detail. Read some of these authors' work and learn the kind of specific detail you should be observing in daily life and jotting in your notebook for later use in fiction—a face, a phrase, a scene. Sometimes the simplest, most personal things are those that can speak direct to the heart.

And the job of distinguishing between the merely personal and the vividly personal is one nobody can do but you.

So your second criterion should be: *Can I work with this idea in a caring but uncompromising way to make it meaningful to somebody else?*

### 3. Is It Going Somewhere?

The third criterion has to do with the nature of the material itself. Supposing the first two criteria have been met, is this an idea with a dynamic? Has it got an engine, or could you put one into it? You could attach a motor to a tree, but it wouldn't go very far. A motor-powered bathtub is still a bathtub.

Does your idea divide itself into a vivid opening, one or more specific developments, and a solid ending? Can you block out in your mind a beginning scene, intermediate scenes, a final confrontation or resolution of some kind?

It doesn't matter if the actual scenes you end up writing are different from the ones you imagine at first. The important thing is that the subject you care about, the subject you think you can make immediate and important to readers, lends itself to being cast into scenes of any kind.

Make a poster and put it up where you write: PLOT IS A VERB.

If what you're writing is nounish or adjectival, a thing or a description, or if it's essentially a lecture or an essay, it's going to be static. It may still be a story, but a relatively formless one aimed at a narrow spectrum of readers. (Nonplot methods of storytelling will be discussed in Chapter 11.) If your story happens over a period of years, with nothing much happening in between, and if you can't see a way to compress the action into a sin-

gle compact tale, even one as long as a novel, you'll have to split
out a smaller piece of it to be your story. If it involves a vast number of people or several major changes of locale, it may be a novel, but not a short story. If it's all beginning, a problem you can
show but not resolve to give the story a conclusion (even an unhappy one), it's not going to work. If it's a sudden turn of events
that nothing seems to lead into, like lightning in the middle of a
bullfight, pure ending, it won't make satisfying reading.

Ask yourself, *Can I dramatize this in a series of scenes with a minimum of explanation? Does it have a plot, or can I create a plot for it?*

## 4. What's at Stake?

Finally, ask yourself: *Is there something quite specific and vital at
stake—not just to me, but to one or more of the characters involved?* Ask
yourself what the central conflict is, the struggle that's the basis
of plot. Ask yourself how you can *show*, rather than tell, why this
is so important to the character, make the reader understand,
empathize, and care about what happens.

If you're writing experimental or literary fiction, you can allow yourself a little more latitude about what's at stake. It can be
the impact of a memory of aesthetic ecstasy experienced in a
time of artistic dryness, as in Thomas Mann's *Death in Venice*. It
can be the downward progress of a deteriorating, obsessive consciousness, as in Poe's "The Fall of the House of Usher." That it's
harder to make such things seem vital issues to the general reader doesn't mean they're not worth doing. But neither does it
mean that you can ignore the issue and just have meandering ruminations about Life and the World.

It's quite possible to make bread with something other than
crushed grain and produce food that's tasty, nutritious, and solid enough so that you know you've eaten something. But whatever your fondness for carrot cake or corn muffins, it's plain old
bread, plot, that's been part of human culture since the beginnings of things. We know plot when we meet it: it's in our bones.
Maybe even in our genes. We say, "But what's it *about*?" and ex-

pect a reasonably concise answer. We want verb bread or we're sure we'll be hungry an hour later.

Any fiction, however literary, still has to possess some dynamic tension, even if it's one of irony, or a surprising contrast. Something has to be seen to matter, and to change—even in a mood piece. The story has to move. If you choose not to have traditional plot, you're going to have to work twice as hard to make your chosen alternate work as compellingly.

If, however, you're writing mainstream or genre fiction intended for a wide readership, it's absolutely crucial that you have and develop a plot and that something quite concrete and definite be at issue. It's what your story is going to be perceived to be "about." Your protagonist wants to gain possession of a ruby approximately the size of New Jersey, become a first-class hockey player, escape from an unsympathetic spouse, get one word of praise from a stern and disapproving parent, or rescue turtles from the zoo and set them free in the all-forgiving sea.

Ideally, you should be able to express the core plot in a sentence or two, in about the same space and style as program listings in *TV Guide*. In fact, it might help to study a few issues of *TV Guide* and one of the several paperback guides to movies on TV, and see how such capsule summaries are done. Practice writing a few about things you've read recently. ("The police chief of a New England vacation community, although terrified of the ocean, sets out to destroy a huge killer shark"—*Jaws*; "A group of British schoolboys, attempting to survive after their plane crashlands on a tropical island, begin reverting to savagery"—*Lord of the Flies*.)

See how brief and direct you can make your summaries. The basic plot of a story (unlike its meaning) ought to be directly expressible in very few words, though playing it out in scenes may take a dozen or a thousand pages.

If the summary of your own story turns out to be one you haven't already seen fifty times, so much the better. If not, don't worry: all the love stories haven't yet been written, nor anything close. And there will be growing-up stories as long as there are people. Some topics, handled in a fresh way, are inexhaustible.

# READY, STEADY, GO!

If you test your ideas against these four criteria, a lot will be tossed out, or saved in your handy notebook for later. Don't let that
upset you. There are a lot more where they came from, and
some of them will pass the test with bells ringing and flags flying.

   All you need is one solid story idea at a time to keep writing
productively, successfully, your whole life. Use these criteria
and you'll have the confidence of knowing you're starting with
good material from the very beginning, material worth the
thought and energy of developing, stories that have the potential of reaching readers. You'll hardly be able to wait to start
working out your ideas on paper, embodying them in scenes, listening to your characters talk.

   Don't wait.
   Start now.

# CHAPTER 2

# GRAND OPENINGS

YOU HAVE A STORY IDEA. You've tested it with the four questions to make sure it's basically sound. You've decided whether it seems to want to be long or short fiction. Now you're going to have to people and dramatize it. How do you start?

The first thing to realize is that generally you're *not* going to begin at the beginning. Your story's start, the actual words that begin the narrative, will be a good way along in the progress of the events you're imagining.

The Greeks, as translated by the Romans, called it *in medias res*: in the middle of things. Starting there, in the middle of things, is even more necessary if your story is going to have negative motivation—that is, if it's one in which your chief character, the protagonist, is reacting against something that has happened. Stories arising from reactions have a past that will try to encumber the story's beginning, if you let it.

That kind of built-in past is called 'exposition'—the necessary explanations that are needed to understand what's going on *now*. Because exposition is, of its nature, telling rather than showing, it's intrinsically less dramatic than a scene. So it needs careful handling.

Maybe you're thinking, Well, I'll avoid the problem of handling exposition by going back to the very beginning of things, when the people involved first met, before there were any problems between them, so there will be no need of background material.

NO!

I say "No" so strongly because exposition very seldom makes good plot. It turns into an explanation. Nothing is happening. Long stretches of exposition tend to get boring very, very fast. I'll talk in more detail about handling exposition in Chapter 4. For now, know that however you handle it, you should do everything possible to avoid encumbering your beginnings with it.

## Departure from a Norm

If what you're trying to show is a change from a pre-existing norm (contrasting before/after or then/now), and that norm is really vital to what is going to happen, you should demonstrate that norm in the briefest possible space, as something already being departed from. A paragraph or two, at most, in a short story; a page or two, in a novel. And neither paragraph nor page should generally be the first one. Get your action rolling *first*, then back off to show the normal state of things.

That's what Dickens does, in *A Christmas Carol*. It starts out, "Marley was dead to begin with." Then we move to an overview of what's normal for Scrooge—his coldly businesslike attitudes, his harshness and callousness—in a series of brief confrontations with his nephew, with businessmen collecting for charity, and with his clerk, Bob Cratchit. His attitudes are all the more shocking in that this isn't just any ordinary day, but Christmas Eve. Then, when Scrooge shuts up shop and goes home, he sees the face of his dead ex-partner, Marley, on his door-knocker and things get rapidly stranger from then on.

The plot gets rolling before Dickens backs off and gives the norm—Scrooge's pre-existing attitudes. This norm isn't explained but instead is demonstrated, shown in a series of brief scenes, after which Dickens returns to the main plot, Scrooge's confrontation with his own past, present, and grim probable future, as embodied by the tortured wraith of Marley, Scrooge's mirror. (More on mirrors and other methods of echoing the main action in Chapter 8.)

You can even set up a character to represent the norm. That's the function Watson serves in the Holmes stories, and the average Ralph as contrasted with ambitious Jack, fat incompetent clever Piggy, and mystical Simon in *Lord of the Flies*. Such a character gives the reader somebody to identify with and judge the other, more unusual characters by.

My strong advice is that if establishing a pre-existing norm isn't absolutely vital, skip it. Leave it out altogether, if you possibly can. Instead, start *in medias res*. In general practice, that means starting your actual narrative just before, or even during, the first major conflict or confrontation: the point at which things start to get serious, when they start moving toward final crisis.

Specifically, that means starting a short story *just before* the main crisis which will provide the story's resolution. Start a novel *during* the first crisis, because you'll have time to draw back and explain how things got that way later in the first chapter, or even in chapter two.

Don't tell how the protagonist decided to go out and buy fireworks, how much they cost, how he brought them home, how he stored them, what his wife said. Begin when the fuse is lit and the reader sees a bang coming any minute.

## JUGGLING THREE BALLS AT ONCE

Every effective beginning needs to do three things. The chief of these is to get the story going and show what kind of story it's going to be. The second is to introduce and characterize the protagonist. The third is to engage the reader's interest in reading on.

Some beginnings do more than this. Some create moods; some introduce narrators who aren't the protagonist, or one or more of the subordinate characters. Some, as just discussed, establish a norm the story will then depart from.

A story can do more than these three things; but it should never do less.

These three special jobs are absolutely vital. To the degree that any short story or novel neglects them, it's risking being dull, uninvolving and possibly confusing reading.

Remember, I'm talking about the *very beginning* here: the first page or so of a short story, the first few pages of a novel.

## Setting the Scene with a Scene

The most economical way of handling these three jobs is to find some way of doing all three at once.

And the best way of doing that, generally, is inventing an appropriate scene: what's going on when the reader starts your story.

Try to think up what situation your protagonist could be in which would directly lead into the final crisis or confrontation, whatever it's going to be. Not an idea, not a description: a situation. A dramatized action with some kind of inherent conflict appropriate to what will follow. The opening situation should be true to the story as a whole, not be (or seem) something tacked on just for the sake of a vivid, exciting opening which, in retrospect, will seem contrived.

Look at the opening of Stephen King's *It*. A child dies, dragged down a grate during a rainstorm by what appears to be a malevolent clown looking up from the sewer. The threat isn't a fake—a child can die, the beginning tells us. And since the rest of the novel involves children trying to understand and defeat the threat that "clown" poses, the opening is valid to the rest of the book. It makes a reader interested in reading on, to learn how this murderous menace will be fought. And it characterizes the protagonist in a brief scene where he makes the paper boat which the boy (the protagonist's little brother) was chasing when the clown got him.

It's an opening which does all its necessary jobs well.

## Characters Busy Being Themselves Before Our Very Eyes

Next, think what your protagonist could be doing, in the context of that situation, which would directly show, with little or no explanation from you, exactly what kind of person he or she is.

In the beginning of *Lord of the Flies*, Ralph finds a conch shell on the beach. Piggy comments on how valuable such shells are and tells Ralph a conch can be blown, like a trumpet. Piggy, being asthmatic, can't blow the shell himself; but his information is what allows Ralph to blow the shell, calling the scattered castaway boys together for the first time.

That shell is the emblem of leadership through the rest of the book. Ralph, finder of the shell, is the leader as long as the shell lasts, with Piggy as his "brain trust"—precisely the pattern set up at the book's opening. When the conch is destroyed, the shell and Piggy both smashed by a huge boulder rolled by Jack's chief henchman, the action represents the destruction of any authority save that of power and of fear. Piggy is dead. The reader knows that the hunt for Ralph won't be long in coming.

Again, this is a masterly beginning in which each character, upon entering, does something that economically and effectively *shows* precisely who and what he is, in this particular context.

And notice how the conch is used to characterize the people who come in contact with it. It becomes a symbol, not because the author arbitrarily assigned some significance to it by a species of novelistic footnote, but because that object has a particular, strong, and important meaning to the people associated with it. The meaning is intrinsic within the story, validly part of the object itself. Even if your objects are less emotionally charged than the conch, or than that novel's later talismanic object, a pig's head rotting on a pole, you can still use them effectively. A man carrying an umbrella is different from a man *not* carrying an umbrella, when an author chooses (and invents) his details carefully and with absolute economy.

## Props and Settings

Give your character objects to be associated with, to carry, to use. In acting, they're called props, and I'll call them that too. Well chosen, well used, props can demonstrate some essential truth about a character without the need of blocks of description slowing down the pace. Think how King uses the paper boat in the opening of *It*, or Golding's conch. Think of the raft in *Huckleberry Finn*, the much sought-after black bird in Hammett's *The Maltese Falcon*. A good prop is a kind of visual shorthand and, like a picture, it can be worth a thousand words, especially at a story's beginning.

And the same thing is true, for the same reasons, about settings. They aren't just backdrops. Just by where you have the action happening will tell a lot about the action itself and the people involved. A scene on a rainy street corner is automatically different from one in a hot, stuffy and claustrophobic schoolroom, or at a county fair, or in an echoing, empty parking garage. You can reinforce the mood and action with your choice of setting, or work against it: a grim thing happening on a carousel, a happy thing happening beside a car nose-down in a ditch. Wherever you set your opening, be aware that where it happens matters, and can matter enormously, if the setting is well chosen to complement or contrast with what's happening there.

It may take thinking over to come up with good props, vivid, meaningful settings. Be ready to think twice, try and discard, until everything seems to be working together in one seemingly inevitable whole with nothing extra and nothing missing.

## Don't Bog Your Opening Down in Descriptions

Have your characters enter talking and doing, in a significant and characteristic way. It doesn't matter when, if ever, you get around to telling what they look like. Some stories do descriptions in just a few sketched details—Sam Spade's "satanic" V of eyebrows, for instance—and some never find it necessary at all: describe Huckleberry Finn. Can you do it? Twain doesn't. Perry Mason, in the numerous novels featuring his wily court maneuvers, doesn't look at all like Raymond Burr: Erle Stanley Gardner deliberately refrained from describing him. Nor does Robert Parker find it necessary to tell more about his private detective, Spenser, than that he's strongly built and well past thirty.

Sometimes the most important thing about a person isn't how he looks, but what he's like, how he behaves, how and what he thinks, how he reacts, even how he talks. Huck Finn, and the characters in Damon Runyon's flavorful short stories, are characterized almost completely by means of their voices—their inimitably slangy way of speaking. Appearance (meaning the kind of crude color-of-hair, color-of-eyes, height/weight/age "police-blotter listing") may not be important at all.

Piggy's weight, asthma, and glasses are crucially important

in the story, and so are carefully detailed. The color of his hair, by contrast, makes no difference at all.

Only spend time describing what it's *important* to describe, what's going to matter in the rest of the story. That may be what your characters look like; then again, it may not. You decide.

And even if your characters' appearance *is* important to you and your story, the story's very beginning may not be the best place to go into any great detail about it. You want your readers to be able to imagine your characters, not describe them for a robbery report. Have your people talking and doing: that will make the stronger impression.

## Opening with a Bang

Some openings are unabashedly melodramatic. Their action is as violent, exaggerated, and mindless as possible. "As I scrambled over the top of the crater, Mount St. Helens cleared its throat and then blew 200,000 tons of its substance straight into the startled sky." Let's call them *volcano openings*. (In Chapter 10, I'll talk about the other half of the equation, *dirigible endings*.)

A volcano opening—a chase scene, somebody falling off a cliff or being attacked by Killer Shrews, a sex scene or mad, passionate love-at-first-sight—makes a statement about what's to follow. The story, such an opening says, is going to be one of exaggerated nonstop action/emotion, lots of excitement and suspense, intended to appeal to the broadest possible spectrum of readers. If you can make good on a promise like that, you could have a best-seller on your hands, and movie rights in the offing.

Assuming that's what you want. . . .

That's one sure thing about a volcano: it gets your attention. But it's also a hard act to follow. And not all writers want to. While some writers yearn for the primary colors and broad sweep of Cinemascope, others have a hankering for the small screen, muted tones, and close ups.

If you don't intend to have a slam-bang action story or scenery-chewing, bodice-ripping forbidden romance following an opening like that, it would have been better to have made a little less noise at the outset and, instead, made a different sort of promise. You could promise an unusual concept ("Big Brother is Watching": *1984*), an especially vivid character (Sherlock Holmes), or maybe an interesting, individual style ("It was love at first sight. The first time Yossarian saw the chaplain he fell madly in love with him": *Catch-22*).

The point is that if you're beginning a short story or novel, you are in fact making a promise the rest of the story will have to fulfill. You don't have any choice about that, because the beginning is, by definition, what gets read first. A reader (and an editor considering publishing it) is going to decide whether or not to read on, based on what that beginning promises. It has to promise something special, or something seen in a special way, to make them want to read on.

And, remember, I'm talking now just about beginnings, not whole plots. Exaggerated events and people are a staple even in literary fiction. Virtually everything by Faulkner has large doses of melodrama—take a look at *Sanctuary*, for instance. The melodrama compensates for Faulkner's characteristically involuted, complex prose style and considerable stretches of philosophizing. So-called Southern Gothic, whether penned by Faulkner or Carson McCullers, has a native streak of the bizarre all through it—freaks, dwarfs, mouldering bodies of old lovers in upstairs bedrooms.

Steinbeck's *East of Eden* and *Of Mice and Men* have adulteries and murders and hard-breathing domestic hanky-panky galore. Dickens' novels have melodrama by the ton. And all are certainly regarded as literature.

But if you look at the beginnings of any of these, you'll find the tone rather quiet, the situations revealing but not characterized by slam-bang action. The melodrama comes later. Virtually no volcano openings.

Better, for hooking the reader, is a *revealing* opening, effectively played out, promising something worth watching to come. Better is something relatively simple and direct, free of encumbering description, explanation, and hype, something a reader can understand immediately by just watching, a situation able to speak for itself. A parent with a hand raised, and a child grimly swallowing tears; a middle-aged woman anxiously scanning the want ads, answering inattentively as a teenager asks when supper is going to be ready; a man and woman stiffly silent or talking about everything except abortion as they wait for a train, as in Hemingway's wonderful "The Hills Like White Elephants."

Find the right scene, one that hits just the right note with a minimum of fuss, and the beginning will take care of itself.

And if it leads to melodrama later on, so be it. You and your story will certainly be in the best of literary company. In Chapter 7, I'll offer some tips on harnessing the fierce power of melodrama to narrative purposes.

## Do You Always Have to Make a Scene?

Scene openings aren't the only way. They're just the simplest, most reliable way, suitable for any kind of writing. If you're just starting to write, they're probably what you should use for your beginnings.

But there are alternatives. Good stories have begun with pure dialogue. Dickens' *A Tale of Two Cities* begins with a philosophical overview: "It was the best of times, it was the worst of times" and his *Bleak House* opens with a wonderful portrait of dense fog spreading through London the same way the foggy intricacies of the case Jarndyce vs. Jarndyce spread to obscure and pollute everything and everyone they touch. Steinbeck's masterpiece, *The Grapes of Wrath*, begins with a splendid description of a dust storm. Du Maurier's *Rebecca* begins, "Last night I dreamt I went to Manderley again," calling up the image of that doomed house.

If you begin with something other than a scene, you'll have to compensate for the loss of immediate action by using something especially striking and powerful. Starting with a description, a philosophical mini-essay, or a dream is dangerous because all will tend to be essentially static if you don't go to heroic lengths to make them something else.

They'll sit and look at you like a fried egg. Your story will stall.

Strong contrast or a strikingly unusual juxtaposition (implied comparison between a law case and a fog, for instance), vivid imagery or wording, a violent or melodramatic event being described, a brooding mood that promises action soon to come—all can help give the reader a *sense* of motion even when nothing is actually happening *right now*.

But such openings are difficult to bring off, and unless your alternative method of opening can somehow contrive to do the required three jobs of all beginnings, your best choice will be a scene.

## IF AT FIRST IT DOESN'T START, START AGAIN

Now if all this discussion makes a beginning sound crucial and complicated, it is. But then, so are middles. So are endings.

If you have a story idea, then don't worry about the beginning. Get your story told, all the way through, at least in first draft.

As I've said before, stories change in the telling. Often you'll find that what you thought was going to be the heart of the story ends up as kind of an appendix, and the story's true motion and true meaning have gone someplace you never expected. And if and when that happens, the original beginning (if you had one) is going to be the wrong beginning anyway. It will need rethinking, re-imagining.

### The Dirty Word

Now I'm going to use a dirty word. Otherwise strong writers shudder and flinch when they hear it.

REVISION.

Any story worth the telling is worth revising. Remember Melville's Bulkington, who fell overboard the first night out of port? If you have such vestigial evidence of a false beginning, be tidier than Melville: go back and change it. Make your story one single solid thing, itself, with nothing left that could stand to be omitted without weakening it, nothing omitted or left sketchy that really needs to be developed for the story to have its proper impact.

Don't assume first thoughts are always best thoughts. Second thoughts, about something already well along in the process of becoming, are often better, more insightful thoughts because they're about something concrete—*this* short story, *this* novel—instead of something vague and theoretical, a set of intentions, a blur of feelings not yet fleshed out into a complex of incident and personality.

Be thinking about your opening, but don't worry about it. If it doesn't come, or come to life, right away, skip over it and write the next scene with just a few notes on what you want the beginning to have done and established, what groundwork it will have laid, for what comes afterward, the part you're working on now. And keep writing away until you have one whole first draft done. Then go ahead and start the kind of invention, addition, and deletion only possible in solid second-draft writing.

I don't know if William Golding knew he was going to need a conch when he began writing *Lord of the Flies*. It's altogether possible that, realizing how important some tangible, visible symbol of leadership was becoming in the story's middle, he went back and stuck the conch on that beach for Ralph to find and for Piggy to identify. Be ready to do the same, once your story has started talking to you and letting you know what *it* needs, instead of what you thought it was going to need.

In other words, a bad beginning shouldn't be the end—not if you realize you'll often need to go back and write it all over anyway, even when you initially thought you got it right the first time around.

## CHAPTER 3

# WOULD YOU TRUST A VIEWPOINT WITH SHIFTY EYES?

WHILE YOU'RE WRITING YOUR OPENING and then going on into the beginning of your story, you'll need to settle two things right away:

Whose viewpoint is going to control the storytelling?

How are you going to fit in (or manage to leave out) background information if, as I've advised, you've begun in the middle?

I can only talk about one of these at a time, but pretend I'm talking about both at once, because both need to be decided at the same time, namely right away. This chapter is on some fundamental choices regarding viewpoint. The next one is on handling exposition.

## HOW MANY EYES ARE ENOUGH?

Sometimes there's no viewpoint character, nobody whose eyes focus the action. Instead, the author tells the story. That's called omniscient (all-knowing) narration. The author narrates, mentioning what this or that character may be feeling or thinking anytime the author pleases.

The trouble with using an omniscient narrator is that all the characters are kept at arm's length, seen equally and from a distance. It tends to be uninvolving. A reader finds it harder to identify with any one character, since the focus and the viewpoint range over all equally.

Unfocused sunlight won't set fire to a piece of paper. It takes a magnifying glass, a single focus, to do that.

So although current fiction may use omniscience in an inconspicuous, sometime way, in the form of narrative summary or other brief, transitional elements, thoroughgoing omniscient narration is now seldom used as the controlling viewpoint of a whole short story (with a few notable exceptions like John Cheever's short fiction), and even more rarely of a novel.

Instead of adopting a broad-focus omniscient narrative voice to be the controlling viewpoint of a whole story, contemporary writers and readers seem to prefer something more like our own experience, in which each of us can know—but not always understand—the inner life of only one person: ourselves. Everybody else is seen from the outside, and known only by what they say and do, and what we think about it. Mirroring our individual experience in fiction means having one central viewpoint character and sticking with him or her.

In short fiction, a single viewpoint character has always been most common, though there are quite a lot of exceptions. Longer short stories, those shading toward novelette length, sometimes will have two or more viewpoint characters. The brevity of short fiction is, naturally enough, the determining factor in whether a given story will support more than one viewpoint without losing impact and immediacy.

But long fiction has space to develop several characters in depth. Intensity rises and falls as the story progresses. Novels also sometimes need to shift locale or show scenes where it would be impractical or impossible for the protagonist to be present, yet which the author doesn't want to relegate to reports or summaries. Or sometimes a writer wants to build suspense by switching the narrative focus from the main plot to a subplot ("Meanwhile, back at the ranch—") or reveal some fact to the reader, yet keep the main character ignorant of it.

In those cases, having just one viewpoint character may be

impractical, even undesirable. So in novels, multiple viewpoints are as common as single focus.

## Winning Reader Identification

The danger of multiple viewpoints is that the reader, lacking just one person to identify with, is likely to become more a detached, uninvolved observer and less a vicarious participant in your story's events. The story, seen piecemeal through several different sets of eyes, may become disconnected, confusing, and incoherent, especially if it contains any other kind of complexity, like flashbacks, many extreme changes of locale, or an intricate or subplot-laden plot.

A story with too many focuses can become a story with no focus at all.

Using a single viewpoint character is the best way to communicate excitement, dread, love, any strong emotion, to the reader, make readers share the feeling and not just the facts your story presents. It's easier to imagine your way into a single character, one on one, than into several in succession.

To the degree you're trying to arouse or communicate emotions in your story, you need to involve your reader; and that means doing everything possible to help your reader identify with the main person that story is about.

Winning that kind of intense reader identification means using the fewest possible viewpoints. If there are no compelling reasons to do otherwise, stay with one viewpoint character from beginning to end. If you really need two, use two. If you can't do without three, then use three. But fight, if you have to, to keep from making it seven or seventeen. Keep it to the absolute minimum.

## SINGLE VIEWPOINT: WHOSE EYES ARE BEST?

If you've decided to use a single viewpoint character, the main choice, the one to depart from only for good reason, is telling the story from the viewpoint of the chief character, the protagonist. He or she is the one the story's events are centered around. He or she is the one who's going to be chiefly affected by what happens.

But don't forget: the protagonist is whoever *you say* the protagonist is; that choice, in turn, determines the nature of the whole story. The story of a flood is a different story if it's told from the point of view of Ginger, a drenched mother clinging to a chimney with five children and an irritated cat, waiting for rescue, than if it's told from the point of view of Fred, her equally drenched husband, a volunteer fireman in a rowboat who is quite content to rescue people on the other side of town and is rather hoping to find himself an unencumbered bachelor again.

Who is really at the story's heart? It may not have been the character you first assumed it was. If you're having trouble with the story of Ginger and Fred and you've been telling it from Ginger's viewpoint, maybe it's really Fred's story and you hadn't noticed. Try looking at the story through another character's eyes—the man in the rowboat instead of the woman on the roof—and see if it makes a better, more satisfying story that way.

Or if it's the story of Ginger and Fred but they're both bores, maybe it's ten-year-old Tiffany's story. Except that Tiffany doesn't yet exist. You have to invent her.

After a story is written, it's hard to imagine it could be otherwise than the way it is. But when you're writing it, all the choices are yours—even, and especially, the one of whose story it is and whose eyes would be best to see it. Because who sees determines in large measure what gets seen: what happens and how it's told about.

## Holmes and Heathcliff: an Outsider's View

A displaced viewpoint character, a narrator other than the main character, is an option. Generally it's used when the writer doesn't want the reader to get too close to the protagonist, maybe to keep the main character strange and mysterious. That's the case, I think, in Fitzgerald's *The Great Gatsby*. The man who called himself Jay Gatsby is full of secrets and private romantic dreams;

Nick Carraway, the narrator, is an onlooker and a thoughtful, moral man. Fitzgerald wanted the story seen by the wise man, not by the dreamer. He wanted to put a filter, a barrier, between Gatsby and the reader, to keep Gatsby a distant figure seen only from and through Carraway's perspective.

Emily Bronte's *Wuthering Heights* also uses displaced narration, partly for the same reason—to emphasize the narrators' rationalism rather than the wild, mystical romanticism of the main characters, Heathcliff and Catherine. But in this book, something else is operating too. You may have a protagonist who's cruel, savage, or hard to understand or like, as Heathcliff certainly is. You may have a Sherlock Holmes, who's so uniquely brilliant and so disinclined to explain, that you need a go-between as a narrator, to act as the reader's eyes and to stand for a norm which the main character violates either for good or for evil. The distance between reader and chief character is already there: what's needed is a bridge.

That bridge, that displaced narrator, may be Watson, who's fascinated by Holmes and communicates that fascination to the reader while letting Holmes produce his amazing deductions like rabbits out of hats. It may be Ishmael, letting us observe Ahab's monomania without having to sympathize with or share it. It may be Lockwood, who shares with a gossiping old housekeeper the narrative chore of revealing the mutually destructive love of Heathcliff and Catherine.

If your story has a highly unusual protagonist, using a displaced narrator the reader can more easily understand and identify with, who can ask questions and bring some objectivity to the protagonist's odd goings on, may be the best answer.

## MULTIPLE VIEWPOINTS: HOW DO YOU SWITCH?

So. You've thought about it and decided your story really needs to be seen through two or more sets of eyes. How do you manage the switches?

A good rule for doing anything tricky in fiction, particularly long fiction—switching viewpoints or anything else—is to do it right away, to let the reader know the rules, and to do it consistently thereafter.

And make no mistake: viewpoint shifts really *are* tricky to handle and are worth all your craft and care. Badly handled, they're as jarring to most readers (*especially* including editors!) as the feeling you get when you thought there were ten steps and there were only nine. Or, worse, when you thought there were ten, there are eleven, and you take a header.

Mangling viewpoint shifts is one of the sirens-howling signals of an utter beginner—as bad as saying "ain't" in front of your strictest teacher. Worse, maybe. It can land your manuscript right back in your self-addressed, stamped envelope as fast as any other beginner's boner I can think of.

Watch out for careless or unintentional viewpoint shifts and cut them out ruthlessly. Treat needed shifts with the utmost respect, the sort you'd accord a loaded gun.

## With Two Characters

If you're going to be switching from Ginger to Fred, there are three main ways to handle the change: scene by scene, chapter by chapter, or part by part.

If you decide to make your switches scene by scene, do your first switch in the first few pages, when one scene changes to another, taking special care that the reader knows the switch has happened. Start the new scene with the new viewpoint and establish it in the very first paragraph with something like, "Ginger was dragging the cat back from the edge of the roof. She . . . ." Then carry on from Ginger's point of view for a *little* while, and switch it back to Fred with a new scene.

Similarly, in long fiction, you may want to have a couple of scene-by-scene shifts in the first chapter to establish the pattern, then go to chapter-by-chapter shifts thereafter.

Whichever you choose, establish the pattern as early as you can. After that, you can stay with Ginger or with Fred more or less as long as you like: you've clued your reader in on the method. There are going to be just two viewpoints, Ginger and Fred, and the story is going to shuttle between them. The reader understands and will bear with you thereafter.

The third way is to have extended sections from each point of view in turn, with no internal switches within sections. In short stories, individual scenes are sometimes grouped into something resembling chapters: these sections are either numbered or otherwise strongly set apart from the rest. Similarly, in long fiction, chapters are sometimes grouped together into larger units, sometimes called parts (for instance, Part I, Part II, etc., but still within the same novel).

If your story is going to have parts, you could have each part told from one point of view, and not change until the next part. With substantial stretches spent in each viewpoint, the danger of confusing the reader would be minimal.

## With Two Viewpoints, Watch Out for a Divorce

The problem with alternating viewpoints is that the story may start to split into two unconnected narratives. That's what happens in Thackeray's *Vanity Fair*, with its two protagonists: scheming, fascinating Becky Sharp and teary, helpless, tedious Amelia Sedley. The book breaks in two, and the Amelia portion pales by comparison. To prevent a similar split, you'll need to take special care to connect the two viewpoints and plot lines every now and again. Bring the main characters together periodically. Make connections of objects, or moods, or continuing action to bind one scene to the next, in spite of the viewpoint shift. Have some subordinate characters appear in sections told from each of the viewpoints. Remember that with a divided narrative, you're going to have to compensate with increased strong connective narrative devices, to make sure one viewpoint character doesn't end up hogging the whole story and most of the reader's interest.

Be prepared for the problem your choice creates, and decide how you're going to compensate for it.

## With Many Characters

If you're going to have several viewpoint characters, what's called rotating viewpoint, the problem is a little different.

You'll find rotating viewpoint exclusively in long fiction. I can't think of a single short story that uses it, though there's doubtless at least one—there are exceptions, and effective ones, to any general rule, when it comes to fiction. Nevertheless, there's usually just not enough space in short fiction to do that kind of switching without fragmenting the story beyond repair.

You can handle your rotation of narrators more or less the same as you would alternating viewpoint, when only two characters are involved. But in this case, it might be a good idea to spend a little more time developing the future viewpoint characters in earlier chapters, *before* they have to take over the responsibility of narration. Let the reader get to know and be interested in them first, before your whole story's viewpoint is turned over to them. If you establish them well, the reader should be able to shift over with no sense of discontinuity when they take over.

If you want to rotate viewpoints frequently, rather than waiting for chapter or part breaks, you should establish the pattern right away. Do at least three or four shifts, briefly, making each scene as self-contained and self-explanatory as possible. The five little paragraphs that make up Ginger's scene have the considerable job of making Ginger and her immediate situation perfectly clear to the reader. The three paragraphs of Fred's scene have to do the same for Fred. When we get to Tiffany, roosting in a treetop by the elementary school, the reader will understand the pattern.

Separate the scenes within chapters either with extra white space, some sort of graphic (* * *), or both. Don't change viewpoints within a scene.

## Build in Connections

You'll remember that earlier in the chapter, I recommended a rule of thumb: if something in a story is complicated, keep everything else as simple and direct as possible. Multiple viewpoints need that kind of compensation, especially at first, or the narrative will fragment and become confusing. So take special care to connect the scenes every way you can think of.

In this hypothetical story of ours, the flood itself could be one such connection. Each little scene, in the beginning of the story, could start with a mention of the water and follow a similar narrative pattern: first water, then the person looking at the water in a particular way, then their immediate situation. (After characters and situations are well established, further along in the story, not so many connections will be needed.)

An additional connection could be one mood which, at that moment, all the viewpoint characters share: they're all frightened, and you're dwelling on the particular *kind* of fright that special person is feeling in his or her individual situation.

Keep to consistency of form, just at first, to compensate for the pogo-stick jumps as much as possible.

You might mention Tiffany in Ginger's piece, and Fred in Tiffany's, to add other connections.

## Another Way to Keep Things Simple

Viewpoints shifts are distracting. The jumps, and keeping the different characters straight, are going to be taking all a reader's attention. At a story's beginning, if the little scenes themselves are complex or involve a lot of individualized characters, or even the *names* of a lot of different characters, the reader is going to be utterly lost and give up.

At the beginning of a rotating-viewpoint story (the sort we've been imagining), keep the *plot* of the first few scenes to things you could understand in a thirty-second commercial. Somebody trying to climb up on a higher branch while ugly water laps over her patent-leathers doesn't need a whole lot of explaining. Neither does the cat descending the roof to investigate a squirrel crouched in the rain gutter. Show simple things, vivid things, and let the switches provide the motion and energy to propel the story forward, there at the beginning.

Don't mention the names of any characters who aren't vital to the scene or to the scene immediately following. You can mention Ginger's husband is named Fred if Fred's section comes next, but don't mention the in-laws or the neighbors or Fred's boss if the information isn't absolutely necessary and the characters don't appear *in that scene*. Develop or introduce extra characters later, when the context calls for them and they have something to do. Don't have your entire cast of characters, and all their relationships, cluttering the narrative at the beginning.

This is a good principle even in single-viewpoint stories. Beginnings should avoid clutter in all ways possible.

## Make Sure the Reader Knows Something's Happening, and Going to Happen

There's another compensation that needs mentioning. Make sure none of your little, simple scenes is static. End them, subtly or obviously, on cliff-hangers. Show something is slipping, something is going wrong, and something is going to happen *very* soon. That, together with the energy the shifts themselves provide, will supply the dynamic force to make the reader want to keep reading and go to the effort of sorting out all the different people, settings, and situations. Make sure that each scene *moves* and is leading up to something quite clear and concrete.

# REMEMBER: YOU CAN CHANGE YOUR MIND

The nice thing about writing is that only the finished product, the final draft, has to be seamless and as nearly perfect as you can make it. The first and intermediate drafts can be scribbled up twenty times, and nobody ever has to know but you.

If you started out with a single viewpoint and want to broaden the focus to other major characters for any compelling reason, build a few shifts into the early sections to prepare, to set the pattern, then go ahead and do your shifts thereafter. If you had several viewpoints but find you end up using only about three, go back and adjust things, assigning the orphaned observations to the chosen characters or to narrative summary.

The basic principle is to use as few viewpoints as you possibly can. If that's seven or seventeen, so be it.

Just don't change your mind in the middle (or, worse, the end!) of a story without doing the necessary tidying and adjustment to make the change fit in.

A case in point: a friend told me recently about a book he'd just read in which the principal character, the viewpoint character, got killed off in the middle of the story. It was quite a wrench, I gather, and rather blunted my friend's enthusiasm for the rest of the book, which concerned an investigation of the startling death. It was certainly an unusual plot twist; but I think I'd feel let down if I encountered it. What do you think?

## NEVER IN THE MIDDLE
## OF A SCENE

Returning now to a point made, briefly, earlier: however many viewpoints you're using—two or several—never never NEVER shift viewpoint in the middle of a scene.

Now, wait before you start yelling you've seen it done. I don't doubt there are instances in published work: you can find examples of any ghastly, incompetent boner you can think of, somewhere or other. Characters change names in mid-story. Protagonists get killed off halfway through. Characters make unconvincing speeches to one another to convey information to readers, or treat us to interminable partisan harangues. Characters peer earnestly into mirrors and inventory their looks as if vaguely fearing their noses might have been stolen. Stories obsessively detail every bite of a meal, every trivial bit of the daily routine of getting up in the morning.

Bad writing, by any standard you care to name, sometimes reaches the printed page.

Print doesn't sanctify it. I've read some really rottenly-written fiction over the years, and not all of it in dog-eared copies with garish covers, from used-book shops—how about you?

But competent writers have their lapses, too. In many cases where a major narrative blunder survives into print, it's tolerated because the story shines like a jewel, flaws and all, and the momentary failure of craft (like the vestiges of Bulkington) is forgiven for the sake of the power of the whole.

Some boners are allowed great writers. Laughably bad technique is often tolerated from very popular writers. But you and I are interested in good craft, in understanding options and making choices on purpose. If you didn't care about craft, you wouldn't be reading this book. So you wouldn't want to cite others' blunders to justify your own anyway—right?

The Prosecution rests.

Therefore. After the beginning of a scene, don't change viewpoint until the scene is over. The next scene can be a continuation of the same action—Ginger on the roof, and little Gertrude, aged 6, also on the roof—but it will have a separate concern, a separate viewpoint, its own miniplot with Gertrude at the center, not her mother. Or it may be a transitional stretch of limited omniscient summary. But in one scene, stay with one viewpoint.

If, for this present scene, you're in Fred's viewpoint, be *very sure* to tell directly only *what Fred himself could reasonably observe and know* about other people. Don't say, in Fred's scene, "Old Mike heard the train whistle." Don't say, "The train whistle told Old Mike the railway embankment, anyway, was above water." *Fred can't know what Old Mike hears*, or what anything tells Mike, train whistles included. Say something more like, "Old Mike cocked his head at the distant hooting of a train. 'Guess the embankment's still above water,' he remarked, smoothing rain out of his mustache."

Don't have characters being happy, or thoughtful, or pleased unless they're specifically *looking* or *sounding* happy, thoughtful, or pleased. Let word choice in dialogue, and expression and gesture, do their proper work. That's what they're for. In Fred's scene, stay absolutely with Fred.

Your narrative's first job, at the beginning of the new scene, is to let the reader know as quickly and economically as possible (1) that the shift has happened and (2) whose eyes he's seeing through now. Don't leave that in doubt a single sentence longer than you have to. Do it right away.

And in second draft, watch out for any unintended shifts and stamp them out like roaches, every one.

# THE EYES THAT MATTER

They're *your* eyes, your coherent vision of what you're trying to say and show. Whether you displace that vision into a narrator or have a viewpoint-protagonist who is a thinly disguised version of yourself, the job is the same: to see things whole and clear and true. To focus on what's important and let the unimportant blur or drop out. To be a photographer of the mind, noting how the shadows are cast by your own private inner sun.

In ancient times, it was believed that the eye sent out rays that illuminated and affected whatever was seen. Belief in "the Evil Eye" is a vestige of that ancient concept of the eye's function. For a writer, it's still true, and always has been. You light up what you see, when you embody it in a story. Then others can see it too. Innumerable learned books are written on this or that author's "vision," the unique worlds created by seeing them and writing about them.

That kind of seeing, insight, is so fundamentally the business of fiction that it's worth taking care with.

And by the way: don't break viewpoint in the middle of a scene. I just wanted to remind you, in case you forgot.

# CHAPTER 4

# "SHUT UP!" HE EXPLAINED— HANDLING EXPOSITION

AT THE BEGINNING OF YOUR STORY, you're going to have to decide how to convey necessary background facts. That's exposition.

Exposition involves breaking away from the ongoing action to give information—for a paragraph, or for a page or more. It's the author telling the reader something—telling, rather than showing.

As I explained earlier, telling is much less effective than showing. It follows that exposition is less dramatic and less vivid than a scene—generally, a *lot* less.

So, as with all major components of narrative, you'll need to recognize the nature of the problem and find effective, appropriate ways of compensating.

## WHY EXPLAIN?

You may be asking, reasonably enough, if exposition is so dull, why not stick to scenes? Well, you can, if you want to and your story will allow it. A good many short stories are one single scene with no more than a phrase or two of exposition or description in any one place. Hemingway's stories are almost all sparse like that. Some novels, like Jack Shaefer's classic western *Shane*, can be all present-time, all surface, and yet be powerful in a stark kind of way.

But doing without exposition can be a problem too. Not all writers want to sound like Hemingway, and not all stories can be limited to immediate, direct action with no past, no context, no overview.

Scenes are, of their nature, close-focus. Having nothing but scenes would be like a movie all in close-up, with no establishing shots, no panning across the landscape to reveal eventual figures far away. That can feel pretty claustrophobic and nearsighted, after awhile.

Well-handled exposition gives perspective, dimension, and needed context that help events in the foreground make sense. Watching only scenes, in long or complex fiction, would be like trying to follow a baseball game through the wrong end of the binoculars. You'd have a lot of motion, all right—but the larger motions of the game would be extremely hard to follow.

In fiction, doing completely without explanations would mean you couldn't describe a person or place for more than a phrase or two. You couldn't skip over periods of time when nothing of importance is happening, not without a jarring break in the narrative. You couldn't take a confusing, close-focus series of events, draw back, and give the reader an overview of what it all means. You couldn't tell about any of the characters' background or previous experience.

Worst of all, maybe, you'd find it very hard to begin *in medias res*, in the middle of things—you couldn't pull back after the initial scene and say how things got that way. That would be a real handicap.

Even scenes, wonderful scenes, have their trade-offs, their problems that require compensation. Even high drama needs relief and context and overview. And that's the special job nothing can supply but the more distant, less immediate, more thoughtful kind of storytelling: exposition.

So in practice, fiction is a balance between scene and explanation—70%/30% or maybe even 80%/20%.

There may not be much explanation, but nothing else can do its work so economically or so well.

There also is nothing else that can kill a story quicker than explanation taking over, exposition badly handled.

Like viewpoint shifts, it needs to be treated with utmost respect, care, and narrative craft.

## BURIED IN FOOTNOTES

I knew a writer who had nightmares about tons of exposition slithering down on her like a landslide. It can feel like that to a reader, too: smothering deluges of fact that prevent any motion at all. Ever read a textbook with lots of footnotes? Remember how you tended to skip or ignore the footnotes? Now, those of you who've read *Moby Dick*: how many of you actually *read* every word of the cetology chapters telling the folklore, anatomy, and habits of whales?

(Being a thorough-going nature nut, I personally enjoy the cetology chapters. Just like a nice National Geographic special. But I know a lot of folk who feel otherwise.)

Exposition is the curse of several of the popular genres, including science fiction, fantasy, and mystery. There are all those facts to be explained: maybe a whole new universe to be accounted for, the languages and customs of the Elven races, not to mention all those suspects and alibis! Westerns and historical fiction, necessarily built on a bedrock of research, are perhaps even more prone to this problem. If these facts, research, and outright invention aren't controlled and subordinated to the plot's needs, they can take over and literally bury a story in footnotes masquerading as narration.

## WORLD-BUILDERS' DISEASE

For a writer, constructing the background material can be so much fun that it's mistaken for writing. Fantasy writers have a penchant for working up histories of imaginary empires that can run to hundreds of pages, full of maps and chronologies and genealogical trees a yard long. It's a common phenomenon: C. S. Lewis, in childhood, chronicled the doings of "Animal Land"; as adolescents, the Brontës produced long histories of an imaginary kingdom called "Angria." The whole of *The Silmirillion* and those long, long appendices are background information Tolkien wisely excluded from his huge trilogy, *The Lord of the Rings*—and certainly not for lack of space.

Similarly, science fiction writers can fall in love with their hardware and want to show it off, like a neighbor's interminable discussion of the gastric workings of his new car. George Lucas has commented that some sf movies are particularly guilty of this—their directors figure they've spent so much on a special effect that they use vital screen (storytelling) time giving a boring guided tour of some particularly elaborate model, relegating plot and character to the background shadows. Seen *Star Trek: the Movie*, with its seemingly interminable shots of the *Enterprise*? Writers can do precisely the same thing on paper.

Or sometimes sf writers can become so immersed in the sociology of the alien race they've invented that they offer glossaries translating native terms, folklore, sayings, and histories stretching back for millennia, in place of a story. Seen any of Ursula Le Guin's recent work, particularly *Always Coming Home*, which comes complete with an audio tape of folk songs?

Mystery writers can spend so much time working out alibis, with lists of suspects, timetables, maps with calculations on how long it would take to go by foot, bicycle, car or even helicopter to the scene of the crime, and the other logistics of detection, that they can't resist reusing these working notes in their stories. Dorothy L. Sayers' *The Five Red Herrings* is (among many excellent things) an exercise in timetable management; so is her *Have His Carcase*.

I call this phenomenon "World-Builders' disease." In its more extreme forms, it's narrative cancer: the unchecked and malignant growth of something that was harmless, even beneficial and necessary, in itself. In all genres, it involves becoming infatuated with the process of invention for its own sake. Exposition, essentially static and undramatic, isn't subordinated to plot and takes over. The story stops dead.

## Pygmalion and Frankenstein

Every writer is Pygmalion, falling in love with his handiwork and wanting it to come alive. And sometimes, that love can be blind, as in the case of Pygmalion's dark counterpart, Dr. Frankenstein.

Writers blinded by the delights of concocting elaborate background material can forget that their primary job is to tell a story, not merely to invent.

Inventing is relatively easy—you take your expertise, whatever it may be, and project it on the universe. Tolkien, a medieval scholar and linguist, invented elaborate languages for dwarves, two races of elves, and several races of men. One of the human languages bore a striking resemblance to Old English, Tolkien's particular area of expertise. A plumber could invent a world full of plumbing, complete with detailed discussions of conduits, fittings, gravity-feed, and so on. A surgeon . . . no, that doesn't even bear thinking on.

As any bored spouse of a card player or a dedicated jogger knows, what's fun for one person to *do* isn't necessarily fun for another person to *watch*. Short of a tournament, chess just isn't a good spectator sport. Neither is working out exposition. Don't rent a stadium and expect crowds to flock in.

Don't assume your enjoyment in *doing* the invention is automatically going to mean the reader is going to enjoy the final product. Inventing is easy—it's storytelling that's hard. And it's storytelling the reader has a right to expect.

## Give Your Reader a Piece of Your Mind—Not All of It

Rightly used, working background notes—what's sometimes called "doing your homework"—is the iceberg, and the story is the proverbial tip. The story is supported, sustained, given solidity and substance by a great mass of information the writer needs to know *but the reader doesn't—and shouldn't*.

The character charts some writing books advise you to make, calling for everything from a character's childhood nickname to his/her taste in furniture, can be useful. They can flesh out characters for you and let you start getting to know them preparatory to writing about them. Such charts are getting-ready exercises, not the race itself. A character in a story should be a character in action, not a walking mass of background data. Don't give in to the temptation to include in your story such working notes, however long, elaborate, and inventive they may be. The iceberg should stay out of sight to anchor the whole, not be on view to weight it down.

## Keeping Exposition Under Control: Tolkien and Adams

To stop the story for long-winded explanations or descriptions is deadly, particularly at the beginning and most especially in the popular genres, where a strong, direct plot that moves along fairly briskly is an absolute necessity.

Follow Tolkien's example. He included the romance of Aragorn and Arwen Evenstar only as an appendix. That's because Tolkien was a storyteller to his very bones. He knew it didn't belong and would, however charming a tale in itself, have been a distraction, an impediment to the ongoing narrative.

Or follow Richard Adams' example. In *Watership Down*, the epic adventures of a group of rabbits setting out to found a new nation, Adams includes several tales of the rabbit folk hero, El-ahrairah. But he compensates. He gets his story well underway first and establishes his main characters before moving to the first tale. He makes sure each tale is brief, fairly simple (as folk tales generally are), and full of action, so it's dramatic rather than static. And he only departs from the main plot at a quiet moment, a lull between crises.

Moreover, each tale is connected by theme, mood, or actual content with the developments of the main plot. For instance, in one of the stories, El-ahrairah imitates the voice of a dog and, by guile, persuades a hostile animal to become his accomplice in stealing food. That's what gives the novel's protagonist, Hazel, the inspiration to lure a dog, as a dangerous but crucial ally, into a battle with invading rabbits, resolving the book's final crisis.

These folk tales are always kept carefully subordinate to the main plot and are never allowed to take over. Handling such an alternation is tricky in the extreme, but Adams brings it off successfully.

(You can see signs of impending world-builders' disease, though, in the fact that Adams includes, as an appendix, a glossary of rabbit language. A glossary, put afterward, when you've already struggled through the book without it, is always a dead give-away that the temptation to worse was there, even though successfully resisted.)

If you can't utterly put away your working notes, make them appendices—or wait until you're dead to issue them in book form, as is the case with *The Silmirillion*. Or keep the interruptions brief and full of action, and build in strong connections with the story proper to compensate.

Put your charts, glossaries, maps, and period newspapers in your sock drawer. Put them anywhere—except, undigested and unsubordinated, into your story.

## The Story Comes First: Everything Else Is a Slow Second

The first, most important part of handling exposition is realizing that *it's going to need handling*. Once you're aware of that, you won't be as easily tempted to break off in the middle of an opening or a crisis to treat the reader to a completely unnecessary lecture on how the protagonist was frightened by a big dog in childhood or on the history of the building where the murder happened to take place.

Second, readers are only interested in explanation *after* their curiosity has already been aroused by something in need of explaining. In the beginning of a story, in particular, drop the people out of the plane and *then* say how they got there in the first place. Introduce your character, let him act and show himself and engage the reader's sympathies and curiosity. *Then* tell his background, if you need to.

In the middle of a story, exposition can serve as preparation for something that won't happen until later. But in its immediate context, it should *seem* called for by what's happened just before that point in the story. Otherwise, the exposition will just seem like a digression with no present relevance, or even like heavy-handed foreshadowing: nudging the reader and hinting obviously about what's coming, which none of the characters know—only the author. That's one form of authorial intrusion and something to be avoided, as I'll discuss further in a few minutes. Don't join the "Little did he/she know" school of writers. Make your hints fit in, inconspicuously, so they'll stay hints, not offensive authorial nudges.

Don't assume your responsibility as a writer automatically includes detailing every trauma, illness, or relationship a character had since birth. Neither does it require you to spell out every detail of sociology of the characters' social milieu or the history of the setting. Only important things, important to understand *this* story, *right now,* should be explained.

Important things. *Not everything!*

Be tough with exposition. Make each piece justify its inclusion—at all, and at that particular point of the story. It shouldn't be any longer than it has to be to do its essential work. Then get back to the plot again, as soon as possible.

# PRESENTING EXPOSITION

So. You've decided what background material is really necessary in your story, and you've been careful to get your story up and running before breaking away for more than a paragraph or so to commit a stretch of exposition.

Now the question arises of how to present it.

## *Build It into the Scene*

If you can, build it right into the scene. If it's important that the protagonist has been married before, invent some prop (a belat-

ed birthday card from ex-spouse? a final divorce decree in the
mailbox?) or a bit of dialogue ("Mommy, is Daddy going to visit
me this weekend?") that *shows* the fact without your having to say
a word directly. Try to make each of your scenes multi-purpose:
introducing or developing characters, moving the plot, and establishing immediately needed background, all at once.

## Put It Between Scenes

If it's not just a fact or two but a mini-essay that's needed, it
would be too confusing and cumbersome to try building it into
the scene. In that case, the simplest way is just to tell it between
scenes, with strong transitional connections to what goes before
and what follows. Use objective narration: you're the all-seeing,
all-knowing (but impersonal and invisible) narrator, and you
just put in the information the reader is interested (you hope) in
learning at that point in the story. That's the obvious choice for
longer stretches of exposition, the one you'll probably use most
often.

## Let a Character Explain

The other choice is to have your characters give the necessary
facts: one asks a question, and the other tells. Or one doesn't ask
a question, but the other tells anyway. Or parts of the exposition
can come out, a little at a time, in a discussion among several
characters, maybe spread across several scenes. All these can
work sometimes, if the exposition involved is brief and has other
work to do at the same time, like revealing something about the
characters involved. If, in other words, it serves a plot or characterization purpose as well as a strictly expositional one.

That has the advantage of keeping the story rolling while
the exposition is going on. It's not as severe an interruption as it
would have been if it were cast as objective narration, the disem-
bodied author/narrator telling the reader directly.

But if the exposition is long or detailed, or if it's something
the characters all know perfectly well, that form of presentation
can be ridiculous and unconvincing. ("As you know, Harvey, our

world was attacked by the eight-armed Arcturans seventy-six years ago and since then, we've all lived in these caves.") Don't ever put into a character's mouth anything that's strictly and obviously for the reader's consumption. Readers aren't fooled, and you've turned your characters into unconvincing puppets, dummies making silly speeches at each other.

## Make It a Character's Interior Monologue

Finally, you can have the exposition as one character's reflections or thoughts—the fiction writer's version of a soliloquy. Your character can think about something, or recollect something, and thereby let the reader know what you want to convey. But be careful with this too. It stops the story; it's subject to the same abuses as exposition in dialogue; and if it's overdone, it can make your viewpoint character seem like a self-important pedant who just can't wait to lecture the reader.

There's a character like that in R. L. Stevenson's uncompleted story "The Wrong Box": a Victorian gentleman others flee because his favorite topics of conversation are things like how many times the word "whip" is mentioned in the Bible. In other words, he's a crashing and voluble bore. Don't let any of your characters turn into information-packed bores. You've undoubtedly met some in life. Why should anybody want to meet one in fiction—unless, like Stevenson's encyclopedic old Mr. Finsbury, they're also very funny?

## THE DREADED AUTHORIAL FINSBURY

This brings me to a related matter: writers turning into Finsburys—lecturers droning on about some esoteric specialty—or into True Believers who see fiction primarily as a soapbox from which to promote some doctrine or belief, whether political, social, ethical, religious, ecological, or whatever.

Partly, this is related to the tradition of the omniscient author, which I discussed in the last chapter. Authorial intrusions—the story stopping dead while the author rambles on about whatever happens to interest him—used to be common-place, a hundred and a half years ago. (Need I again mention Melville's cetology chapters?)

Now, though, they're much disliked.

Although a story is of course nothing from first to last but an author's ideas anyway, we forget that, while we're reading. We treat the story as real, the characters as people we care and are concerned about. We imagine our way into it and don't want to be reminded it's an elaborate lie, a made thing, a puppet show in which some author is yanking the strings. To the degree that we're conscious of the puppeteer, that awareness keeps us from holding on to our conviction that words on a page can be worth our tears, our laughter, or our love.

Probably, any lecturing author is showing more than a few signs of world-builders' disease, too.

Don't become a Finsbury or a True Believer.

No matter how worthy your doctrine or how important or insightful your inside knowledge of the territorial battles of Siamese fighting fish, neither is storytelling. And storytelling is the primary business of fiction. Everything else comes second. It has to.

Does that mean I'm contending you shouldn't ever try to cast your convictions or your expert knowledge in the form of fiction? Of course not. Since the very beginnings of fiction, there have been wonderful, moving stories demonstrating some evil, social or personal. Think of Dickens and his attacks on Chancery, cruel schooling, the condition of the urban poor, and the "businesslike" barbarities exemplified by such characters as Scrooge, Mr. Dombey, and the elder Mr. Nickleby. Think of Hawthorne's *The Scarlet Letter* or Hardy's *Tess of the D'Urbervilles*. Think of Judith Rossner's *Looking for Mr. Goodbar* and Shirley Jackson's classic fable, "The Lottery." It's not hard to think of a dozen stories frankly embodying their authors' views on some social or moral issue.

Likewise, specialist information, carefully subordinated and sparingly doled out with a minimum of jargon, has given conviction, believability, and a unique slant to everything from stories about art-critic/detectives to fiction set on exotic plantations or in astronomical observatories, or featuring a protagonist who's a leper. Specialist detail comes under the heading, "If you've got it, flaunt it!" with just the recognition that flaunting doesn't involve letting it bury the story in footnotes.

If you want to include informational or polemical exposition, treat it as you would any problem element. Subordinate it, and compensate with all the narrative craft you've got.

Build it into the story, wherever the story will stand it.

Make it come alive so the reader can see it happening and mattering rather than being lectured by an author, either directly or by proxy, through some character.

Integrate it so thoroughly into the fabric of your story and your characters that it becomes part of their rightful structure and substance, bone and flesh, not just a series of labels, speeches, or footnotes.

## KEEP OUT OF THE PLOT'S WAY

However you decide to handle exposition, of whatever kind, remember: the plot is paramount. Plot is the engine drawing everything else along. If you weigh it down with too much exposition, it's going to grind to a wheezing halt.

Limit exposition to the absolute essentials. Introduce it the least conspicuous, most natural-seeming way. Keep it as short as possible in any one place. Spread it across different scenes, if you can, according to where it's actually relevant and needed. And always make sure the present, immediate story is running strongly before breaking away from it for more than a paragraph or so. Leave your plot as unencumbered as possible. Let it move.

### Judging the Balances in Popular Fiction

It's a question of proportion, of balance. The stronger, simpler, and more melodramatic your plot is, the more exposition it will stand (within reason) once the plot is rolling. If there's a murder on page one, readers will wait quite a few chapters, while the detective investigates this or that possibility and interviews suspects, until the next major event. That initial murder isn't forgotten. Once you've earned readers' confidence by an economical, powerful opening, readers will trust you not to let them down. They'll have faith that the buildup wasn't for nothing: something important is going to come of that first murder and there'll be more exciting dirty work afoot in the very near future.

The more complex, strange, and actionless your story is, the more you'll need to limit, digest, and subordinate your exposition, doling it out very sparingly indeed. That's particularly true in the most exposition-prone genres: science fiction, fantasy, mystery, and historical fiction of all sorts. If you're working in any of these forms, you're going to need to be particularly careful not to let unsubordinated exposition bog everything down.

## *With Literary Fiction, You Have to Make Your Best Judgment*

Literary fiction is often complex, and isn't normally characterized by slam-bang zippy melodramatic plots. Readers of literary works are a more tolerant audience in some respects than are readers of popular fiction, though they're apt to be more exacting in others. They're remarkably patient with fairly long stretches where nothing much seems to be happening, provided they like the characters, or the writing style, or *something* about the story enough to keep reading.

There are folk like me who *like* the cetology chapters in *Moby Dick* and the long, bizarre ruminations in Mervyn Peake's *Gormenghast* trilogy, and folk who think of *War and Peace* or *Finnegans Wake* as a pleasant evening's entertainment. (All right, a weekend, then.) Plot isn't as crucial to such readers as it is to devotees of genre or popular fiction. As will be discussed in Chapter 11, literary fiction occasionally substitutes some other kind of strong motion or contrast for plot, so there may not even *be* a plot to subordinate the exposition to.

If, in your story, something else is substituting for plot—juxtaposition, contrast, collage, whatever—then keep *all other el-*

*ements out of its way.* If it serves plot's purpose as the bones, the dynamic engine of your story, then it's *that* which should be the basis of your choices of what to subordinate and what to leave clear, unencumbered, and dominant. If your story is built on a nested series of flashbacks, then character and plot come second. Exposition should be no more than a distant third in your narrative priorities.

Exposition is the thing in fiction most like thought, least like action. Decide how much thought your story will support, in proportion to its dominant element, and still remain compact, direct and readable. Then write it however it seems to need to be written.

## Add Emotion and Stir Vigorously

Here's a tip based on a psychological quirk: we tend to remember best the information that comes to us surrounded by highly charged emotion. That's why so many people can remember precisely where they were and what they were doing when they first learned of the assassination of President Kennedy and how they spent their very first date.

Applied to exposition, this means that otherwise undigestible chunks of explanation will move faster, and be absorbed more easily, if they're put in a highly emotional context.

If you have some character really desperate for this information, the reader will tend to catch the infection and really want to know too. If you position the information in such a way that it has a strong and immediate emotional impact on somebody in the scene, it will become part of that scene's framework—hardly exposition at all. Or you can immerse your exposition in melodrama—whole situations which are emotionally charged—as I'll explain more in Chapter 7.

So now you know all the basic rules of effective exposition-cookery: move it fast, don't let it pile up too much in any one place, subordinate it to a strongly moving plot, and dip it in emotion whenever possible. Then, whenever you can, cut it out.

## Become a Plot Surgeon

When you've got one whole first draft in hand, one of your first chores in beginning your second draft should be going back and cutting every scrap of exposition you find you can possibly do without.

There's an ancient joke that runs: *Want to lose ten pounds of ugly fat? Cut off your head.* Well, don't cut off your story's head. But in second draft, cut absolutely everything your story can do without—and that especially includes exposition.

# CHAPTER 5

# EARLY MIDDLES: NEW DIRECTIONS AND SUBPLOTS

REMEMBER AWHILE BACK, I WARNED YOU that every plot will try to go wrong after the first big scene?

It's true. Generally, it's because fiction fatigue has set in. You've been concentrating intensely, and now your beginning is complete, doing all the jobs that beginnings need to do.

Back off a day or two, catch your breath, before going any further.

But leave your beginning alone.

That's terrifically important. You'll be inclined to tinker with it, unsure that the hard choices of intuition and craft were the right ones, after all. And much of your second-guessing will be wrong. When you've just finished something is not the right time to revise it. You don't know where it all fits in yet—what it's leading up to. Your story doesn't have a real shape yet that can resist insecure tinkering.

Leave your beginning alone, at least until you have one whole first draft, in the case of a short story; or until you're past the middle, in a novel. Until then, you're not in a position to judge the fiction as one unified thing and make informed decisions about the individual sections.

If you have ideas for revision, fine. Jot them down, staple them to page one. Start a file of afterthoughts. But don't try to implement them—not yet. Your beginning may well benefit from revision; as I warned you earlier, you may even find you have to scrap it and start over. But not now.

I think more stories have collapsed from premature tinkering than from any other single cause.

Fiction fatigue: expect it, and don't let it ruin your story.

Let the beginning cool off enough to stand poking and prodding, before you go back to it. Instead, after a healthy rest mowing lawn or going to your job, start gearing up for the special tasks that middles involve.

# AFTER THE OPENING, TAKE YOUR BEARINGS

I'll talk about short stories first because novels have to do exactly the same thing, only more so. (Novels have to do extra things, too, but don't worry about that now.)

If you followed my advice, you began *in medias res*. So there'll be things the reader will now be interested in knowing, to understand how matters came to be the way they were in the opening.

So you may decide to insert some exposition at this point or even a dramatized flashback, where past temporarily becomes present. These can do any of a variety of chores.

## A New Perspective on Your People

You can broaden the reader's understanding of a character by giving a highly selective account of his past, distant or immediate. Emphasize just the two or three (or so) things which are going to be of significance in your story's present context. As I've said before: Important things—not everything.

Or you may follow the character as he goes about his present business, as Dickens does with Scrooge: trudging home through the holiday streets from his frigid office to his frigid house, starting to eat his wretched supper.

You can get into a full-blown character sketch, establishing some contrary facet of your protagonist that wasn't apparent in the opening. The huge, wilfully unattractive protagonist of Flannery O'Connor's "Good Country People," lumbering around on her artificial leg, is shown to be a highly intelligent, sardonic observer of her rapacious and hypocritical circle of rustic acquaintance.

## Naming the Norm

If you're going to establish departure from a norm or a then/now contrast, it's a good time to lay the groundwork for it.

After its beginning, Katherine Anne Porter's *Noon Wine* shows the newly-hired and mysterious stranger at work in the fields and playing his cherished harmonica, at peace with himself and his surroundings—a peace that will be broken when the farmer discovers the hired man is on the run from a murder. This second section establishes a norm the story's later developments can be contrasted against.

Or the norm may be environmental—the character's society he or she is at odds with. In many of the stories in *Dubliners*, James Joyce follows that pattern: first giving a close focus on the protagonist, then showing the character's social world, demonstrating common attitudes and customs to present the protagonist in clearer social perspective. If your story has the main character in conflict with his immediate society and social norms, you may want to try this kind of opening-out too.

## Switch Viewpoints?

The shortest fiction can seldom support more than one viewpoint. But now the first scene is over; if you're going to change viewpoints at all during your story, here's where you should do it for the first time to establish the pattern for the rest of the story. Thus your character sketch may center, instead, on the story's antagonist, profiling him or her in a way that shows why a collision course with the protagonist is inevitable.

## Driving Right for the Cliff

Of course, you may plan a story that maintains tight focus to the end, with scarcely any exposition at all and perhaps just two characters. Many of Poe's short stories follow that pattern; I think of the narrator and doomed, foolish Fortunato, who provide the entire cast of "The Cask of Amontillado." And the plot is down the stairs and down the stairs, pausing only to collect wine and brandish the necessary mason's trowel as the narrator prepares to wall his victim up in the ancestral wine vaults to avenge a (perhaps) imagined insult.

That's the pattern in most genre short stories. The story flies like an arrow and hits the target at maximum speed.

If your story is going to have a direct, unencumbered narrative line with no digressions or shifts and virtually no exposition of any sort, then from the opening you'll continue the same scene or move right to another, with no interval at all.

## The Janus-Faced Interval

Whether you're writing short or long fiction and whatever the section following the beginning is, it's got two chores: to open up the beginning by looking backward or simply around, adding context; and to look anxiously forward and lay the groundwork for what's to come. The Roman god Janus, the god of doorways for whom January is named, had two faces so he could look both ahead and behind. That's what you need to do, after a story's first beginnings. I'll talk about methods of doing that kind of necessary spadework in a minute. But this part of your story is where it starts in earnest.

## GEARING UP FOR THE LONG HAUL

Now, the good news for the novelists out there: everything I've just been explaining applies to you too, but you've got more space to do it. You can devote a whole chapter or two to this second part, if you want. Probably there'll be scenes as well as straight exposition, to keep things rolling; but a strong effective beginning will win your readers. They're on your side now.

They've picked up the book. They know everything isn't going to be over in three or four pages. That's the way they want it, if they like novels. They'll stay with you now, unless you do something to lose them.

The looking-forward aspect of early middles is even more important for you, though, than for the short story writers. There's short-term plot and long-term plot, and both have to be running at once, either together or in alternation.

## Stages in the Journey

Remember, *plot is a verb*. Something is happening, and going to happen. But there are stages to plot, and in long fiction there should always be some specific event in the not-too-distant future the reader can anticipate. The main or long-term plot ideally runs through the whole story from the beginning. It's what the opening centers on; it provides the final climax or confrontation.

In *Lord of the Flies*, the castaway boys' immediate problems are, in sequence: establishing order, lighting a fire, hunting a wild pig, exploring the island, and dealing with their dread of "the Beast" they believe is on top of the mountain. More problems follow. But each of these intermediate problems is a stage in the larger problem of staying alive, and civilized. The whole long-term problem is broken up into a series of actions, each of which has its crisis and resolution. For instance, the problem of gathering the castaway boys together is solved by the finding and blowing of the conch. The problem of making fire is solved by Piggy's glasses, concentrating the sun's rays. But the solution sets up a later problem, when the breakaway tribe led by Jack steals the glasses and deprives Ralph's group of fire and Piggy of sight/vision (not precisely the same thing, in this book).

One problem or crisis builds to another, and another yet beyond. You need to have the main plot firmly in mind all along and be building toward the final crisis—in *Lord of the Flies*, the murderous pursuit of Ralph by painted, screaming savages driven by fear and superstition. You may not, at the early stages of the story, know precisely what that final crisis is going to be. That's all right. I'll offer some advice about endings in Chapter 10. Early in the story, just know that you should be building toward that ultimate crisis and that it should derive from the main plot as it was in the beginning, not from something weird and unexpected that turns up someplace along the way.

## Setting Up Subplots

Often long fiction will have more than one plot. The subplot(s) may run just a while before coming to resolution, or may continue through almost the whole story, being tied up just before the story's end. Sometimes subplots center on the main plot's protagonist, and sometimes they focus on one of the subordinate characters.

Well handled, they can deepen the story's context, offer ways to mirror or contrast with the main action, and be used in pacing to offer foreground motion while the main plot is in a temporary lull. When the main plot is busy, they can generate suspense when the narrative splits off to follow the subplot for a while before rejoining the main action, generally with added momentum and impact when they again converge.

If you're going to have one or more subplots centering on the main characters, start the first one running right after the beginning. For instance, your protagonist, Fred, not only wants to avoid rescuing Ginger from the roof—he also wants to prevent anybody else from rescuing her. This involves sabotaging the walkie-talkies before they're issued, one per boat crew. Or Fred is in fact a concert violinist and is worried that his flood rescue efforts will mean he won't be able to get to his solo appearance in Detroit. And he's worried Ginger may not have taken his centuries-old Stradivarius to safety up onto the roof with her. He wants to rescue the Strad, but not Ginger. Conflict!

But if you're going to have a subplot centering on somebody other than the protagonist, don't treat it separately just yet. (Remember Tiffany, stuck in the tree?) Instead, introduce the subordinate characters central to the subplot so the reader can get to know them before the narrative line splits off to follow them.

Maybe a flashback to the last argument between Ginger and Fred, when Tiffany ran out shouting that she wanted to live with Grandma. Then, when main plot and subplot are running simultaneously, you can switch off to follow Tiffany all by herself. Maybe she got caught in the tree while trying to run away to Grandma's house forever. Maybe she's worried about Grandma, or having second thoughts about running away. Maybe Grandma's up in the tree with her.

Whatever, it's an independent (though closely related) subplot. Lay some groundwork and establish your main plot firmly before splitting off to follow another line of action.

## Try a Braid

In long fiction, plots don't merely alternate with subplots: they're often woven together in something very like a braid. One strand loops around to the outside, out of sight, then warps in or under to briefly become the central point before warping off for another turn.

Once you have your initial situation running, with the major characters established and facing some crucial problem the reader can tell isn't going to go away, a braided plot won't just continue on. You'll bring in a new subject, one that has some new plot thread which you make clear but leave unresolved so that the reader can see that there are more developments to come.

You can braid that way two, three, even four times before you pick up strand A again and continue to new developments in that plot for a little while. Then C loops back, and B perhaps crosses over it to make a new pattern. Aha! Here comes D!

The stronger and clearer your individual plot threads are, the thicker the braid you can make. But a braid, like a chain, is only as strong as its weakest element. If one plot thread—especially your main one—is fragile, delicate, subtle, even confusing, be careful not to warp it more than it will stand or strangle it with subplots pulling this way and that. A braided plot can have so many twists and turns that it becomes something like a lump of fouled fishing line no sane reader's going to try to disentangle.

Be sure there's always a strong central narrative thread the reader can follow in spite of diversions and interruptions.

If your central plot is built on hints and slow unfoldings rather than on a series of clear and decisive developments, cut the number of subplots way back, maybe even to none. Conversely, if your main plot is as direct as a falling piano (something like boy meets girl, boy loses girl, boy and girl find one another), then braiding can broaden your story's scope and add narrative interest to an otherwise thin, straight-line, and predictable tale.

Multiple-strand plotting can yield a good solid braid if you watch out for dangling loose ends and keep tension strong at all times. Try a two or three strand braid, to start with. Then, as you learn the feel, you can expand to as many strands as you have pages and plot enough to spin out of your imagination.

## Don't Forget to Knot as You Go

Remember what I said about alternating viewpoint: that the story will try to split in two? That's even more true when it comes to subplots. Knot the different strands of your narrative together from time to time. Build in all the connections and convergences you can. Show events in the main plot affecting what's happening in the subplot, and the other way round. Have characters overlap, figuring in both main plot and subplot, although perhaps more important in one than the other. For instance, in *Wuthering Heights*, Heathcliff is one of the main protagonists of the plot as a whole; but in the subplot detailing the successive romances between young Cathy and her two cousins (one of them Heathcliff's son), Heathcliff becomes a background figure, like a thunderstorm grumbling in the distance.

Build in connections of mood, event, props, setting, and narrative pattern, as I'll discuss more in Chapter 8.

Finally, remember that like main plots, subplots need developments, crisis, big scenes, and resolution. Even if a subplot is only going to run for thirty pages or so before coming to final crisis, it deserves the same care, in miniature, as does your main plot. Don't neglect it. Refer to it from time to time. If possible, make the subplot's crisis coincide with, and be directly involved in, an important crisis in the main plot. Converging plot lines will add to the whole scene's impact and meaning.

For instance, you shouldn't kill off your protagonist in mid-plot; but you can kill off an important subordinate character who's been the center of a subplot. The implied threat to the protagonist will be intensified. And if you really like the subordinate character, you can write him or her a wonderful death scene and maybe throw a spectacular funeral.

## Parallel Plotlines

Sometimes judging which is main plot and which is subplot is about like tossing a coin. Both seem about equal. Perhaps the most familiar example of that would be the contrasting adventures of Han Solo, Princess Leia, and Chewbacca, on the one hand, and of Luke and Yoda, on the other, in George Lucas' movie *The Empire Strikes Back*, the second segment of his *Star Wars* trilogy.

All the characters are initially established together, at the secret rebel base tunneled into the ice. Since the ending of the story will involve Luke's rash and unsuccessful attempt to rescue Han from Darth Vader, a similar situation is set up in the beginning, where Han rescues Luke from being frozen to death. By no coincidence, Han's peril from Vader also involves his being frozen, although in something called "carbonite," not ordinary ice. The opening crisis mirrors the ending.

Likewise, Luke's initial resourcefulness in killing a snow monster and in singlehandedly destroying a huge, walking tank mirrors his lone battle with Vader at the movie's end. Since in the middle Luke is shown failing, blundering, whining, and not doing too much exciting, the action-filled beginning and end prevent him from looking like an incompetent wimp.

The beginning provides contrast and context for the middle. It's also strongly tied to the ending, to help hold the middle together.

The middle needs all the tying it can get, because in the middle, two plots split apart to follow different protagonists. The narrative line cuts back and forth between them. The part of the story focused on Han & Co. is a fairly straight chase/adventure with a romance thrown in. Luke's plot, more subtle and thoughtful, involves his education by Yoda in the nature and use of the Force—a more interior plot with hardly any action at all and certainly no romance.

I've found it interesting which among my friends prefers the Han plot and which the Luke plot, in this movie. Whichever you like better, notice the differences in subject, pacing, and tone in the divergent sections. Pains were taken to balance the comparatively less dramatic account of Luke's education with the lasers-blasting escaping and hiding and capture involved with Han & Co. Each plot is the richer and stronger for being contrasted with the other.

And notice how connections were built in. Although Han & Co. are completely occupied with their own problems, Luke becomes aware of them through a vision. That awareness and feeling of connectedness is what prompts Luke to leave although his training hasn't been completed. So Luke's awareness is a bridge between the two plot lines. Another is the fact that Han & Co. are captured by Darth Vader primarily as bait, to bring the real target—Luke—into Vader's reach.

But there are even more obvious connections—events repeated in slightly different form in each plot line. For instance, both plots involve the sudden and unexpected appearance of Darth Vader. For Luke, Vader appears as a malignant vision of possibility and identification (the illusory Vader has Luke's face), laying the groundwork both for the later duel and for the revelation that Vader is Luke's father; for Han & Co., Vader appears as an even more malignant reality. Both plots involve journeys. Han & Co.'s journey is primarily across space, whereas Luke's is mainly one of interior growth and insight—to and through the dark spaces in his own soul, moving from self-doubt to confidence (maybe even overconfidence). Both protagonists meet old friends: Han encounters Lando, and Luke finds he's still under the not-quite-ghostly oversight of Obi-Wan Kenobi, the dead (?) Jedi master. Both plots involve a cave where things aren't quite what they seem. Han parks his souped-up space jalopy somewhere in the interior of a mammoth space worm which, open-mouthed, fills the cave—the cave is a monster in literal fact. In Luke's cave, he finds the dreadful shadows of his own interior made manifest: his own fear and hatred take form as the figure of Vader, the threatening monster.

In each case, what in the Han plot is external, a physical reality is, in the Luke plot, internal—a realization or a vision. Internal and external balance, connect.

Then, after this middle section, the plots converge again in Luke's attempt to rescue Han & Co. and his first face-to-face confrontation with Vader. Luke joins the Han plot.

Together, apart, together. But even during the separation, many connections and echoes keep the two plots strongly interconnected and related. And suspense is created as the narrative line shifts from the one to the other, typically at cliffhangers in the Han plot, so we're kept waiting to find out how things are going back in the asteroid belt or in the Cloud City.

This is a story that could easily have fragmented; but it's held together by strong and effective narrative rivets so that the whole works as one single connected action.

Even though I assume most of you aren't planning to write space-opera melodrama, the structure of this story serves as a valuable demonstration of the basic techniques of handling parallel and equal plot lines. Reviewing it on videotape, if you have a VCR, can reveal still other connective devices, echoes, mirrors, and pacing techniques you'll find useful no matter what kind of fiction you're interested in.

Though there are all kinds of fiction there's only one craft. What works for one story will likely work for another, and all good works of craft repay thoughtful study.

If you're contemplating a divided plot structure, spend this after-beginning section strongly establishing your characters and their relationships, and creating scenes and events you can echo later on, to be a solid basis for the coming split.

Because after this, things are going to get *really* interesting. In just a few paragraphs or pages, you'll be looking toward your first major crisis, your first Big Scene, where the plot is really going to thicken and knot and spit sparks in all directions.

# CHAPTER 6

# BUILDING THE BIG SCENES: SET- PIECES

THE JOB OF A MIDDLE is to build toward and deliver crisis. That's true whether you're working in long-form or short-form fiction.

And since scenes are the foundation of fiction, the foundation of plots are special scenes, big scenes. They're generally called set-pieces—I'm not sure why. Maybe it's because they need setting up to be effective.

## SLOWLY IT TURNS, STEP BY STEP

Stories, especially long fiction, need to be divided into stages, intermediate short-term plots, each with its own build-up, crisis, and resolution. Before Frodo and Sam can reach Mount Doom to destroy the terrible Ring, they have to reach Rivendell and Lorien and pass through Shelob's lair. Before Sam Spade can find out who killed his partner, he has to disarm Joel Cairo and the gunsel, dodge his partner's jealous wife and the police she sets on him, and find out who the Fat Man is and what this black bird is that everybody seems so interested in.

Even if your story is a journey through time or one of realization and revelation, rather than one across distance, it's still a journey. There need to be destinations, memorable landmarks, and even rest stops, several of them, before it reaches the final goal.

## Set-Pieces

These intermediate moments of climax and partial, temporary resolution are what set-pieces are designed to provide. A set-piece is a big scene the reader can see coming and can look forward to awhile, either in fear or in hope, before it's reached. The duel between Luke and Darth Vader is a set-piece. The burning of Atlanta, in *Gone With the Wind*, is another. In *Lord of the Flies*, Simon's journey up the mountain to see what's *really* up there, monster or not, is a set-piece, as is his return into the middle of the hysterical tribal dance by which the boys are trying to drive out fear. Simon is mistaken for the Beast and killed. We could see it coming, even though Simon didn't. We weren't sure—we hoped for the best, but suspected the worst.

Seeing a scene like that coming, watching it build to crisis, is one of the major ways of creating tension, drama, and suspense in a story.

The earliest set-pieces will be the hardest, because they'll still have expositional chores to do—developing the characters, demonstrating the nature of the conflict, establishing the setting, and so on. They'll also have the briefest preparation. The later ones can be more streamlined and direct. You'll have your little world set up fairly completely in all its complexities by then; the reader will already know your characters and appreciate what's at stake, and you'll have had time to lay your groundwork to build toward the set-piece that's coming.

Being more direct, and carrying the whole foregoing story's momentum behind them, these later set-pieces will gain in impact and drama. You and your story will be up to speed then: in third gear, and rolling fast. Later set-pieces will be easier to write.

Remember that and take heart: after the beginning, and after the sections immediately following, it gets easier. The story itself will be on your side, helping you to create and move.

If you choose your set-pieces well, build up to them so that the reader can see what's coming, *and deliver on them*, your story will be good reading from beginning to end.

# Delivering on Set-Pieces

I emphasize *delivering* because far too many beginning writers get terminally shy about their set-pieces. They dodge away into talk, or skip the scene and maybe refer afterward to what happened. They'll do every blessed thing except actually *write the scene*.

I don't know how or why this kind of fundamental narrative timidity originates (although, rereading my own early stories, I see that I suffered from a touch of it too, here and there). I only know I've seen quite a lot of it, mostly in unpublished work.

Maybe intuitively such beginners realize that a set-piece is the third most important part of any story, after the opening and the ending. Maybe they realize their story is going to stand or fall by the scene coming up, and they just can't face the responsibility of writing it and being judged by it. They're afraid to commit themselves and go for broke. So instead, they skitter off into exposition or summary, and the story sags.

Face up to set-pieces. Make up your mind to write them, even if—*especially if*—you're afraid to. If you see that things in your story are heading toward a blowup between Ginger and Fred pretty soon, show the tension building up, show the hurt feelings accumulating, and then blow everything sky-high. Make their blowup happen at a party, on a train station, or someplace where neither can get away until they've both had their hurtful say. Use the setting to complement or contrast strongly with the action. Write the battle as though it were a new beginning, with that much clarity and intensity.

Write the scene.

Notice and polish every legitimate, intrinsic bit of drama inherent in the scene until it absolutely glitters. Embody that drama in action—things done, things said, in a *scene* happening right before the reader's eyes.

## Not All the Scenery Has to Show Tooth Marks, Though

When I say "write the scene," I don't mean overwrite it. If what you're writing is a domestic quarrel, don't throw in a burglar or attacking commandos or the kitchen sink just because it would make the scene dramatic. That sort of overkill will only push the scene over the edge into farce.

What I mean is that, whatever your set-piece is, you should bring out all its facets and polish it like a jewel. Make it the best domestic quarrel anybody ever wrote, one the neighbors would buy tickets to watch, not a garbled, hodgepodge screaming match with tanks bursting in.

Write the scene so that something has completely happened, every bit. More will undoubtedly come of it later on, but this one scene shines. Frodo really does resist the Dark Riders at the ford, at least long enough for wizardly help to arrive. Simon really does see, clear and plain, what horrible, pitiable thing actually is on top of the mountain.

## Setting Up What's to Come

Now, after the beginning that set up the major narrative and structural patterns, and after the opening section where your plot really got rolling, you should start imagining where, in the short run, your story is going. What major event, several pages or chapters ahead, is going to happen? Start imagining it. Who will be there? What's going to lead to it? And what's going to happen? What will you need to establish beforehand, so that set-piece can have its full weight and impact? How can you go about laying that necessary groundwork now, where you are in the story?

As I've said before, stories—especially live, convincing stories—will change under your hands. That's the reason I've never been persuaded of the usefulness of outlines. By other writers' experience and my own, I judge that you generally won't know how a story's going to go until you get close to the place where something is just about to happen. It will take its own shape and tell you how it wants to go, if you listen and watch attentively for the ways it's telling you.

My advice is that you should always know what your next set-piece is going to be. You should be laying the groundwork for it right up to the time it happens. You should start that groundwork either from the story's beginning, or lay down the first seeds back before the previous set-piece, to mature and bloom later. And you should be thinking of how that set-piece relates to your main story and making sure it won't seem grafted on, invented on the spot, but is a natural outcome of everything that's gone before.

It can't be just any scene, either. You'll have only about a dozen set-pieces in a whole long novel; in a more compact book, there will probably be more like six. In short fiction, perhaps three: beginning, middle, and end. Or, in the tightest and most focused of short stories, maybe only one. These set-pieces are going to be your story's high points; the scenes a reader will remember when the build-up, transition, and explanation have all been forgotten; the scenes where your plot rises to crisis.

So choose them well. As much as possible, let your story generate them. Let them arise out of who your people are, what problems they're facing, what they're trying to do—the story's central conflict. After they're in place, they'll seem inevitable, as if nothing else could possibly have happened. But you have to make them up: not quite out of nothing, but out of the body and bone of your story as it takes shape under your hands.

## Things Get Blacker and Blacker

In long fiction, scene builds on scene, set-piece on set-piece. The impact isn't isolated, but cumulative. It becomes a story's momentum, its pace (about which, more in Chapter 9.)

Very often, several or even all of the intermediate crises will be disasters, with matters apparently much worse than before. The protagonist will be defeated, though not quite utterly. This increases tension and suspense, acting as build-up for the final crisis. But each of the intermediate crises also should open a new door, present a fresh opportunity, offer a revelation as to the real nature of the problem the protagonist faces. In Charlotte Brontë's *Jane Eyre*, the attic conceals brooding Rochester's first wife, and every crisis in Jane's romance brings her nearer that crucial discovery. Daphne du Maurier's *Rebecca* is also founded on a fundamental lie—that Rebecca, Maxim's dead first wife, was a paragon whom Maxim loved profoundly and now mourns continually. Every major crisis the young protagonist faces unravels part of that lie to disclose the truth: that Rebecca was an unfaithful and unfeeling wife whom Maxim came to hate deeply, perhaps to the point of murder.

To the degree that your plot is a mystery, your set-pieces should provide, not only crisis, but unfolding revelation of a central truth concealed at the story's beginning and not completely demonstrated until the final crisis.

But it's not just mysteries which set-pieces can reveal. Remember, plot involves actions with meaningful consequences. Such consequences evolve, one step at a time. Each set-piece (after the first) should be set in motion, at least in part, by what happened in the previous one. This present scene should dramatize and arise from the effects created by what's gone before, and in turn have effects played out in the story thereafter. Cause sparks effect, which in turn becomes cause, right up to your story's end.

Using the existing story as a step from which to find and reach the next level of tension and crisis is what creates unity in long fiction: the feeling that all the parts are necessary to the whole and are meaningfully connected, each with the others.

## Outlining from Inside

When you've written your set-piece, you should be looking ahead to the end, to see if you can see its shape any more clearly from this vantage point than you could before. And if you can, make adjustments to make this scene lead more clearly, more precisely, toward the last cliff, with fewer possible turnings-away, so that the story, crisis by crisis, narrows down to a point that seems inevitable when it comes.

I call it outlining from inside. Blocking out the story, one set-piece step at a time, from inside it, taking due account of what it seems so far to be trying to become. That much outlining, I believe, every writer needs if his story is not to appear a funhouse, a random series of events sprung on the reader for no particular reason, gone too fast to have impact, leading from nothing to nothing. You need some kind of an outline, some idea of where you're going and how, if you're going to keep your story out of the funhouse which, in fiction, is no fun at all.

Look ahead at least to your next major scene and get ready for it. Then deliver.

## But Don't Hint It to Death

In your build-up, though, take care not to try to write the set-piece before it's ready, before it's had a chance to simmer properly. Establish that it's coming, and maybe hint at the basic nature of the confrontation. You've established your characters, so the reader has some idea how each will react in crisis. But don't give away the exact crisis, or the outcome. Leave that for the scene itself. Grant the reader not only the enjoyments of looking forward but the enjoyments of discovery, scene by scene, as well. Write your set-pieces boldly and thoroughly, but keep some of your cards hidden right up to the end.

## Or Serve It With a Twist

If the outcome, or the crisis itself, seems too predictable, like the traditional western gunfight, you can throw in maybe one surprise element—not attacking guerrillas, but something you've carefully refrained from hinting about. If you've set the stage for a duel, deliver a duel, all right—but fought with dynamite instead of guns. If your build-up has promised an explosion at a bank, deliver an explosion—but one that not only opens the safe but sets fire to the thieves' getaway car.

Never fail to deliver what, implicitly or explicitly, you've promised your reader. But don't assume you have to serve it up in the same, predictable old dish, either.

Your sudden twist mustn't change the basis of the confrontation itself, like guerrillas in the middle of a domestic argument (unless, of course, you're writing surrealistic farce, in which case all bets are off, anyway: even twittering nine-armed Martians are legal, then, if they work). The mood and meaning should be the same, regardless of the twist. Don't make the scene anticlimactic, like a duel that's fought with wet spaghetti or water balloons, or a

ball where friends try to keep the feuding male and female protagonists apart—and succeed, so nothing happens after all.

Play with Murphy's Law. Try to think of what, within that
fundamental situation, could go surprisingly wrong, yet seem
believable and reasonable, within that context, when it happens.

For instance, on the mountain, Simon finds, not a monster,
but a dead pilot. But since Jack's tribe is in the process of turning
into warriors, and since the irrevocable step in that transformation is their killing of Simon, a dead soldier isn't a neutral thing
either. It's the essential savagery and warlike inclinations of humanity that's the Beast in the book. So it's a real Beast, *the* real
and only beast, which Simon discovers. It's just not the sort of
beast either Simon or the reader had expected.

The scene throws in a twist, but it works. It delivers true
monsterdom, in the book's special context, and monstrous
things come of the discovery. It works better than it would have
if Simon found nothing, or Godzilla. And part of its being better
is the surprise twist that makes more sense than finding either
nothing or a trampling reptile, because it's appropriate to its
context. We couldn't have predicted it, but it fits. It works. It's a
masterly twist—one of many in the book. There's another at the
end. And, no, I'm not going to tell you how it all comes out.

Read *Lord of the Flies*, if you haven't already. It's not cheery,
but you'll learn a lot about laying evidence, build-up, and delivering set-pieces from it. Also, if it's any inducement, it's short. . . .

## LAYING THE GROUNDWORK

There are ways to prepare for an upcoming set-piece. Some of
them are obvious, some less so.

One obvious thing you need to do is simply naming the approaching event—the visit of the wealthy but irascible grandfa-
ther, the trip to the zoo, the battle at the river, the big dance or
exclusive party your protagonist yearns to be invited to. It would
seem just common sense to mention the event before it happens
and indicate, through characters' words and attitudes, why it's
likely to be climactic, but I'm always surprised how many writers

neglect this basic chore.

Maybe they figure if they spring their set-piece on the reader without preparing the ground, it'll be even more of a surprise. And it is—but not a good one. Without anticipation, a sudden crisis has all the drama of slipping on the ice and thumping your tailbone. There's no suspense, no anticipation—just the jolt, and it's over. Big deal. At least half the fun of any holiday is the looking forward. Apply that to your fiction, and prepare for your big scenes.

These no-build-up folk are the opposite of those I mentioned earlier: the ones who enjoy the hinting and the looking forward, but hate arriving, whose idea of effective surprise is that, after considerable preparation, *nothing* happens. Wow. Surprise. I trust you won't be tempted to join that coy and anticlimactic crew. You may have heard the saying, "It's better to travel hopefully than to arrive." Maybe so. But in fiction, you'd better do both or take up another trade, like fan dancing. There's only just so much hopeful traveling you can expect readers to do before they give up in annoyance and disappointment. After a strong beginning, you'll have some credit to draw on, but there are limits.

## Use a Preview Scene

Another way to lay groundwork is to have a small preview scene where some form of the actual events of the coming set-piece are set up—a small duel or clash anticipating the big duel or clash. There's an instance of this in *The Empire Strikes Back*, which I discussed in the previous chapter: Luke has a laser-sword fight with an apparition of Darth Vader conjured in an evil cave (a fight Luke loses *because* he wins). Those few seconds are setup for the actual duel enacted in several distinct stages near the movie's conclusion. In that later duel, Luke loses but escapes defeat by casting himself into the unknown rather than allow himself to despair and surrender—a reverse mirror of the earlier fight where victory paradoxically meant defeat. Here, defeat leads to Luke's coming to terms with the truth, that Vader's his father: the pivotal insight which powers the trilogy's eventual and climactic reconciliation between them in *Return of the Jedi*.

If your set-piece is going to hinge on the fact that your protagonist has lost his glasses, show them being lost (and eventually found) a time or two beforehand. It will provide foreshadowing as well as make the important loss of the glasses, in the set-piece, entirely believable and convincing.

## Use Contrasts and Make Things Get Much Worse or Much Better

Your set-piece will have the most impact if you lead up to it with scenes of varied length, but all brisk and relatively short. Then, when your set-piece arrives, your reader will be ready to settle down to something more substantial and intense.

If your set-piece is going to be a grim disaster, you have a choice—your lead-in scenes can be cheery, hopeful, or peaceful (suspicious readers will immediately start suspecting the worst) or else more and more troubled and disturbing. Then the scene will need to be not merely the confirmation of the characters' worst fears, but beyond anything they'd even imagined. (Merely confirming suspicions has little drama; finding out things are even worse than you'd thought leaves whole new vistas of unpleasantness to explore.)

But if your big scene is going to turn out wonderful and happy, the lead-in should probably be as black as possible. Cheer followed by more cheer, cute upon cute, can make even the non-diabetic among us wince. A touch of sour gives tang and helps ward off banality. Unrelieved sweetness, thoroughgoing uplift, becomes stronger and more persuasive by the addition of a dash of bitters, at least in anticipation, though your set-piece may open all sunny and go on to become positively idyllic and full of implicit happily-ever-afters.

## Make Room for the Aftermath

How you lead your narrative out of a set-piece is just as important as how you lead it in.

The outcome of the set-piece has to *matter*, and needs to

have narrative and emotional space to matter in. After the big scene, the story should be changed and the characters meaningfully affected by what's happened. If everything goes on as before, the set-piece will seem much fuss and bother about nothing—empty, irrelevant, and finally disappointing, no matter how well written and dramatic in itself. It should not only arise from the story that goes before, but be a determining factor in the story that comes afterward.

Crises are sometimes called turning points. Make sure that, after a set-piece, the story does turn—into something even more absorbing and important. With each round, all bets are raised and more is at stake and at risk. By the story's end, everything of importance to the protagonist, in that particular context, should be at hazard, win or lose.

## A Matter of Life and Death

In fiction for the widest readership, what's at stake will probably be life, love, or both, in the most literal and direct way. Somebody, or somebody's lover, could get killed. In less melodramatic fiction, the stakes may be self-respect, reconciliation, being true to oneself or to an ideal or a relationship. But these more subtle, interior stakes must in fact be just as high as those in stories where the protagonist faces purely physical and external threats.

The death of the self is also death, though the body may live on. An interior death is still a death to be feared and fought with all one's energy and wit. So is the death of the heart—the capacity to feel, as distinct from the threatened loss of a relationship or of a particular lover. The risk of becoming what one hates, committing the one unforgivable act, speaking the lie (or the truth) that can never be unsaid, are dangers perhaps more terrible than that of facing a loaded gun.

Whatever the actual terms of the risk, it should finally always become and be a matter of life and death—however life and death have been defined in this particular context, your own unique world. And the risk should escalate and intensify from the opening crisis right up to the end. With the whole weight of the book's context, the characters' development, and the building momentum of the crises along the way to give it force and meaning, what seemed perhaps a minor threat or a small personal desire at the beginning should, by story's end, be felt by the reader to be as profound as a clash of suns, in which all light will either fail or blaze triumphant.

Where everything's on the line, and that line keeps getting nearer the edge—that's a set-piece.

# CHAPTER 7

# HARNESSING MELODRAMA

MENTION MELODRAMA AND ALL IT CONJURES UP for some people is a wide-eyed heroine being tied to the train tracks by a moustache-twirling villain. But that's not it. Not by half.

If drama releases the electricity implicit in small events, melodrama calls down lightning.

Melodrama is the equivalent of a blinding flash accompanied by a loud noise. It can be a bony hand creeping from behind a curtain, a grand passion, someone teetering on a high ledge, or any of a thousand vivid situations and characters. Their meaning is right out in the open; they seem special, unusual, exciting. Such events speak directly to our imaginations and emotions.

Some people seem larger than life. Who and what they are is recognized at once. It's similar to the way a good caricature of a President or a celebrity can be more easily identified than an ordinary snapshot: a caricature draws in bold lines those features most associated with that person and downplays the unimportant ones. Some fictional characters seem larger than life: strong, interesting, dramatic. They too speak directly to our imaginations and emotions.

Melodrama is a technique of revealing reality by concentrating on the ends of the spectrum rather than the middle, the remarkable rather than the ordinary.

Events and individuals whose appeal and significance speak directly in this way, that don't need explaining, can immediately involve readers and arouse their sympathies. Using them in fiction can lead to forceful plots relatively unencumbered by exposition and peopled by vivid, colorful characters. For that reason, melodrama is the foundation of popular (genre) fiction, aimed at the broadest possible range of readers and intended primarily (but not solely) for entertainment.

Melodrama is also used, selectively and often with even greater impact, in literary fiction, which aims at a narrower readership and is intended primarily to present the author's view of the world/life/people. Because it's heightened, exaggerated reality, melodrama lends itself easily to symbolism, allegory, and surrealism, a different but related kind of exaggeration whereby the meanings implicit in objects, people, or events become more luminous and accessible than meanings normally are in the chaotic muddle of our everyday world. Sometimes visionary, heightened reality is the most real of all, because all the transitory, trivial details have been stripped away to reveal the fundamental essence of things.

## The Power and Problems of Melodrama

Because melodrama ignores the ordinary to concentrate on the unusual and unlikely, it often creates a credibility problem. Because it chooses the heart over the head, the snap reaction over thoughtful consideration, emotion can go over the edge into sentimentality, tear-jerking, thrills or scares for their own sake, as empty of meaning as a whoopie cushion. Melodrama can therefore seem *or be* sensation-mongering, appealing to the lowest common denominator and our least intelligent responses; so it also has a respectability problem. But carefully managed, it has power.

At the best, it's as fundamental and useful as salt, heightening and bringing out the flavor of whatever it's added to; at the worst, it takes over and drowns all lesser seasonings and renders the dish uneatable. Such built-in power isn't something any writer can afford to dismiss or ignore without risking blandness. But it's not something to toss in by the handful, either.

Like myth, legend, and fairy tale, melodrama is a part of our common emotional and cultural language. Judiciously used, it can create instant rapport between writer and reader. It can be casting an effective spell—or it can be a curse, a pitch as blatant, annoying, and obvious as somebody stridently hawking used cars on late-night tv. It's a question of degree, and of craft.

Whether a given melodramatic event or character is effective or becomes a kind of emotional and literary cliché, trivializing the story in which it appears, is just a matter of how it's handled, set up, shown.

If your story is founded on melodrama—the death of a child, first love, God running a society of secret agents (Chesterton, *The Man Who Was Thursday*), a vampire opening red eyes, a maniac stalking and slaughtering teenagers—it will need to be handled with special care if it's to avoid being or seeming clichéd, overdone, or outright silly and weird.

## TAMING WILD MELODRAMA

Curses are melodramatic—the ancient kind, especially in mysterious symbols on parchment, especially involving mummies. Especially curses that work. (Boasts Shakespeare's pompous Glendower, "I can call spirits from the vasty deep," to which Hotspur retorts sardonically, "Why, so can I, or so can any man; but will they come when you do call to them?")

So how can you have something like, say, a real working curse, something that actually *comes*, in your story and make the reader want to believe in it while the story lasts?

How can you encourage what literary critics have called "the willing suspension of disbelief" when your story is founded on something intrinsically unlikely, strikingly unusual, or even impossible?

Melodrama, what I'm going to call "the curse" as a kind of shorthand for discussion, can be any of a variety of events, horrible or wonderful: love, death, or both together. It can be the supernatural, the exotic, the strange, the highly improbable coincidence. It can be a monstrous or magical character, divorced from the usual range of human experience or capabilities.

Melodrama is extremes of any kind, things intended to rouse strong emotions and invoke implicit shared attitudes. Like Jacob wrestling with the angel, you can't let go of such powerful material until you've come to terms with it, turning the curse into a blessing.

## Taking the Curse off the Curse

There are straightforward ways of setting your curse in the middle of solidly credible things and declaring it right from the beginning. There are other methods of misdirecting attention so that the curse has already happened and been accepted before the reader has a chance to holler, "Hey, now, wait a minute!"

I'll start with the front-loading ways first—putting the unusual right up front and making it part of the story's fundamental reality.

1. Show that it works, right away. Have your curse actually operating (or your vampire stalking, your magician performing prodigies, or whatever) right on page 1, so the reader knows that in this story, one of the rules is going to be that your particular curse works. Show it, don't tell it.

*Star Wars* starts out with a backdrop of stars and two spaceships blasting colored rays at another. Anne Rice's *Interview with the Vampire* starts out with a vampire talking into a tape recorder. Either way, you know pretty clearly what you're in for from the beginning. Each story demonstrates its central premise: modern vampires, or shoot-'em-up spaceflight. What you see is what you get.

If your story will be playing by rules other writers have used before—that vampires exist, that faster-than-light travel is possible—this may be the best way. Introduce your premise with as little fuss as possible and get on with your story, what you're going to be doing within that accepted convention.

If you're embarking on thoroughgoing surrealism, then make *that* clear from the outset. The unfortunate protagonist of Kafka's *Metamorphosis* doesn't turn into an insect halfway through but in the very first sentence. State the premise, make the rules of your fiction clear, and go on from there.

2. Show that the curse has worked in the recent past. Sometimes this way is better, particularly if you're working with an unusual premise that will be entirely new to your readers and that they'll therefore be more resistant to than a familiar one. That way, your curse becomes, not a possibility, but an accomplished fact.

We know there's no arguing with the past: it's over. That psychological quirk, our willingness to accept something that happened in the past more readily than something claimed in the present, can work for you.

This can include having your curse (or unusual character or event) talked about before he/she/it actually appears, to prepare the ground. That's the way Melville sets up Ahab.

Or you can have a past event for which no satisfactory explanation has ever been found. The story then demonstrates the cause in the present, which also explains the past, retroactively. The real and undoubted past event anchors and renders credible the present investigations, revelations, and developments.

You can also tie in the *in medias res* advice I gave earlier, in this regard—showing curse #2 threatening first, then dropping back to let the reader know about curse #1 (or the fact that three teenagers have already been found mysteriously hickory-smoked to death or whatever your improbable premise may be).

3. Establish a reasonable character, and have him take the curse seriously. Don't have anybody doubting it, at least not for long. As readers, we're used to fictional conventions. We'll accept that in one story there's a secret door to elfland, and in another, killer tomatoes are thumping toward New York. It doesn't really do any good, anymore, to have some stooge still claiming on p. 183, "It can't be: another head growing out of her WHAT?"

The reader gets annoyed at such a character, who's still resisting what the reader has already accepted as a basic premise. A resident Doubting Thomas doesn't defuse incredulity, as he once served to do in earlier fiction for a more literal-minded age; he just looks like a dolt.

Instead, have your whole cast of characters either ignorant of the curse, or worried/hopeful about it—just the one, or the other. Once the reader has accepted your premise, anybody who stubbornly refuses to do likewise is obviously a jerk (and you might want to use that fact to undercut a character at some point). Show that in your story, ordinary, reasonable people—not just those privy to the Secret Knowledge of the Ancients, like Dr. Van Helsing—take your premise very seriously indeed.

4. Surround your curse with tangible everyday objects and activities, described in detail. Paraphrasing the trenchant observation of a former Dr. Who, the Yeti (Abominable Snowman) you surprise in your suburban bathroom is a lot scarier than the one encountered on a glacier in exotic Tibet.

Realistic details make for realism. Alfred Hitchcock knew this, and made ordinary things the springboards for horrifying and unlikely occurrences: remember the shower scene in *Psycho*? Remember the birds roosting patiently (and in ever-increasing numbers) on the jungle gym, waiting for school to let out?

Things can get more and more bizarre as your story progresses, but if you anchor your improbability solidly in the everyday to begin with (nice urban professional couple—husband a little moody, wife pregnant: Ira Levin, *Rosemary's Baby*), the reader will accept it.

If you're going to have, as a character, the eight-armed ambassador from the Wobbly Worlds, don't introduce him/her/it doing something alien and incomprehensible. Open the story with him/her/it swearing at a cabdriver in midtown Manhattan or searching myriad pockets for change of a ten. Or have the alien doing something plain and simple, like watching the sunrise or playing a flute. Balance the extraordinary with the mundane to give the reader a solid point of contact.

5. Use just one curse at a time. Don't have more than one major improbability per story. If there are a whole lot of odd goings-on, as in Peter Straub's *Ghost Story*, they should all have, finally, a single cause. That one cause accepted, all the rest follows: the other oddities fall into place. But don't turn your story into Abbot and Costello Meet Frankenstein, the Wolfman, Dracula, and the Smog Monster. That just turns into embarrassed giggles, not serious (if temporary) belief.

Don't cross genres, either. Don't have what, for 2/3 of the

story, we're led to believe is a normal (if insane) mass murderer, in a police-procedural sort of story, and then change gears and reveal that the murderer is a filthy Arcturan spy after our electromagnetic secrets or a Neanderthal thawed from a handy nearby glacier. State your rules, make your promises, at the outset; then stick to them.

However, you're free to extrapolate, as Stephen King does in *'Salem's Lot*. His premise is your basic vampire. His extrapolation is that, in an isolated town with only so many bite-ees available, one vampire with one victim per night would lead very shortly, by geometric progression, to virtually everybody in town's becoming vampiric. (One bites one; two bite two, the following night, for a total of four; four bite four more, and now there are eight, just in three days, and so on.) That's a valid, reasonable extrapolation from the initial premise. Science fiction does a lot of similar extrapolations—one speculative hypothesis, and then the rest solidly logical and reasonable, given that initial premise.

Keep to one central premise, and what hangs by it. Refrain from throwing in kitchen sinks.

6. Don't undercut your curse. Don't play it for laughs, ever, if you want it otherwise taken seriously. Don't show it was all a dream, or not really a curse at all, or all due to a fever hitherto unknown to science. A contemporary reader's belief isn't too hard to earn, but can be lost in a flash. Don't explain your curse away or make fun of it. Your monster can show up wearing a Mickey Mouse watch (or, as in the case of King's *It*, a clown suit)—but it'd better be a *very sinister* Mickey Mouse watch, worn for a solid and serious reason, not because you're laughing at your own story and making it look silly. That has all the charm of a comedian getting hysterics over his own gags while the audience prepares to pelt him with week-old kumquats.

Your readers can't express their indignation quite so directly; but they'll flip the page or do something more interesting, like sort coupons. And they won't come back. Ever. Why risk that, for the sake of a few authorial chuckles at your story's (and your readers') expense?

7. Especially at first, don't talk about the curse yourself, in

narrative summary. Show it in action and dialogue, in scenes. As
the characters discern what odd thing is going on, the reader will
be finding out along with them. And the characters provide a
solid anchor (if you don't make them unbelieving fools). The
reader will tend to accept what they accept, if you've established
them as credible people the reader is willing to identify with.

Dialogue is more believable than summary. We overhear it.
We assume the characters believe and mean what they're saying,
unless they're visibly foolish or obviously lying. The dialogue is
shown (heard), not told about in summary, and therefore has
greater immediacy and impact. We may not be inclined to credit
what the author claims (until we've seen it for ourselves), but
we'll believe the characters if they've been made credible as people to begin with.

8. Don't let the curse either take over, rendering the whole
story weird and uninvolving, or become commonplace. If you've
got a magical character, don't have him or her casting spells every few pages, or the reader will find it too hard to make contact
with the reality the fiction presents. A story where literally anything can happen is a story where nothing makes sense. It has no
internal coherence, no rules, no dramatic tension. If anything
can happen, it all happens for no particular reason and leads to
no particular result. No build. No momentum.

Similarly, an all-powerful character, one who can do anything he or she chooses, kills drama and suspense. That's the
trouble the original creators of Superman ran into—nothing
was a real challenge, the way Superman's character and powers
had been defined. *Voila*: Kryptonite!

If the extraordinary character is somebody other than the
protagonist (usually a good choice: remember what I said about
bridge characters, back in Chapter 3), keep that character offstage most of the time and center attention on the more credible
protagonist. That's why Tolkien kills off Gandalf fairly early in
the first book of the trilogy and doesn't resurrect him for several
hundred pages. He wanted to focus on the hobbits, who have to
make hard choices, not on a wizard who just has to wave a wand
and speak some words to get out of trouble. And he shows the

limits on Gandalf's power throughout, to bring out the wizard's human qualities and counterbalance the magical ones.

Make the magician or elf (or whatever) very normal and ordinary 99 percent of the time, but with the potential of being extraordinary once in a while. That builds credibility and also suspense, since the reader is always waiting for the specialness to come out.

Michael McDowell has a remarkable multi-volume novel titled *Blackwater*. It's an account of the doings of a fairly ordinary southern family, except that the protagonist turns, every now and again, into something apparently indistinguishable from the Creature from the Black Lagoon. The rest of the time, she's an interesting but by no means remarkable housewife. Sometimes, just once in a while, she transforms and eats people who annoy her. That gives, as you might well imagine, heightened drama to arguments with her in-laws and makes readers take a particular interest in her children's adolescent difficulties.

If you've got a monster, don't trot it out in every chapter or the reader will start to yawn. The monster you imagine, as a reader, is much more frightening than the monster you see. The reality will tend to be a letdown, simply because it's a determinate object and no longer The Unknown.

*Waiting* to find out builds suspense, drama. Actually finding out should be reserved to a climax, a set-piece. Afterward, if the story continues beyond that first face-to-face revelation, you'll need some new source of drama because the monster won't be quite so scary anymore.

Doyle knew this in *The Hound of the Baskervilles*: he let the reader hear the hound's howling but didn't give more than a glimpse or a hint until the very end. He avoided undercutting his monster, too. The hound isn't supernatural, but it's still quite capable of tearing somebody's throat out. It's not the same threat as was feared, but it's a legitimate threat all the same. Remember what I said about twists, back in Chapter 5? That applies here, too. Your twist (if you use one) must satisfy and improve upon what it substitutes for, not just change it to something else. That's anticlimax, letdown, disappointment.

# FAKING OUT THE READER

The other way of winning conditional belief in your curse, especially after the story's initial section, is to keep the reader watching the right hand while the left hand is doing the funny business.

Here are the major techniques:

1. Introduce the melodramatic element by the back door in a scene ostensibly dealing with something else. ("Charlie, I'm getting a divorce. I'm sick of your father's drinking, the way your brother Greg seems to disappear into the wallpaper, and your mother's flute playing." *Disappears into the wallpaper?* Hmmm.) Make the curse seem innocuous at first, until the reader is solidly hooked. Then develop it.

2. Have one or two previews, or false alarms, before the *real* curse shows up. Introduce, just casually, some apparently trivial elements that have a buried, hidden connection to your as-yet unrevealed curse.

Don't have any important plot element or character revelation depend on these false alarms, so the reader's resistance isn't alerted or raised. Don't make them carry any immediate narrative weight. The elements are just there, seemingly incidental, hardly noticed at the time.

In *To Kill a Mockingbird*, as Scout and Jem Finch are trudging through woods toward the schoolhouse for the pageant, another child jumps out and frightens them. On the way home, Scout thinks she hears following footsteps and believes it's the same child trying to startle them again. She calls out, but gets no reply. She and Jem begin to walk faster, still expecting the malicious child. When the backwoodsman who hates their father suddenly attacks them, the emotional groundwork has been laid.

Again, the reader is surprised—nobody expected the man to attack the Finch children (despite an oblique warning from the sheriff)—and not surprised, since Scout was expecting somebody to jump out at her. She just didn't expect an adult with a big, sharp knife.

An effective false alarm leaves the reader both prepared and unprepared—surprised, but believing. Even though the reader didn't realize the false alarm was groundwork, it's been laid and will sustain the strangeness when it comes.

In general, because readers take plot seriously and follow most attentively what at least *seem* to be plot developments rather than incidents, misdirecting their attention (now that you know what they'll be paying special attention to) isn't all that hard.

3. Have a character expecting something even more extraordinary, so that when the real curse comes, it'll seem credible by comparison. In *Wuthering Heights*, the initial narrator, Lockwood, is confronted by several extremely crude and unfriendly people on his first visit to Heathcliff's house. He's shortly attacked by some savage dogs which Heathcliff, entering, drives off. By contrast to what he's met so far, Lockwood takes Heathcliff to be a rare good fellow—a little harsh, but clearly a gentleman. It takes Lockwood a while to realize Heathcliff is the most savage, wild creature in the place. Far from being a gentleman, Heathcliff is an embodiment of amoral and practically demonic energies—hardly even human in the usual sense of the word, much less a social being of any sort. But by that time, the emotional groundwork of surrounding savagery and Lockwood's error has prepared for this extraordinary character.

But be careful, if you use this method, that your actual curse is *really* worse (or better) than what's expected, even though it doesn't seem so at first. Otherwise, it will be a letdown.

4. Alternatively, have a character expecting a smaller and more credible version of the thing you actually intend to spring on him. In Flannery O'Connor's "Good Country People," the homely and highly intelligent protagonist thinks the boyish traveling Bible salesman is out to seduce her, and rather patronizingly decides she's willing to let him. She looks forward to his shock when she tells him she really doesn't believe in anything. Seducers are a common and relatively routine sort of predator she can handle easily enough, she thinks.

It's another matter when she realizes, too late, that what he's really after is her artificial leg. He steals it, expressing his contempt for her supposed superiority and a cynicism and lack of belief far deeper than her own. She's left stranded, in humiliated helplessness, in the barn.

It's a real seduction, and a real psychological rape, though not the sort she expected and felt so confident of handling.

It's a weird and melodramatic story—the clichéd Traveling Salesman and the Farmer's Daughter, for heaven's sake—and yet it works beautifully. The groundwork—preparing to handle a seducer when the man is really something much darker and more cruel—is well and unobtrusively laid. You don't see it coming until it happens. And then you believe it.

# COMPENSATIONS FOR COMPENSATIONS

In many ways these four techniques of displacement and misdirection contradict the eight methods of putting your curse right up front and toughing it through with all the compensations possible, which I discussed earlier.

I'd tend to use misdirection in situations of gradual revelation, when a mystery is involved and finding out the exact nature of the curse is the basis of the story (as in *The Hound of the Baskervilles*). I'd also use it when a melodramatic element is so outrageous that it needs considerable preparation, or when I wanted the reader to be expecting one thing when in fact I was planning to pull a switch (a satisfying, valid one, remember).

But, really, these are mix and match techniques—especially if your story is going to be novel-length. You may want to use one of the straightforward techniques early in the novel and some of the double-fakes later on, or the other way around. It depends on what you're trying to do in each particular section of your story.

And just as there are all sorts of melodrama—of events and of characters—these techniques can be used to prepare for and "take the curse off" any strong element in your story, whatever it be.

If the strong element is a very complex prose style, you may want to balance it with vivid, direct happenings and simplified, exaggerated characters, the way Faulkner often does. If it's a lot of unavoidable and concentrated exposition, as often happens in mysteries, science fiction, and fantasy, melodrama may come to your rescue, keeping the story moving until the necessary explanations are done.

Melodrama can be a compensation for any narrative element which tends to distract attention from the story and the characters. It's so strong that it's impossible to ignore, and the story falls back into an effective balance between showing and telling.

But melodrama, in turn, needs compensation because the reality it presents is so exaggerated and intense. Whether you choose techniques of straightforward preparation or buried preparation, you can use melodrama to show a heightened reality even truer than our more mixed and muddled everyday existence, where things seldom show as clearly what they are and what they mean as fiction can, and life is seldom so interesting and exciting as a story.

# CHAPTER 8

# PATTERNS, MIRRORS, AND ECHOES

I'VE SAID THAT EVERY STORY makes promises to its readers, promises the writer has to take care to keep. Mostly, those promises are unspoken ones. And some are made indirectly, through pattern.

Just by writing, you're choosing what happens and what doesn't, what's possible in your little world and what isn't. What your characters are concerned about becomes, automatically, your story's concern as well. The kinds of people whom you select as your characters—their attitudes and capacities, the kind of relationships they get into—all are going to add up to something.

Detail on detail, incident on incident, character on character, the pattern begins to form: the implicit rules and realities of your fictional world. A reader may not notice the patterns at first, at least not consciously; but if they're carefully orchestrated and controlled, they're what hold your story together, give it both diversity and unity, and make it specially your own.

With enough accumulated detail, a shape starts to form. Any two dots define a line; any three, a triangle. Even yarrow stalks, tea leaves, and random Tarot cards fall into patterns from which people attempt to read meanings. It's part of the way the human mind works: finding faces in clouds, seeking shape, seeking meaning. So how could your story, which certainly has more intrinsic significance than a few soggy tea leaves, hope to escape?

Patterns are going to happen. The question is whether you're going to guide them into symmetry and significance, or whether they're going to spring up, sprout branches in eleven-teen contrary directions, and then slump like weeds.

The problem, at its simplest, is recognizing your tentative, partial patterns as they accumulate and strengthening them, making them coherent, getting other things out of their way to let them stand straight and tall. The next and harder stage is going beyond basic weeding to cultivating: creating patterns deliberately, to gain for your writing the immense but subtle power of recurrence, the second level of meaning that can only be spoken in echoes.

## MANY HAPPY RETURNS

In school, you were probably taught, as I was, to avoid simple verbal repetition—using "however" or "interesting" too often in a single paragraph.

That's not what I'm talking about.

The kinds of repetition that work in fiction, that make buried but not-quite-hidden connections that can hold a story together, aren't a matter of single words. They're part of a writer's larger vocabulary: image, incident, situation, character. Narrative structure. Plot in the largest sense—not just what happens, but precisely *how* the incidents are presented and the patterns they make.

### Return with Us to the Thrilling Days of a Galaxy Far, Far Away

I'll ask you now to flip back to Chapter 5, near the end, where I did a bit of commentary on the structure of *The Empire Strikes Back*. Reread that section, then meet me back here.

OK? You're back?

There, I was talking about parallel plots, and how they can be held together with echoing incidents. Now, the focus is on the incidents themselves.

A threat of freezing, in the beginning of that story, mirrors a threat of freezing at the end. A cave in one of the parallel plot lines is mirrored by a cave in the other. A meeting with an old friend or with a terrible adversary, a buried truth finally spoken and acknowledged (Leia: "I love you" and Han: "I know" the counterpart of Darth Vader's disclosure of paternity)—each has its match, its echo. And there are even more connections than I have space to list. And that was a movie for the widest possible audience, aimed primarily at teenagers, for heaven's sake—not a story built with the intricate craft possible in literary fiction, for a readership of discerning adults.

Yet look at the number of connections there, if you stand back from the story a little and take the time to notice them. Look at how thoroughly all the threads are gathered into neat knots, how thoroughly the story belongs to itself.

Lots of fiction uses that kind of internal riveting. If you stop thinking in terms of *things* and start thinking in *categories of things*, you'll see more resemblances, echoes, and outright repetitions in your favorite fiction than you'd ever have suspected. Start thinking categories rather than individual, isolated pieces, and the family resemblances start showing up—an author's characteristic concerns, the larger elements of style that connect diverse fictions as the works of a single guiding consciousness.

That's what you need to start doing with your own fiction. Start noticing the patterns your initial scenes and set-pieces have set up and think of ways to echo and reinforce them in other scenes, later on.

## A Case in Point: What's in the Living Room?

To illustrate, rather than cite a finished, set story, I'll use my experience with one of my own short stories, so you can see how the method works.

The protagonist of "A Sense of Family" is a lanky middle-aged woman named Val, a sculptor. The initial scene shows how Val tends to lose track of the hours and the days, absorbed in her current project, a block of marble—a tombstone discarded for commercial use—that she's turning into a bas-relief horse. That first scene is Val alone in her drafty loft wandering vaguely around after a concentrated session of carefully carving and smoothing, as she reconnects by degrees with the realities of time, neighbors, weariness, not having eaten.

In the middle of the floor is the half-carved horse and the intense personal silence around it.

That dark quiet room, of which Val is barely aware except for the horse, seemed to me a good image of what and who Val was. So I repeated the pattern in the story's other two major scenes—one with a cheerful busybody of a neighbor, one with a man she seeks out to collect an almost-forgotten debt. Both men are sculptors too.

A week-old letter Val opens turns out to be a wedding invitation from her stuffy younger brother, who lives across the country. Nudged by her neighbor, Jerry the Welder, Val makes up her mind to reclaim the lapsed family connection and go, but lacks the money for bus fare.

Jerry's whole apartment is filled with a metal and neon construction with lots of sharp edges, reflective surfaces, and flashing lights, which he proudly calls "a social construct"; Val's terrified of it, but braves edging through it to use his phone (naturally, she doesn't have one: she's cut off from people and has just begun to notice it). Platz, the man she tries to phone and then crosses the dark city to confront, owes her money. In the center of Platz's room a slatternly woman repeats, "It's got nothing to do with me," several times, echoing Platz's refusal to pay what he owes, since Val got nothing in writing, no security, at the time she lent him the money. It was a loan of unconsidered but real trust, as one member of the artist "family" to another, which Platz has no qualms about betraying. He refuses to acknowledge either the responsibility of repaying the debt or the implied relationship that prompted Val to give him the money in the first place.

The first image (Jerry's "social construct") is one of involvement; the second (Platz's wife or lover) is a refusal to be involved. Val's reaction to each helps to show who she is.

The pattern was that each of the major people was characterized through what was in the middle of the room, mirroring situations that brought out what I felt to be the central truth of the people in this story's context.

The story's end returns Val to her loft with a bad cold, fussed over and nagged by assorted hippie neighbors who do, after all, supply something like a sense of family.

I think this basic method will work for you too. Look at your initial scene and what's important in it. Try to identify what the basic emotional dynamic is and how it's shown: what objects, what ideas, what words. Then repeat the pattern through the rest of the story—once, or more than once—to show what the meaningful differences are, scene by scene.

Alternatively, think of ways to contrast the initial scene and situation in what follows. Setting up pairs of opposites, or the continuum that connects such a pair, is also a kind of connecting, even when it's not repeating the identical pattern. The road to Rome is still the road to Rome, whether you're headed toward the city or away. The emotional connections continue.

That's the first thing to realize. Although the individual situations in your story may be different, even vastly different, from one part to another, if the emotional resonances of the scenes are at all similar or contrast on the same continuum, there's a way to build in even stronger mirrors and echoes so the reader will see the scenes as linked.

Heightening what's there—that's the beginning.

## MIRRORING SINGLE SCENES

Once you've got two situations tagged for connection, how do you go about building in recurrences?

You do it by continuing some specific element(s) of the first situation in the second. Going from simplest to most complex, you can:

1. Keep the second situation almost identical to the first, except (perhaps) for one crucial element. The characters involved, the place where it happens, the props mentioned, the nature of the confrontation itself, can all continue. Simply because the sto-

ry will have developed since the first incident happened, the second one won't be seen as a simple (boring) repetition of the first unless it goes on too long—it will be in a new and richer context; the reader will know the characters better and know more clearly what's at stake. It will deepen emphasis, like saying "No. *NO!*" The second time, your hearer knows you really mean it.

2.  Repeat one or more lines of dialogue in the same or similar form.

3.  Repeat a brief description of emotion or action ("He looked his father square in the eyes"; "He felt the old, bitter taste of anger and frustration") in the exact same words you used before.

4.  Make sure the *subject* or the *terms* of the second situation are the same as the first. For instance, two disputes about money, or coming home when he pleases, or doing his homework; or the situation arising unexpectedly, when the protagonist didn't anticipate trouble, and reacting with anger: the *way* the situation develops being the same.

5.  Have the two situations go through the same stages.

6.  However they arise, have the two situations *come out* the same way.

7.  Use similar imagery to connect the two scenes. For instance, in our hypothetical argument, the person the protagonist is arguing with could be described with animal-like words (growled, pawed at the air, whinnied, bellowed, etc.) in both scenes. Or you could focus on a feeling of constriction (mentioning walls, or that the protagonist is finding it hard to breathe, is pulling at his collar, is getting red in the face, is gasping, feeling weighed down, etc.) Whatever imagery is used in the first scene is repeated in the second. By imagery, I mean the implied comparison between the present situation and something else, in terms of the wording you choose. (Saying somebody "burst into a rage" suggests explosion; saying they "smoldered with anger" suggests fire. The two are *not the same thing*. The precise words matter, and have distinct, separate meanings. Getting conscious control of imagery is one of the very hardest and most delightful chores a writer tackles: it requires you to make friends with words and use them with a diamond-cutter's precision.)

8. Have the overall dynamic and polarities of the two scenes be the same—the same emotional content, the same basic opposing forces. For instance, rebellion against authority; a plea for understanding and love refused; an attempt to be rational defeated by strong emotion. The opposing forces in the scene, *rather than the individuals involved*, are continued from the earlier scene to the later one.

You can mix and match any of these techniques, depending on how strong and plain you want the connections to be. (In "A Sense of Family," I mostly used methods 4, 6, 7, and 8. Each scene involves Val deciding to make contact and being defeated, and both attempt and defeat are represented by whatever is displayed in the middle of the room.) And there's no need to limit the number of mirrored scenes to just two: three is a good number, as I'll explain in a minute.

As you move up the list, away from direct repetition of words and toward repetition of patterns or ideas, the connections will be less noticeable—but they'll still be there, and the reader will be affected by them, even if the recurrences aren't consciously noticed. As I said before, we like repetitions, coherent shape. The reader will feel the story's unity, even if he can't, at first, point to what made him feel that way.

But, you may be saying, if I *do* repeat some elements of one situation in another, isn't a reader going to notice and be bored? And I assure you, not unless you go about it in the most heavy-handed way possible and repeat the earlier scene virtually word for word and at length. On first reading, readers are absorbed in details and emotion, plot and character. Though pattern has its effect, it's just about invisible to a reader, at least the first time through.

Think back to something you read in which, after repeated readings, you can now see narrative patterns the author set up. And honestly think back to that first reading. How many of those patterns were you aware of? Any? One? But weren't the patterns, the *kind* of events that happened, truly one of the reasons you cared enough about the story to read it a second and maybe a third time?

You already knew the plot, so you certainly couldn't have been rereading the story to find out what happened. You knew the characters, so it wasn't discovering them, though you may have liked visiting with them again for a while. No, I strongly suspect that when we reread any fiction out of liking, rather than on assignment, it's because of the *kind* of thing it is, the shape it makes in our minds, the growing discovery of how it belongs to itself and is one connected thing. It's the patterns that the incidents and the people make, not the incidents and the people themselves, that give stories richness the second and twentieth time around.

Patterns may seem abstract at first, compared to crises and characters, but it's the patterns that last.

## The Experiment, the Variable, and the Rule of Three

In item #1, above, I suggested you could repeat virtually the whole situation with just one significant change. I'll explain a little more what that involves.

In a scientific experiment, a researcher will generally have two groups: the test group, and the control. Both groups are as identical as it's possible to make them, and they're treated exactly the same, except for one item—the thing that's being investigated, altered with the test group to find out what effect that single change will have. Whatever difference there is in the two groups at the conclusion of the experiment will presumably be caused by the one thing that was different—the variable.

This is the basis of countless folk tales involving three related individuals in similar circumstances. The first one leaves home, is rude to the ugly old witch, and is turned into stone. The second one leaves home, is rude to the ugly old witch, and ditto. But the third one leaves home, shares his baloney sandwich with the old witch, and gets tons of gold and jewels, a magic ring for warding off dragons, and makes a royal marriage.

Recognize the pattern? It's Cinderella and her wretched stepsisters. It's three little pigs, building houses of straw, sticks, and solid wolf-proof bricks. It's the three bears.

Why all this fuss about threes?

One is an incident. Two is a pattern. Three breaks it.

One tells us what the risk is. Two confirms what wrong behavior is. At three, we know the rules, and so can appreciate what the smart third person is doing differently, to break the unsuccessful pattern and win.

If that folk tale was about just one pig who built a house of bricks in the first place, and the wolf couldn't get in no matter how he huffed and puffed, where would the story be? Conflict, but no drama, just stalemate. Success for the pig, but no suspense. Anticlimax. No story.

Three is suspense, pattern, and contrast, all in one nifty little technique as old as storytelling.

It's the scientific technique of the variable, with third time lucky.

If somebody fails twice, in similar circumstances, there's going to be more tension and drama when he tries the third time because we've already seen him fail and know it can happen. We know what doesn't work, we know the situation; now we're focusing on what he's doing differently this time. We're aware of the pattern, the apparent rules, and are concentrating on the one thing that changes.

Instead of two repetitions, you can use the Rule of Three. The first time the bell coincides with the painful electric shock, you're too busy being shocked to notice. The second time, you think uneasily that maybe it wasn't a coincidence. The third time, you've started jumping before the bell is even done ringing.

If you want your reader interested and involved in the scene before it's fully begun to happen, there's nothing like a triple setup to get things rolling. It gives added drama. It directs the reader's attention where you want it directed. And it makes the scene's meaning clear in a way it could not have been in isolation.

Choose and control the variable with care, keep the situations visibly comparable so the reader will be aware of the bell/shock pairing and be anticipating the outcome, and all three scenes will gain in impact and effectiveness.

Or, in Henny Youngman's memorable phrase, "You had it

before? Well, you got it again."

## Patterning for Contrast

Taking the concept of the one variable a little farther, it's possible to set up scenes as contrasts with one another. Repeated elements let the reader know the two situations are similar; but something in the situation has radically changed.

This is the basis of then/now, before/after pairings.

Consider Scrooge, early in *A Christmas Carol*, nagging Bob Cratchit about using excess coal and requiring holiday pay for no work. Watch him show no interest whatsoever in Bob's family or personal problems. Then consider Scrooge, after his experiences with the spirits, anonymously donating a large holiday goose for the Cratchits' Christmas dinner, raising Cratchit's wages, promising to help Bob's struggling family, and commanding Bob to go out and buy a new coal scuttle.

Not only is Scrooge a kinder man: he's kinder *in the very same terms, on the very same subjects, and to the identical person in the identical circumstances* as he was callous and selfish before. The basic situation and terms of the two scenes are repeated, step by step, so that the degree of Scrooge's change of heart is put into the clearest possible focus and contrast.

The same correspondence of scenes is used with Scrooge's initial refusal to contribute to the poor and to go to his estranged nephew's home for Christmas dinner. At the story's end, Scrooge has accepted his nephew's invitation and has made a substantial contribution to the poor. The whole of the initial situation is played out again, point for point, at the story's conclusion.

At the beginning, the succession of Scrooge's confrontations demonstrated the norm, as I discussed earlier; the identical succession, with changed results, demonstrates the new norm at the end.

If you want to set up any strong contrast, whether it's a then/now, a before/after, or something more complex—how a character treats his dog (with perception and compassion) and his child (with indifference)—there's no stronger way to do it than by setting up mirror situations which echo each other's terms and conditions as closely as possible, so the one crucial difference stands out in sharp focus.

## MIRRORING CHARACTERS

Two children, one rich, one poor, who look just alike, change places. That's the basis of Twain's *The Prince and the Pauper*. He uses the boys, alike in everything but expectation and upbringing, to show and satirize the conditions of both rich and poor during the reign of Henry VIII.

Two men, alike enough to be brothers, love the same woman. One goes to the guillotine in the other's place, because the other is the woman's husband. Dickens' *A Tale of Two Cities*.

Two men inhabit the same body. One is a monster loving pleasure and cruelty, the other an altruistic physician trying to destroy the evil in the human psyche—Stevenson's *Dr. Jeckyll and Mr. Hyde*.

It's like the experimental variable I just discussed. Two characters who in some meaningful sense are reflections of one another can highlight either the differences or similarities between them. Or, with foreground figures who are almost alike, contrasts in the backgrounds—their societies or circumstances—are demonstrated more clearly.

Sometimes, though, the resemblance isn't one of appearance but something more subtle: attitude, upbringing, or experience.

### Scrooge's Mirrors

I mentioned some chapters back that Marley was Scrooge's mirror. By that, I meant not only that Marley was Scrooge's partner; more importantly, he shared the materialistic values which are Scrooge's central characteristic. ("You were always a good man of business, Jacob," says Scrooge in an attempt to placate the ghost, rousing an irate howl from the spectre.) This qualifies, I think, as a legitimate and significant similarity between the two.

Therefore, we can assume Marley's warning is valid: what's happened to him, dying unrepentant in his businesslike, uncharitable attitudes, will also happen to Scrooge if he dies without a change of heart. Marley is, in some meaningful sense, what Scrooge represents seen from a different angle, in slightly different circumstances, inasmuch as Marley is now dead and Scrooge isn't—yet.

Accepting the resemblances, we accept the implications. The visible (if ghostly) chain Marley bears does, indeed, correspond with the even heavier, longer chain Scrooge has forged for himself, even though neither we nor Scrooge can see it. What Marley is, Scrooge may become—*will* become, if things continue unchanged.

Finally, their attitude (their chief point of similarity) sets them apart from the story's other major characters, who are typically models of good-heartedness, cheer, and selfless concern for others. Scrooge and Marley are more like one another than either is like anybody else in the story.

Those are my rule-of-thumb criteria for an effective mirror character. There must be one or more points of plain connection or resemblance; what happens to one must have an effect on or implication for the other; and their similarity must be a unique one, not shared by other characters in the story.

That's why I call Marley Scrooge's mirror.

But there are other mirrors than Marley. Scrooge, we are shown, had a deprived, loveless childhood and felt set apart from others. His life was stunted; he became an emotional cripple. What was true of Scrooge inwardly is true of Tiny Tim in physical fact. Tim's childhood is deprived by poverty (unlike Scrooge, who apparently was born into middle-class circumstances); Tim's materially poor but emotionally rich. So Tim echoes Scrooge's combination of poverty and wealth, but with reversed meanings. Tim has a crippled leg, and is thus set apart from other children—a different cause from Scrooge's isolation, but a comparable result. Tim's condition is deteriorating, and he is likely to die. Scrooge's emotional isolation is also hardening, he also is likely to die, as the story proceeds to demonstrate.

Those implicit connections are important if Scrooge is to believably identify with Tim and take Tim's life and death to heart as having implications for himself.

The visions of Tim's much-mourned death and of Scrooge's miserable end, his only attendant filching his bed-curtains and even his shroud, unmourned even by his daily associates, constitute the plainest possible case of two scenes deliberately set up to contrast with one another. They show the difference, in this case, that being a lovable and beloved person can make, as compared to being "a good man of business."

Tiny Tim, in his way, is also Scrooge's mirror—a contrasting one.

The whole story is full of echoes, showing many examples of harsh business callousness contrasted with gentle fellow-feeling—situation after situation, with a consistent emotional dynamic which increases in power as the story progresses.

That's what can happen when a writer is really in control of his fiction and its patterns.

## Some Applications

But you're not writing about Scrooge or Marley. What can mirror characters do for your fiction?

They can highlight some central thing about a main character you want to bring out, as Scrooge's mirrors focus attention on the conflict between materialistic selfishness, however socially acceptable, and emotional involvement with others, however profitless. Is there some one trait of your protagonist you want to make plain in a way that's showing rather than telling? Then set up a mirror character who shares that trait in even more visible form and let the reader draw his own conclusions.

Is there something about the protagonist's present circumstances that's specially helpful or destructive? Then show somebody more or less comparable, but even *more* able (or more desperate) being helped/destroyed by it. That will underline the threat or hope as it relates to the protagonist. In the very simplest terms, sidekicks get bumped off right and left in detective fiction so that the author can maintain a sense of threat without ever having to *really* kill off his detective. (Doyle killed off Holmes, but only because he was sick of that insufferable know-it-all, and he was sorry afterward and wrote him back to life.)

What you can't afford to do to your protagonist, you can do to the mirror character, showing that it's possible, it's a real threat or hope. Drastic things, irrevocable things, often happen to mirror characters in fiction for just that reason. Like Marley, they can very suddenly become "dead as a doornail" or, like the foolish younger sister in Jane Austen's *Pride and Prejudice*, they can marry most unsuitably to show the protagonist the way to a better, wiser choice.

If you don't want to go into your protagonist's background, or want to keep some other element of the protagonist's life a secret, set up a mirror who's explained in more detail and again let the resemblance carry its own implications.

Things you let readers figure out for themselves are sometimes more powerful than those you spell out in so many words.

## MIRRORING PLOTS

We've already discovered several examples of plots which are parallel, in whole or in part. In addition to *The Empire Strikes Back*, I've talked at least a little about Thackeray's *Vanity Fair* (which splits awkwardly in two, between the Amelia Sedley plot and the Becky Sharp plot) and *Wuthering Heights*, with its parallel love stories involving Catherine and Cathy, the wild older generation and the tamer, younger one.

Developing two independent main plot lines takes quite a lot of narrative space; it's mostly done in long—and I do mean *long*—fiction. Family sagas provide more than a few instances. For instance, Steinbeck's massive *East of Eden* involves two stories of conflict between sets of brothers over a single, wicked woman. In the first, one brother eventually marries the woman and fathers the two sons who are the protagonists of the book's second half, with the wicked mother as a pivotal figure if no longer the romantic interest. This book was arguably improved for the movie version by cutting the entire first half.

A contrasting and generally more successful technique is shown by Stephen King's *It*. Like *East of Eden*, it has a double plot line, one past, one present, basically concerning the same characters and the same situation. In one plot, the protagonists are children; in the other they've become adults. The stories are intercut—the narrative line switches back and forth between them, rather than handling them in sequence, one after the other. That helps maintain the whole novel's unity. Both stories rise to generally similar climaxes near the book's end.

So it's not just space that's required: quite a lot of narrative muscle and control is needed, too, to bring off so complex a plot structure successfully without the book's breaking in half. Double stories that run concurrently or through alternating flashback narration tend to be easier to handle than those that run in sequence, one after the other with no intercutting. It's easier to build in connections and convergences among people and events existing in the same fictional time—both present at any given section of the story, even though in alternation—than when one set is dead and gone and over before the other set takes up.

The plots must be very carefully balanced to keep one from taking over and making the other seem weak and boring by comparison. Pacing has to be very carefully handled so one plot doesn't get lost while you're dealing with the other. Connections between the two plots have to be riveted in brass, using every kind of echo and mirror I've described in this chapter, and likely others nobody has even thought of yet, to keep the two plot lines from splitting the story completely apart.

If you intend to embark on a double, fully-mirroring plot line, remember these techniques of compensating—they may help.

Watch *The Empire Strikes Back* a few more times. Read *Wuthering Heights* or *The Lord of the Rings*. (Speak about parallel plot structures! It's got at least three, maybe four!) See how ambitious and able authors have kept strong, complex stories together with carefully chosen and positioned repetitions of scenes, people, and even whole plots.

# BEYOND FORMULA AND INTO LITERATURE

There's another advantage of looking hard into your story's heart and bones to create mirrors and echoes based on what's gone before. It can help you use but transcend formula, if you're working in one of the genres with a fairly rigid and restrictive set of rules about how stories can acceptably be shaped. Detective/ mystery fiction is one; gothic and romance fiction are others. Gothic, for instance, absolutely requires a female protagonist menaced/wooed by a dominating male. Yet within this restriction, wonderful and individual fiction has been written. The same is true of the other formulaic genres.

Finally, formulas are only as limiting as you let them be. There are few formats as rigid as sonnet form, but great diversity is possible within it.

You don't (and shouldn't) violate or ignore the formulas—not if you intend your work to be published. Instead, fulfill and go beyond them, making your stories uniquely themselves.

One way to seek and create that specialness is to look to your story itself, stage by stage, for its shape, its proper development. Use it as your crystal ball, to see the shapes of what's to come. Make your story grow from what it, in part, already is. Then no matter what restrictions you're working within, your story can't possibly turn out to be like a hundred others.

Look in. Also look out—to the world of literature, myth, and legend. Many stories are structured as quest/adventures. That too is a kind of formula, even if it's one you choose. Other stories hark back to the classics—*West Side Story* to *Romeo and Juliet*, for instance—and embody their essential truths in new flesh, new events. Other stories draw on myth and religion—the Greek story of Pygmalion is the foundation of *My Fair Lady*; *Paradise Lost* and *East of Eden* draw on Biblical sources. John Cheever's "Metamorphoses" translates legends from Ovid into Westchester settings. The travels of Odysseus are one foundation of Joyce's *Ulysses,* with specific events and characters reappearing in fresh guises. But I don't believe I've ever heard *Ulysses* referred to as "formula fiction."

Sometimes what's mirrored in your story won't only be what's in it: you may, like Joyce, choose some external source as the formula to honor in the way your fiction is constructed. For instance, I patterned a science fiction novel concerning a husband's attempts to revive a dead wife on the myth of Orpheus' attempt to rescue Eurydice from the underworld, which seemed to me a natural connection that might give my imagined world greater power, significance, and emotional depth. If readers notice the implicit connections, fine; if they don't, still fine: the "Orpheus formula" had already done its job in guiding and helping me in making tough narrative choices as the book was written. Such a formula isn't a code to be broken but a set of guidelines, a shape to reflect in a new mirror.

Formula, choosing or accepting some external guidelines for the shape or content of fiction, has been the basis of everything from the worst hokey imitative junk to the finest and most subtle literature. It's all a matter of technique, insight, and craft. The formulas are all there for you to breathe fresh life into, if you choose.

Learn to recognize your hidden, implicit fictional promises and do your best to keep them. Look hard and long into your mirrors, and fulfill and reinforce the recurrences you see there. Because in them, you can begin discovering the power beyond plot: pattern.

# CHAPTER 9

# PACING, TRANSITIONS, FLASHES, AND FRAMES

THE FARTHER YOU GO IN YOUR STORY, the more things each individual scene will be doing. It will be looking forward and back. It will be taking account of the consequences of previous crises and building toward other crises, both near and distant. It will be further developing your characters, showing them in new contexts, new situations.

But a string of scenes, however good, isn't a story. The story as a whole, to be effective, has to develop a rhythm. That's pacing.

## TRANSITIONS

Rhythm is composed of many things: the interweaving of plot and subplot, the build to set-pieces, the introduction of new elements and surprises and the knotting off of old plot-threads, the amount and placement of exposition, the unifying effect of narrative mirrors and of a strong, distinctive theme, and the nature of the plot itself—complex and intricate, or direct and uncomplicated. It depends on the amount and degree of melodrama, the number and relative complexity of characters, and the balance between scene and summary. Some of these things speed a story up, and some slow it down. A story needs both speed and deliberate build, fireworks and thoughtful times.

To unite all these disparate elements, these different speeds, into one coherent story, you need strong, judicious, and effective transitions.

Scenes that run directly into other scenes can be like beads on a string, isolated and bumpy to follow. Sometimes a span of time needs bridging or a change of viewpoint or setting needs preparing for. Sometimes you need to give an overview to compensate for a series of close-focus events, to show an overall meaning or development.

That's the job of transitions.

They come in all sizes. Transition can be a carefully chosen sentence at the end of a scene and another at the beginning of the next. It can be a lead-in paragraph to a new section. It can be several pages of narrative summary, or even a scene that will develop things your story is going to need soon. A stretch of exposition can also serve transitional purposes.

## Something Continues

When you've completed one scene and are ready to begin the next, especially when there's likely to be a rough shift, a jagged change, choose something to continue. Following a single viewpoint provides some connections, but that's usually not enough all by itself. Your chosen element can be a connected action, begun or planned in the previous scene and carried on in the subsequent one. It can be keeping to the same setting, though perhaps exploring/establishing a new part of it. It can be a simple verbal repetition or echo, like having "going" in the final sentence of the last scene and "coming" in the first sentence of the next. It can even be a more diffuse connection like mood, or some facet of the background environment such as rain or wind.

Whatever it is, choose something to continue beyond the gross details of the plot and the continuity of character. These, alone and not reinforced by narrative craft, aren't enough to hold the pieces of your story together.

## Balancing Scene and Summary

Anything other than a scene is telling rather than showing, and slows things down. Sometimes, you may want to slow things down; or you may have exposition or description which previous scenes require or without which following events will be bare and sketchy.

If you've had a series of brief and emotionally intense scenes, it's probably time for summary—at least a paragraph or two, or a page or two in long fiction. This overview can come from the story's narrator or, if you're not holding to one strictly limited viewpoint, from you as impersonal, objective author. It may cover the events of a day or two, a week, to bridge the distance from here to there without laboriously following every step in between. It may account briefly for the doings of several different characters, doings that, while important, don't merit full-blown scenes. It may describe present but distant events that have a bearing on the immediate situation.

All such narration stays close to the story, but looks from a broader perspective and a greater distance from the characters' minute-to-minute affairs. It helps readers not only follow what's happening, but understand it, too.

## FLASHBACKS AND FRAMES

If you tell of bygone events in narrative summary, it's exposition. If you dramatize them as a scene, it's a flashback.

Flashbacks can be as brief as a single line of past dialogue or as extensive as a whole independent plot.

The virtue of flashbacks is that, unlike exposition, they're showing, not telling. They have action, drama, immediate events. But they're not as strong or vivid as present-time scenes, simply because they're past. I mentioned in Chapter 7 that we tend to take the past less seriously than the present because, for good or ill, it's over. We're only hearing about it rather than seeing it happen—*even though it's presented as a scene*. It's history, even if dramatized history.

*Real* matters. *Now* matters. And what's real, and now, is what we *perceive* as being real and now.

There's a tricky corollary to this insight. Nearly all the stories ever written happen in the past. That is, the story's present timeline is the reader's past. Anything that wasn't set, written, and published in this present year is, to a greater or lesser degree, historical fiction of this kind.

Some stories don't age well. References get dated, styles and expectations change, society has different concerns from one decade to another. Stories about our own pasts, times we've lived through, paradoxically seem more dated than those that occurred during our parents' generation, or even longer ago.

So why aren't all these stories seen as flashbacks, as things with marginal relevance to our current interests and concerns?

Some of them are. The adjustments needed to read, say, Shakespeare or Chaucer with comprehension and enjoyment can be radical. And without a lot of footnotes, much of the fine detail and topical references still get lost. And there were hundreds of other writers in Shakespeare's time, or Chaucer's, or Dickens', whose work is virtually unknown now, except by scholars who aren't reading primarily for enjoyment.

But there's also fiction that's lasted, that we can still imagine ourselves into despite sometimes radical differences of time and culture. And those stories are set in something I'll call the *absolute past*. They're complete, reflecting one small slice of everything there is or might be, requiring little or nothing beyond themselves to make sense. Each is a self-contained and independent fictional world.

That fictional world, existing in the absolute past, has its own timeline, its own stated present. While we read, that present is ours. Nothing is over until the final fat lady sings, no matter how many hundreds or thousands of years ago or ahead the events (even imagined events) are supposed to occur.

It's part of the willing suspension of disbelief I talked about earlier, part of the *Once Upon a Time* syndrome. It's a fictional convention we're so used to that, as readers, we scarcely notice it.

And this is just as true of science fiction and fantasy, with only the most tenuous claims to connect with historical reality, as it is of more ostensibly realistic fiction. Each has its own timeline, its own hermetic present which doesn't need to connect to anything outside itself.

Therefore, what's present is whatever the story's central timeline *shows* being the present. Anything that departs from that is a flashback or, more rarely, a flashforward.

## Flashbacks

Flashbacks are past, in the story's context. Therefore they disrupt the story's timeline and are, individually and collectively, less effective than "present" action. If there are a lot of them, they can leech the vividness out of the whole story and invalidate the story's present.

If you think your story is going to have just one or two substantial flashback interruptions, it's probably not worth disrupting the timeline to include them. They're not enough to set and maintain a narrative pattern, so they're anomalies, freaks in an otherwise sequential story. Turn the essential information into exposition. Don't dramatize it. Your story's timeline is already no more than a convention between writer and reader—why put a needless and avoidable strain on it?

If your story is going to have several extensive flashbacks, particularly if it's long fiction, then the technique is roughly like leaning off a roof: make sure you're solidly anchored and the footing is reliable, then go ahead and lean.

Make sure the running plot in your story's present is strong, clear, and well established before splitting off to do *anything* else, whether following a subplot, interjecting a chunk of exposition, or embarking on a flashback. Make sure the flashback is vivid and interesting in itself—if it's not, it would be better as exposition. Compensate with as many echoes and mirrors, to connect the flashback plot with the present plot, as seem reasonable and judicious. Use strong but inconspicuous transitions to help the shift along. And remember that a past story is also a story, and needs to develop characters and situations just as any story does, even if it's only a single scene long.

To compensate for the ending being known (remember, it's the story's past), you might state the past resolution right out and then use your flashback to show what led up to it. That's especially appropriate when the story hinges on some major historical event whose outcome is presumably already familiar. In *The Day of the Jackal*, Frederick Forsyth managed to bring off a cliffhanger thriller about a plot to assassinate de Gaulle during the Algerian crisis, although readers presumably already knew that de Gaulle survived to an irascible old age. I suspect the interest was in knowing the attempt was going to fail, yet wanting to find out precisely *how* it failed.

The same problem arises if your narrator is telling the events of his youth from the perspective of greater experience and more years. After all, he survived to tell the story, didn't he? So you can't create suspense about whether or not he's going to survive. But you *can* create suspense about the manner of his survival—did he fail or succeed? Did he pay too great a price for survival? The *style* of his surviving is still open to narrative embellishments.

You can also displace the narrative interest from the known to the unknown, focusing not on who won the Battle of Midway, for instance, but on whether one particular seaman survived and won the Navy nurse of his choice.

Of course, sometimes the problem of known outcome doesn't even arise: in entirely invented worlds; with minor historical events the reader is likely to be unfamiliar with (quick, now: who won the War of Jenkins' Ear? Gotcha!); or in really strange or exotic societies, invented or borrowed. Instead, another problem takes its place. If the situation is already complicated by some major strangeness, like an alien world or an invented future society, it's risky to throw in any more and merely structural complications. If your story's present is apt to be difficult for a reader to follow for whatever reason, you'll probably be better off just staying with the main timeline and avoiding any flashback longer than a paragraph or so, to keep avoidable complications to a minimum.

If your flashbacks are going to run through the whole of a

novel, treat them as what they are: another parallel and relatively equal plot, or as main plot and subplot, one running in the present, the other in the past, as I discussed in the last chapter.

## Frames

What if you only want two flashes—one at the beginning, and the other at the end? The narrator, at the age of 40-some, is going to tell the events that happened when she was 20. Then we leave the narrator and jump directly into the story, with no other departures. The story's main timeline is therefore anchored in the 20-year-old events. *That's* the story's present. The 40-year-old who introduces things exists in that curious construction, a flashforward.

An introductory flashforward of this sort is used in du Maurier's *Rebecca* to set this gothic story's mood of brooding uncertainty. Then the timeline drops back a few years and proceeds sequentially until it again reaches the time the story opened with. King's *'Salem's Lot* uses the same technique.

Other stories have no overlap (save perhaps the continuing narrator) between opening flash, story, and closing flash. The flashes are one time; the story is another. In either case, it's the story's main plot that establishes what the timeline is, regardless of any introductory flash.

All these kinds of arrangement constitute what's called a frame. It's used when an author feels some kind of bridge to the story's basic situation is needed—to put things in the proper perspective (as in Conrad's *Lord Jim*), establish a social context to which the main protagonist will be a stranger, provide solid credibility for a story otherwise likely to be taken as fantasy (James' *The Turn of the Screw*), hint at a climax the reader can thereafter look forward to reaching, or do some other important narrative chore the story itself will be too busy to do as economically or strongly.

To get technical for a minute, an opening flash with the "past" story following sequentially thereafter is a flashforward, sometimes called a prologue; an end-flash is an epilogue. A prologue or epilogue stands aside from the story and comments on it from a different perspective.

Matching and connected flashes at beginning and end, mirroring one another—which may or may not be actually labeled as prologue and epilogue—constitute a frame.

Stand-alone prologues are still fairly common; epilogues are less so—in part, I think, because they've been so severely abused in the past. Epilogues in which the author rambles on self-indulgently about everything that happens to the main characters for the rest of their natural lives, or tries (generally unconvincingly) to tie up all the loose threads of an untidy plot, became justly notorious in the past century.

And there's another problem with epilogues: the story is already over. Epilogues which aren't part of a frame presenting an independent miniplot therefore have no drama and are pure talk. Pure exposition. Soggy anticlimax.

If there's no overriding reason to do otherwise, get the story done and then close the curtain as quickly as possible, while the reader is still halfway wanting more, as I'll discuss in more detail in the next chapter.

Don't dither. Avoid weak, throat-clearing closes, just as you'd avoid throat-clearing, inconclusive openings. Let the ending be the ending, without waffling afterthoughts.

But if there's some solid narrative reason (not just trying to do in five pages what you failed to do in 200) to have a stand-alone epilogue, make it a scene rather than exposition and make sure it has a point, some new insight the story would be incomplete without (please: not "It was all a dream"! It's far, far too late, at that point, to change the rules!). Follow the good manners of departure: say goodbye firmly and briskly, then get yourself gone.

The only trick to creating a frame, prologue, or epilogue is to keep it brief, direct, and interesting. The frame isn't the picture. It's just support and context for the picture. Keep it to that, and you shouldn't have any trouble.

## In Search of Elegance

All this structural hanky-panky isn't something to engage in just for the fun of it. Any departure from linear, sequential storytelling is going to make the story harder to read and call attention to the container rather than the content, the technique rather than the story those techniques should be serving.

There's a principle called "elegance" which means that a theory or an object has no excess parts. It may be very complex, but it's as simple as it can be and still work. This applies to fiction, too. Don't use a frame or a flashback if the story can be well told by following the King of Hearts' advice: "Begin at the beginning, and go on till you come to the end: then stop."

Keep your transitions strong; be as simple as you can; strive for elegance.

# CHAPTER 10

# WHEN YOU COME TO THE END, STOP

ENDINGS COME IN TWO BASIC SHAPES—circular and linear—each with potential strengths and dangers. They also come in three major flavors—happy, unhappy, and a mix. Which combination of shape and flavor will be right for your story is the final major structural decision you'll have to make. And your choice will depend on what kind of a story you're trying to tell: one that rises to a point of climax, or one that returns home to tell the tale.

## WHEN BEGINNING AND END CONNECT: CIRCULAR STORIES

The end of a story is much more like the beginning than it's like the middle. Middles have ups and downs, characters coming and going, intermediate crises. But a beginning focuses down from vague, cloudy Everything to a particular Something—a single vivid problem, a situation, a central character. The middle broadens out to create a diverse reality. Then the end brings Everything, all the story's varied motions, down to a particular Something again: a single, crucial action.

Because ends are so like beginnings, many writers deliberately invite readers to compare the two, with similar situations, the same characters involved, perhaps even echoes of dialogue or imagery at both ends of their stories. Or beginning and end may contrast in selected, significant ways while still remaining visibly comparable, related, as I discussed in the last chapter. Beginning and end then touch, connect, form a circle.

With circular strategy, the story becomes visibly one thing, united, a trip away and a return rather than a linear journey ending at a foreign destination unguessed at the start.

Now, I'm not talking about frames here, but the story proper. Frames are like bookends, supporting the story from outside and made of a visibly different substance. With circular stories, the main plot curves back to connect, in significant ways, with the beginning.

Quest-adventure stories usually have this shape. The major character sets out to find or learn or do something, passes through trials along the way, and finally succeeds (or at least survives), often at great personal cost. But that's not the end. Having won through, such characters then return home—in part to be rewarded, but in part to share the benefits of their experience with their family, tribe, or nation, whether those benefits be tangible treasure or intangible insight and wisdom.

That's the shape of many fantasies, which are frequently structured as quest-adventures. Alice, having dismissed the characters of Wonderland as "nothing but a pack of cards," wakes to find herself again at home. Dorothy, having learned that "there's no place like home," returns to Kansas and is reconciled with ordinary life. Although the bulk of *The Lord of the Rings* chronicles the hobbits' travels to very exotic places indeed, the trilogy ends in Hobbiton, in the same place and among the same characters with which it began.

If your story shows someone going out to grow or change or achieve and then bring that growth, change, or achievement to alter his or her pre-existing everyday life, then it's a circular story. And it needs a solid and appropriate ending to bring things full circle.

## Techniques of Circular Endings

The circular ending is a kind of before/after, then/now contrast. Since beginning and end are comparable but not quite identical, there are clear opportunities for mirroring, for running a kind of experiment with a particular variable, as discussed in Chapter 8. Circular strategy offers possibilities for irony and satire—the disproportion between the way things are and the way they either ought to be or the way we wish they were—because the reader is encouraged to compare the before and the after. The contrast, bitter or sweet, is plain to see.

Establishing the new norm, the way things are going to be from here on, needn't mean coming home in a strictly literal sense. As all of us know who have changed houses, cities, and even states more than once in our lifetimes, "home" is a state of mind. It's where you live, what means "home" to you. Similarly, if the mood, meaning, and emotional dynamic of two places or situations are the same, in some sense they're subjectively the same place, the same situation. They're experienced more or less the same, even if the addresses are different. "Coming home," in a circular story, just means returning to a place, mood, or situation that's related in clear, meaningful ways to counterparts in the story's beginning.

Circular stories tend to end quietly, in repose. If there's a slam-bang action scene, it's not at the story's absolute end—rather it's the scene immediately before the end. It provides the crisis, the change, that makes the new norm possible.

Setting up a clear contrast (before/after, then/now) highlights the variable, the thing that's changed, the story's turning point. That's the pattern in *A Christmas Carol*, highlighting Scrooge's change of heart brought about by his experiences among the spirits. That's also the pattern in Richard Adams' *Watership Down*. After the defeat of the invading army of rabbits, the story doesn't end. It goes past, into peace, into the "new norm" which Hazel's good leadership, Fiver's visions, and Bigwig's bravery have made possible. The ending, showing life in a contented rabbit community where visions are respected and the weak protected, is contrasted implicitly with the opening, which showed a warren where visions were ignored and ridiculed, and the weak were bullied. We see what Hazel and his followers have achieved. The story is circular, even ending at the same season of the year in which it began.

If you want the quiet strength which a circular story can lend, build in mirrors as strongly as you can. Build in circular and recurring things: seasons turning and returning, day opening and dropping into twilight, holidays or other special events that faithfully recur. Show that the beginning and the end belong to one another, and show that without the middle, nothing would have changed—that the middle, up to final crisis, was a turning point.

A circular story is all one motion. If beginning and end aren't strongly tied, the result will be inconclusive, unsatisfactory, a letdown, however interesting in itself. It's *not* by itself: it has the whole weight of the story resting on it, and must reflect the coming to a dynamic stability of all the major forces that produced it, now in repose. It's not just the final scene: it's the culmination of the whole story—beginning and middle—and should reflect that entire progression.

If beginning and end are tied but there's no turning point in the middle, your story will, in retrospect, seem to have been a great deal of fuss about not much of anything—a long journey to get no place in particular. Although Dorothy may start from and return to dull, commonplace Kansas, in between, she's been to Oz. Make sure your story has been somewhere worth the reader's journey too, and that the end isn't just a replay of the beginning but is changed by what's happened in the meantime.

## When Circular Endings Go Wrong

The most likely problems—beginning and end poorly connected or lacking a definite turning point—aren't all that can go wrong. Some problems can happen to any kind of story, and I'll get to those in a minute. But there are two other problems to which circular stories are especially prone. Knowing what they are will help you watch out for them.

### Lost in exposition

One problem is assuming that, because the story continues beyond the final confrontation, it doesn't have any plot chores to do. Such an ending can turn into something like a Victorian epilogue, babbling on about what happens to major (or even minor) characters for the next thirty years or so. There's no development, no plot, nothing but the author droning on until eventually the story falls dead of exhaustion.

Circular endings *do* have a job: showing the homecoming, the new norm; establishing how the middle (turning point) matters; bringing the story full circle.

After they've done their proper work in as direct and compact a way as possible, they should shut up.

## No homecoming

Another problem is stopping the story short at the conclusion of your final confrontation, your Big Scene. Ending with a bang is fine for a linear story, but it short-circuits the potential strengths of structure and of resolution which make circular stories special.

After the gunfight and the defeat of the hired killer, Shane pauses for a moment to reassure the boy who's the story's narrator and then rides off alone, mirroring the story's opening in reverse order. *Shane* ends as it began, with a lone horseman in the distance, being watched by a young boy; but neither Shane nor the boy is precisely what he was at the outset. They're no longer strangers—to each other, or to the reader. The reader knows how each has changed the other's life for the better. Peace is now possible—the new norm.

Although we don't expect either man or boy to live blithely happily ever after, and although the story ends with a parting, a final farewell, we know both Shane and the boy are going to be all right now. This story is over, and it's a positive resolution even though not precisely a "happy" ending. We don't need the details. We know that something of importance has happened and now is resolved.

The close of *Gone with the Wind* seems even grimmer, if we consider only the gross facts of the situation. Rhett has finally left Scarlett for good. Her sole child has died. She has no husband and no way of supporting herself. None of these things is developed any further. They're left as flat facts, final.

But the story's main issue was Scarlett's resiliency and courage in defending and maintaining Tara, her home, and only secondarily her stormy romance with Rhett. Rhett's walking out is the crisis which leaves Scarlett alone again at the story's center— again the sole mistress of Tara. Whatever she may have lost, she still has that. And when she echoes the line that's helped her survive so many past crises, "I'll think about it tomorrow," we believe that somehow she'll cope and survive, and so will Tara, just as they always have.

That's all the resolution needed to make the ending a complete, satisfying one. The important things are settled—not every possible thing the author might have dragged the story out to explain.

And ending with an implicit reminder to the reader of Scarlett's proven (sometimes ruthless) ability to survive makes this story's close, like that of *Shane*, upbeat and positive in mood. It emphasizes Scarlett's essential identity—the lady of Tara, then, now, and always—and her characteristic refusal to accept defeat, even amid the wreckage of her life. We know she'll get by somehow—dead child, no money, lost lover notwithstanding. And that makes it a happy ending.

If you want the power of circularity and connectedness for your story, bring it back, bring it home first. Then let it be over.

## LINEAR ENDINGS

Many stories demonstrate a more linear strategy. The story is a jagged, uphill journey, with building suspense, sudden slides, and occasional diversions in one direction or another, until at last it reaches the summit: the highest point of conflict, the make-or-break confrontation. Companions on the journey have come and gone, and finally it's just the two major opposing forces left and the characters who exemplify them. Once the result is known, the story is over. Anything afterward would be just downhill, anticlimax.

Most genre fiction, particularly mystery, adventure, and

suspense, has this pattern: drive straight toward a single goal and stop when it's been achieved. Ending right after the crisis, which would be a fault in a circular story, becomes a strength and a virtue in a linear one.

*The Maltese Falcon* centers on Sam Spade's involvement with what we gradually learn is the ongoing search for "the black bird." The story begins with a mysterious client and the soon-following murder of Spade's partner, Miles Archer. Finding the falcon doesn't settle things. Even revealing the falcon to be a fake doesn't settle things. The falcon is a fictional prop, a pretext, not the story's central issue. We know that because when the matter of the falcon has been resolved as far as it can be in this present story—the falcon's a fake, the real falcon has yet to be found—the story still isn't over.

Remember that. What finishes a linear story is going to be seen, by the reader, as its main issue. Be sure that in your story, it *is*. Otherwise the ending will be an anticlimax, something tacked on when the story really was already over.

In the present case, not until the final confrontation between Brigid and Sam in which Brigid, Sam's client, has been thoroughly unmasked as the liar and killer she is (that mystery solved) and the circumstances of Archer's death are revealed (the other mystery solved), is the story over, its central issue, the one that continued all the way from the beginning, satisfactorily tied up.

## Clear the Decks for Action

Linear strategy, even more than circular strategy, requires a narrowing down as the end approaches, so the ending can happen cleanly and decisively.

All the narrative clutter possible should go.

Any subplots and side issues should be resolved beforehand, along the way (as is the revelation the present falcon is a fake). If you had a divided plot, either both major plot lines should already have converged into a single narrative line (as in *The Empire Strikes Back*), or the less vivid of the pair should have reached climax and resolution (as with Stephen King's *It*), leaving the other unencumbered and clear to provide the whole story's ending.

All the subordinate characters possible should be shuffled offstage, their work done, as the ending approaches, to leave the major characters alone in the central spotlight.

## Settle the important things—not everything

With a linear story, one that ends immediately after crisis, it's absolutely vital to focus only on the story's central issues at the end. There's not going to be any follow-up scene, as in a circular story, to tidy any flapping loose ends. They need to be tied off securely before the final crisis commences. Trying to yank them into knots during crisis will only clutter and confuse your narrative line. Your story should then be looking straight ahead—not back, not around. It should be all forward motion toward crisis and resolution.

The moment the central questions, the focus of the final crisis, are settled—not necessarily explained, but shown to be resolved, so there's no more dramatic tension—that's the moment your story is really over and you should type "THE END."

Just as good openings start *in medias res*, with something already in progress, good linear endings don't wait till every bit of the dust has settled. Show the explosion but don't wait until every bit of debris has thumped into the dirt or until the smoke fully clears. If the brick that rose fifty feet has reached the top of its arc and is coming down, we don't need to *see* it hit the ground to know that it *will*.

The moment the situation is over and things have assumed their final shape, that's the end of the story. Not a paragraph, not a word more.

## No faraway places with strange-sounding names

Don't introduce a new or complex setting for your ending if that's going to mean stopping the story for exposition. Linear endings are no place for exposition.

If the place is new but simple—a high ledge, the woods in a

rainstorm, a circus, a supermarket, a rush hour expressway where your characters dodge through the lanes on foot—then it won't need explaining or extensive description. Such a setting can be created by citing just a few effective details; readers can fill in the rest from their own experience. A setting like that, even if it's a new one, can heighten your drama without becoming a distraction.

But if your ending itself is going to be fairly complex no matter how you narrow it down, then keep all other elements as simple as possible in compensation. That includes setting. With a complex ending, you might better keep the characters in a setting already familiar, one that's been thoroughly described earlier in the story.

But that kind of decision can be made retroactive. What's new is what's new to the reader, no matter when you actually created it. If you find that for your ending, you've found/invented a perfectly wonderful place you refuse to do without, a new place that would be confusing or ineffective without description, then pre-wash it to get the new out. Go back in your story and use it as the location for some other scene, with whatever description or explanation is then appropriate. Then you'll be able to re-create it at the end with just a phrase or two, maybe echoing a piece of the original description, maybe mentioning some memorable feature you invented for the purpose, to help the reader's recollection.

## No new characters

By the same token, don't introduce any additional characters except cardboard walk-ons (a driver leaning to shout curses as he blurs by; a checkout clerk who hands a character some change and then discreetly disappears from the narrative). Keep to the principals.

## Making a scene

Be sure your final scene *is* a scene. Not a discussion, not an interior monologue. Make something happen.

Just as scenes generally provide the most effective openings, they make the most powerful endings. And just as you needed to think of an opening which would demonstrate exactly who these people are and what's at stake, you now need a situation that shows so clearly what the final conflict involves that you won't need to do any explaining or have any character do it either, as your proxy.

As in the story's opening, create/select and use good props. Use things a reader can see going on.

Even if your story is more about attitudes than actions, think of some concrete thing your protagonist can *do*—not just think about, not merely realize or comment on in dialogue—to *show* the reader both the nature of the final conflict and its resolution. Actions still speak loudest. So invent an appropriate action to demonstrate internal realities.

## No new plot!

Most important of all, though: don't introduce a new plot. Stay with the main plot.

As you write the ending, it may seem to you to be just another scene, even if a Big Scene, a set-piece. What it's easy to forget is that, from the reader's point of view, the whole story is bearing down on this moment. It has the potential for immense weight and power, just because it's the end.

If you don't keep to your main plot line, to what you've been developing all through the story, you forfeit all that momentum and make the reader feel all that build-up was for nothing. You'll be trying to start a new story in the closing minutes of the old one, and no matter how good the scene is as a scene, the reader is going to feel let down, disappointed.

When you're moving at high speed, it's dangerous to try to take a sudden right-angle turn. You have to realize the velocity your story has built up, by now, and not throw your ending into a devastating skid by trying to turn aside at the last moment. This is as true for circular stories as for linear ones.

Whatever forces you established, at the beginning, as the center of your conflict, whether internal, external, or a blend, they should be the forces in conflict at the end. What's at stake should be essentially the same thing that's been at stake from the beginning, even though it's gained added meaning and dimension in the story's developing context. The characters involved should be the main characters and as few of the subordinate ones as absolutely have to be there too.

Your story has already established a context, the rules, the personalities, the stakes: everything you need to make your ending meaningful. You've got all that accumulated power working for you. Use it, guide it, keep that momentum. There's no stopping now, short of the end.

In all ways, keep the ending as simple and direct as you can.

## OFF-CENTER ENDINGS

It doesn't seem fair, but an ineffective ending can invalidate, for a reader, an otherwise fine story. If the ending is bad, the whole story can become a letdown, even though the opening was involving and the middle was entirely satisfying while they were happening.

As readers, we generally don't notice parts of a story as separate things. We consider the apple we're eating as a unit without stopping to analyze the texture and taste of each individual bite. We're enjoyers and appreciators, not judicious, objective critics. We either like the story-apple, or we don't.

The more we liked the first few bites, the opening and the middle, the more disappointed and angry we'll be if the ending falls flat. If the last bite of the apple makes us notice that half a worm remains, we're not going to say to ourselves, "Well, the first three bites were nice." We're going to toss away the apple in disgust and remember the worm.

It probably *isn't* fair. But it's true.

### Changing Focus

A writer I know had an enjoyable fantasy dramatizing the education of a girl in the disciplines of wizardry. The story culminated in a magical battle between the girl's mentor (a good wizard) and his enemy (an evil wizard). The girl looked on.

It was a bad ending.

It didn't lack drama, action, or very literal fireworks. The problem was that the protagonist of the story wasn't the protagonist of the ending. The story had changed focus, right at the end. And so it was uninvolving and surprisingly empty, considering all the potentially exciting pyrotechnics going on.

This is something you can avoid fairly easily, if you realize the danger. Though it's necessary to have the main protagonist present during the story's final crisis, that's not enough all by itself. Be sure he or she is at the center of the ending, and that what he or she does *determines* the outcome. Bystanders and onlookers don't count.

When my friend realized this, she crafted a new ending that put the young protagonist right in the middle of the battle. What the girl did, though small, was appropriate to what had gone before and proved crucial: distracting the evil magician so that he lost concentration. His own spells turned on him. And the girl was responsible, breaking the wizardly stalemate and bringing about victory.

With that change of focus and action, it became a good, effective ending.

## Dirigible ex machina

Another writer I knew didn't know how to end his story. It involved a self-styled prophet who convinced his followers to sell all their belongings and meet him on a certain hill on the night he promised them the world was going to end. Good build-up. But the writer couldn't decide how to resolve things. So he dropped a dirigible on them, killing the lot.

Dramatic? Yes. Credible? Not even a little.

The author's problem was that he imposed a giant piece of melodramatic improbability on his story without any preparation at all. It ended the story, all right: killed it dead in its tracks.

That kind of weird ending that comes, as it were, out of the blue for no particular reason except that the author wants to settle things, is called a *deus ex machina*. The Greeks, as translated by the Romans, coined the term to describe the practice of cranking gods out over the stage to settle otherwise insoluble tangles of human affairs. The whole idea creaks.

Take your ending from within the story itself. Make sure it grows from the characters and the nature of the conflict as it's been presented up to that point.

Whether it's a dirigible descending or convenient lightning striking the villain dead (as happens at the end of the movie version of *The Bad Seed*), the reader isn't going to buy it for a minute. Of course, as with any bit of real unlikeliness, you can prepare beforehand in some of the ways I suggested in Chapter 7.

Keep any major improbabilities to the opening and the middle: keep them out of the ending, except to the degree that they're a reasonable development of premises you've already established. If you've got a vampire, a beam of sunlight can legitimately wither it into a pile of ugly dust; but not if you've got an otherwise realistic (if unsavory) little girl who's been known to murder another child to steal a school spelling prize.

No lightning. No dirigibles, please.

## Trick Endings

Since O. Henry popularized them, trick endings have been a temptation and a danger to all writers but especially to beginners, to whom such gimmicks can be perilously appealing. Some tricks, like dirigible endings, are born of incompetence and the failure of imagination. Others, although unexpected, legitimately arise from within the story itself and are validly startling—on the first reading, anyway. And some tricks are solutions to narrative problems, trapdoors to let a story escape the trap of cliché.

Sometimes, at a story's conclusion, plots can run into a dead end, with no good way out. A trapdoor can't save a dying story any more than a dirigible can: that takes rethinking from the beginning. But it sometimes can make a basically sound story better, acting like a chute to use the story's built-up momentum and deflect the plot line with even greater force and speed in an entirely new and intriguing direction.

Maybe the only possible ending seems too predictable—too much like fifty other stories, or telegraphed so far in advance that the writer gets bored just thinking about it, let alone writing it. For these or other reasons, the writer thinks the ending won't work unless something really startling happens: a real surprise, a trapdoor, a trick.

I've talked before about valid tricks, about substituting something else *of the same general kind, with the same emotional significance*, for what you led the reader to expect. You can do that, if you choose, even in an ending—though I don't advise it. It's generally too risky to be worthwhile, if you don't know precisely what you're doing. If your gimmick doesn't work, your whole story goes down the drain, not just the ending. And endings are such crucial times anyway that tricks become even trickier to bring off than they normally are, when everything isn't riding on their success.

All the same, with great care, trick endings can be made to work. As I discussed in Chapter 7, effective tricks and switches depend on proper preparation beforehand. If, in spite of the risks, you decide to build one into your ending, you can't just spring it, or drop it like a bomb (or a dirigible): you'll need to go back into your story and lay the groundwork—not enough to give your trick away, but enough to make it seem at least plausible when it happens.

## Chute-out in outer space

*The Empire Strikes Back* seems to be leading toward a climactic duel between Luke and Darth Vader—the science fiction version of the noon shoot-out on Main Street. Predictable. Dull. But it would be disappointing if, after all that build-up, protagonist and adversary never meet, or meet but don't fight.

George Lucas decided to build himself a chute from the materials at hand, from the context the story had already established.

Groundwork about Luke's father had been laid from the beginning of the series. The elder Skywalker was evidently an accomplished Jedi warrior; like Luke, he was the student of Obi-Wan Kenobi—indeed, one strongly suspects Luke undertakes the Jedi training to follow in his father's ways. Obi-Wan, whom one takes to be a reliable source, reports that the elder Skywalker was killed by Vader—as Obi-Wan himself later is, before Luke's eyes.

From all these accumulated details, by the time we reach the part of the story where the duel commences, we know Luke's father means a great deal to him. It's the personal, rather than the political, part of his motivation for seeking out the duel: to avenge his father's murder, as well as that of his fatherly and beloved mentor, Obi-Wan.

And these details might have rested there, just like that: perfectly acceptable as background information about Luke, explaining and justifying his hatred for Vader. And then the duel could come, and Luke could win or lose, and we could all yawn and munch our popcorn and admire the special effects in a vague, abstracted fashion until the duel was done.

But rather than just grind out the expected clichéd duel, Lucas saw the possibility for an effective switch. In his original stories, on which the screenplays were based, he laid the groundwork that would bear more than the one obvious interpretation. Lucas decided to go ahead and build on it.

He couldn't avoid the duel altogether: that would be anticlimactic, since Luke's motivations for fighting Vader had been demonstrated so strongly. The duel is played out. All the expected swashes are buckled and the legitimate expectations satisfied. But the duel is less climax than build-up to a startling switch that changes it retroactively in our imaginations—not a worm in the apple, but a hissing fuse. It's not just a change in plot—it's a change in meaning and relationship and therefore more powerful and convincing than mere externals could be. Vader's revelation that he himself is Luke's much-idolized father—not dead, but corrupted and evil—turns the duel, and all Luke's attitudes, right around. The world changes, and that changes everything.

The chute, the trick, wasn't simple reporting of fictional "facts": George Lucas constructed it. Though we see the final product which now seems inevitable, as though it couldn't be other than it is, there was a time when anything in the story could have been changed and we'd never have known the difference.

Darth Vader didn't *have* to be Luke's father. In an interview, Lucas has admitted thinking about whether to go ahead with the revelation or not. No, George Lucas *made* Vader Luke's father. He didn't merely reveal the fact: he invented it, out of the details of plot, characterization, and background the story had already established.

Just as easily, Vader could have turned out to be Han Solo's father. Nothing rules it out—as far as I can tell, Solo was found under a cabbage: no parentage, no home is ever mentioned. But no groundwork had been laid, to give such a revelation resonance and emotional power: to make it *matter*. Can you visualize Vader declaring himself to be Solo's father, and Luke saying blankly, "So?"

Not any chute would have done. Only one that followed the story's essential dynamic, one that immediately and instantly *mattered*, could use the story's momentum and shoot it off in a new direction without slowing.

A switch can be sudden to the reader, but it must be foreseen and carefully planned by its author. And like all effective endings, it must grow out of what the story has become, up to that point.

It must not be an escape from labored plotting, but a fulfillment of careful plotting. It's not a thing to do in desperation, because you can't think of anything else.

If you're in doubt, don't do it. The wrong chute will do nothing but zip your story straight through onto some editor's reject pile.

If you're going to have to go back into your story anyway in order to construct a valid and effective trick ending, look around while you're there. Consider the moods and attitudes and other elements that might be adjusted to lead to a different conclusion than the one you're contemplating with dread and boredom. Maybe you'll find you don't need a trick after all. And maybe that will be for the best.

## Happy Endings

A happy ending isn't necessarily one that makes the characters grin a lot and start cracking jokes at one another. It's not even one that promises marriage, true love, or victory to the protagonist.

In a very meaningful sense, a happy ending is one that satisfies, and that kind of happy ending, any story can have—even one that ends up with virtually everybody dead on the floor, like *Hamlet*.

The traits that make an ending satisfying are fittingness (the characters seem to have gotten the ending they earned by their actions during the story, for good or ill) and definiteness (the story's resolution is clear, appropriate, and decisive: it's really over).

But even though this is true, it doesn't address the issue of traditional happy or downbeat endings all writers have to confront and settle in every story they write.

Most genre fiction of all sorts tends to be upbeat, ending on what at least seems a positive note—the murderer identified and caught, the lovers reunited, the kidnaped child rescued—no matter what miseries were suffered in getting there.

In its extreme form, this can be a mindless, saccharine cheeriness that makes us want to go out and kick a small fuzzy kitty into next week.

By contrast, literary fiction tends toward the opposite extreme, as if there were something inherently suspect and superficial about happiness or contentment. If popular fiction sometimes falls off the fence on the right, with resolute, offensive uplift and fake happily-ever-afters, literary fiction is apt to fall off on the left, serving up suffering, squalor, and trashcan angst that's as fully a violation of our sense of life's diverse possibilities.

It's important to realize that formula moroseness and despair can be just as trite and unconvincing as doctrinaire, regulation happiness and cases of the terminal cutes. Gloom isn't intrinsically any more honest, courageous, or intellectually respectable than joy. Either has to be rendered credible in the context of a particular story. Each needs to be earned. And each works the better for a dash of the other, like Yin and Yang, opposing swirls that divide a circle, each containing a spot of its opposite.

Better, in the long run, to be honest than either vapidly "happy" or churlishly scowling and grim. Let the story shape its natural ending no matter where on the spectrum of blessing or bane it may fall.

But, with deliberate craft, it's possible to have things both ways. Unless you're committed to unmitigated cynicism and despair, there's going to be something readers can contrive to interpret as a positive note in your ending. Let them.

If 99 percent of your ending is wretchedness, gloom, and doom, if the whole world has been destroyed except for the two lovers and they're not feeling any too healthy, readers will still nod and say to themselves, "Well, at least they have each other." They'll notice the positive 1 percent if you focus on that and keep the gloom and doom no less black, but off to the side a little, where it can be ignored if a reader is so inclined.

Remember Scarlett O'Hara. Remember that Ishmael survived the meeting with Moby Dick, even though nobody else did.

Even death can be positive, if it's sentimental enough and worth a good cry, and has a healthy chunk of true, unselfish love and sacrifice mixed in. Look at *A Farewell to Arms*, *Romeo and Juliet*, or *A Tale of Two Cities*. Tears, accepting the sadness and passing beyond it, can be a healing thing too.

Likewise, that a character can win or recover a capacity for joy, in spite of great and convincing suffering, makes that joy stronger and more believable. Such a stance doesn't pretend that the hurts, the cruelties, and the disappointments don't exist. It accepts them, but says that joy is nevertheless still real and valid in the world as well, unquenchable as grass. And that's more powerful than unrelieved niceness and empty bliss that escapes the dark only by keeping its eyes resolutely shut.

If you can refrain from depressing the living daylights out of your readers, they'll probably like your work more. But if, in a given story, you find you really have to choose between happy and satisfying, take satisfying.

It lasts longer.

## *No Ending*

Remember back in Chapter 6, I told you about how some writers hesitate, waffle, and try to dodge set-pieces? The same thing can happen, only worse, with endings.

No-ending stories happen a lot. They've happened to me, and lately. In my drawer I have a few beginnings I haven't been able to grow middles from yet, let alone endings. Some stories stall because they really weren't ever going anywhere to begin with. The fault was in the concept, from the first. It just takes writers a few scenes, or a hundred pages, to realize their story has run out of gas and feel it wheezing to a halt.

The only possible cure is going back and starting over. And I will, one of these days, on some of my tail-less stories. Some, I'll just leave, or cannibalize for parts, realizing that probably they weren't my stories to tell after all.

That's not what I'm talking about now.

It's the stories that seem to end, but really don't. There's no final climax, nothing that seems worth all the build-up or seems as if the whole story has led up to it. There's a little talk, a little action, maybe a little scene. Then all the characters just wander away like kids playing sandlot ball whose mothers have called them home to supper in the middle of an inning. Everything's left unfinished, inconclusive.

Such a story seems one segment of a potentially endless tube of cheese, arbitrarily cut at some point to make an end. There doesn't seem to be any reason it shouldn't be twice as long, or half as long. It just goes on for awhile. Then, for no particular reason, it stops.

Some writers claim to consider such formless finales more artistic. "Let the readers imagine their own ending," I've heard them say loftily. On that rationale, a writer could not bother to write the story at all and let readers imagine the whole thing.

Saying a story should have a definite conclusion doesn't mean it ought to have a moral, or spell out every nuance. Ambiguity, with two or more valid meanings, can work; willful vagueness, with no particular meaning at all, doesn't.

A fiction writer's business is to tell a story. The story can be as complex, interior, and subtle as you choose, or as plain as a pie in the face. No matter what it is, whether the most ambitious and literary of fiction or utter and unredeemed formula schlock, a story that just stops, that doesn't come to a head in conflict and resolution, is a story that's not there yet.

Write the scene. Make it happen.

## KNOWING WHEN TO STOP

So. You're done.

Often, after all that intense work, it's hard to let a story be over. You've lived with your characters so long. You know them so well now—better than you do your closest friend, your dearest lover. Even if the story has a happy ending, if it's over, you've still lost them *as your characters*. Their decisions and actions are in the past, fixed, finished, not living and fluid as they were while you were imagining the story into words and scenes. They're not waking you up in the middle of the night with dialogue, or creating fresh new situations in your mind while you're driving to the grocery, the way they used to.

It's as if they'd died. You're going to miss them, even through all the rereading and revising. It will never again be quite the way it was when you were writing the story and imagining it out of nothing.

You're suffering from the most virulent form of fiction fatigue: fictional withdrawal.

It takes various forms, all destructive.

### *Dithering*

Some writers won't let a story be over. They burden the conclusion with meandering afterthoughts, Victorian epilogues, explanations. Some of them have even gotten away with it.

Detective fiction, particularly the older, British kind with butlers, used to be particularly subject to talky, expositional endings after the real issues had been settled. Once the murderer had been named and officially led away, or had decently committed suicide in the drawing room, everybody sat around for maybe a dozen pages while all the loose threads were methodically knotted up and the improbabilities rationalized. Sometimes that required the detective to tell practically the whole story all over from the beginning. And everything drifted into anticlimax. But that was an accepted convention at one time, though it's little used now.

## Sequel-Fishing

Another way of refusing to let a story be over is to write an inconclusive, foggy conclusion that doesn't really settle things at all. I just discussed the "no-ending" problem, and that's one form this inconclusiveness may take. In its more extreme forms, it can be a cliff-hanger ending that cries out for a sequel because the present story isn't really done. It just stops.

I've read stories like that, and I expect you have too.

Before I had any idea that there were three volumes to *The Lord of the Rings*, I picked up a copy of the first book, *The Fellowship of the Ring*, at my neighborhood library. I was furious for weeks at the book's conclusion, which left all the major issues unresolved and the characters scattering in every direction but up. I felt cheated. I'd gotten involved with these characters, I'd read all those pages, and *now* look what the author had gone and done to me!

*The Lord of the Rings* is exceptional (I know now): it's one huge novel arbitrarily packaged as three separate volumes for no better reason than that one standard paperbound book physically *can't* be made big enough (or priced low enough) for the "trilogy" to be what in fact it is, one novel. I was furious, not at the end of a novel, but at a legitimate "part" break. It wasn't the author's fault that it took me about seven years (until I ran into the first of the paperback boxed sets) to get past that part break into the rest of the story.

What Tolkien did to me, by accident, don't do to your readers on purpose.

Don't go fishing for a sequel if you haven't constructed, in your present story, solid and honorable bait.

Stories that spark effective sequels do so *not* because the original story was left hanging, but because there's more than one good story to be told in the world they've created. The possibilities of Sherlock Holmes weren't exhausted by *A Study in Scarlet*; there was more to Oz than Dorothy saw in her original journey to see the Wizard.

If your world and your characters are rich enough, diverse enough, original enough, perhaps you'll be able to make them wholly live for you again in another story, some other time. But not by hanging on to this present story so hard that you strangle it. Let it be done. Let it go.

## *Revising . . . and Revising . . . and Revising. . . .*

A third way of not allowing the story to be finished is by diving immediately into endless, destructive revisions that tear the story up by its roots and hack away at its branches.

New scenes! New climaxes! Wonderful new dialogue muttering inside your head!

As long as you're working on it, you tell yourself, it's not really over. And you really don't have to send it out or risk the trauma of somebody else looking at it and (horrors!) maybe not liking it as much as you do. It's all for the story's own good, you tell yourself, after months or years have passed and you're still revising. After all, it's not done yet.

With any luck at all, it never will be, either. It will sit with all your other mangled fragments and drafts and redrafts on the desk where somehow nothing ever really gets completed.

Partly, it's like what I warned you about in regard to beginnings: rushing into revision. Don't try to rework your story while it's still hot from your handling. Let it cool and set into its own form. Let yourself get a little emotional and intellectual distance from it. Let it be over, and be happy with it: a finished thing, one whole first draft.

But partly this problem has another cause. Some writers, losing the vivid excitements of first-draft writing, mistakenly believe the story has died. Because it's no longer interesting in exactly the same way as when it was growing and changing, they think there's something wrong with it. They start on an endless autopsy or, worse, refuse to look at it anymore and send it out the way it is with no revisions at all, in lieu of a funeral.

There are probably things in it that can be improved, but what's happened is normal and necessary. There's nothing wrong with the story—not wrong *that* way, anyhow.

That it now seems solid, dry, and definite, rather than flowing quicksilver in your fingers, just means it's grown up. It's started to become its own thing, rather than being just an extension of your living imagination that can't be severed and survive. But it's only started. It still needs your help, your care, your craft to become fully itself.

Love the child it was. Love the adolescent it is. Help it become the independent living thing it ought to be, free of you, able to stand on its own and ready to meet its readers.

Revision has its excitements and its pleasures too, though they're different from the pleasures of first-draft writing. They include seeing buried connections you can bring out, strong scenes you can make stronger, ideas or intentions you now see ways to embody in character, scene, and action. There's also the delight of seeing the symmetrical patterns of the story you've made, with all its interconnectedness, which you couldn't discern while originally writing the story because you were holding it too close.

But these very real and legitimate joys of revision have nothing to do with procrastination or refusing to let the story have a final shape and be what it is, even with a few flaws of characterization or narration that, maybe with ten years' more experience, you might be able to improve. The story doesn't have to be perfect. It just has to be the very best story you can write now. That's all you have a right to expect of it, or of yourself.

Once it's cooled, let it sit for a reasonable time. A week or two. Then set about your second draft. After that, maybe try it out on some readers, as long as you ask them specific questions and get specific answers you consider yourself entirely free to ignore completely. ("Did you like it?" is *not* a specific question; "Where did it get confusing or slow?" *is*.)

Third draft next, working with *what's there*, not just yanking things out and jamming things in haphazardly. And when it all fits together the very best you can make it, type up a good clean draft (remember to keep a photocopy) and send it out to the first appropriate market on your list.

If it comes back, don't retreat into anxious tinkering. Make a fresh copy, if the original has coffee-cup rings on it, but send it out to the next market that same day, barring illness or accident. And do the same a dozen times more, if it's needed. Do it like clockwork, as if the story were no more than a bill you're paying.

And then, if it still comes forlornly back, *then* look over the accumulated rejects for any insights they may offer, reread the story, and find out whether you can see it with fresh eyes. *Then* revise once more, if you can see a way to make the story better, stronger, *as the story it is*, not as some other story you might try to wrench it into becoming. It has a right to be itself.

If it's a true story, true to people and their experience, and if it's constructed with at least moderate narrative craft, it will be published, sooner or later, somewhere.

Stories are for sharing. Not for gathering dust in pieces on your desk or hiding in some bulging file. Let this story be done and start thinking about the wonderful next one you can't wait to get started on, bringing to it all the craft and insight you've developed and will develop still further as long as you're writing.

# CHAPTER 11

# BEYOND PLOT

NOT ALL FICTION IS FOUNDED on the falling dominos of cause and effect. Some stories concern being rather than doing, states rather than processes. Rather Eastern, really.

The writer's problem is to make something essentially static, something that doesn't change, *seem* to move and develop before the reader's eyes. Otherwise the resulting story will be about as absorbing as watching a puddle.

The writer has to select or create some structure that's appropriate to the material and that will act just as plot would, as an organizing principle to which he or she can refer questions of what to put in and what to leave out, what to develop and what to pass over, when to move and when to stand still.

The three strategies this chapter discusses—mosaic, collage, and revelation—can all happily coexist with plot, and with one another. Particularly in long fiction, collage or mosaic may be used as an additional element or variation within an otherwise plotted story, as are the newsreels in John Dos Passos' *U. S. A.* or the extended character sketches in Faulkner's *The Town*. (Then, they should be handled like exposition, which is also static and a potential distraction from the plotline: they should be kept brief and interjected only when the plot's running strongly and will carry the reader through the interpolation.) Revelation, a mystery gradually disclosed, is part of the archetypical Story we've been telling one another since we began to be people.

But in literary or experimental fiction, non-plot techniques are sometimes the main organizing principle of a whole short story. The story may contain a few incidents, but these aren't linked to one another in a cause/effect way. They're not plot. And a short story, being compact, can better sustain lots of technical "special effects" than can a whole novel: imagine watching five hours' worth of *Laugh-In* or MTV, or read about the first thirty pages of *Finnegans Wake*, and you'll see what I'm getting at.

All these techniques manipulate a story's surface, make it move, to compensate for the fact that the essential content doesn't move or change. And coping with a complicated surface can be as difficult, for a reader, as trying to make out what's being reflected in a choppy lake or trying to read by strobe light. Remember that, when you're writing. Balance motion and stillness at least enough so that the reader can figure out what the situation is, who the people are, and why the story will be worth puzzling out.

## MOSAIC STRUCTURE

The first strategy depends on selection and recurrence, as discussed in Chapter 8. Things repeat, and that repetition can be seen as a kind of motion. Patterns of images, of symbols, of repeated situations and attitudes, have a cumulative impact. Detail adds to detail, each clarifying the adjacent details, like putting together a puzzle. Not until all the pieces are in place is the whole picture at last revealed.

Each piece is complete and has a shape of its own, but its fascination is in how it relates to all the other pieces, the picture slowly emerging that's not contained in any one piece but is the sum of them all.

This strategy is like that of the Impressionists, who built up pictures out of colored dots. If you don't have any Seurat handy, look at a newspaper photo through a magnifying glass to see the clusters of tiny spots that, at the proper distance, resolve themselves into a face.

Let's call this technique "mosaic structure."

It comes in five major formats: mood piece, character study, slice-of-life, theme and variation, and allegory. All depend on the accumulation and arrangement of carefully selected detail. Although the individual pieces may be static, the energy comes from seeing how they relate and make a whole, and from guessing toward the final picture as each piece is added.

## Mood Piece

Poe's "The Fall of the House of Usher" is primarily a mood piece. True, things happen in it—the house does fall down, and Usher's sister does apparently rise from her crypt—but these events aren't related in a linear, literal, cause-effect way. Horrible revelations don't normally affect one's architecture. There's a strong element of surrealism and perhaps even loose allegory (of which, more in a minute) in this story, but the descriptions of people and setting serve less to characterize Roderick Usher, his sister, or the narrator than to create a mood of feverish foreboding which comes to crisis for dreamlike reasons, not literal ones.

A lot of horror fiction—"tales of terror" and of "lurking dread"—and atmospheric gothic fiction are structured more to build and sustain a particular mood than to develop plot. At the other end of the spectrum, inspirational and religious fiction does the same thing in terms of uplift and reassurance that all's well with the world. A mood has to be a strong one, to sustain even a whole short story, with minimal or no help from plot.

Mood pieces tend to be closed and rather claustrophobic worlds in which the major objects become luminous, significant to each of the major characters. There's much opportunity for symbolism. This often takes the form of some object standing, either for the whole spectrum of attitudes being considered, or for one particular element in that spectrum. Roderick Usher's house is more than a house—it's a kind of emanation of his personality, a larger skin his spirit inhabits. When the spirit fails and Roderick dies, the house falls down as one's body collapses at death. It's perfectly reasonable, given what the house has come to represent by the end of the story. An inner fact or process is made literal—the basis of most surrealism.

It's important, in a mood piece, to pick a strong mood and to choose appropriate characters, settings, and objects to represent and reinforce it. Using mirroring characters, each demonstrating some facet of the story's central attitude or situation, is a common technique. Another is making the landscape and physical surroundings appear nearly alive, so that they can seem imbued with menace or hope, haunted for either good or ill, to project the inner state or mood onto the world at large. When you feel gloomy, the whole world looks drab; when you're anxious, the world seems bright-edged, sudden, and threatening, as though it were about to pounce. A phone's ringing can blast like a fire alarm.

This kind of projection, sometimes called "the pathetic fallacy," serves to make a story's mood seem part of reality itself, not just a personal and idiosyncratic quirk of the protagonist. It's no accident that the house of Usher is located on the precarious edge of a menacing and oily-looking tarn.

Moods are fragile things. If you strike one wrong note, the mood will collapse and dump the reader back into hard-headed rationality. Don't let into your story any character, situation, or object that doesn't contribute to and share the chosen mood. In gothic romance, nobody has an itch or visits the orthodontist. In horror fiction, nobody Has a Nice Day. Except for the briefest of comic relief that ends up reinforcing the mood (the orthodontist has fangs; the Nice Day is a sinister mask for Something Else), keep to your mood from first to last.

## Character Sketch

A character sketch employs much the same strategy as a mood piece, except that the subject involved isn't a feeling, but all the important facets of a given person in his or her particular context. So the strategy is often to present a series of situations that bring out the character's possibilities and essential attitudes—all the relevant parts of who that person is. Each of these situations may be fragmentary—not a complete scene in the usual sense of the word—because its purpose isn't to develop a plot but to let the character demonstrate his or her basic nature.

That's the overall strategy of Salinger's *Catcher in the Rye*, in which Holden Caulfield shows who he is through a journey that involves successive meetings with adults and finally with his sympathetic sister.

Relationships are confined to those which add further detail to the developing picture of the character. If his dead father is important, then there may be recollections or even flashbacks of that relationship; if her interest in architecture is the guiding force in her life, the story might be structured in terms of her visits to different buildings, showing what a school, a church, a theatre mean to her and therefore precisely who she is in that particular context. If she cares more for architecture than for people, each building might be empty, or filled with strangers the story shows her ignoring or misunderstanding.

Each piece of the story should be either a new facet of the character's being or an effective repetition and development of one already shown.

My story "A Sense of Family" was much more a character sketch, showing the nature and possibilities of its protagonist, than it was a plotted story, since all Val's actions end up short-circuited and frustrated. She never does collect the money she's owed or get to her brother's wedding. If plot were the only interest, the story would probably be a letdown to most readers. But the gradual revelation that what keeps Val from relating to people in more effective personal ways is her very strength, her ability to live on her own terms without compromise but also without anger or love, provides a fuller and more ironic picture than the plot alone could communicate.

Character sketches can be structured from the outside in, developing first the most external and commonplace of the character's doings and relationships, then dealing with ones successively closer to eventually show the one thing at the center. Alternatively, they can be structured broadly, mixing the important with the more trivial so that a pattern can emerge. Or they can be a species of collage built around strong contrasts and perhaps the gradual revelation of unexpected or unusual traits.

## Slice-of-Life

Although a single character or a cluster of characters—say, a family—may be at the center of a slice-of-life story, the story's main concern is not to explore their personalities. Rather, it's to use them as ways to demonstrate their social context. They tend to be representative characters, chosen because they demonstrate a given social situation so well rather than primarily because they're so interesting as people.

Steinbeck's *The Grapes of Wrath* is a portrait of the Okies displaced westward by the dust bowl disaster of the thirties. It's the Okies as a group who are important, rather than the Joads in particular. They're significant as a typical family who, through their travels and trials, show what Steinbeck conceived to be the main facets of that social upheaval as a whole.

That they're typical, though, doesn't mean they're not highly individualized. Ma Joad, in particular, is as memorable a character as ever was written. Rather, they're a way of making concrete and immediate the human dimension of economic and social disaster.

Similarly, James T. Farrell's *Studs Lonigan*, Heller's *Catch-22*, Dickens' *Oliver Twist*, and much of the short fiction of Cheever and Roth, are attempts to reveal a certain way of living—a time, a place, a social context—as demonstrated by the experiences of a given set of characters. The characters and the plot elements (if any) are less important for their drama than for their representative qualities, persuading the reader that the small reveals the large and that each character and event has a significance beyond the merely individual.

The danger with slice-of-life stories is that, in the absence of a plot to keep things moving, the small incidents of individual lives intended to demonstrate a larger social reality will just seem trivial and boring. A friend of mine describes slice-of-life, not altogether jokingly, as stories where a woman in carpet slippers goes out to buy a loaf of bread and then comes home again. It's crucial, in such stories, that the events chosen be vivid and interesting in themselves and be arranged and presented in such a way that the reader can't help noticing they mirror a reality larger than the merely personal.

Melodrama can come to your rescue here, as it did for Steinbeck and Dickens. Virtually a whole state uprooted, dust storms, cruelty and hope, strong family relationships put to the ultimate test, violent events of many kinds, prevent *The Grapes of Wrath* from ever seeming mundane, boring, or everyday. Similarly, *Oliver Twist*'s colorful details of life in London's underworld of child exploitation and the vividness of individual characters like Fagin, Bill Sikes, and Nancy compensate for Dickens' exceedingly improbable plot weakened, at most crucial points, by the extensive use of coincidence.

Slice-of-life has a tendency to yawn. Don't let it.

## Theme and Variation

*Moby Dick* is an exploration of humanity's relation to the infinite and the eternal. *Hamlet* has been characterized by Lawrence Olivier as being about indecision. *A Christmas Carol* is about the cost of a selfish alienation from humanity.

In some stories, a single essential concept appears in a variety of forms and is demonstrated in successive situations. While plot can and often does help organize that demonstration, a strong enough theme can sustain a story by itself.

The subject being examined and revealed isn't a character or a setting or a mood. It's a cluster of related ideas.

Faulkner's *The Bear* illustrates the method. This novelette presents a spectrum of attitudes concerning Nature, maturity, and manhood in the context of a boy's experiences when he is taken hunting by assorted adult kinfolk. As is the case with the conch and the Beast in Golding's *Lord of the Flies*, each character is defined by his relationship with the story's main totem, the bear, and the ideas of wildness which the bear gradually, through successive and layered detail, comes to represent. And that spectrum of gradually developed and revealed attitudes— each of them static and unchanging, except the boy's—constitute the story's structure.

As with the other kinds of mosaic, careful selection of scene, character, and detail are crucial. What doesn't fit the theme doesn't belong.

Faulkner's story doesn't include anybody who thinks bear hunting is a waste of time, anybody interested in electronics or gourmet cooking or European politics. The setting is the timeless forest, though civilization and urbanization have begun to have an impact on both place and people. Everything in the story contributes to the central theme and the recurring limited spectrum of attitudes, developed piece by piece as the boy interacts with the various characters. Things that don't relate to that spectrum are deliberately excluded. But the range of characters is so rich, the almost mystical rapport with Nature so intense, that the other things aren't missed. They're not part of this story's presentation of a particular way of seeing the world and humankind's place in it.

If you intend your story to be taken as a credible, albeit heavily edited and arranged, version of everyday reality, it will be important that characters not make obvious speeches spelling out the theme to one another. If everybody in your story is suffering through some phase of divorce, the story's implicit subject will show itself, just by what's included and what's kept out. The larger picture will form, from the individual parts chosen.

To the degree that your story is surrealistic, it's shading into the next category, allegory, and the appropriate caveats discussed there will apply.

Theme stories are difficult to carry off without plot, because the story's essential subject, being abstract, intangible, and often highly intellectual (as well as static), is hard to make immediate and involving for a reader.

Again, melodrama to the rescue.

Vivid, exaggerated happenings can hold the eye and the interest while the meaning penetrates more subtly. And credibility can be maintained using some of the techniques discussed in Chapter 7.

Remember, *Moby Dick* is also an adventure story; *Hamlet* has duels and murders galore, as well as a semitragic love story; *A Christmas Carol* has ghosts, a sudden transformation, and judicious tear-jerking; *The Bear* has the excitements and tensions of the hunt, a first hunt seen through the eyes of a boy. Even without plot, melodrama can compensate and help bring theme to effective life.

But the extremes of melodrama aren't the only answer. There's also the solid middle-ground of human imperfection and everyday experience: drama.

As theme stories shade toward plot, toward a pattern of meaningful cause and effect, a story's essential conflict will often be cast in terms of opposite forces contrasting and colliding. Polarities. Not just simplistic, unmixed Good against absolute Evil, but more subtle shadings of two essential principles each with some claim to validity. One partial Good, as it were, contrasted with another partial Good—individuality and self-fulfillment against responsibility to family or community, for instance, or the conflicting demands, on a parent, of helping two very different children.

The closer such polarities are, the finer the distinction that can be made between what a given story presents as better or worse modes of action or being, and the emotional cost of each. For instance, in the overall field of Charity, can you imagine two conflicting ways of helping people—both well intentioned, but one basically arrogant and humiliating, the other more compassionate but perhaps less effective? Can you imagine two genuine loves—one of which dominates the loved one, the other of which liberates but ends in the lovers' separating?

Some of the most profound stories aren't about absolute right and wrong, the melodramatic extremes, but about forces nearly alike, both credibly strong, valid, and humanly imperfect, distinguished by one crucial difference. Does it begin to sound at all like the control and the experimental group and the one variable, discussed in Chapter 8? Because that's what it is, only on a grander scale.

It's been said that no one knowingly does Wrong: people always think they have a Good reason for what they do. Those who make wrong choices generally aren't monsters, freaks, or devils—they're only people, sharing the flaws we all possess. Thus, battles between blatant Good and obvious Evil often aren't the most persuasive or involving ones—it's the battles between rival Goods that lead to the special insights and the really hard choices that are the basis of drama.

If your theme story is going to be developed at least in part in terms of plot, you may want to identify for yourself the story's essential dynamic, the polarity working itself out through the principal characters, and then strengthen it and eliminate clutter. That will clarify not only the terms of the characters' choices, but the value placed on those choices in your story's special world, among the alternatives you show to be possible and available.

If you do, you may find that you've constructed, not just drama, but literature.

## Allegory

Like a theme story, allegory has a subtext, a pattern of meaning beyond what's evident on the surface. Just more so. Allegory involves creating a fairly thoroughgoing pattern of symbolism in which all major events and characters in a story have a meaning beyond themselves and those meanings can be put together to make some sort of overall sense.

In its simplest forms, allegory can be a fable like that of the dog in the manger or the fox and the grapes, in which dog, fox, grapes and manger stand for some reality of human experience—that some people who can't use a thing nevertheless are reluctant to let others enjoy it; that some people rationalize their disappointment at being unable to get something by claiming the thing is no good anyway.

*Lord of the Flies* is, in large measure, a fable of this sort. Each of the major characters represents one particular facet of human possibility as Golding conceives it. The characters are stranded on an island to limit them to their own resources. They're schoolboys (some are choirboys) to underline that they're as close to innocence as human beings are apt to get. And all are male, I assume, to keep any question of sex from muddling the experiment, since it's not part of what Golding wants to examine.

They're boys. But boys plus. Simon, for example, is a fully realized individual. But he also stands for and demonstrates the mystical and hopeful tendencies in all people. He's the only mystic on the island, just as Piggy is the only intellectual, Jack the only natural hunter, Roger the only sadist, and so on.

Other fables are more complex, and whole groups of characters stand for some concept or idea beyond their role purely as characters. Consider the pigs in Orwell's fable, *Animal Farm*—capitalists and totalitarians. Consider the great lion, Aslan, in C. S. Lewis' Narnia stories.

This kind of structural symbolism lends itself to social satire, political polemics, fantasy, and religious fiction. There are innumerable examples of each. Some are plotted; some derive their energy from the tension between symbol and reality, the character and what the character stands for, the gradual revelation of larger meanings.

Allegory can also be the basis of surreal and absurdist fiction, in which the literal meaning (characters living in trashcans or turning overnight into insects) isn't at all realistic but, through its bizarre unlikeliness, strikingly portrays some equivalent real situation.

Hardly anybody lives in trashcans; but people live in slums, and we speak of "throwaway children," those who are unwanted by society. And isn't living in a trashcan a reasonable equivalent or image for either of those real situations? And which of us, at some time, hasn't felt completely alien within our family, as though we were of some entirely different species—say, an insect? As with Roderick Usher's anthropomorphic house, the surreal elements, if well chosen, can become a metaphor demonstrating a core truth by exaggerating and making literal its essential emotional dynamic.

There are two main dangers with this kind of fiction. One is that the message, the larger meaning, will take over, making the characters seem like lifeless puppets and the story, however organized, a mechanical thing determined by forces imposed from outside—a political stance, a religious or social ideology. The fiction has a blatant ulterior motive. In extreme cases, the events and people of the story, as presented, make no surface sense at all. Only what they stand for is of any significance; and that's not enough to make the story readable or coherent.

The second difficulty is establishing the system of symbols itself. The pattern must make sense, rather than seeming an arbitrary authorial whim (umbrella = ambition; galoshes = passionate love; fish = space travel). The symbols chosen must be appropriate both to what they represent and to one another. The connections should be valid and reasonable in a plain literal sense as well as a metaphorical one, and be consistent through the whole story. A knife can be a symbol; but it also better be able to cut string. And if it represents cutting free, cutting loose, in the story's beginning, it better not be used to prop up a bookcase and then forgotten, later on.

In practice, this makes characterization and plotting doubly hard, since each element of the story carries an added weight of meaning and invites interpretation, as though it were a code to be broken rather than a story to be enjoyed.

Both difficulties, combined with allegory's tendency to become preachy and polemic and its requirement that the reader put in extra work discerning the second level of meaning, have diminished its popularity over the centuries. Strict allegory, in which virtually every word must support a double meaning and fit into a coherent interpretation, has produced few examples since the Middle Ages. But loose allegory, in which only major events and characters must fit the chosen ideological pattern, still appears with fair frequency and is a staple of experimental, literary fiction, and fantasy.

## COLLAGE

Collage is closely related to mosaic. But it doesn't tend to yield an overall picture. Its component parts remain parts, individual and isolated.

Imagine a picture that's composed of a few newspaper clippings, a pair of scissors and a plastic doll's head glued to the canvas, some big blurs of red paint, and some mustard-colored corduroy cut into oblong shapes with threads dangling out. That's collage.

The energy comes either from various kinds of violent, extreme contrast—surprising juxtapositions (things not ordinarily related, side by side: for instance, a department store dummy with a hinged door in its torso that reveals a photo of a fetus in a jar), or disjunctions (things normally related which are separated or distorted, like the features of a person in a Picasso painting)—or a great deal of intricate detail within the parts (like a Rube Goldberg drawing of an incredibly and ridiculously complicated machine for getting you up in the morning, including a chicken pecking grain, a rising balloon hitting a nail, a chute down which marbles scamper, a dog trying to catch a cat, and so forth).

Because any collage is a diverse collection of disparate elements, it's hard to characterize the form except in the most general fashion. Each work is unlike all others. The classic example is probably *Don Quixote* by Cervantes, consisting of more-or-less random adventures and confrontations, built on the contrast between the way the Don sees the world and the way his more hardheaded companion Sancho perceives it. Another classic is Sterne's unique *Tristram Shandy*, with its blank pages, marbled pages, disquisitions on the deeper meanings of a falling hat, and so on. Some modern examples would be Heller's *Catch-22*, and much of Vonnegut's fiction, including *Cat's Cradle* and *Slaughterhouse Five*.

There are collage components in Dos Passos' *U. S. A.*, with its "Camera Eye" newsreels and profiles interspersed with the various plots. Another contemporary and very unsettling example is Jerzy Kosinsky's *The Painted Bird*, a succession of awful people and experiences a child encounters while wandering around rural Poland during the Second World War. (Or maybe it's a slice-of-life or a theme story, or maybe a bit of all, combined. Collage is such a catchall that few stories are pure collage. They tend to shade into other forms, if only to gain some semblance of structure.)

The Rube Goldberg school of intricate detail is demonstrated by Peake's *Gormenghast* books, with their bizarre explorations of architecture, weird characters, long, meandering discussions of the habits of owls, and endlessly convoluted plots. Herbert's *Dune* also comes close, with its scraps from future histories, royal journals, sayings of philosophers past, present, and future, and multiple alien cultures, in spite of a strong and melodramatic central plot. Ursula Le Guin's *Always Coming Home*, with its myths and folk song tape, is another science fiction work which is much more a collage than a plotted work.

The diversity and endless invention of this kind of grab-bag fiction can create an impression of great exuberance—that there's a place for shoes, ships, sealing wax, cabbages, kings, and even a kitchen sink or two. And according to the poet Blake, "Exuberance is Beauty."

The tricky things in collage are holding it together within a single frame, giving it even the appearance of unity, and knowing when it ought to be over.

The strengths of collage are the startling quality of its fragmentary images, the sudden jumps and quick cuts, the diversity of the elements it assembles and uses.

Collage may *seem* random, but should never actually *be* so. The connections between and among the flashing scenes and images should come clear if one reads hard enough. But it's definitely not a form for a beginner.

## More About Contrast and Juxtaposition

Strong contrasts and startling resemblances are the major structural principle in collage. But they also have more general applications.

Then/now pairings, mirroring events and characters, and the Rule of Three have already been discussed in earlier chapters, in terms of how they can be used in plotted fiction. They can also become the main strategies of works with little or no plot. Such stories depend on the energy of like/unlike pairings, on the same principle that red is redder against a bright green background, or that a cardinal seems especially vivid pecking in the snow.

Often this technique will be combined with revelation, which I'll discuss in a minute, to show that things aren't as they seem—unmasking hypocrisy, shattering illusions people have about themselves or others, or showing perhaps that apparently dissimilar people are more alike either than they'd guessed or would like to admit. A bookish minister working among convicts with serene detachment who discovers in himself a capacity for cruelty or a love of the power he has over his flock, might be the basis of a contrast story.

I discussed earlier the story "Good Country People." The plot, though minimal, is effective—a traveling Bible salesman steals a woman's artificial leg on pretext of seducing her. But the antagonist is what he is all the way through the story—we readers (and the protagonist) just don't know it until the end, because he's a hypocrite. And the protagonist always had an inflated sense of her own cynicism and insight into people; again, she and we don't discover her real naivete until she meets someone far more cynical and shrewd than she is.

In other words, the story is a process of revelation of static things, rather than something actually happening, short of the theft that provides the story's resolution. It's a contrast between false cynicism and the real thing, two attitudes, two states of being—and that's the dynamic of the story far more than its plot is.

Another story, Hawthorne's "Young Goodman Brown," has a similar pattern. Brown has faith in the goodness of his neighbors in colonial New England and the center of that faith is his love for his wife. He meets the devil, who tempts Brown with the claim that commerce with the devil is quite commonplace. The devil asserts that not only have Brown's ancestors been "associates" of his, but all the respectable townspeople, Brown's friends and neighbors, are corrupt as well. He invites (tempts?) Brown to spy on a witches' sabbat, where Brown sees arriving the respectable townspeople in whom he had such faith. He is even given reason to suspect that his wife has participated in the satanic celebration. He runs away in horror and the experience poisons his whole life thereafter: he doesn't trust anybody, including his wife, not to be of the devil's party, believing himself the lone holdout, the one righteous man in his community. The devil didn't convert Brown—or did he?

Contrast—seeming and being. That's what drives this classic story.

# REVELATION

Both "Young Goodman Brown" and "Good Country People" demonstrate another technique, that of revelation. It's the basis of much plotted fiction, especially any story containing a mystery—and that includes far more than detective or mystery fiction. When a story's main dynamic is to have the protagonist find out something, or realize something, that's been true for some time, the story's motion is in the finding out, not in the discovered fact itself. Except for the secret, the mystery, the story would be quite static.

An investigation is the basis of Conrad's *Heart of Darkness*, in which a man goes deeper and deeper into the jungle to discover the final evil embodied by the unspeakable Kurtz, and of that novel's modern-day counterpart, the movie *Apocalypse Now*.

Often the framework of this kind of mystery/revelation story will be very simple: a quest or journey which involves meeting people, getting into one situation after another, each demonstrating the story's central theme but otherwise unrelated to the others, each supplying some new information on the story's central mystery.

Much gothic fiction is founded on such a central mystery—*Jane Eyre* has Rochester's insane first wife in the attic all the while Rochester is romancing Jane; the story is Jane's gradual discovery of the unchanging but hidden state of things. Likewise *Rebecca*, whose plot is the disclosure of dead Rebecca's real nature and how her widower, Maxim, actually felt toward her.

Most of the central part of *Lord of the Flies* is the developing answer to the question, "What is the Beast?" Most of the drama of Poe's "The Cask of Amontillado" is the reader's realizing, along with the strikingly unfortunate Fortunato, just why the narrator is carrying that trowel and showing his hated enemy through the family vaults.

Some long fiction has mystery and revelation as a subordinate element, but very often they stand alone as a novel's main motion.

The important thing to realize is that *revelation is seen, by the reader, as motion*, even if nothing has changed but knowledge or insight. Plot elements can develop and reinforce that revelation, and show how it matters to the story's world, giving it added importance and force, but they're not absolutely needed to make it work.

In *The Empire Strikes Back*, the duel is far less important and has far less impact than does Vader's revelation of paternity.

If you choose to use revelation either as a substitute for plot or as a subordinate element within a plotted story, these are the things you should watch out for:

1. The secret must be something worth knowing. It must have a direct impact on the immediate situation. It has to matter, and matter intensely, within the story's context. Were Jane Eyre not a lonely girl in love with Rochester and on the point of marrying him, whether or not he had an insane wife upstairs would make little difference to her—or to the reader. Simon's decision not only to investigate the Beast but *to tell the other boys what he's found out* costs him his life. The revelation matters.

2. The build-up should give the secret a context and demonstrate part of its meaning, as well as providing clues. That Kurtz participated in unnameable savage rituals, if presented as a fact in the book's first few pages, would have virtually no impact. The story's journey develops the differences between savagery and civilized attitudes through the interaction between the civilized narrator/investigator and the increasingly disturbing tribespeople and debased Europeans he encounters. It establishes the "line" so that when we find out Kurtz has crossed over that line, the revelation has meaning.

3. The secret should be a simple thing, recognized the instant it's met, its impact not blunted by somebody explaining. The developing context should be arranged so that all except the fact itself has been made clear before the climactic revelation. Vader says, "Obi-Wan never told you what happened to your father." Luke says, "He told me enough. He told me *you* killed him." Vader says, "No. *I* am your father," and the thing's done, the secret is out. It doesn't need qualifying or explaining to have its full impact. That's because the needed groundwork had been laid.

4. The secret can and should be hinted at, as part of the needed preparation; but it should never be telegraphed or disclosed even as a possibility until the actual moment of unveiling. Don't make it one of two possible alternatives considered from the beginning, and the revelation consists of disclosing which of

the alternatives it is: that falls flat. Instead, as discussed in Chapter 7 in regard to valid tricks, you may want to hint at something different but related, or something considered as bad (or good) that proves to be only a pale reflection of the actuality. Misdirect the reader's attention and assumptions, but come through with something satisfying that's a genuine surprise.

Most stories founded on revelation have a double plot structure. The story moves both forward and back (sometimes, but not often, by means of flashback). The unraveling of the secret, perhaps against opposition, is paralleled by the move backward from the beginning to the source of the mystery itself. So the story begins at the literal middle, the point at which the investigation is set going. Like an archeological expedition unearthing successively more ancient settlements the farther down they dig, the story progresses by going back. Both motions should complement one another, so that the moment of revelation is also the moment of the deepest penetration into the past, the point at which the past's implications on the present become fully known.

If your story is founded on some static reality, some buried truth strong enough to speak for itself and have immediate emotional impact on the story's characters and situations when it's finally revealed, then the techniques of revelation may be all that you need.

## STYLE AND SUBSTANCE

To the degree that it's not plot, any experimental structure will call attention to itself and often seem visibly artificial. So it has to be managed carefully or the story, the human content, will become secondary to the style. The story may even disappear altogether, lost in the clever externals of its presentation.

One of the most damning things that can be said about a story is that it's an amazing technical achievement. That's admiration for craft, not enjoyment or appreciation. Whole books have been written whose text omits one or more letters of the alphabet. Undoubtedly that was a difficult achievement, one at least equal to making a scale model of the Empire State Building out of hundreds of thousands of toothpicks.

But is that really what you want to do?

Do you want your readers to marvel at all the work that went into your invention or be impressed with how clever and unusual the technique is, or do you want to share some vision of what it means to be human and alive in the world?

Like quick cuts and computer imaging in movies, non-plot techniques are gadgety. Such gadgets can end up being yawn-making, uninvolving tricks as soon as the novelty wears off, if they're all the story has to offer.

Compare two Disney projects, *Bambi* and the recent *Tron*. Each was an immense technical achievement at the time it was made. *Bambi* is a classic, a perennial children's favorite; *Tron* disappeared to the netherlands of video rental almost as soon as it was released. The difference was in the ability of each movie's content, apart from the gadgetry of cartooning or computer graphics wizardry, to reach and move its audience.

Craft and invention shouldn't, I believe, become ends in themselves. They should serve the story, the human vision conveyed in words. Unless they do that, any story becomes a dry technical exercise, without heart.

As with world-building, manipulating the surfaces of stories is often more fun to do than to watch. Remember that the job of a writer is less to perform than to communicate. Don't get so caught up in technique that the style becomes more important than the substance. Subordinate. And simplify.

Use the simplest possible structure that conveys what you want to convey, presents what you want to present. And, as with other matters of technique like viewpoint shifts or changes of locale, clue the reader in on the method, the structural rules of *your* story, right away in as direct and clear a manner as you can manage. Then follow the pattern you've set, whether that pattern uses plot occasionally or not at all.

Finally, it's not the form but the content which will determine whether your story will reach and move its readers, whether it will be good fiction or just another quirky experiment that disappears without trace.

Style is important. But it's not everything.

Now, quit reading. Go write.

# INDEX

## A

Adams, Richard (*Watership Down*), 48-49, 122
allegory. *See* mosaic structure
anticlimax, 89, 102, 118, 123, 125, 126, 129, 130-132, 134, 148
Austen, Jane (*Pride and Prejudice*), 107

## B

*Bambi*, 162
*Bambi Meets Godzilla*, 10
before/after pairings, 103, 121, 151-152
beginnings, story, the necessary chores of, 21. *See also* openings
belief, winning readers', 83. *See also* disbelief
Believers, True. *See* intrusion, authorial
Benchley, Peter (*Jaws*), 17
Boles, Paul Darcy, 6
Bradbury, Ray, 14
braided plots. *See* subplots
bridge characters. *See* characters
Bronte, Charlotte (*Jane Eyre*), 73, 159
Bronte, Emily (*Wuthering Heights*), 34, 65, 91, 107, 108
and "Angria," 46
Bulkington. *See* Melville, Herman

## C

Capote, Truman (*In Cold Blood*), 11
character sketch. *See* mosaic structure
characters
charts used in developing, 48
representing a norm, 20-21
serving as a bridge, 33-34
establishing credibility, 88-89
mirror, 104-107, 157
Cheever, John ("Metamorphoses"), 109, 149
Chesterton, G. K. (*The Man Who Was Thursday*), 83
clutter, eliminating/avoiding narrative, 38-39, 126-128, 153
collage structure, 155-158
defined, 155-156
diverse nature of, 156-157
contrast important in, 157-158
compensation
for complex endings, 128
for exposition, melodrama serving as, 56, 93
for needed complexities in story structure, 37
for multiple viewpoints, 39
for static stories. *See* melodrama

conflict
distinguished from drama, 102
as "fair" opposition, 9
as "wrestling," 6
connections
in parallel plots, 108
between plotlines, 65, 67-68,
95-96. *See also* transitions
between scenes where
viewpoints shift, 37
Conrad, Joseph
*Heart of Darkness*, 159
*Lord Jim*, 117
contrast, 78, 157-158
credibility. *See* belief, winning
readers'. *See also* disbelief
crisis, 66
criticism, asking for, 142

**D**
descriptions, being economical
with, 24. *See also* settings
detail, as an aid to realism, 86
*deus ex machina. See* dirigible
ending
dialogue, as an aid to credibility,
88
Dibell, Ansen ("A Sense of
Family"), 12, 96-98, 148
Dickens, Charles, 14, 53
*Bleak House*, 27
*A Christmas Carol*, 20, 59, 103,
104-106, 122, 150, 151
*A Tale of Two Cities*, 27, 104, 137
*Oliver Twist*, 149
dirigible ending, 131-132
disbelief
techniques of defusing, 84-91,
114
the willing suspension of, 83,
114
dithering. *See* fictional withdrawal
Dos Passos, John (*U.S.A.*), 156
Doyle, Arthur Conan, 34, 107,
141
*The Hound of the Baskervilles*, 89,
92
drama, distinguished from
melodrama, 7, 81, 151-153

Du Maurier, Daphne (*Rebecca*), 27,
73-74, 159
dynamic, the need for in story
ideas, 15-16

**E**
early, starting a story too, 19
elegance, 119
endings
circular
defined 120-121
problems with, 123-125
techniques of, 121-123
turning points used in, 123
dirigible, 131-132
expositional. *See* fictional
withdrawal
focus-switching, 130-131
happy, 136-137
inconclusive ("sequel-fishing"),
140-141
linear
narrative economy necessary
in, 127
new places/people/plotlines
undesirable in, 127-129
problems with, 129
stop immediately after crisis,
125-126
satisfying, 136-137
trick, 132-135
unhappy, 136-137
unsatisfying ("no ending")
138-139
epilogues. *See* frames
experiment. *See* Rule of Three,
The
exposition
amount appropriate in literary
fiction, 55-56
amount appropriate in popular
fiction, 54
character charts used in, 48
creating, not a spectator sport,
45-47
cutting, 57
definition of, 19
distinguished from flashback,
113

emotion useful in, 56
inappropriate in epilogues, 118
interrupts and delays action, 43
limiting, 54
melodrama a compensation for,
93. *See also* melodrama
placement of, 51
place of opinions in, 52-53. *See
also* intrusion, authorial
as preparation for following
events, 50
a problem in genre fiction, 45
rules for handling, 49-50, 56
specialist information used in,
53-54. *See also* intrusion,
authorial
subordinate to plot, 54-56
use of dialogue to convey, 51-52
usefulness of, 44-45
as "world builders' disease" 45
*Empire Strikes Back, The. See* Lucas,
George
extrapolation, 87. *See also*
premises

**F**

fact-based fiction, difficulties of, 1,
14
fallacy, pathetic, 147
Farrell, James T. (*Studs Lonigan*),
149
Faulkner, William, 92
*The Bear*, 150-151
*Sanctuary*, 26
*The Town*, 144
fiction fatigue. *See* revision
fiction, genre
happy endings in, 136
suitable exposition for, 54-55
fictional withdrawal, 139-143
Finsbury, the dreaded authorial.
*See* intrusion, authorial
Fitzgerald, F. Scott, 6
use of displaced narrator by, in
*The Great Gatsby*, 33-34
flashbacks, 32, 59, 108, 113-117
distinguished from exposition,
113
preventing distraction by, 115

flashforwards. *See* frames
focus, changing, 130-131
formulas, fictional, 109-110
Forsyth, Frederick (*The Day of the
Jackal*), 116
frames
defined, 117-118
as epilogues, 117, 118
relationship of, to main plotline,
117
as prologues, 117, 118

**G**

Gardner, Erle Stanley (Perry
Mason books), 24
genres, crossing, 86-87
Goldberg, Rube, 156
Golding, William
(*Lord of the Flies*), 7, 20-21, 159
allegorical elements in, 153
characters described in, 24-25
conch used in, 22-23, 29, 150
opening of, 22-23
set-pieces in, 70, 76
stages in the plot of, 62, 72
use of twist in, 76
Good vs. Evil, 152
"Good Country People." *See*
McCullers, Carson
groundwork, laying. *See*
preparation

**H**

Hammett, Dashiell (*The Maltese
Falcon*), 23, 69, 126
Hardy, Thomas (*Tess of the
D'Urbervilles*), 53
Hawthorne, Nathaniel
*The Scarlet Letter*, 53
"Young Goodman Brown," 158
Heller, Joseph (*Catch-22*), 14-15,
26, 149, 156
Hemingway, Ernest, 44
"The Hills Like White
Elephants," 27
Holmes, Sherlock. *See* Doyle,
Arthur Conan

**I**

ideas, story, how to develop and
test, 11-17

identification, readers', how to
win, 32, 81-83, 102. *See also*
melodrama
imagery
defined, 99
used as a patterning technique,
99
*in medias res*, 19, 44, 59, 85, 127
incidents, distinguished from plot,
5
information, specialist. *See*
intrusion, authorial
intrusion, authorial, 50, 52-54
involvement, readers'. *See*
identification

**J**

Jackson, Shirley ("The Lottery"),
53
James, Henry ("The Turn of the
Screw"), 117
Janus, 61
Joyce, James
*Dubliners*, 60
*Ulysses*, 109

**K**

Kafka, Franz (*Metamorphosis*), 84
King, Stephen
*It*, 22, 23, 87, 108, 126
*'Salem's Lot*, 87, 117
Kosinsky, Jerzy (*The Painted Bird*),
56

**L**

Le Guin, Ursula, 46, 156
Lee, Harper (*To Kill a
Mockingbird*), 5, 90
Levin, Ira (*Rosemary's Baby*), 86
Lewis, C. S. (Narnia novels), 46,
154
literary fiction
alternative narrative structures
used in, 144-163
suitable exposition for, 55
unhappy endings in, 136-137
*Lord of the Flies*. *See* Golding,
William
*Lord of the Rings, The*. *See* Tolkien,
J. R. R.

Lovecraft, H. P., 9
Lucas, George
*The Empire Strikes Back*, 66-68,
70, 77-78, 95-96, 107, 108,
126, 133-135, 160
*Star Wars*, 84

**M**

Mann, Thomas (*Death in Venice*),
16
McCullers, Carson, 26
McDowell, Michael (the *Blackwater*
novels), 89
melodrama
as compensation for exposition,
56, 92-93
as compensation for static
stories, 149-150
credibility in. *See* disbelief
defined, 81, 83-84
detail useful in, 86
distinguished from drama, 7, 81
in openings, 25-27
overkill ineffective in, 88-89
relation of to symbolism &
allegory, 82
as sensation-mongering, 82
wins readers' identification,
81-83
use of dialogue in, 88
use of, in popular fiction, 82
use of, in literary fiction, 82,
151
use of, in theme/variation
stories, 151
Melville, Herman (*Moby Dick*), 2,
3, 9, 34, 40, 45, 55, 85, 150,
151
Mitchell, Margaret (*Gone with the
Wind*), 10, 70, 124-125
monsters, establishing credible,
87-89
mood piece. *See* mosaic structure
mosaic structure, 145-155
defined, 145
varieties of
allegory, 153-155
character sketch, 147-148
mood piece, 146-147

slice-of-life, 148-150
theme and variation, 150-153
mystery, role of revelation in. *See* revelation

**N**

narrative clutter. *See* clutter
norms, presenting, in fiction, 20-21

**O**

O'Connor, Flannery ("Good Country People"), 60, 91-92, 158
Oedipus, 10
omniscient viewpoint. *See* viewpoint
openings
  implicit promises made by, 25-26, 34-35, 84, 94
  melodramatic, 25
  revealing, 26-27
  revising, 28-29. *See also* revision
  volcano, 25-27
Orwell, George
  *Animal Farm*, 154
  *1984*, 26
outlines, 3, 72
  outlining from inside, 74-75
overwriting, 71-72

**P**

pace, 73, 78
  in parallel plots, 108
Parker, Robert (Spenser mysteries), 24
patterns, fictional, 94-109
  imagery as a technique of creating, 99
Peake, Mervyn (*Ghormenghast*), 55, 156
persistence. *See* rejection, handling
personal, stories that are too (blind spots), 13-14
plot
  defined, 5, 6, 74
  distinguished from incident, 5
  stages of. *See* set-pieces
  as a verb, 15, 62

plots, double, 7, 36
  parallel, 66-68, 107-108
Poe, Edgar Allan
  "The Fall of the House of Usher," 16, 146
  "The Cask of Amontillado," 61, 159
Porter, Katherine Anne (*Noon Wine*), 60
popular fiction. *See* fiction, genre
predictability, avoiding, 75, 132. *See also* endings
premises, establishing fictional, 84, 87
preparation ("laying groundwork") for future events, 72, 75-78
preview scenes. *See* scenes
prologues. *See* frames
promises, implicit fictional, 25-26, 110
props
  defined, 23
  as a means to minimize exposition, 50-51
protagonist, killed off in mid-plot, 40
Pygmalion, 47, 109

**Q**

questions, to test a story idea, 11-17

**R**

repetition, effective. *See* patterns
rejection, handling, 143
revelation, 73, 85, 92, 144, 148, 157-161
  methods of setting up, 160-161
revision
  to change viewpoint structure, 39-49
  disastrous effect of fiction fatigue on, 58-59
  to eliminate excess exposition, 57
  endless, 141-142
  need to delay, limit, 58-59, 141-142

of openings, 28-29
pleasures of, 142
rushing into, 141-142
Rice, Ann (*Interview with the Vampire*), 9, 84
Rossner, Judith (*Looking for Mr. Goodbar*), 53
Roth, Philip, 149
Rule of Three, The, 101-103, 152, 157
Runyon, Damon, use of dialogue by, 24

**S**

Salinger, J. D. (*The Catcher in the Rye*), 147-148
Sayers, Dorothy L., 46
scene, defined, 8
scenes
balancing with summary, 113
mirroring, techniques of, 98-101
preview, 77-78, 90
purposes of, 8
relation of, to flashbacks, 113
used to begin a story, 22. *See also in medias res*
used to end a story, 128-129
Scrooge, Ebeneezer. *See* Dickens, Charles, *A Christmas Carol*
set-pieces
aftermath of, 78-79
anticipating/planning, 72-73
avoiding excess in, 71-72
contrast in, 78
defined, 69-70
delivering on, 70-71, 75
effective impact in, 79-80
number of, 73
pacing in, 78
preparing for, 75
settings, creating effective, 23-24
Shaefer, Jack (*Shane*), 44, 124
Shelley, Mary (*Frankenstein*), 11
show, don't tell, 7, 8
simplicity, how to achieve, 27, 38. *See also* clutter; elegance
slice-of-life. *See* mosaic structure
specialist information. *See* intrusion, authorial

stake, what's at, 16-17, 79-80, 130
Steinbeck, John
*East of Eden*, 26, 107-108
*The Grapes of Wrath*, 27, 149
*Of Mice and Men*, 26
Sterne, Lawrence (*Tristram Shandy*), 56
Stevenson, R. L.
"Dr. Jeckyll and Mr. Hyde," 104
"The Wrong Box," 52. *See also* intrusion, authorial
Stoker, Bram (*Dracula*), 9, 86
story ideas, testing, 11-17
Straub, Peter (*Ghost Story*), 86
structures, alternative narrative, 144-163
artificiality of, 161-163
subplots, 32
braiding, 64-65
building connections among, 65. *See also* transitions
developing, 65-66
establishing, 63-64
nature of, 63
use of multiple viewpoints in, 31
summaries, the usefulness of, 17. *See also* outlines
surrealism, 146, 151
suspense, techniques of creating, 63, 68, 89, 102
switches. *See* twists/switches
symbolism, 153-155

**T**

Thackeray, William Makepeace
*Vanity Fair*
use of double plot structure in, 107
use of two viewpoints in, 36
theme. *See* mosaic structure
then/now pairings. *See* before/after pairings
Thomas, Doubting, the ineffectiveness of, 85
Tolkien, J. R. R.
*The Lord of the Rings*, 2, 3, 14, 47, 48, 69, 72, 88-89, 108, 121, 140
*The Silmarillion*, 46, 49

transitions, 41, 65, 111-113
*Tron*, 162
turning point. *See* endings, circular
Twain, Mark
*Huckleberry Finn*, 23, 24
*The Prince and the Pauper*, 104
twists/switches, effective, 75-76, 89, 92. *See also* endings

**U**

undercutting
characters, 86
melodrama, 87, 89
unity, 100-101

**V**

vampires, 9, 83
variable. *See* Rule of Three, The
victims, helpless, 9, 10
viewpoint
consistency in, 39, 41
multiple
handling switches in, 35-37
avoiding confusion about, 37

omniscient, 30-31
single
establishing, 32-34
reasons for choosing, 31
use of "bridge" characters in, 33-34
switches, unintentional, 35, 37, 41
switches in the middle of a scene, 35, 37, 40
volcano openings. *See* openings
Vonnegut, Kurt, 156

**W**

Who, Doctor, 86
world-builders' disease. *See* exposition
"write what you know," 12
writers, great, boners allowed to, 41

**Y**

yeti, 86
your story to tell, is it, 11-12

# CHARACTERS
# AND VIEWPOINT

BY

*ORSON SCOTT CARD*

# ABOUT THE AUTHOR

No one had ever won both the Hugo and the Nebula Award for best science fiction novel two years in a row—until 1987, when *Speaker for the Dead* won the same awards given to *Ender's Game*. But Orson Scott Card's experience is not limited to one genre or form of storytelling. A dozen of his plays have been produced in regional theatre; his historical novel, *Saints* (alias *Woman of Destiny*), has been an underground hit for several years; and Card has written hundreds of audio plays and a dozen scripts for animated videoplays for the family market. He has also edited books, magazines, and anthologies; he writes a regular review column for *The Magazine of Fantasy and Science Fiction*; he publishes *Short Form*, a journal of short-fiction criticism; he even reviews computer games for *Compute!* Along the way, Card earned a master's degree in literature and has an abiding love for Chaucer, Shakespeare, Boccaccio, and the Medieval Romance. He has taught writing courses at several universities and at such workshops as Antioch, Clarion, Clarion West, and the Cape Cod Writers Workshop. It is fair to say that Orson Scott Card has examined storytelling from every angle.

Born in Richland, Washington, Card grew up in California, Arizona, and Utah. He lived in Brazil for two years as an unpaid missionary for the Mormon Church and received degrees from Brigham Young University and the University of Utah. He currently lives in Greensboro, North Carolina, with his wife, Kristine, and their three children, Geoffrey, Emily, and Charles (named for Chaucer, Brontë, and Dickens).

To Gert Fram,
alias Nancy Allen Black:
You never had any trouble
finding an attitude or point of view,
and as for inventiveness,
you wrote the book.

# ACKNOWLEDGMENTS

I owe thanks to the editors at *Writer's Digest* and Writer's Digest Books, especially:

Thanks to Bill Brohaugh, who accepted my proposal for a brief article on using the "implied past" to help in characterization—and then accepted what I actually turned in, an article on making characters memorable that was so long it had to run in three issues of the magazine.

Thanks to Nancy Dibble, who as my editor on this book was both patient and helpful, far beyond what could fairly have been expected.

Thanks to all those who delayed the launch of a major and important publishing project while waiting for Card to get his act together.

And to those outside Cincinnati who helped, namely:

Thanks to my good friends Clark and Kathy Kidd for putting me up and putting up with me for two weeks in February and March 1988 as I finished the final draft of this book.

Thanks to the students in my writing class at the Center for Creative Arts in Greensboro, North Carolina, who forgave me—or kindly pretended to forgive me—for canceling two classes so I could finish this book.

Thanks to all the other writing students who have been the victims of my developing understanding of fiction; I learned from their successes and failures as much as I learned from my own.

In particular, I thank my teachers: François Camoin of the English Department at the University of Utah; Clinton F. Larson and Richard Cracroft of the English Department and Charles W. Whitman of the Theatre Department at Brigham Young University; Ida Huber at Mesa High School in Mesa, Arizona; and Fran Schroeder at Millikin Elementary in Santa Clara, California.

Thanks to my sister Janice for her help with art and copying.

And, above all, thanks to my wife, Kristine, for making all my work possible and all my life joyful.

# CONTENTS

INTRODUCTION • *1*

PART I: INVENTING CHARACTERS • *3*

1. WHAT IS A CHARACTER? • *4*

2. WHAT MAKES A GOOD FICTIONAL
   CHARACTER? • *14*

   *The Three Questions Readers Ask • You Are the First
   Audience • Interrogating the Character • From Character to Story, from Story to Character*

3. WHERE DO CHARACTERS COME
   FROM? • *25*

   *Ideas from Life • Ideas from the Story • Servants of
   the Idea • Serendipity*

4. MAKING DECISIONS • *41*

   *Names • Keeping a Bible*

PART II: CONSTRUCTING CHARACTERS • *47*

5. WHAT KIND OF STORY ARE YOU
   TELLING? • *48*

   *The "MICE" Quotient • Milieu • Idea • Character •
   Event • The Contract with the Reader*

6. THE HIERARCHY • *59*

   *Walk-ons and Placeholders • Minor Characters •
   Major Characters*

**7.** HOW TO RAISE THE EMOTIONAL STAKES • *68*

*Suffering • Sacrifice • Jeopardy • Sexual Tension • Signs and Portents*

**8.** WHAT SHOULD WE FEEL ABOUT THE CHARACTER? • *75*

*First Impressions • Characters We Love • Characters We Hate*

**9.** THE HERO AND THE COMMON MAN • *93*

**10.** THE COMIC CHARACTER: CONTROLLED DISBELIEF • *99*

*Doing a "Take" • Exaggeration • Downplaying • Oddness*

**11.** THE SERIOUS CHARACTER: MAKE US BELIEVE • *105*

*Elaboration of Motive • Attitude • The Remembered Past • The Implied Past • Justification*

**12.** TRANSFORMATIONS • *119*

*Why People Change • Justifying Changes*

## PART III: PERFORMING CHARACTERS • 125

**13.** VOICES • 126

*Person • Tense*

**14.** PRESENTATION VS. REPRESENTATION • 134

**15.** DRAMATIC VS. NARRATIVE • 140

**16.** FIRST-PERSON NARRATIVE • 143

*Which Person Is First? • No Fourth Wall • Unreliable Narrators • Distance in Time • Withholding Information • Lapses*

**17.** THIRD PERSON • 155

*Omniscient vs. Limited Point of View • Making Up Your Mind • Levels of Penetration*

**18.** A PRIVATE POPULATION EXPLOSION • 173

*INDEX • 174*

# *INTRODUCTION*

Writing fiction is a solitary art.

When an orchestra performs a symphony, it's a shared effort. Not only are there many musicians playing their instruments, there's also a conductor helping them sound good together. Yet before any of them plays a note, a composer has to write the musical score.

There's even more teamwork with a play or movie. Lots of actors, of course; a director to guide, suggest, decide for the group; designers of sets, costumes, lighting, and sound; technicians to carry out those designs. In film, add the vital work of the cinematographer, camera operators, and editors.

But before any of this work can be done, a writer has to put together a script.

Script or score, those group performances existed because somebody had a plan. Somebody composed the music before ever a note was heard; somebody composed the story before ever an actor spoke a word. Composition first, then performance.

We who write fiction have no team of actors or musicians to do our bidding, so it's easy to forget that our work, too, has a composition stage and a performance stage. We are both composer *and* performer. Or rather, we are both storyteller and writer.

The actual writing of the story, along with the creation of the text, the choice of words, the dialogue, the style, the tone, the point of view—that is the performance, that is the part of our work that earns us the title "writer."

The invention of the characters and situations and events, along with the construction of plot and scene, the ordering of events, the complications and twists, the setting and historical background—that is the composition, the part of our work that earns us the title "storyteller."

There is no clear separation of our two roles. As we invent and construct our fiction, we will often do it with language—we jot down notes, tell scenes to our friends, write detailed outlines or synopses. And as we are performing our stories, writing them out in our most effective prose, we also invent new details or motivations, discover new relationships among characters, and we revise the construction of the story in order to make a scene work better, by adding a new fillip of suspense or horror or sentiment, or presenting a startling new idea that only just now came to us.

There is no "right" way to arrange the two roles of storyteller and writer. I often work for years on a story, inventing, outlining, mapping, constructing, before I feel that I'm ready to write it down. Writer Larry Niven tells his stories aloud to his friends, letting each tale grow and take shape with a live audience to help guide him. I know other writers who can compose only while performing, like an actor improvising a monologue—they have to be writing the story in order to bring ideas to mind, discovering and shaping the characters and plot as they go along.

Regardless of how you mingle the roles of storyteller and writer, though, you *must* do both jobs well. If you don't invent and construct well, then all your beautiful prose will be no more effective than a singer vocalizing or a clarinetist warming up—very pretty technique, perhaps, but music it ain't. And if you don't write well, readers will be hard put to discover the wonderful story you want to tell—just as bad acting can ruin a good script, or out-of-tune, clumsy, underrehearsed musicians can make Mozart sound like a mess.

Effective characterization requires careful attention at every stage in the writing of fiction. You must invent your characters carefully, to avoid cliche and to provide your story with rich human possibilities; as you construct the story, you must determine exactly how much and what type of characterization to use for each character. Later, as you set out to write the story, you must make decisions about point of view—which character or characters will be the lens through which the reader sees the story.

So I have divided this book into three parts: Invention, Construction, and Performance. Don't imagine for a moment that the actual process of characterization will ever be as neat and tidy as the chapters and sections of this book. I doubt that you could use the chapters of this book as a checklist, "characterizing" mechanically as you go. Instead you should bring the questions and ideas in each chapter to your own work, the stories you believe in and care about. See which aspects of characterization you already handle well and which you might have overlooked; examine your handling of point of view to see whether you're helping your readers or confusing them. You don't improve your storytelling by turning characterization into a mechanical process. You improve your storytelling by discovering and nurturing the characters, by letting them grow.

In other words, this book isn't a cupboard full of ingredients that you can pull out, measure, mix, and bake into good fictional characters.

This book is a set of tools: literary crowbars, chisels, mallets, pliers, tongs, sieves, and drills. Use them to pry, chip, beat, wrench, yank, sift, or punch good characters out of the place where they already live: your memory, your imagination, your soul.

# PART I

# INVENTING
# CHARACTERS

# CHAPTER 1

# WHAT IS A CHARACTER?

THE CHARACTERS IN YOUR FICTION are people. Human beings.

Yes, I know you make them up. But readers want your characters to seem like real people. Whole and alive, believable and worth caring about. Readers want to get to know your characters as well as they know their own friends, their own family. As well as they know themselves.

No—better than they know any living person. By the time they finish your story, readers want to know your characters better than any human being ever knows any other human being. That's part of what fiction is for—to give a better understanding of human nature and human behavior than anyone can ever get in life.

So let's go through the ways that people get to know each other in real life, and see how each method shows up in fiction.

## A CHARACTER IS WHAT HE DOES

If you're at a party and you see the same guy spill a drink, talk too loudly, and make inappropriate or rude remarks, those actions will lead you to make a judgment of him.

If you see a man and a woman meet for the first time, and then a few moments later see him stroking her back or see her with her hand resting on his chest as they engage in intense close-up conversation, you reach conclusions about them.

If you tell a painful secret to a friend, and within hours three other people act as if they know that secret, you have discovered something about your friend.

People become, in our minds, what we see them do.

This is the strongest, most irresistible form of characterization. What did we know about Indiana Jones at the beginning of *Raiders of the Lost Ark*? He was a taciturn guy with a wry smile who took an artifact out of an ancient underground temple. When he was left to die, he figured out a way to escape. When a huge boulder rolled toward him, he didn't freeze— he ran like a madman to get away. None of this required any explanation.

Within ten minutes of the beginning of the movie, we knew that Indiana Jones was resourceful, greedy, clever, brave, intense; that he had a sense of humor and didn't take himself too seriously; that he was determined to survive against all odds. Nobody had to tell us—we *saw* it.

This is also the easiest form of characterization. If your character steals something, we'll know she's a thief. If he hits his girl friend when he catches her with another guy, we'll know he's violent and jealous. If your character gets a phone call and goes off to teach a third-grade class, we'll know she's a substitute teacher. If he tells two people opposite versions of the same story, we'll know he's a liar or a hypocrite.

It's easy—but it's also shallow. In some stories and with some characters, this will be enough. But in most stories, as in real life, just knowing what someone does while you happen to be watching him or her isn't enough to let you say you truly *know* that person.

# MOTIVE

When you watch the guy at the party who spills a drink and talks loudly and rudely, would you judge him the same way if you knew that he was deliberately trying to attract attention to keep people from noticing something else going on in the room? Or what if you knew that he had been desperately hurt by the hostess only a few minutes before the party, and this was his way of getting even? You may not approve of what he's doing, but you won't necessarily judge him to be an ignorant boor.

What about your friend, the one who told your secret to others? Wouldn't it make a difference if you found out that she thought you were in serious trouble and told others about it solely in order to help you solve the problem? You would judge her very differently, however, if you were a celebrity and you discovered that she tells your secrets to other people so they'll think of her as the closest friend of a famous person.

And the man and the woman who met and moments later were stroking and touching each other with obvious sexual intent: You'd judge them one way if you knew that the woman, a government bureaucrat, was lonely and had a terrible self-image, while the man was an attractive flatterer who would do anything to get this woman to award his company a valuable contract. You'd judge them very differently if you knew that his wife had just left him, and the woman was rebounding from a failed affair. The same acts would take on a completely different meaning if you knew that she was passing government secrets to him while they only pretended to be romantically involved.

What about a person who tries to do something and fails? He aims a gun at the governor and pulls the trigger, but the gun doesn't fire. She dives into a pool to pull out a drowning man, but he's too heavy for her to lift. Don't we then think of him as an assassin and her as a hero, even though he didn't actually kill anyone and she didn't actually save a life?

Motive is what gives moral value to a character's acts. What a character does, no matter how awful or how good, is never morally absolute:

What seemed to be murder may turn out to have been self-defense, madness, or illusion; what seemed to be a kiss may turn out to have been betrayal, deception, or irony.

We never fully understand other people's motives in real life. In fiction, however, we can help our readers understand our characters' motives with clarity, sometimes even certainty. This is one of the reasons why people read fiction—to come to some understanding of why other people act the way they do.

A character is what he does, yes—but even more, a character is what he *means* to do.

# THE PAST

Knowing a person's past revises our understanding of who he is today. If you're introduced to a man at a dinner, all you know about him is what he does and says at that dinner.

But what if, before meeting him, a friend had whispered to you that this man had been a prisoner of war for seven years, finally escaped, and recently made his way to safety by crossing 300 miles of enemy-controlled territory?

What if your friend told you that the man was the corporate raider who had just caused the layoffs of many of your friends who worked for a company he tried to take over?

What if, as you conversed with him at dinner, he told you that he was just getting over the death of his wife and infant boy in an automobile accident several months before?

What if he mentioned that he's a critic for the local paper, and you realize he's probably the same critic who wrote that vicious review of your last book?

Wouldn't such bits of information about a person's past cause you to look at him differently?

People are what they have done, and what has been done to them. That's how we construct our image of ourselves. We all carry around in our memory our own story of what has happened in our past. Some events we disregard—oh, yes, I did that, but I was such a *child* then—whereas others loom over us all our lives. Our past, however we might revise it in our memory, is who we believe that we are; and when you create a fictional character, telling something of her past will also help your readers understand who she is at the time of the story.

# REPUTATION

Isn't it awful when you're introduced to somebody who says, "Oh, *you*— I've heard so much about you!" It's an unpleasant reminder that people are talking about you when you aren't there—and you can be sure that not everything that gets said is nice.

You have a reputation. If enough people tell stories about you, we call it fame; but even if it's just your neighbors, the people in your workplace, or your relatives, stories are being told about you, shaping other people's judgment of you.

We all take part in the process of building up or tearing down reputations. We do it formally sometimes, as with letters of recommendation or employee evaluations. Mostly, though, the process is informal. When others do it, we call it gossip. When *we* do it, we call it conversation.

"Wasn't it terrible about poor Mrs. Jones getting sent to the sanitorium? To think her son did that to her after all those years she took care of him."

"Did you hear Bill's been hitting on JoBeth for a date? What a waste of time—she's such a cold fish. She probably bathes with her clothes on and waters down her ginger ale so it doesn't get her too high."

"Don't bother asking Jeff to contribute. He's such a tightwad I heard he wouldn't even help buy flowers when Donna's husband died."

You "know" a lot of things about people you've never met, just from what others say about them. The same process works in fiction—your readers will form attitudes and opinions about characters they haven't "met" yet, just by what other characters in the story say about them. When you finally bring the character into the story in person, readers think they already know him; they already have expectations about what he'll do.

As a storyteller, you have the option of fulfilling those expectations, or violating them—but if you violate them, you also have to show your readers how the character got such an incorrect reputation. Maybe he's a con man who deliberately created a positive image. Maybe he was the victim of jealous gossip, whose perfectly innocent or well-meant behavior was misinterpreted. Maybe he made a serious mistake, but can never seem to live it down. Whether his reputation is deserved or not, however, it must be taken into account. Part of a character's identity is what others say about him.

# STEREOTYPES

The moment we see a stranger, we immediately start classifying her according to the groups we recognize she belongs to. We also, unconsciously, compare the stranger to ourselves. Is the stranger male or female? Old or young? Larger than me or smaller? My race or another? My nationality or another? Richer than me or poorer? Does he do the same kind of job as I do, or a job I respect, or a job I think little of?

The moment we have identified the stranger with a certain group, we immediately assume that he has all the attributes we associate with that group. This is the process we call prejudice or stereotyping, and it can lead to embarrassing false assumptions, needless fears, even vicious unfairness. We may wish that we didn't sort people out this way, that we could be color-blind or gender-blind. Indeed, in our society most of us regard it as uncivilized to *treat* people differently because of these stereotypes, and most of us try to live up to that standard. But no one can keep his mind from going through that sorting process.

It's built into our biology. Chimpanzees and baboons and other primates go through exactly the same process. When a chimp meets another chimp in the wild, he immediately classifies the stranger by tribe, by sex, by age, by relative size and strength. From this classification the chimp will decide whether to attack, to flee, to attempt to mate, to share food, to groom the stranger, or to ignore him.

The difference between us and the chimp is that we try to keep ourselves from acting on all our immediate judgments. But make the judgments we will, whether we like it or not—it happens at an unconscious level, like breathing and blinking and swallowing. We can take conscious control of the process, when we think about it, but most of the time it goes on without our noticing it at all.

The more like us a stranger is, the safer we feel, but also the less interested; the more unlike, the more we feel threatened or intrigued.

Strangeness is always both attractive and repellent. Chimpanzees show the same contradiction. A stranger is frightening at first, yes—but as long as there is no immediate attack, the chimp stays close enough to watch the stranger. Eventually, as the stranger causes no harm, the chimp's curiosity overcomes fear, and he approaches.

Readers do the same thing with characters in fiction. A character who is familiar and unsurprising seems comfortable, believable—but not particularly interesting. A character who is unfamiliar and strange is at once attractive and repulsive, making the reader a little curious and a little afraid. We may be drawn into the story, curious to learn more, yet we will also feel a tingle of suspense, that tension that comes from the earliest stages of fear, the uncertainty of not knowing what this person will do, not knowing if we're in danger or not.

As readers, we're like chimpanzees studying a stranger. If the stranger makes a sudden move, we bound away a few steps, then turn and watch again. If the stranger gets involved in doing something, paying no attention to us, we come closer, try to see what he's doing, try to understand him.

Characters who fit within a stereotype are familiar; we think we know them, and we aren't all that interested in knowing them better.

Characters who violate a stereotype are interesting; by surprising us, they pique our interest, make us want to explore.

As storytellers, we can't stop our readers from making stereotype judgments. In fact, we *count* on it. We know of and probably share most of the prejudices and stereotypes of the community we live in. When we present a character, we can use those stereotypes to make our readers think they understand him.

> The old man was wearing a suit that might have been classy ten years ago when it was new, when it was worn by somebody with a body large enough to fill it. On this man it hung so long and loose that the pants bagged at the ankle and scuffed along the sidewalk, and the sleeves came down so low that his hands and the neck of his wine bottle were invisible.

\* \* \*

She heard them before she saw them, laughing and talking jive behind her, shouting because the ghetto-blaster was rapping away at top volume. Just kids on the street in the evening, right? Walking around outside because finally the air was cooling off enough that you could stand to move. One of them jostled her as he passed. Was it the same one who laughed? A few yards on, they stopped as if they were waiting for her to catch up with them. The one with the boom box watched her approach, a wide toothy grin on his face. She clutched her purse tighter under her arm and looked straight ahead. If I don't see them, she thought, they won't bother me.

Both of these descriptions—of the old man, of the city kids—rely on stereotypes. You immediately recognized the old man as a bum, a wino. And if you're a white American in the 1980s, you probably thought of the kids in the second paragraph as black, even though I never actually said so. I gave you enough subliminal clues to awaken the stereotypes in the contemporary white American mind: "jive," "ghetto-blaster," "rapping," the city setting, the "wide, toothy grin," and the woman's fear—all of these draw on the countless movies and television shows and news stories that have played off of and reinforced racial stereotypes.

As writers, we find stereotypes are useful, even essential—but I'll discuss that more in another place. It's important to remember that you can also play against stereotypes. For instance, what if the paragraph describing the old man were followed by this passage:

"Hey, old man," Pete said. "You've lost some weight."

"It wasn't the cancer, Pete, it was the cure," he answered. "I'm glad you're here. Come on upstairs and help me finish this Chablis."

Kind of turns our understanding of the old man around, doesn't it? That's part of the power of stereotypes—they set up expectations so you can surprise your reader. To use stereotypes, either by working with them or playing against them, you have to know what they are. Keep in mind that while no stereotype will be true of every member of a group, most stereotypes grew out of observations that are true as far as they go.

Jobs: Plumbers generally work with plumbing. Doctors usually wear stethoscopes when making rounds or doing physical exams. Barbers and hairdressers usually chatter as they work. Most newscasters take elaborate pains to make sure they look good for the camera.

Sex: Adult women generally have developed breasts and fuller hips than men; adult men usually have more facial hair, are generally taller, and, in our society, have less elaborately coiffed hair. The sexes usually dress differently. People of opposite sex often judge each other according to sexual attractiveness.

Age: Old people are generally more frail, more likely to have poor hearing and eyesight, more likely to forget things or lose the thread of the conversation. Little children are more likely to fidget, to say embarrassing things, to wander off, to misunderstand or ignore instructions.

Family role: Parents usually tell their children what to do. Siblings usually quarrel with each other. Teenage children are usually rebellious, or chafing under parental rule.

Racial or physical type: Blacks usually have dark skin, full lips, and wide noses, and, in America, have commonly had some experience with racial discrimination; a higher percentage of blacks live in poverty. Orientals usually have straight black hair and epicanthic folds. Redheads usually freckle and turn bright red when they blush or get angry. Navaho and Hopi Indians tend to be heavy-bodied as adults.

Ethnic and regional traits: Italians tend to gesture a lot as they speak. Oriental Americans are disproportionately successful in mathematics and science. To northerners, southerners seem to drawl; to southerners, northerners jabber. Westerners speak with a twang. Foreigners usually speak English with an accent.

All of these stereotypes have a few—or even many—exceptions. The actual stereotypes a community believes in will change over time, as community needs and fears and other attitudes change. What doesn't change is the fact that humans identify people according to stereotypes, whatever they happen to be, and you will, consciously or not, use stereotypes as part of characterization in every story you write.

However, in fiction as in life, the better we come to know a character through other means, the less important those initial stereotypes will be.

# NETWORK

When I was growing up, my mother used to tell us that you never know a man until you see how he treats his sister. The immediate purpose of this was, of course, to get us boys to treat our sisters better. But the deeper truth is that we are different people in different relationships.

Children experience this most sharply in their teens, when they start putting on a different persona with their friends. A girl whose friends call her "Rain" and who is cool as can be would rather die than let her friends come home, where Mom calls her "Lorraine" and tells her that her room's a mess, and where her little sister still wants her to play dolls sometimes. She's a different person with her friends than she is with her family.

The same is true, to one degree or another, of almost all of us. We have one personality at work, another on the phone, another with the children, still another alone with our spouse. This can become hypocrisy, if we deliberately try to deceive somebody into thinking we're something we're not. But usually it isn't hypocritical at all. With each set of relationships, we have a different history, different in-jokes, different shared experiences. We act with different motives. We do different things.

Our "self," then, is a kind of network, many threads connecting us to many different people, who are always shifting. We grow within any relationship that remains close; when relationships are interrupted or fade away, the self that belonged in that relationship stays the same. Getting together with old buddies you haven't seen since school, you tend to become the same person you were when you all used to hang out together.

So you may think you know a person because of frequent contacts in one setting, but in fact the taciturn fellow at work may be a cut-up at the bowling alley; your tough-guy buddy may be embarrassingly sentimental with his kids; your quiet, polite daughter or son may curse like a truck driver (note the stereotype) with friends.

It is also one of the most startling and effective devices in fiction to take characters out of one setting and put them in another, where different facets of their personality come to the fore. The character himself may be surprised to realize who he becomes when circumstances change.

## HABITS AND PATTERNS

A person's habits and patterns of behavior are definitely a part of who he is—especially if those habits drive you crazy:

She always drums on the table with her fingers.

He always clips stories out of the paper before anyone else has read them, and then leaves the clipped stories lying around in piles, saying he's going to file them someday.

She never replaces the toilet paper roll when she finishes it.

He always stops at the newsstand on the way home and spends fifteen minutes deciding whether or not to buy a magazine.

She finds your half-worked crossword puzzle and fills it in, incorrectly, in ink, because she can't stand to see empty squares.

He always insists on saying grace, loudly, in restaurants.

Other habits aren't necessarily annoying, but they tell you something about a person:

She carries a can of Mace with her wherever she goes.

He always parks his car on the dividing line between two spaces so it won't get dented by other car doors.

She always takes the garbage out on Tuesday night.

He always washes a dish or glass as soon as he's through using it.

When she writes a check, she always draws three lines after the amount.

Every one of these habits or patterns implies things about a person. You may not know why or how a habit began, but you come to count on the person always acting the same way in the same situation. The habit is part of who he is.

It works just the same way with characters. Habits not only make the character more realistic, but also open up story possibilities—a change in pattern might show an important change in the character's life; other characters might take advantage of her habits; curiosity about or annoyance at a habit might lead to an interesting relationship between characters.

# TALENTS AND ABILITIES

A large part of who you are is what you can do. Often a person can seem quite ordinary and uninteresting—until you hear him play the piano, or get a look at her paintings, or see him stuff a ball through a hoop, or watch her give a dynamite sales presentation. If a person has an extraordinary ability that sets him apart from most other people, that ability becomes who he is, at least to people who don't otherwise know him well.

Your readers will also perk up when a fictional character turns out to be unusually good at something. A certain kind of fantasy and science fiction depends on the hero who has some unique gift that enables him to do great things. But talents don't have to be extreme to make them a vital part of a character's identity. Superman can leap tall buildings in a single bound. On the other hand, Robert Parker's series character Spenser doesn't strain credulity, yet he is very good with his fists. We see him work hard to stay good at boxing; we also never see him perform feats beyond what we'd expect of a tough middle-aged former cop in Boston. After reading all of Parker's Spenser novels, I feel like I know Spenser very well; and when I think of him, one of the first things to come to mind is his ability as a fighter.

# TASTES AND PREFERENCES

Another thing about Spenser that sticks in my mind is his penchant for quoting poetry. You don't know Spenser until you know his love of literature. You don't know Rex Stout's great detective Nero Wolfe until you know that he's a gourmet and that he spends certain hours every afternoon tending his orchids.

Nero Wolfe's tastes border on obsessiveness, so that they dominate his character. But in real life, with ordinary people, our tastes are part of who we are. If you happen to love Woody Allen movies, don't you feel an instant kinship with somebody who says, "I walk through the valley of the shadow of death—no, I *run* through the valley of the shadow of death." "*Love and Death*," you say, and then the two of you toss favorite scenes and lines back and forth for a while.

What somebody likes does not define who they are—I mean, what do you really know about me when I tell you that my favorite modern play is *Who's Afraid of Virginia Woolf?* and that my favorite movies are *Far from the Madding Crowd* and *The Lion in Winter?* Somebody could like all the same things as you and still not be the kind of person you would allow to babysit your children.

Still, real people do have preferences, and so should fictional characters. Not only do such tastes help the reader feel like he knows the character better, they also open up possibilities within the story.

On a trivial level, knowing your character's devotion to wines will give her something to chat about at dinner; a chance to show a flippant attitude—or resent someone else's flippancy; a reason to disdain another character's lack of taste or knowledge. A character's tastes can even be endearing, like Dagwood Bumstead's mammoth midnight-snack sandwiches.

On a more significant level, a character's love of skiing gives you an excuse to get her into the mountains in the winter; gives her at least a few friends she met on the slopes, friends who might phone or visit during the story; allows you to show her escaping from someone on skis without the reader doubting for a moment that she could do it. Skiing is already part of who she is—it's perfectly in character for her to ski away from trouble.

# BODY

It's no accident that I've listed physical appearance last among the ways we come to know other people. A person's body is certainly an important part of who he is. Physical handicaps can force changes in a person's life. More minor physical problems—weakness, thinness, overweight, lack of beauty—can have powerful effects on how a person feels about himself and on how others treat him.

This sort of thing is vital for a writer to know about his or her characters. A character with arthritis or a metal plate in his leg or a severe case of sinusitis is going to behave differently from one with no physical problems or limitations. Chronic or permanent physical problems—or physical strength and beauty, for that matter—will shape all the character's actions and relationships throughout the story.

The reason I listed the body last is not because it's unimportant, but rather because far too many writers—especially beginners—think that a physical description of a character *is* characterization. If they have a woman stand in front of a mirror and comb her long brown hair with the comb delicately balanced in her slender fingers as she looks into her own flashing brown eyes, such writers think they've done the job. I put the body last on the list so it would be clear that physical description is only one factor among many in getting to know a character.

And such matters as hair color, complexion, eye color, length of the fingers, size of the breasts, or hairiness of the body—those are usually pretty trivial, unless there's something exceptional about them. If readers know a character's actions, motives, past, reputation, relationships, habits, talents, and tastes, they can often get through a whole story without ever knowing a character's eye color, and they'll still feel as if they know the person.

Remember that of all these different ways of getting to know people—and therefore getting to know characters—the most powerful of them, the ones that make the strongest impression, are the first three: what the character does in the story, what his motives are, and what he has done in the past.

# CHAPTER 2

# WHAT MAKES A GOOD FICTIONAL CHARACTER?

REAL PEOPLE ARE WHO THEY ARE—you love 'em or leave 'em. But fictional characters have a job to do. And if they aren't fulfilling their purpose, they've got to change until they do—or another character has to be found to do the job.

If they're major characters, they've got to be interesting and believable enough for people to want to read about what they do.

If they're minor characters, they've got to advance the story line or twist it or relieve tension or convey information—and then they've got to get out of the way.

## THE THREE QUESTIONS READERS ASK

When readers pick up your story or novel, they want it to be good. They want to care about the people in your story. They want to believe. They're on your side. That honeymoon with the readers lasts about three paragraphs with a short story, two pages or so with a novel.

Within that time you need to give the reader some reason to read on. You need to answer the three challenging questions that all readers unconsciously ask throughout every story they read. When each question is adequately answered, readers go on with the story. When a question isn't answered well enough, doubts begin to rise to the surface.

### Question 1: So What?

Why should I care about what's going on in this story? Why is this important? Why shouldn't I go downstairs and watch TV? I've seen this kind of thing happen in stories a thousand times before. If this is all the story's about, I'm through with it.

### Question 2: Oh Yeah?

Come on, I don't believe anybody would do that. That isn't the way things work. That was pretty convenient, wasn't it? How dumb does this author think I am? Give me a break. This author doesn't know anything. I'm through with this story.

## Question 3: Huh?

What's happening? This doesn't make any sense. I don't know who's talking or what they're talking about. Where is this stuff happening? I don't get it. This is just a bunch of words, it doesn't amount to anything. Either I can't read or this author can't write, but either way I'm through with this book.

Sounds pretty hostile, doesn't it? Well, as long as you do your job as a storyteller and a writer, most of your readers will find you ready for these basic questions.

Whenever they unconsciously ask "So what?" your story will give them a reason to care.

Whenever a doubt comes into their mind and they're about to say "Oh yeah?" your story will include a clue or an explanation that persuades the reader to go on trusting you.

And, of course, you'll make sure there's never a moment of confusion or inclarity in your story. On those rare but vital occasions when suspense requires you to withhold a bit of information, you'll make sure your readers know exactly what the question is, even if they don't know the answer. Even the uncertainties in your story must be clear, so readers will know you meant it to be that way, so they'll continue to trust your competence to deliver the story you promised them.

Your characters must deal with these three audience questions from the beginning. With rare exceptions, stories are about people and what they do, and, with even rarer exceptions, a story should focus on only a few characters. (As a general rule, the longer the story, the more characters it can deal with well.) These major characters are the ones who must satisfy those three questions the audience is constantly, unconsciously, asking.

Not every reader will care equally about every character. When you've answered the questions well enough to satisfy Group 1, there's still Group 2 that won't care and Group 3 that won't believe, and Group 4 that never gets what's going on at all.

## YOU ARE THE FIRST AUDIENCE

A lot of this book is devoted to helping you learn how to make characters more interesting and believable to your readers. But the starting point, the most important factor of all, is whether they're interesting and believable to *you*. You are the first audience for the tale.

If you don't care about a character, you can't possibly write an interesting story about him. If you don't believe in a character, there's no chance that you can make your readers believe in him either.

This isn't something you decide intellectually. It's a feeling, a gut-level response. When you think of an idea for a character (or for any other part of a story), you either get interested and excited and know that you want to write about it, or you don't. And if you don't, if a character or story idea bores you or sounds silly to you, you can't possibly write a convincing or engaging story—unless you find something else about the character or story idea that *does* intrigue you.

Throughout the rest of this book, I'll be making suggestions about ways to improve story ideas. I'll often give examples. Sometimes those examples will appeal to you—you'll care about the scrap of story I tell, you'll believe in it. More often, though, you'll intellectually understand what I'm doing, but it won't ring true to you, or it will seem a bit dull. That's OK. This book can't possibly give you the exact answer to every story problem you're going to run into. All I can give you are the questions you must ask of your characters, the demands you must make of your story material. Then you must keep asking those questions and making those demands until you finally come up with an answer that works for *you*, that makes you hungry to tell the story.

No two authors would ever tell a story the same way, because no two people ever care about and believe in the same things to exactly the same degree. Every story choice you make arises out of who you are, at the deepest levels of your soul; every story you tell reveals who you are and the way you conceive the world around you—reveals more about you, in fact, than you know about yourself.

That's what it means when people tell you that you can only write to please yourself. If you don't care about a story, you can't possibly write it well. It's like writing down a long lie that doesn't convince even you.

But once you have a story that rings true to you, a story that feels important and worth telling, then you *don't* write just to please yourself. At that point you must use every ounce of skill you have, every technique you've learned through experience—and through this book—to help your readers discover how important and truthful your story is, to help them understand what's going on, to bring them into the world of your story and let the events unfold before their eyes, in their imagination, in their memory.

Some readers will be so in harmony with you that they'll receive your story no matter how clumsy your efforts; for other readers you'll never succeed no matter how good a writer you are. But that doesn't mean you should shrug and write however you like. You owe it to other people to give them the best possible chance to receive this important, truthful story. You owe it to them to make it as clear as possible, to give them every possible reason to care, every possible justification for belief.

Belief. Emotional involvement. Understandability.

I like to remember these principles by paraphrasing St. Paul: *Faith, hope, and clarity.*

I don't think it even has to be paraphrased. Because if your story really does matter, if your made-up tales have any real value at all, then it truly is an act of charity, of brotherly love, to open up that story to as many people as can possibly receive it.

Some techniques I'll tell you in this book can be used mindlessly and mechanically, and they'll still work, to a degree. But I hope you won't use them that way. I hope you'll only use them when they really belong in your story, when they won't damage the truth and power of the tale.

Our objective as storytellers and writers isn't to make money—there are faster and easier ways of doing that. Our objective is to change people by putting our stories in their memory; to make the world better by bringing other people face to face with reality, or giving them a vision of hope, or whatever other form our truthtelling might take. You want the widest possible audience to receive this message; when you use your best skills to open up your story to other readers, you aren't "pandering to the masses," you're freely giving your best gifts. If your stories happen to reach a very wide audience then yes, money will come. But it isn't the money that makes the work worth doing; too many of us make too little for that to be the motive that pulls us along.

The moment you use a technique that doesn't belong in your story, solely for the sake of appealing to some imagined reader who wants a bit more sex or a tad more sentimentality or some tough action, at that moment your story dies a little, becomes a little more lie and a little less truth. For every reader you might gain that way, you'll lose the power to influence a dozen others who will recognize the falseness in your story and reject it.

## INTERROGATING THE CHARACTER

I'll talk in a minute about where ideas for characters come from. But before you go in pursuit of ideas, it's good to know what to do with an idea when you find one.

You ask questions.

### *Causal Questions*

The questions you'll need to ask are mostly about causes and results. Why would he do such a thing? What made him do it? If he does it, what will happen as a result?

Let me give you an example. I recently conducted a workshop I call "A Thousand Ideas in an Hour." I've done this with adults and children, professional writers, aspiring writers, and people who have no particular interest in writing. It's always an exhilarating, creative hour.

This time I was working with a group of fourth-graders in my son's school. I asked questions; they came up with answers.

Do you want a story about a boy or a girl?
—*A boy! No, a girl!*

OK then, we won't decide yet. How old is this person?
—*Ten! No, twelve!*

Twelve? Why twelve? What happens to you when you're twelve?
—*You can stay up later.*

Oh? What do you do when you stay up later?
—*Watch TV!*
—*The good shows!*
—*Scary shows!*

What else can you do?
—*Go places by yourself!*

Where would you go?
—*The mall!*
—*Friends' houses!*
—*Wherever I want!*

Heck, I'm thirty-seven and I can't do *that*.
—*When you're twelve you get more money.*

How does that happen?
—*Bigger allowance.*
—*Babysitting.*

So twelve-year-olds can babysit. Have any of you ever done any babysitting?
—*My brothers.*
—*The baby.*
—*I have.*

What can go wrong when you're babysitting?
—*The house burns down.*

Yeah, but that doesn't happen very often.
—*The kids start a fire!*

What do you do then?
—*Put it out!*
—*Call the fire department!*
—*Get out of the house!*
—*Get the kids out of the house!*
—*Leave the one who started the fire!*

Oh, you're all heart. A fire would make an exciting story, but I don't feel like doing that one right now. What else can go wrong when you're babysitting?
—*Messy diapers.*

That's just part of the job.
—*The baby crying.*

OK, the baby's crying. What do you do?
—*Change his diaper.*

You changed the diaper. He's still crying. What do you do?
—*Feed him.*
—*Burp him.*
—*Tell him to be quiet.*

You do all that, he's still crying.
—*Maybe he's sick.*

There's a chance of that. What do you do?
—*Call your mother!*

She isn't home. She had a meeting that night.
—*Call the people. The people you're babysitting for.*

They're driving somewhere and they don't have a car phone.
—*Go next door!*

You don't know those people, and it's dark and there are a lot of trees and they aren't home anyway.
—*You're cheating!*
—*You won't let us do anything!*

It's no fun if it isn't hard. All these things you're telling me, they're part of the story. You try everything, and it doesn't work. What do you do now?
—*Put it to bed and let it cry.*

You do that, and it screams louder and louder until it starts choking and coughing and you pick it up again. What next?
—*Call the doctor.*

His office is closed.
—*Call the hospital!*
—*The emergency room!*
—*They* never *close.*

You've got me; I can't weasel out of that. They never close. So you call. What happens? They tell you to try doing all the stuff you've already tried. They tell you to call all the people you already tried to call. Then what?
—*Woooooooo!*
—*Ambulance!*

OK, you called an ambulance. It pulls up, siren going, lights flashing. What happens?
—*The baby stops crying.*
—*The parents come home!*

Wonderful! The baby stops crying *and* the parents come home. They see an ambulance at their house, they come inside—
—*The baby's sleeping.*
—*Like a baby!*

What do you do?
—*Tell them what happened.*
—*They won't believe you.*
—*They never believe kids.*
—*They yell at you.*

Maybe they do, maybe they don't. But do they ever hire you again?
—*Never!*
—*Nobody does!*
—*They tell your parents!*
—*Your mom never lets you babysit again.*
—*You go back and smack the baby!*

You want to, anyway.
—*This isn't a fair story! It wasn't your fault!*

Right. It *wasn't* your fault. So what do you do about it?
—*Make your parents believe you.*

How do you do that?
—*Have your mom babysit the stupid kid.*

Great idea! Only you don't make her do it. Let's say that a couple of months later the parents call and ask your mom to watch the baby for a while. You don't even go downstairs to see them, you're so embarrassed. You just sit in your room, studying, reading, whatever.
—*Listening to tapes.*
—*Watching TV.*

What happens?
—*The baby starts crying.*

The baby cries. You can hear it up in your room, you listen, you enjoy. You know your mom's changing the diapers, feeding it, all the stuff you did. Trying to call the parents. She even tries to call *her* mother.
—*She calls an ambulance!*

Maybe! But I think it's enough if she comes upstairs, opens your door, holding the baby screaming its head off, and says, "OK, kid, you were right. You can babysit again."
—*Not if it's that baby!*

Right! That's what you tell her. And the story's over.

Notice the process that's going on here. We started out knowing nothing more than the character's age. But that gave us enough that we could start asking *why* and *what result.*

*What happens because you're twelve?* There were several answers. Any one of them would have been useful—in fact, later in that same session we went back and got another story out of the idea of twelve-year-olds staying up late and watching scary movies. But I happened to choose babysitting.

*What can go wrong?* This is a fundamental story question, asking for complications and difficulties. But it's also a *what result* question—only I slanted the question to get negative answers. After all, there's no story if nothing goes wrong. The idea of a fire was too melodramatic for me, though of course a wonderful story could be told about saving the children you're babysitting. But it just wasn't what I felt like working with then, so I kept asking the same question till I got an answer that I liked.

Once we had the idea of the baby crying, I again asked a *what result* question. What do you do to *stop* the baby from crying? Each time they came up with a possible solution to the problem, I agreed that the babysitter would try that, but kept saying that it didn't work. Why? Because the minute something worked to stop the crying, the story would be over.

If one of them had suggested that the babysitter should examine the baby's body, then I would have asked what the babysitter found. Maybe a bruise, maybe a horrible bug—who knows what they would have come up with? It might have led to the babysitter finding out the cause of the crying. But since nobody came up with any suggestions except the obvious and uninteresting ones, I made them keep going—I wouldn't let the baby stop crying.

I could have asked more sophisticated motive questions. Why doesn't the babysitter just put the kid to bed, close the door, and ignore the screaming? Then they might have said such things as: The babysitter was once locked in a dark room when she was little and she can't stand to leave anybody else alone. Or: She can't stand to hear babies cry.

Or: She's afraid the baby might die.

Why would she be afraid of that?
—*Her little brother died.*
—*He cried all the time before he died.*

Do you see how the answer to this simple *why* question opens up new possibilities in the story? The version we actually came up with was fine. It would be a cute, funny story. But coming up with a reason why this crying baby would mean far more than annoyance to the babysitter adds an element of urgency, of poignancy. Now the glib ending might not be enough. Now the babysitter's mother might understand why the babysitter called an ambulance, might explain to the baby's parents. We might even want to have it end with the paramedics discovering that there really *was* something wrong with the baby. Or we might want to lead up to the babysitter's mother driving them both to the little brother's grave, and talking about it in a way they never had before.

But such possibilities only emerge when we demand more from the idea, when we ask more *why* and *what result* questions. If you stop with the first acceptable answer, the first "good enough" version of the story, you lose the chance to move from shallowness to depth, from simplicity to complexity, from a merely fun story to a fun but powerful one.

## Exaggeration

Notice also that as I kept insisting that *nothing* would stop the baby's crying, I was building the baby up to mythic proportions. It had ceased to be an ordinary baby, one that can be comprehended by the normal human mind, and had started to become the archetypal Baby, the unfathomable barbarian who emerged from the human womb but now rules the family with its whimsical, unintelligible demands; the Baby as a devil-god no sacrifice will ever satisfy.

A little exaggeration helps turn an ordinary, believable, dull person into an interesting one. A little more, and the person becomes more archetypal, but a bit less believable as an individual. Even more exaggeration, and a character becomes a cartoon, a caricature, perhaps useful for laughs or satire, but not for poignancy or real belief. Exaggerate too much, and the character becomes utterly useless: unbelievable, unrecognizable.

## Do the Twist

In the story idea the class and I worked out together, we assumed that the babysitter was a responsible human being, trying to do a good job. But what if the babysitter has a racket? What if the parents *always* come home to find the baby crying, so they'll feel guilty for the awful time the babysitter had and pay extra?

The method here is to take an assumption about a character and give it a good sharp twist. I was conducting a thousand-ideas session at a convention in Chattanooga that happened to be attended by Gene Wolfe, the most brilliant writer of speculative fiction in the 1980s. The group had invented a fantasy character—a young king who had to abstain from all sexual activity as a kind of sacrifice; if he ever achieved any kind of sexual fulfillment, his kingdom would weaken, the magic that sustained it would slacken or fade. We had all assumed that the young king would be restive under his obligatory limitations, yearning for sex and trying to find a way to escape his guardians. But Wolfe said, "No, no, you don't understand. This young man thinks they don't restrict him *enough*. He's absolutely terrified that he'll accidentally slip into some form of sexual release and cause some dire consequence to his people. He'd make sure they watch him all the time."

The character the group had invented was believable, certainly—a lot of teenagers in real life expend considerable effort trying to escape sexual limitations. But Wolfe's twist led to a character no less believable, but a great deal more interesting, and from there we asked a lot of *why* and *what result* questions that made for one of the best stories ever to emerge from such a session.

## The Cliche Shelf

Never let an idea pass through your mind without giving it the third degree. Shine a bright light on it. Demand that it answer your questions.

And let your questions, again and again, be Why? What caused that? For what purpose? What's the result of that? What would happen then?

Be brutal. Don't let your idea sit there without answering. Don't believe the first answer that comes to mind, either. Chances are very good that the *first* answer you come up with will be a cliche. The second one, too. Keep asking the questions, trying for more answers—eventually one will come along that really comes alive for you. Or if the one that works best for you is one of the first ones you thought of, then fine, go back to it.

And then, when you think the idea is just right, when the character is exactly what you want her to be, exaggerate an aspect of her that nobody else has ever thought of exaggerating. Or give the character a little twist. Or both.

Everybody—not just writers—has a little library of cliches, stock story elements. We all pick these up from our reading, from jokes and stories people tell us. Most of these are public cliches—events and characters that everybody has seen a lot of over the years. Some are private cliches, personal quirks or obsessions that you aren't even aware of.

When you're writing along, or outlining a story, or simply interrogating an idea that just came to you, chances are very good that when you ask one of these *why* and *what result* questions, the first answer that pops into your mind will be a cliche. It's as if, without even looking up, you reach onto that cliche shelf and pull down the first thing that comes to hand. And if you aren't paying attention, you'll settle for it, and your story will be weaker and shallower because you made do with a cheap and easy answer and didn't keep asking questions until you came up with something really good.

# FROM CHARACTER TO STORY, FROM STORY TO CHARACTER

There are some specific questions that will help open up possibilities in your mind as you interrogate your ideas.

In that thousand-ideas session, when we just had a twelve-year-old kid we didn't have a character, really. Once we got a job for the kid, then we had a stereotype: babysitter.

A simple stereotype isn't much to build a story on. But that question I asked—*What could go wrong?*—is one of the basic questions you ask to get a story or situation out of an idea for a character.

Often you'll find yourself in the opposite position. You'll have an idea for a setting or situation for a story, and you won't have any idea about who the characters ought to be. Then the question you ask is: *Who suffers most in this situation?* Your interrogation of the idea will then focus on the person who has the most need to change things—that will almost always lead you to the most possibilities, and it usually happens that the character you find this way will end up as the main character of the tale.

Actually, for practical reasons the question should usually be: Who suffers most in this situation without dying or being incapacitated? The story usually can't be about somebody who dies at the beginning, or who is rendered incapable of doing much throughout the rest of the tale.

This whole chapter has been about questions, hasn't it? There are questions the audience asks:

So what?

Oh yeah?

Huh?

You ask those questions, too, but you ask many more. There are the causal questions:

What made this happen?

What is the purpose?

What is the result?

Then there are the questions that open up story and character possibilities:

What can go wrong?

Who suffers most in this situation?

Finally, there are two processes that wring the last drop from a character or story idea:

Exaggeration

The Twist

There. Now that we've got a plan for what to do when we find an idea, let's go get some.

## CHAPTER 3

# WHERE DO CHARACTERS COME FROM?

TO GET IDEAS FOR CHARACTERS, you don't have to go searching until you find the Holy Grail. There's no mystical process involved. All you have to do is turn your mind into a net for ideas, always casting out into the waters of life and literature, and gathering in the ideas that are there waiting to be noticed.

Because, you see, ideas are cheap. They're around you all the time. You can't get through a day without running into hundreds, even thousands of ideas for characters or stories.

Not *me*, you say?

Yes, *you*, says me.

If you don't notice these ideas, it's because you aren't paying attention. You let them slide on by without ever realizing they were ideas at all.

So let me take you through some of those sources of ideas, so you can see how an idea net can snag characters and get them to where you can interrogate them, whip them into shape—bring them to life.

## IDEAS FROM LIFE

Oh, yes, you know all about mimesis—how art is supposed to derive from life. But not *your* life. Nothing happens around you that isn't ordinary, dull, uninteresting.

How wrong you are. What seems ordinary to you will seem strange to someone else. Furthermore, something that seems ordinary to me will seem strange when you describe it, because you'll see it from a different perspective.

I think immediately of a couple of fantasy novels I read that concern some ordinary teenagers in the hill country of Georgia. These teenagers get involved with visiting elven-folk, or Sidhe, who think of America as the magical land of Tir-Nan-Og. The effect is somewhat like the *Iliad*, with godlike beings manipulating human affairs for their own benefit. Not until I read the second book, however, did I realize the author didn't seem to understand what was really interesting about these stories. The author, to whom the Georgia setting was ordinary, was fascinated with the Sidhe, and in the second volume had a lot of the movement of the story take place in their world. But to me, the Sidhe lived in a stock fantasy Neverland, a place I've seen so often in fantasy fiction that it bores me silly. What I loved was the part of the story that took place in Georgia, showing people who were at once believable and strange. What seemed like ho-hum stuff to the author was fascinating to me.

So when you're looking for characters, cast your net first in your own life—the people you see, the people you know, the person you are.

## Observation of Strangers

Some writers have resorted to carrying a notebook or tape recorder with them to record observations or snatches of dialogue. You'll be at the gas station, standing in line at the grocery store, in a waiting room before an appointment, and you'll hear someone tell a story or express an attitude or perform some act that strikes you as funny or annoying or weird—or exactly typical. Such an observation can be the root of a fascinating character.

For instance, I was recently at the local Big Star supermarket during the after-work rush and needed to check out quickly. I got in the shortest line, immediately behind a woman with only a few items in her basket, thinking that she wouldn't take long. But while we waited in line, her husband and three children all arrived with armloads of other items. OK, I'll tell the truth: there was only one kid, and the father and the kid each had only one or two things to add. But the minute I caught on to what was happening, I started exaggerating it in my own mind. The idea net was operating without my even realizing it. And a little exaggeration sure made for a better story, didn't it?

Anyway, the result was a family I'm going to use in a story sometime. I'm not sure of their motivation yet, but I think it has to do with one parent's obsession with avoiding wasted time—or perhaps it's the family's cooperative answer to the problem of doing housework when both parents work and all the kids are in school. Anyway, they divide up the grocery list on the way to the store. Each person gets a section of the store. Mom gets a cart and stands in line. Each person has time for exactly two armloads of stuff before she gets to the checker. If anybody fails to get his whole list, he suffers deep embarrassment at the meal where that item was supposed to be on the menu.

This isn't a story yet, of course. It's just a comic family situation. But I can imagine using, as my main character, one child who is deeply embarrassed about this whole process. But then, maybe I'll give it a half-twist and write about the kid who thought this system up and believes the others don't do it half well enough. I might have the family members compete with each other to see who can get the most items on the list—and then have my main character always win by scanning other shoppers' carts as he scoots through the store, snatching items he needs from their carts instead of having to search them out on the shelves. There are a lot of character possibilities from that one rather ordinary observation.

However I end up using the idea—if I use it at all—it came from watching people converge on a cart in the grocery store.

Remember, though, that the words you hear or the event you observe are rarely usable exactly as they happened. You don't have to exaggerate as much as I did in this case, but you do need to demand more from the idea than the plain facts.

When somebody says something intriguing, you need to ask yourself why somebody might say something like that, why someone might have that attitude. Don't settle for your first guess as to motive. An interesting observation is nothing more than local color, a bit of background—until you wring from it all its story and character potential.

## People You Know

I know a lot of authors who use their friends or family members as models for characters in their stories. I've occasionally done it myself.

And why not? You *know* these people. You know their quirky way of talking, the odd things they do, their virtues and weaknesses. Besides, it's easier to simply describe someone you know than to invent someone new.

All true. But let me give you a few warnings, too. There are two categories of Things That Can Go Wrong.

1. Taking characters "from life" can lead to bad fiction.

You may not know these people half so well as you think you do. After all, you are never inside their memory, inside their soul—you don't really know *why* they do the things they do. You know why they *say* they do them; you know your own guesses. But when it comes to writing your character, you have to know a lot more than you'll ever know about your friends or family. So it isn't just a matter of copying. You've still got to do a lot of invention before a real-life character—even one you know well—is ready to hold down a job in your fiction.

Also, when you use real-life incidents, it's easy to forget that your readers don't know that the incident really happened to a friend of yours. If the event is particularly strange or intriguing, your readers are going to need some serious justification before they believe it. You, however, may not realize this, and so you'll expend no effort trying to show how such a thing could happen, or justifying why your character does what she does. The result is that at exactly the points where your story is most factual, it will be least believable.

Remember that believability in fiction doesn't come from the facts—what *actually* happened. It comes from the readers' sense of what is plausible—what is *likely* to happen. And the further you stray from the plausible, the more time you have to spend justifying the event, piling up details to show the process, explaining motivation and cause and result, so that the reader *will* believe. "But it really happened like that" is no defense in fiction.

2. Taking characters "from life" can lead to personal problems.

If your friends or family members recognize themselves, you can be in deep trouble, and not just when you do a hatchet job on them. You may even think you've treated them "nicely" or (shudder) "fairly." But remember, all the time you've known them, they didn't know they were being "interviewed" or "filmed" for inclusion in your fiction. They may have confided things in you—hopes and fears, memories and motives—that were just between friends. When you put them in the pages of a story or book, they have every right to feel betrayed.

Asking their permission first can be even worse. Then they start to feel a proprietary interest in the story; they call you up with new reminiscences. You'll very soon find yourself having to say, "I'm sorry, I'm only using a few bits from your life, and I just don't need any more." Worse, when the story comes out you'll get the Phone Call: "I can't believe you showed me doing *that*. I never would have done *that*." Very few friendships can stand the strain of an author-character relationship. The whole point of being an author is that your characters do what you tell them to do. Your friends and family just don't follow that pattern.

The solution to all this is simple. Use your family and friends as the starting points for characters—but then use the full process of interrogation to transform them from the people you think you know into the characters you *really* know. In other words, make new people out of the old ones.

Then discard all the extraneous details. Just because you're modeling the character on your sister doesn't mean that the character has to *look* like her, or have the same career, or the same taste in clothes, or the same childhood experiences. Jettison anything about the real-life model that isn't essential to the new character, and disguise everything else that you can.

Then if your sister or father or friend later asks you, "Was this character supposed to be me?" your answer can be, in complete honesty, "I'm glad he seemed so real that you thought he was like you. But you're much nicer (prettier/more sincere/gutsier) than that character." If you've taken bits out of your friend's life that can't be fully disguised, you can say, "I might have taken some bits out of the lives of people that I know—that sort of thing can't be helped, it happens without a writer even noticing—but the characters are meant to be themselves. None of them are modeled on any particular person." If you have done the job of fully inventing your characters, this statement will always be true.

I learned all these lessons the hard way. When I was in college, I wrote a play based on my mother's family. My only source was Mother's own reminiscences of childhood and adolescence, told to her children as we grew up. I loved the stories—and besides, I had been told, time and again, "Write what you know."

The result was a pretty good little play, given the state of my skills at the time. But when my mother saw it, she was aghast. She made me promise *not* to invite any of her brothers or sisters to see it.

Why? There were no villains in the story. Everyone was sympathetically portrayed.

The problem was that my mother knew something I had not thought of: She and her siblings weren't likely to remember these events quite the same way. Even though these things had all happened more than thirty years before, feelings would be hurt, questions would be raised, and old family tensions would be revived.

And the funny thing was that the best things about these characters were not the elements I took from Mom's stories. The best things were the motives and misunderstandings, the dialogue and the details that I had invented to flesh out the tales.

That is *always* true. Modeling characters on life is not a method, it's a starting point. The characters who come to life on the page or on the stage are the ones that have passed through the storyteller's imagination. Your readers already "know" people as well as real people ever know each other. They turn to fiction in order to know people *better* than they can ever know them in real life. If your story tells them nothing more about people than they already know, you've let your audience down. By sticking to the facts, you cheat them out of the chance to learn the truth.

## Yourself

OK, you've never murdered somebody, and your character is a murderer. Does that mean you've got to go interview people on death row in order to find out how they think?

No. Of course you *can* interview them, and you might get some interesting insights—though all the warnings about modeling characters on friends and family also apply to modeling characters on interview subjects. There's an added problem, too: Interview subjects never tell the truth. Oh, they may *think* they're telling the truth, but in fact their stories and statements are altered by the fact that they're telling them to someone else. They want you to think of them a certain way, and so they'll emphasize certain things and leave out others that don't make the right impression. If you believe everything you're told in an interview, your story may be less true than if you never interviewed a soul. At best, an interview will be a starting point—you will still go through the whole process of character invention.

There is one person you can always interview, however, who will tell you much more of the truth than others ever will—yourself. You can *imagine* what it would take to get you to behave in a certain way.

So what if you've never murdered somebody? Haven't you ever been blindingly angry? Haven't you ever longed for cold revenge? You've felt all the emotions, all the motives. All you have to do is imagine those feelings and needs being even stronger, or imagine your inhibition against violence being even weaker.

Was it a crime of passion? Then imagine what kind of provocation it would take for you to be filled with murderous rage, and then find the sort of provocation that would get that same reaction in your character.

Was it a calculated murder in order to win some objective? Then figure out which of your own attitudes you'd have to change before you'd come to regard murdering somebody as a reasonable way to get him out of the way in order to achieve your goal. What if you were fighting for some desperately important cause? What if you had grown up in a situation where killing was commonplace? What if you had cause to think other people were all beneath consideration?

## Analogy

What if you just *can't* imagine yourself doing something? Then, instead of trying to think of what it would take to get you to do what your character does, think of something you actually *have* done that is *like* what the character does.

For instance, Michael Bishop faced this problem in his brilliant 1988 novel *Unicorn Mountain*, in which one character, Bo, is a young homosexual who is dying of AIDS. Bo and another character are at a motel swimming pool when three muscular young men come to swim. Bo might have had any of several responses: envy at their health and strength; resentment that these boorish young heterosexual men don't have to pay a price like AIDS for their sexual activities. But what Bishop chose to show was simple lust. These three young swimmers had attractive, muscular bodies. Having AIDS hadn't stopped Bo from being a homosexual. He still looked at these young men with desire.

I believe that Bishop, who is not a homosexual, based this scene primarily on analogy. What is it like to be a homosexual with AIDS? This question surely came up again and again as he worked on *Unicorn Mountain*. I think it led him to this analogy: It is very much like being a heterosexual with a fatal disease that has cut you off from having sex with anyone, but hasn't yet made you impotent or weakened your desire.

Bishop knew what we all know, that swimsuits reveal people's bodies a great deal more than business suits do, and that nowadays swimsuits are designed to emphasize sexual attractiveness. It just happened that Bo was interested in and aroused by the men at the pool. Yet he was not affected the way a woman is usually affected when watching men in swimsuits. He was affected as heterosexual men are affected when they watch *women* in swimsuits.

Complicated? Yes. And yet it led Bishop to write a quiet but startling scene that rang true—with *me*, at least. I did not realize that I had been asking the question: What is it like to be a homosexual? But when Bishop showed me this scene, showed his character's attitude toward these young men, I realized the question had been answered, at least in part—and that it was an important question, one that would matter to me even after the story was over, because it gave me a new way of looking at and understanding other human beings. In other words, Bishop had achieved one of the primary purposes of fiction.

So if you can't imagine doing what your character must do, then compare that act with something you *have* done. Is my character going to kill somebody to get her out of the way? Then I might think of a time when I carelessly disregarded someone else's feelings because I was rushing to get a job done. I lost a friendship. I didn't *kill* anyone, but I did feel that same single-minded focus on my goal that left no room for regarding another person's needs. In my mind, that former friend had ceased to be a person. And, remembering that painful event in my past, I can then, by analogy, show how my character completely disregards the value of other people's lives.

## Memory

I've come to this last, because this is a deep well, but one that can quickly become exhausted. Whether you mean to or not, you will constantly draw on your own memory for incidents and characters in your fiction. In fact, all these other sources of characters arise out of memory—your memory of your friends and family, your memory of strangers.

All these memories are distorted by time or your own needs and perceptions. No less distorted is your memory of yourself—what you did, what you meant to do, what caused you to do things, what the results of your actions turned out to be. Yet, distorted or not, your memory of yourself is the clearest picture you will ever have of what a human being is and why people do what they do. You are the only person you will ever know from the inside, and so, inevitably, when your fiction shows other characters from the inside, you will reveal yourself.

This will happen unconsciously, whether you plan it or not. Sometimes it will startle, even embarrass you, when you look back on a story you've written and suddenly realize how much you have confessed without even meaning to. I once handed the manuscript of early chapters of one of my novels to a friend and fellow magazine editor. She read it, and when she gave it back, among her comments was this one: "It's an interesting exploration of self-alienation. This guy really hates his own body."

I smiled and nodded, as if that had been precisely my intent. But the fact was that I had no idea that such a theme was emerging in the story. Yet I knew at once that she was right, that without even meaning to, I had created a character whose situation exactly mirrored the cause of many of my deepest injuries and much of my personal anguish during my teenage years. It made it hard to go on writing the novel, in fact, because I was afraid that my novel was exposing more of me to my audience than I ever intended. In fact, it was. But I finished it and published it, and despite many flaws, the book remains one of the truest stories I've told.

Whatever obsessions you have, whatever memories are most important to you, either negatively or positively, they are going to show up in your work no matter what you do.

However, just because your memory will be an unconscious source of characterization doesn't mean you can't also mine it consciously. When I needed to show a child character's attitude toward his older brother and sister, I remembered how I felt toward *my* older brother and sister when I was little; I even used incidents that showed what those relationships were like. In no sense were the characters of the brother and sister based on my own brother and sister—but the child character *was* based on my memory of what it was like being myself at that age. I know far more about myself than I'll ever know about any other human being—it only makes sense that my most truthful material will usually come from my own recollections.

The danger of delving into your own memory is that you've only lived one life. You're going to keep coming up with the same incidents and attitudes over and over again, without even realizing it. This is where personal cliches come from, constantly mining the same spot in memory, the way a child will keep picking at the same sore. You have to make a conscious effort to keep from remembering the same things in the same way. In other words, even when you take a character directly out of yourself at some particular time in your life or in some particular situation, you *still* have to invent that character—ask the causal questions, exaggerate, twist.

## Finding "New" Memories

What I'm about to suggest smacks of self-psychoanalysis, and for all I know it may have therapeutic value. But I suggest that one way for you to discover good characters is to search randomly through your memory, just as you move randomly through the world around you, with your idea net extended.

The way you do this is to pick some arbitrary starting point. It might be a point in time: seventh grade, for instance. What school were you in in seventh grade? Who was your homeroom teacher? Who were your other teachers? I immediately remember Mr. Arella, the science teacher—a man I haven't thought of in twenty years, yet his name was there, waiting to be dredged up. His was the last class of the day for me, and I recall staying after school the first few days, talking to him, asking questions. Partly it was because I really was interested in science, but mostly it was because I was waiting for my mom to pick me up—I couldn't walk home carrying my tuba. By the end of the second day, he started calling me his "lab assistant" and talking about how I'd stay after school and help him clean test tubes and jars—not at all what I had in mind. I soon stopped staying after class; but I remember that later in the school year, I heard him refer to someone else as his lab assistant, whereupon he affixed me with a steady gaze for a few moments before moving on to talk about something else. Without meaning to, I had apparently hurt his feelings or let him down somehow—though he had never asked me whether I *wanted* to be his lab assistant.

I also remember that in the encyclopedia I happened upon a description of how to separate water into hydrogen and oxygen using an electric current. I talked to Mr. Arella about it, telling him what I had figured out about how to conduct the experiment. He encouraged me; I went to a great deal of trouble to find batteries, strips of copper, and a way to hold everything in place while hydrogen arose from the water to fill an overturned jar.

I set up the experiment for the first time in front of the class—it never occurred to me to rehearse in private. The experiment didn't work. I don't know why, and neither did Mr. Arella, but we never got that little puff of an explosion from a lighted match that tells you isolated hydrogen was present. It was frustrating and embarrassing.

But that was nothing compared to the frustration when, a month or so later, he got to the electrolysis section in the textbook, opened the cupboard, and took out a complete prefabricated electrolysis device. All the elements were there, professionally designed, preassembled, and ready to use. After class I demanded to know why he had let me go to all that trouble when he had the experiment already in hand. "I wanted you to learn from your own experience," he said. A noble thought. But at the time all I could see was that he had let me waste a ridiculous amount of time and caused me much public embarrassment, when he could have said, "Want to see electrolysis work? I've got the whole setup right here in the cupboard."

My only consolation was that his professional setup didn't make any more hydrogen than my amateurish one did.

All these memories came flooding back the moment I typed the words "seventh grade" into my computer. Are any of them usable for a story? Probably not directly. I have no idea how interesting this story is, but I suspect your eyes were beginning to glaze over before I had finished. Still, if I interrogate the character of Mr. Arella—or of myself—I may find an interesting story there:

I didn't do anything to "get even" with Mr. Arella, but what about a student character who *did* plot vengeance?

Or what if the teacher character has a different motive for letting the student embarrass himself? What if he's getting even for the student's failure to serve as his lab assistant?

Or what if I choose a different experiment, one that causes even more embarrassment than simple failure?

Or what if I change the relationship and make it a husband and wife? The wife is going into the same line of work as the husband; she gets a terrific idea and sets to work on it. He encourages her, and she goes to great effort, but fails. Only later does she discover that he knew exactly how to do the whole job, even had key pieces of equipment or information that might have allowed her to succeed. When she confronts him, he says, "I figured you'd want to do it on your own."

"I didn't care about doing it on my own! I cared about doing it right, and you could have helped me do that!"

"What kind of career is it if your husband steps in and makes it easy for you?"

"I put you through college, you jerk! What kind of education would you have had if I *weren't* the kind of wife who stepped in and made it easy for *you*? People in business sometimes help each other. *Nice* people do, anyway. They don't let somebody drown while they've got a life preserver in their hands!"

"OK, I'm sorry, I made a mistake!"

"It wasn't a mistake. You meant me to fail. You wanted me to blow it, because if I did it right then I'd be a threat to you!"

"Oh, I see, I'm not just a husband who made a mistake, suddenly I'm a symptom of the whole male conspiracy against women. The trouble is, if I *had* helped you, that would *also* be part of the male conspiracy against women, since I would have been plotting to prove to you that you couldn't succeed without my help!"

And so on. This relationship has some story potential, though the scene itself is far too abstract to be useful—real people don't stick to the subject so relentlessly while they argue. This scene would never end up in a story, but these characters, this relationship, might. And if such a story ever comes to be, who would guess that it emerged from the incident with Mr. Arella and the electrolysis experiment, which came to mind solely because I was randomly exploring through times and places in my memory.

# IDEAS FROM THE STORY

As you work on a story, it will suggest characters to you—as long as you know how to look for them.

## Who Must Be There?

Let's say you're telling the story of a young princess who's being held captive in the top of a tower. If fairy tales don't appeal to you, update it: A young girl who has been kidnapped off the streets of New York and is being held captive in an abandoned building. Or if melodrama doesn't appeal to you, a girl who has to spend the summer with somebody unpleasant while her parents are off on a long working vacation in Australia.

The story idea itself will imply certain characters. Since the girl is being held somewhere against her will, there has to be a person who is holding her—a "villain" who has caused her confinement. Also, there must be some people she was kidnapped *from*. If she's a princess, by implication there must be a king or queen—or both—who want her back. Or perhaps she feels that her parents wanted to be rid of her. Either way, one or both parents must figure into the story.

If she's staying with relatives, then those characters must be added as well. A bossy aunt? A boring uncle? Or, more sinisterly, an aunt who is always off "shopping," while the uncle stays around home like a couch potato, sleeping in front of the television; only it turns out that the uncle is mixing up hallucinogenic chemicals in the basement all night, while the aunt makes drug deliveries during the day. No, no, you say—you're getting melodramatic again. All right, the aunt is always away because she's supporting the family, and the uncle is every bit as lazy and dim-witted as he seems. He's even dumb enough to think that his young niece will appreciate suggestions for a relationship closer than nepotism.

Whether any of these ideas interested you, you can see how the process works. The basic idea of the story requires certain people to be present. Once you know the story roles that must be filled, you can use the process we've already talked about to create interesting, well-rounded characters for those roles.

## Who Might Be There?

Besides the people who must be there because of the story, there are also characters who might be present simply because of the setting. Let's take the girl living with her aunt and uncle for the summer. They might have children. Younger ones that the girl is required to tend? Older ones, who exclude her from their good times or otherwise make her miserable? One exactly her age who resents having her there—or who is horrible and boring and wants to be with her all the time?

The aunt and uncle must live in a *place*, of course, so is it a town? Are there neighbors? A local 7-11 store, with a clerk she befriends, or kids who hang out playing pinball or video games there?

Maybe the aunt and uncle live at the beach—there are always people coming to the beach. Could she meet an interesting person who takes an early morning walk along the beach every day?

She came *from* somewhere, so could she be writing letters to a friend back home? Trying to carry on a long-distance romance with a boyfriend who is actually dating her best friend now?

Could she be attending summer school? There are teachers and students there. Or maybe she gets a summer job—proofreading at the local weekly newspaper? Then there'll be an editor, a typesetter who might resent all her corrections, an eccentric society columnist, maybe another kid who doubles as delivery boy and cub reporter.

Or maybe the aunt and uncle live on a farm, and there are some migrant workers who come for the midsummer cherry picking. Or maybe they live in the mountains, and she meets a poacher, or a forest ranger, or some interesting hikers—or some dangerous ones.

This process is a simple one, but it's amazing how many writers forget to do it. All you have to do is take your eyes off the main characters long enough to see who else is nearby. Most of the characters you discover this way will remain minor ones, or even background characters. Still, by using them you'll enrich the story and make it more real.

These other characters will also add possibilities for conflict or complication, or sources of help for the main characters. And some of them will become so interesting that you'll have to move them into major roles in the story after all, even though they were never part of your original plan.

But if you don't look to see who *might* be there, you'll never find these people, and your story will be the poorer for it.

## Who Has Been There?

Even though your main focus will be on the characters who are present in the story, it's also important to look into the story's past to find the characters who are no longer around, but who still helped shape the characters who are present. So often we see stories with heroes who seemed to come from nowhere—they never remember anybody who isn't present, never meet anybody they knew from long before, never even refer to parents or old jobs or anyone else. Yet in real life you are constantly remembering people who aren't present, bumping into old acquaintances, and responding to present situations in ways that clearly grow out of old relationships.

When the teenage girl in our story becomes friends with the funny-looking clerk at the 7-11, does she gradually and uncomplicatedly fall in love with him? Or does he remind her of a slick exploitative guy she knew at school back home? Maybe she's trying to stay faithful to her boyfriend back home, so she has constant thoughts of her boyfriend even as she gets more and more attracted to the 7-11 clerk. Those guys from back home are never "present" in the story, and yet her relationship with them is very important.

Or perhaps as she tries to get along with her aunt and uncle, she finds that the real difficulty is her long-dead grandmother—the mother of her father and her uncle, a woman who always favored the girl's father and disapproved of the uncle. At first the girl will agree with the grandmother's assessment of the uncle, especially because the uncle clearly feels a strong antipathy toward the girl. Gradually, though, she'll come to appreciate some aspects of her uncle's character that neither her father nor her grandmother ever saw. In fact, the story might come to focus on the relationship between the girl and her dead grandmother, with the girl becoming angrier and angrier at a woman who exists now only in her memory. Finally, she has it out with her *uncle*, in a complicated scene in which she is angry at *him* for acting out the grandmother's image of him. It might end up transforming both of them.

Yet that story would be impossible to tell if we hadn't first wondered about characters who might have been there in the story's past, but who are not physically present in the story.

# SERVANTS OF THE IDEA

Often a story emerges, not from characters or events, but from an idea that you want to put across. Maybe you're concerned about the danger of pollution, the arms race, the escalating cost of medical care, or the unfairness of American immigration policy. Maybe you worry about abortion, women's rights, racism, or poverty. Maybe you want to speak for disarmament, more humane prisons, justice for an oppressed people, or the rights of intelligent marine mammals.

All of these are causes that many wise and concerned people find to be worthy and important. But the first thing you must decide is whether to write a polemic essay or a story.

These are not mutually exclusive forms. That is, if you decide to write an essay—for a newspaper's op-ed page, a pamphlet, or even a book-length essay—you will find that stories are effective tools in persuading people to pay attention. No amount of philosophizing about the rights of dolphins will have as much effect on readers as a simple story of the life of one dolphin—his birth, upbringing, family life, playfulness, all leading to his senseless drowning when he is caught in a tuna net. One story is worth a thousand abstractions or statistics, when it comes to having an emotional impact on people.

And if you decide to write a story, this doesn't mean you can't also make your point.

The problems arise when you forget that you're writing a story, and let the idea take over. Forget about fully inventing characters! I'm going to show how bad pollution is, so I'll have all the polluters be evil conspirators so eager to make a buck that they don't care how many people die because of the poisons they put in the ground or in the water.

The trouble is that when such a story is finished, who will want to read it? People who already agree with you, who already think polluting corporations are run by inhuman monsters, will think the story is right on the mark; but what about the people who *don't* yet agree with you, the ones who have never thought much about pollution? If your characters are too one-dimensional to believe in, you won't persuade anybody. Your uncommitted readers will sense that they're being lied to. "Nobody's *that* evil," they'll say. Few will be convinced. You'll end up preaching to the choir.

When you have a point to make, an idea to put across, it is all the more important to be a good storyteller, to examine every character and wring from him all possible truth. If you want to write a story that makes the dangers of industrial pollution really come home to people, you don't make the "bad guys" into villainous conspirators. Instead, you focus on a "bad guy" who thinks of himself as a good guy. His factory makes a product that people need, and he's following all the regulations. He's also trying to keep costs down so the product will be affordable and competitive. When people start complaining that the company is polluting the community's water, he doesn't oppose these people because he's evil, he opposes them because he thinks they're wrong. To him, they're just extremists who think that nothing but distilled water should ever be emitted by any factory; to him, these people would rather see everybody live in caves than allow any modern progress.

And, in fact, some of the people attacking his factory *are* just as mindlessly anti-technology as he thinks they are. But there is one of them who means more to him than any of the strangers. It might be a neighbor; or perhaps it's a lab technician that he hired because he knew her folks years before, but now he has to fire her because she has leaked the contents of lab reports to the press. He knows that he's right to fire her—she violated company regulations—but he also worries that her reports might be right. After all, he knows *she* isn't crazy, and so he talks to her, learns from her, gradually comes to realize that while his factory isn't causing the death of civilization as we know it, the pollution problem might be real. He works to solve the problem from the inside.

Do you recognize this story? You should, at least if you've seen the movie *The China Syndrome*, about the violation of safety regulations at a nuclear power plant, leading to a dangerous near-meltdown. The situations are not identical, but the basic movement of the stories is similar. *The China Syndrome* did settle for a few trite and obvious villains—which weakened the movie—but all the people we focused on were ordinary and decent, neither perfectly good nor perfectly evil. That movie turned out to be effective persuasive writing, precisely because the characters were so believable. Of course, it helped believability when the nuclear accident happened at Three Mile Island around the time the movie was released.

Polemic—persuasive writing—only works when it doesn't feel like propaganda. The audience must feel that you're being absolutely fair to people on the other side. If you depict them as devils, the uncommitted members of the audience will be disgusted, and you'll convince none of them. But if you show all the characters as human, you have a good chance of bringing many audience members to your point of view or increasing their commitment to your cause.

The same is true when you are telling a story in order to put across an idea. This often happens in science fiction, where the writer wants to show readers a neat gadget or scientific discovery, and uses characters only to convey information. The same can happen in historical fiction, where certain characters exist only to demonstrate particular historical attitudes; or in academic/literary fiction, when a character is introduced solely to be a symbol of something, or to speak key words that explicate the story's theme.

All of these are legitimate starting points for a character—but if you actually expect your reader to get emotionally involved, to respond to your story *as a story*, you must wring more life from the character, so that she isn't so obviously being manipulated by the author to produce results that have nothing to do with the events of the story itself.

Of course, this can be done wrongheadedly. I've seen many writers "characterize" by having their one-dimensional cardboard character hop into bed with another one-dimensional cardboard character and have the cardboard equivalent of sex. You don't "flesh out" a character whose role is to put across an idea or point of view by having the character do a lot of things that have nothing to do with the story.

Instead, you must follow where the original idea leads. *Why* does the character care so much about this particular idea? And don't settle for the first answer, either. Why does Nora care so much about pollution? Because her father died of pollution-caused cancer! No, no. Let's twist that around. Let's say instead that her father used to spray the defoliant Agent Orange out of his helicopter in Vietnam. It never had any ill effect on him, but he has become increasingly despondent, knowing how much harm he might have done. No, no, let's twist it again. Nora only found out he sprayed Agent Orange by accident, overhearing him talk with some war buddies. When she challenged him, he answered with hostility, swearing that the chemical was harmless, and all the people claiming to have been damaged by the chemical are just trying to collect from the government to pay for health problems that have nothing to do with Vietnam. Now as she fights industrial pollution, she's really fighting her father—or, perhaps, trying to atone for his sin, though he refuses to admit he did anything wrong.

Isn't the character of Nora a lot more interesting now than she was when she was anti-pollution because her father died from it? Not that the death of a parent isn't good motivation. It's just too *easy*. "My father died of it," said Nora. It explains everything—it explains nothing. Do all the children of people who die from pollution go out and crusade against it? No. So we still haven't answered the question of why Nora reacted to her father's death by devoting her life to the crusade against pollution. The simple answer is never the complete answer.

To create effective persuasive or educational fiction, you must have believable, interesting characters. That means that you must be even more careful to make your characters balanced and well-rounded, not less so. If you're in doubt, go back to Chapter 1 and see how much you know about the character in each of the categories listed there. Go back to Chapter 2 and ask those questions of the character. The idea may be the source of your character, but it better not be the *only* source, or your story won't be either good fiction *or* good polemic.

# SERENDIPITY

There are many other chance sources of character ideas. You aren't necessarily looking for stories or characters, but because your idea net is out, you catch them anyway. Some people get ideas from dreams, some from news stories, a letter to Ann Landers, an anecdote from a history or biography, the headline on a supermarket tabloid, a line from a song. Sometimes characters seem to come out of nowhere—they just start talking inside your head.

In every case, you'll need to examine them carefully, invent them fully, help them come to life.

## Two Ideas from Unrelated Sources

It's important to remember that ideas don't have to come at the same time for them to belong together. I've often been struggling with a problem in one story, only to find the solution by remembering a character or idea from a completely unrelated story, one I may have worked on years and years before. For instance, the basic idea for my novel *Speaker for the Dead* was going nowhere until I realized that my title character had to be the main character from another story, *Ender's Game*. Suddenly I knew the character's past, knew *why* he was "speaking for the dead," and the story unfolded much more easily.

My experience is that I have never done well writing a story from one idea or developing a character from one source. Only when I put together two previously unrelated ideas or characters do they come to life; it is in the process of connecting the unconnected that my stories grow. This may be true for some of you, also.

## Wondering

You can help ideas come "by chance," however, by simply keeping your mind working—by often filling your mind with speculation. What if?

What if I lost my eyesight? What would I do then?

What if I accidentally threw away something priceless? Who might find it? How would *I* go about finding it? What could you possibly throw away without realizing it had value? A lottery ticket, of course. Anything else? A letter by someone famous. A priceless book. A jewel you thought was fake. An alien from another world who happened to look just like a paper clip. What then?

What if a person who had worked in an office all his life suddenly got assigned to work at home on a computer terminal, doing the same job without even leaving his house? How would his family respond? Would he miss the office life? Revel in the new freedom to determine his own schedule? Would his wife start expecting him to be a househusband while she continued going off to work?

Or look at the landscapes you drive through or live in or remember, or landscapes you've seen in *National Geographic*. Wonder about them. Who lives here? Who has died here? How did they die?

What do children do to play here? Where would they find books? What would they daydream about? What are they afraid of? Where do they refuse to go after dark? What do they dare each other to do?

What is likely to be the first job of a person who grows up around here? What do parents fear and hope for their children? Where do people shop or trade? What is the worst thing the weather here does to people?

Where do their kinfolk live? What songs do they hear coming through the window on a hot summer night? What do they smell? And how do they feel about the smells, the songs, the weather, their jobs, each other, themselves?

There isn't a landscape on earth where you can't find wonderful stories in the answers to these questions.

"Wonderful stories." Exactly the right word, *wonderful*.

The stories that fill a reader with wonder are the stories that came from a wondering mind, *your* mind, constantly speculating, exaggerating, questioning, challenging, twisting, searching. Good stories and characters will wander through, by and by. You'll find them in your idea net, and you'll breathe on them and bring them all to life.

# CHAPTER 4

# MAKING DECISIONS

SO FAR, I'VE BEEN TREATING CHARACTERS as if everything about them were negotiable. This is true, as long as the story still exists only in your head or in outline form. But at some point you're going to start writing the story down, and then you've got to make some decisions and stick to them.

## NAMES

One of the earliest decisions to make is a character's name. I have a friend who doesn't name his characters at all, until a story or novel is almost through. He just names them things like XXX and YYY. Then, when he knows them better, he decides what their names should be and uses his word processor's global search-and-replace command to turn all the XXXs into Marions and the YYYs into Ednas. That just wouldn't work for me. A name is part of who a person is. It's the label that stands for everything you've done and everything you are.

### *What a Name Means to the Character*

A name has many associations. Your last name links you to your family. If your character is a married adult, did he take his wife's name; did she take her husband's? If she's divorced, did she keep her husband's name or return to her maiden name? Or perhaps the character's parents were divorced, his mother got custody of the children, and she later remarried. Did he keep his birth father's name or take his stepfather's name? Surely these decisions had repercussions.

Your last name also suggests ethnicity. Wozniak does not have the same associations as O'Reilly, Bjornson, Redfeather, Goldfarb, Fitzwater, or Robles. The moment you choose a last name, you bring to the character a load of ethnic, national, even racial baggage. You will almost certainly find that the name opens up all kinds of character possibilities, inviting you to speculate on the character's upbringing. How much did his ethnicity make him who he is?

You might be named *for* someone, too. Is your character a junior or II? Named for an uncle, aunt, grandparent? He's going to have an attitude toward his own name in part based on his attitude toward the person he's named for. What about a girl growing up as Scarlett or Meryl, or a boy named Elvis or Lennon? Not only does the name tell when the character was probably born, it would also have caused a lot of teasing from other kids. Maybe the girl named Scarlett O'Hara Watt insisted that her friends call her So Watt, from her initials? The name is almost too cute to stand—but that, too, may be a part of her character.

Robert Parker's best-known character is named Edmund Spenser. He at once follows his name, being a lover of poetry, and rejects it, insisting that people call him Spenser. He insists on people spelling the name correctly, with a middle *s* instead of *c*; yet having a name like Edmund when he was growing up may be why he always regarded it as essential that he be in top physical condition and know how to fight. Indeed, most of Spenser's main character attributes seem linked to his name—it's quite possible, though I have no way of knowing, that the choice of the name Edmund Spenser was how Robert Parker came up with the idea for his character in the first place.

## You Can't Tell the Players Without a Program

There are other considerations involved in naming a character, however, besides the effect on the character himself. The name of a character is also the label the reader uses to help keep the characters straight. That's why it's always helpful to give characters memorable—and very different—names.

One rule I try to follow is to make sure all my major characters' names start with a different letter. I won't have a Myron in the same story with a Milton, unless there's some compelling reason to violate that rule.

I also try to vary lengths and sound patterns. It's hard for the reader to remember who is who if all the names follow the same pattern. Monosyllables like Bill, Bob, Tom, Jeff, Pete lead to boredom and confusion. These particular examples are such common-sounding names that the reader begins to feel that you gave these characters the first name that came to mind—it leads to a subliminal message that the characters' identities don't matter.

However, it also becomes distracting when you choose a lot of flamboyant, bizarre names, unless that is an important part of a story. If you're writing about a street gang, you might give them all odd nicknames like Mud-eater, Wall Man, Slime, and Lick. But you'll lose a lot of belief if all beautiful women in your stories have phony but euphonious names. And make sure your characters don't all have names that *mean* something, unless you are writing allegory and deliberately want them to be tagged with symbolic names, like the characters Patience, Will, and Angel in an allegorical fantasy I once wrote.

It's easy to fall into a rut, repeating the same patterns: Jackson, Waters, Deaver, Rudman. Change the number of syllables: Waters to Waterman. Change the accent position from the first to second syllable: Deaver to Despain. Start one name with a vowel instead of a consonant: Rudman to Urdman. Change one name so they don't all sound like WASPs: Jackson to Giaconni or Kabuto.

## One Name Per Character

Have you ever read a Russian novel? The Russian pattern of naming is different from ours—everybody has a first name, a family name, and a patronymic. Thus Ivan Denisovitch is Ivan the son of Denis—but the author might also refer to him by a completely unrelated name, like Dobrinin, which is his family name. The character might also have a nickname—and Russian authors feel no qualms about having characters refer to each other by any or all of the names in any combination, or so it seems. This is often hopelessly confusing to English-speaking readers.

Yet many a writer does exactly the same thing to his readers, with far less reason.

> Bill heard the all-stations siren and wondered whether he was going to get in trouble this time. Well, too late to worry now. Lieutenant Waterman would help him if he could, and if he couldn't, well, that was the breaks. He got out of his berth and put on his clothes.
>
> Johnson walked down the corridor until he got to the bridge of the ship. The executive officer was asking, "How much time do we have?"
>
> The captain quickly surveyed the situation. "About three minutes, I'd say. Not enough time to avoid a collision. But we've got to try. Hard port, full speed."
>
> Howard immediately relayed the command to the engine room, while his mentor made sure everyone else knew what to do.

OK, folks, guess: How many characters have we just seen? There are seven different names or tags here—yet this passage could just as easily refer to only two people. Lieutenant Howard Waterman is the executive officer of the ship; his mentor is Captain Bill Johnson.

This is an extreme example, but a lot of beginning writers (and some who should know better) make almost as bad a mess of naming.

The rule of thumb is that the narrator of the story will refer to each character the same way *every time*. You introduce the character by the name he's going to have most of the time through the story. For instance, you might decide to always refer to Captain Bill Johnson as Johnson. His junior officers, of course, will always call him Captain or Sir; his wife will call him Bill; his children will call him Dad. But the alert writer will make sure that we are constantly reminded who we're talking to. The first time somebody calls Johnson "Captain," make sure he calls him "Captain Johnson." From then on, the reader can make the connection. But "Captain Johnson" won't help if the only name we've seen so far is "Bill." It takes a little thought, but your job is to help your reader keep clear who is who, and you can't do that if you're busy playing musical chairs with the characters' names.

Sometimes amateurs play "musical names" because they're afraid that using the same name over and over again will become "repetitive."

What they don't realize is that repetition is rarely a problem with names—names aren't a stylistic device, they're a signpost to guide us through the story, telling us who's doing what. On those rare occasions when it really would be awkward to repeat the name, we already have a solution: the pronoun.

Sometimes amateurs play "musical names" because they're trying to convey information with the replacement nouns:

> Johnson went to the bridge. The captain barked his orders. The Annapolis graduate wasn't going to take any nonsense from these youngsters. A sixty-year-old has to fight to get respect in this navy, thought the grandfather of nine.

If it's vital for us to know that Johnson is a sixty-year-old Annapolis graduate who is captain of the ship and has nine grandchildren, then tell us—but don't do it by using all these taglines *instead* of Johnson's name:

> Johnson went to the bridge and barked his orders. He knew these youngsters didn't have much respect for a sixty-year-old like him; who cared anymore that he graduated first in his class from Annapolis? He knew that whenever he gave an order, his executive officer thought, "What's an old coot like him doing as captain of a ship? He ought to be sitting on a park bench boring people to death with pictures of his nine grandchildren."

The second version takes a little longer—but then, it conveys a lot more information and attitude as well, and you always know who Johnson is. Remember, if you lose clarity, you've lost your reader, and the consistent use of names is one of your chief tools in keeping the reader clear on what's happening in the story.

## KEEPING A BIBLE

Besides names, you'll make a lot of other decisions about your characters. Some you'll make before the story begins—a lot of facts about the character's past, about things he's going to do in the story, and so on. But you'll make many other decisions as you go along. And it will help you a great deal if, from time to time, you jot down these decisions.

For instance, when you showed the character getting dressed, you had him choose a striped tie. No particular reason—it was just a detail to give reality to his morning routine. Ten pages later, though, you forgot that. You have him pull his shirt off over his head before he goes in swimming—but not a word about loosening or removing his tie. Why did you forget? Because it isn't all that important, and because you wrote the first page three days ago, and because writers forget. We're human.

Most of your readers are human, too. But they're reading the story all at once, and for them page one and page ten are minutes apart, not days.

During the shooting of a movie, there's a person whose whole job is making sure that if an actor's cigarette was two inches long in the establishing shot, it's also two inches long in all the closeups and reaction shots. You don't have anybody to help with that. You have to do it for yourself.

The best way is to keep a bible—a notebook (or a separate computer file, if your computer allows you to open two files at once) in which you jot down each decision you've made. If it's too distracting to do this while writing, don't interrupt the flow; you can simply wait till you're through writing for the day and take a few minutes to scan through the day's output, jotting down all the things you've decided. The method I find best for me is to *begin* each day's work by scanning the work I did the day before, jotting down things I've decided on papers beside the computer. This not only helps me maintain consistency, it also gets me back into the story and makes me think about each decision, wondering if it was right, seeing if perhaps it makes me discover new things about the character.

The decisions you make aren't all as trivial as the color of a character's tie, either. When I wasn't creating a bible as I went along, I once changed a character's name between chapter 5 and chapter 15. I forgot that I made him an orphan and had him telephone his mother. I've changed a minor character's race, I've changed other characters' professions, I've changed my hero's hair color, age, height, birthday—it's easy to do when a character isn't the focus of the action or when a lot of pages have intervened.

Fortunately, editors—or my wife, Kristine, who reads everything in manuscript—have caught most of these mistakes. When they have, I've had to choose which version is correct. This has forced me to rethink many decisions that I had made arbitrarily, on the spur of the moment, and I've realized that many of these decisions were careless, that with a bit more thought I could come up with something much better. I had reached up and grabbed the first idea from my stock of cliches, when on second thought I was able to come up with a better decision that enriched the story and the character and brought them to life.

Keeping a bible helps make you aware of the decisions you're making. The very fact of jotting down your decision makes you think about it again, allows you a chance to do some wondering, some questioning. Whether you do it right at the moment, at the end of the day, or the next morning, you have a chance to improve on the decision while the story is still fresh, before you have gone ten or fifty or a hundred pages beyond that moment.

Even a bible, however, won't keep you from the occasional mistake, and for every decision you realize you're making, there are hundreds or thousands of others you'll never even notice. That's all right. The idea isn't to make every single aspect of storytelling a conscious decision—then no one would ever finish writing anything. Most of your decisions will remain unconscious. But the ones you *are* aware of allow you to open up your story with more invention, more possibilities, more space, more people for your unconscious mind to play with.

In fiction, necessity isn't the mother of invention. It's possible to have a career without inventing very much at all. You don't *have* to be inventive.

But the stories that astonish us, the characters that live forever in our memories—those are the result of rich imagination, perceptive observation, rigorous interrogation, and careful decision-making.

When it comes to storytelling, invention is the mother of astonishment, delight, and truth.

# PART II
# CONSTRUCTING
# CHARACTERS

# CHAPTER 5

# WHAT KIND OF STORY ARE YOU TELLING?

WHEN YOU INVENT A CHARACTER, YOU DEPEND on your sense of what is important and true to make your decisions. This will continue throughout your telling of the tale—but once you start setting down words, you also have to make many decisions based on what is right for the whole story. Now it's time for these newly created characters to get to work.

## THE "MICE" QUOTIENT

It is a mistake to think that "good characterization" is the same thing in every work of fiction. Different kinds of stories require different kinds of characters.

But what are the different kinds of stories? Forget about publishing genres for a moment—there isn't one kind of characterization for academic/literary stories, another kind for science fiction, and still others for westerns, mysteries, thrillers, and historicals. Instead we'll look at four basic factors that are present in every story, with varying degrees of emphasis. It is the balance among these factors that determines what sort of characterization a story *must* have, *should* have, or *can* have.

The four factors are *milieu*, *idea*, *character*, and *event*:

The *milieu* is the world surrounding the characters—the landscape, the interior spaces, the surrounding cultures the characters emerge from and react to; everything from weather to traffic laws.

The *idea* is the information that the reader is meant to discover or learn during the process of the story.

*Character* is the nature of one or more of the people in the story— what they do and why they do it. It usually leads to or arises from a conclusion about human nature in general.

The *events* of the story are everything that happens and why.

These factors usually overlap. Character A is part of the milieu surrounding character B. The idea in the story may include information about the nature of a character; the idea we are meant to discover can be some aspect of the milieu, some previously misunderstood or overlooked event, or the nature of a character. The events of the story are usually performed by characters or emerge from the milieu, and the discovery of an idea can also be an event in the tale.

Each factor is present in all stories, to one degree or another. Every factor has an implicit structure; if that factor dominates a story, its structure determines the overall shape of the story.

# MILIEU

It has become a figure of speech to say that a story "takes place." But it is quite true: The characters must have a place in which to perform the acts that make up the story—the setting, the milieu of the tale. The milieu includes all the *physical locations* that are used—one city or many cities, one building or many buildings, a street, a bus, a farm, a clearing in the woods—with all the sights, smells, and sounds that come with the territory. The milieu also includes the *culture*—the customs, laws, social roles, and public expectations that limit and illuminate all that a character thinks and feels and says and does.

In some stories the milieu is very sketchy; in others, it is created in loving detail. Indeed, there are some stories in which the milieu is the primary focus of attention. Think of *Gulliver's Travels* or *A Connecticut Yankee in King Arthur's Court*: The point of these stories is not to explore the soul of a character or resolve a tense and thrilling plot, but rather to explore a world that is different from our own, comparing it to our own customs and expectations.

The structure of the pure milieu story is simple: Get a character to the setting that the story is about, and then devise reasons for her to move through the world of the story, showing the reader all the interesting physical and social details of the milieu. When you've shown everything you want the reader to see, bring the character home.

In most pure milieu stories, the main character is a person from the writer's and readers' own time and place, so that the character will experience the world with the reader's attitudes and perceptions.

In a pure milieu story, the *less* you characterize the main character, the better. Her job is to stand in the place of all the readers. If you make the character too much of an individual, you draw the readers' attention to her and away from the milieu; instead, you want to keep the readers' attention on the milieu. So the main character's reactions to everything that happens must be as "normal" as possible (what the reader would expect *anybody* to do in those circumstances). The character might have a wry humor or a particular slant to her observations, but the more you call attention to the character, the less the story tends to be about the milieu.

Few stories, however, are "pure" milieu stories. Travelogues, utopian fiction, satires, and natural science tend to be the only genres in which the pure milieu story can be found. More often, stories emphasize milieu but develop other story factors as well. Although the setting might be the primary focus, there is also a strong story line. The reader then absorbs the milieu indirectly. In these stories, the major characters don't have to come from the readers' own time; usually, in fact, they'll be permanent residents of the story's milieu. The characters' own attitudes and expectations are part of the cultural ambience, and their very strangeness and unfamiliarity is part of the readers' experience of the milieu.

Such stories will seem to have the structure of another kind of tale—but the author will reveal that the milieu is a main concern by the close attention paid to the surroundings. The characters will be chosen, not just for their intrinsic interest, but also because they typify certain kinds or classes of people within the culture. The characters are meant to fascinate us, not because we understand them or share their desires, but because of their strangeness, and what they can teach us about an alien culture.

This kind of story is fairly common in science fiction and fantasy, where the milieu, the world of the story, is often the main attraction. Frank Herbert (*Dune*), and J.R.R. Tolkien (*The Lord of the Rings*) are most noted for works in which the story line is not tightly structured and the characters tend to be types rather than individuals, yet the milieu is carefully, lovingly drawn. In such milieu stories the author feels free to digress from the main story line with long passages of explanation, description, or depiction of the culture. The reader who isn't interested in the milieu will quickly become bored and set the story aside; but the reader who is fascinated by the world of the story will read on, rapt, through pages of songs and poetry and rituals and ordinary daily life.

How much characterization does a milieu story need? Not very much. Most characters need only be stereotypes within the culture of the milieu, acting out exactly the role their society expects of them, with perhaps a few eccentricities that help move the story along. It is no accident that when Tolkien assembled the Fellowship of the Ring in his *The Lord of the Rings* trilogy, there was only one dwarf and one elf—had there been more, it would have been nearly impossible to tell them apart, just as few readers can remember the difference between the two generic hobbits Merry and Pippin. Because *The Lord of the Rings* was not a pure milieu story, there are some heroic major characters who are more than local stereotypes, and some that approach full characterization—but characterization simply isn't a major factor in the appeal of the book.

Besides science fiction and fantasy, milieu stories often crop up in academic/literary fiction ("This story absolutely *is* contemporary suburban life") and historical fiction (though most historicals nowadays focus on the romance rather than the setting), while milieu plays an important role in many thrillers. Milieu is the entire definition of the western.

Are you writing a milieu story? Is it mostly the setting that you work on in loving detail? That doesn't mean that you can ignore character, especially if you're trying to tell a compelling story within the milieu; but it does mean that a lot of fully drawn characters aren't really necessary to your story, and might even be distracting.

# IDEA

The idea story has a simple structure. A problem or question is posed at the beginning of the story, and at the end of the tale the answer is revealed. Murder mysteries use this structure: Someone is found murdered, and the rest of the story is devoted to discovering who did it, why, and how. Caper stories also follow the idea story structure: A problem is posed at the beginning (a bank to rob, a rich and dangerous mark to con), the main character or characters devise a plan, and we read on to find out if their plan is in fact the "answer" to the problem. Invariably something goes wrong and the characters have to improvise, but the story is over when the problem is solved.

How much characterization is needed? In puzzle or locked-room mysteries, there is no need for characterization at all; most authors use only a few eccentricities to "sweeten" the characters, particularly the detective.

In classic English mysteries, like those of Agatha Christie, characterization rarely goes beyond the requirement that a fairly large group of people must have enough of a motive for murder that each can legitimately be suspected of having committed the crime. .

The American detective novel tends to demand a little more characterization. The detective himself is usually more than a tight little bundle of eccentricities; instead, he responds to the people around him, not as pieces to be fitted into the puzzle, but as sad or dangerous or good or pathetic human beings. Such tales, like those of Raymond Chandler or Ross MacDonald, require the detective to be a keen observer of other people, and their individual natures often twist and turn the story line. However, such characters—including the detective—are rarely *changed*; the story only *reveals* who they are. In these novels, the characters' true natures are among the questions that the detective—and the reader—tries to answer during the course of the story.

Caper stories, on the other hand, generally don't require that their characters be much more than charming or amusing, and only rarely is there any attempt to show a character being transformed by the events in the tale.

In fact, it is the very lack of change in the characters in mystery, detective, and caper stories that allows writers to use the same characters over and over again, to the delight of their readers. A few writers have fairly recently tried to change that, developing and changing their detective characters from book to book. But that very process of change can end up severely limiting the future possibilities of the character.

When the title character of Gregory Mcdonald's *Fletch* series became very rich, it made it very difficult to put him in situations where he actually *needed* to solve a mystery; Mcdonald finally resorted to writing the prequels *Fletch Won* and *Fletch, Too,* which took place *before* Fletch got rich, and has announced his intention to stop writing Fletch novels.

Robert Parker took his character Spenser even further, showing him with ongoing and developing relationships, with friendships and transformations that begin in one book and are not forgotten in the next. The result, however, has been a tendency in recent years to reach for increasingly far-fetched plots or to repeat story lines from the past. It's *hard* to do full, rich characterization in an idea story.

Don't get me wrong, though—I don't think it's a mistake to attempt full characterization in idea stories; Fletch and Spenser are two of my favorite mystery characters precisely because of the richer-than-normal characterization and the possibility of permanent change. You simply need to recognize that if you choose to do full characterization in an idea story, complete with character transformation, there is a price.

There are idea stories in other genres, of course. Many a science fiction story follows the idea structure perfectly: Characters are faced with a problem—a malfunctioning spaceship is one of the favorites—and, as with a caper, the story consists of finding a plan to solve the problem and carrying it out, with improvisations as needed. Characterization is not needed, except to make the characters entertaining—eccentricity is usually enough.

Allegory is a form in which the idea is everything. The author has composed the story according to a plan; the reader's job is to decode the plan. Characters in allegory are rarely more than figures standing for ideas. While allegory is rarely written today, many writers of academic/literary fiction use symbolism in much the same way—characters exist primarily to stand for an idea, and readers must decode the symbolic structure in order to receive the story.

Does all this mean that idea stories require "bad" characterization? Not at all. It means that appropriate characterization for an idea story is not necessarily the same thing as appropriate characterization for another kind of story. Characters stand for ideas, or exist primarily to discover them; a character who fulfills her role perfectly may be no more than a stereotype or a bundle of eccentricities, and yet she'll be characterized perfectly for that story.

# CHARACTER

The character story is about a person trying to change his role in life. It begins at the point when the main character finds his present situation intolerable and sets out to change; it ends when the character either finds a new role, willingly returns to the old one, or despairs of improving his lot.

What is a character's "role"? It is his network of relationships with other people and with society at large. My role in life is father to my children—with a different relationship with each; husband to my wife; son and brother to the family I grew up with. I have a complex relationship with each of the literary communities I write for, with the full assortment of fans and critics; I also have a constantly shifting role within my religious community, for which I also write. Like every other human being, I have some interests and longings that aren't satisfied within the present pattern of my life, but in most cases I foresee ways of fulfilling those desires within the reasonably near future. All of these relationships, together, are my "role in life." I'm reasonably content with my life; it would be difficult to write a character story about me, because stories about happy people are boring.

The character story emerges when some part of a character's role in life becomes unbearable. A character dominated by a vicious, whimsical parent or spouse; an employee who has become discontented with his job, with growing distaste for the people he works with; a mother weary of her nurturing role and longing for respect from adults; a career criminal consumed by fear and longing to get away; a lover whose partner has been unfaithful and can't bear to live with the betrayal. The impossible situation may have been going on for some time, but the story does not begin until the situation comes to a head—until the character reaches the point where the cost of staying becomes too high a price to pay.

Sometimes the protagonist of a character story cuts loose from the old role very easily, and the story consists of a search for a new one. Sometimes the new role is easy to envision, but breaking away from the old bonds is very hard to do. "Cutting loose" doesn't always mean physically leaving—the most complex and difficult character stories are the ones about people who try to change a relationship without abandoning the person.

Needless to say, the character story is the one that requires the fullest characterization. No shortcuts are possible. Readers must understand the character in the original, impossible role, so that they comprehend and, usually, sympathize with the decision to change. Then the character's changes must be justified so that the reader never doubts that the change is possible; you can't just have a worn-out hooker suddenly go to college without showing us that the hunger for education and the intellectual ability to pursue it have always been part of her character.

Remember, though, that not all the people in a character story must be fully characterized. The protagonist—the character whose change is the subject of the story—must be fully characterized; so, too, must each person whose relationship with the protagonist is part of his need for change or his new and satisfactory role. But other people in the story will be characterized less fully, just as in many milieu, idea, and event stories. Characterization is not a virtue, it is a technique; you use it when it will enhance your story, and when it won't, you don't.

# EVENT

Every story is an event story in the sense that from time to time something happens that has causes and results. But the story in which the events are the central concern follows a particular pattern: The world is somehow out of order—call it imbalance, injustice, breakdown, evil, decay, disease—and the story is about the effort to restore the old order or establish a new one.

The event story structure is simple: It begins when the main characters become involved in the effort to heal the world's disease, and ends when they either accomplish their goal or utterly fail to do so.

The world's disorder can take many forms. It can be a crime unpunished or unavenged: *The Count of Monte Cristo* is a prime example, as is *Oedipus Rex*. The disorder can be a usurper—Macbeth, for instance—who has stolen a place that doesn't belong to him, or a person who has lost his true position in the world, like Prince Edward in *The Prince and the Pauper*. The disorder can be an evil force, bent on destruction, like Sauron in *The Lord of the Rings* or Lord Foul in *The Chronicles of Thomas Covenant The Unbeliever*—that is also the way Nazis, Communists, and terrorists are often used in thrillers. The disorder can be an illicit love that cannot be allowed to endure and yet cannot be denied, as in *Wuthering Heights* and the traditional stories of Lancelot and Guinevere or Tristan and Isolde. The disorder can be a betrayal of trust, as in the medieval romance *Havelok the Dane*—or the romance of Watergate that was enacted in America's newspapers and television news during the early 1970s.

I think that the event story—the structure at the heart of the romantic tradition for more than two thousand years—might well be the reason for the existence of Story itself. It arises out of the human need to make sense of the things happening around us; the event story starts with the assumption that some sort of order should exist in the world, and our very belief in order in fiction helps us to create order in reality.

How important is characterization in the event story? Most of the time, it's up to the author. It's possible to tell a powerful event story in which the characters are nothing more than what they do and why they do it—we can come out of such tales feeling as if we know the character because we have lived through so much with her, even though we've learned almost nothing about the other aspects of her character. (Although Lancelot, for instance, is a major actor in the Arthurian legends, he's seldom been depicted as a complex individual beyond the simple facts of his relationship to Arthur and to Guinevere.) Yet it is also possible to characterize several people in the story without at all interfering with the forward movement of the tale. In fact, the process of inventing characters often introduces more story possibilities, so that event and character both grow.

# THE CONTRACT WITH THE READER

Whenever you tell a story, you make an implicit contract with the reader. Within the first few paragraphs or pages, you tell the reader implicitly what kind of story this is going to be; the reader then knows what to expect, and holds the thread of that structure throughout the tale.

If you begin with a murder, for instance, and focus on those characters who have reason to find out how, why, and by whom the murder was committed, the reader can reasonably expect that the story will continue until those questions are answered—the reader expects an idea story.

If, on the other hand, you begin with the murder victim's wife, concentrating on how widowhood has caused a sudden, unbearable disruption in the patterns of her life, the reader can fairly expect that the story will use the character structure, following the widow until she finds an acceptable new role for herself.

Choosing one structure does not preclude using another. For instance, in the first version of the story, the murder mystery, you can also follow the widow's attempts to find a new role for herself. The reader will gladly follow that story line as a subplot, and will be delighted if you resolve it along with the mystery. However, the reader would feel cheated if you began the novel as a mystery, but ended it when the widow falls in love and remarries—without ever solving the mystery at all! You can do that once, perhaps, for effect—but readers will feel, rightly, that you misled them.

On the other hand, if you establish at the beginning of the story that it is about the widow herself and her search for a new role in life, you can also weave the mystery into the story line as a subplot; if you do, readers will expect you to resolve the mystery, but they won't regard that as the climax of the story. They would rightly be outraged if you ended the book with the explanation of the mystery—and left the widow still in a state of flux.

The rule of thumb is this: Readers will expect a story to end when the first major source of structural tension is resolved. If the story begins as an idea story, the reader expects it to end when the idea is discovered, the plan unfolded. If the story begins as a milieu story, readers will gladly follow any number of story lines of every type, letting them be resolved here and there as needed, continuing to read in order to discover more of the milieu. A story that begins with a character in an intolerable situation will not feel finished until the character is fully content or finally resigned. A story that begins with an unbalanced world will not end until the world is balanced, justified, reordered, healed—or utterly destroyed beyond hope of restoration.

It's as if you begin the story by pushing a boulder off the top of a hill. No matter what else happens before the end of the story, the reader will not be satisfied until the boulder comes to rest somewhere.

That is your first contract with the reader—you will end what you began. Digressions will be tolerated, to a point; but digressions will almost never be accepted as a substitute for fulfilling the original contract.

You also make a second contract all the way through a story: Anything you spend much time on will amount to something in the story. I remember seeing one of Bob Hope's and Bing Crosby's road movies when I was a child—*The Road to Rio*, I think. In it, the director constantly interrupts the main story to show Jerry Colonna, their mustachioed comic sidekick, leading a troop of mounted soldiers to rescue our heroes. In the end, however, the story is completely resolved without Colonna's cavalry ever arriving. The director cuts one last time to Colonna, who pulls his horse to a stop, looks at the camera, and says something like, "It didn't amount to anything, but it *was* thrilling, wasn't it?" It was very funny—but the humor rested entirely on the fact that when a story spends time on a character, an event, a question, or a setting, the audience expects that the main thread of the story will somehow be affected by it.

Examine your story, either in your head, in outline, or in draft form. What is it that most interests you? Where are you spending the most time and effort? Are you constantly researching or inventing more details about the setting? Is it the detailed unraveling of the mystery that fascinates you? Do you constantly find yourself exploring a character? Or is it the actual events that you care about most? Your story will work best when you use the structure demanded by the factor that you care most about.

If you love the mystery, structure the tale as an idea story—begin with the question and devote the bulk of your story time to answering it. If you care most about the milieu, let the reader know it from the start by beginning with a character's arrival in the new world (how long does it take Alice to get down the rabbit hole or through the looking glass into Wonderland?) or by concentrating on the details of the place and culture; then spend the bulk of your time discovering the wonders and curiosities of the milieu. If you care most about a character, begin with his or her dilemma and spend the bulk of your time on the effort toward change. If you care most about the events, begin at the point where the characters become involved with the world's sickness, and spend the bulk of your time in the story on their efforts to restore balance.

The techniques and structures of the other story factors are always available to you for subplots or complications, but keep them in a relatively subordinate position. In *The Lord of the Rings*, there are several event stories going on within the overall milieu story—Aragorn, the out-of-place king, coming to take his rightful throne; Denethor, the steward who reached for power beyond his ability to control, threatening the safety of the kingdom and the life of his son until Gandalf finally succeeds in stopping him; Frodo, Samwise, and Gollum, the three hobbit ringbearers, in their twisted, braided paths to the cracks of doom where, by casting in the ring, they will be able to put an end to the evil, destructive power of Sauron.

Yet when all these story lines are resolved, the reader is not disappointed to find that the story goes on. Tolkien begins a completely new story line, the Scouring of the Shire, which is related to the other stories but is barely hinted at until the hobbits actually come home.

Even then the tale is not done—Tolkien still has to show us Frodo sailing west, along with the elves who can no longer live in Middle Earth, at least not in their former glory. Was this the resolution of a question raised at the beginning of the book? No. Nor was it the resolution of a character dilemma—Frodo was quite content when the story began. And Frodo's and the elves' presence in Middle Earth was not, when the story began, a disequilibrium that needed to be resolved.

So why are we still reading? Because *The Lord of the Rings* is a milieu story. The author establishes from the beginning that he is going to spend large amounts of time simply exploring the world of Middle Earth. We are going to have detailed accounts of birthday parties, village life, customs and habits of the people; we will visit with Tom Bombadil, who has almost nothing to do with the story, but has everything to do with the underlying mythos of Middle Earth; we linger with the Ents, we pass through the Mines of Moria, we visit with the Riders of Rohan, travel with the legendary dead; and while Tolkien weaves all these places and peoples into a story that is generally interesting, sometimes creating characters we care about, there is no story line or character that becomes our sole reason for reading. It is the world itself that Tolkien cared most about, and so the audience for the story is going to be those readers who also come to love the world of Middle Earth. So it is no accident that the story does not end until we see, clearly, that Middle Earth has ceased to exist as it was—we are entering a new age, and the milieu we were exploring is now closed.

All the MICE factors are present in *The Lord of the Rings*, but it is the milieu structure that predominates, as it should. It would be absurd to criticize *The Lord of the Rings* for not having plot unity and integrity, because it is not an event story. Likewise, it would be absurd to criticize the book for its stereotyped one-to-a-race characters or for the many characters about whom we learn little more than what they do in the story and why they do it, because this is not a character story. In fact, we should probably praise Tolkien for having done such a good job of working creditable story lines and the occasional identifiable character into a story that was, after all, about Something Else.

I'm dwelling on these structural matters at some length because this is a book on characterization, and for us writers to characterize *well*, we must characterize *appropriately*.

Character stories really came into their own at the beginning of the twentieth century, and both the novelty and the extraordinary brilliance of some of the writers who worked with this story structure have led many critics and teachers to believe that only this kind of story can be "good." This may be a true judgment for many individuals—that is, the only kind of story they enjoy is the character story—but it is not true in the abstract, for the other kinds of stories have long traditions, with many examples of brilliance along the way.

However, character stories have been so dominant that they have forced storytellers in the other traditions to pay more attention to characterization. Even though a story may follow the idea, milieu, or event structure, many readers expect a deeper level of characterization. The story is not *about* a transformation of character, but the readers still expect to get to know the characters; and even when they don't expect it, they are willing to allow the author to devote a certain amount of attention to character without regarding it as a digression. This is the fashion of our time, and you can't disregard it.

But it's a mistake to think that deep, detailed characterization is an absolute virtue in storytelling. You have to look at your own reason for telling a story. If it's the puzzle—the idea—that attracts you, then that will probably be the factor in your story that you handle best; your natural audience will consist of readers who also care most about the idea. A certain amount of attention to characterization may help broaden your audience and increase your readers' pleasure in the story, but if you go into characterization as an unpleasant chore, something you must do in order to be a "good writer," chances are your characterization will be mechanical and ineffective, and instead of broadening your audience, it will interfere with your story. If you don't care about or believe in a character's deepest drives and troubled past, neither will your readers.

So if you choose not to devote much time to characterization in a particular story, this won't necessarily mean you "failed" or "wrote badly." It may mean that you understand yourself and your story.

And because you chose to tell one story in which characterization played a lesser role doesn't mean you "can't characterize." A good understanding of characterization includes knowing when it's appropriate to concentrate on character—and when it isn't.

# CHAPTER 6

# THE HIERARCHY

NOT ALL CHARACTERS ARE CREATED EQUAL.

In earlier chapters we've talked about major and minor characters, without defining the terms. You must know—and let your readers know—which characters are most important to the story, so they'll know which are worth following and caring about, and which will quickly disappear.

It's hard to measure the exact importance of a character—importance doesn't come in quarts or by the inch. But there are three general levels of importance, and the distinctions can be useful.

1. Walk-ons and placeholders. You won't develop these characters at all; they're just people in the background, meant to lend realism or perform a simple function and then disappear, forgotten.

2. Minor characters. These characters may make a difference in the plot, but we aren't supposed to get emotionally involved with them, either negatively or positively. We don't expect them to keep showing up in the story. Their desires and actions might cause a twist in the story, but play no role in shaping its ongoing flow. In fact, a rule of thumb is that a minor character does one or two things in the story and then disappears.

3. Major characters. This group includes the people we care about; we love them or hate them, fear them or hope they succeed. They show up again and again in the story. The story is, to one degree or another, about them, and we expect to find out what happens to them by the end. Their desires and actions drive the story forward and carry it through all its twists and turns.

Remember, though, that there is no wall dividing one level from the others. In your story, Pete and Nora may be the main characters, but their friends Morry and Dolores and Pete's boss Edgar and Nora's brother Shawn are also fairly major, and we expect to know more about them; and then there's Pete's secretary and the doorman, who both do some pretty important things in the story, though we aren't aware of deep personal dilemmas in their lives; and we certainly will remember the weird taxi driver and the Indian cop and . . .

So where is the dividing line between major and minor? There isn't one. But we know that Pete and Nora are the most important; Morry, Dolores, Edgar, and Shawn are somewhat important; Pete's secretary and the doorman are somewhat important but still pretty minor; and the weird taxi driver and the Indian cop are definitely minor but certainly not mere walk-ons. The different levels shade into each other. And as you master the techniques appropriate to each level, you'll be able to create each character at exactly the level of importance the story requires.

# WALK-ONS AND PLACEHOLDERS

Unless your story takes place in a hermitage or a desert island, your main characters are surrounded by many people who are utterly unimportant in the story. They are background; they are part of the milieu. Here are a few samples that show what I mean.

Nora accidentally gave the cabby a twenty for a five-dollar ride and then was too shy to ask for change. Within a minute a skycap had the rest of her money.

Pete checked at the desk for his messages. There weren't any, but the bellman did have a package for him.

People started honking their horns before Nora even knew there was a traffic jam.

Apparently some suspicious neighbor had called the cops. The uniform who arrested him wasn't interested in Pete's explanations, and he soon found himself at the precinct headquarters.

Notice how many people we've "met" in these few sentences. A cabby, a skycap, a hotel desk clerk, a bellman, horn-honkers in a traffic jam, a suspicious neighbor, a uniformed police officer. Every single one of these people is designed to fulfill a brief role in the story and then vanish completely out of sight.

## Part of the Scenery

How do you make people vanish? Any stage director knows the trick. You have a crowd of people on stage, most of them walk-ons. They have to be there because otherwise the setting wouldn't be realistic—but you don't want them to distract the audience's attention. In effect, you want them to be like scenery. They really aren't characters at all—they're movable pieces of milieu.

So you dress them in drab or similar clothing, and make your main characters' costumes contrast sharply with the crowd. If possible, you make the walk-ons hold absolutely still; if they have to move, you make them move as smoothly and gently as possible. You do not allow them to make noise except when you want general crowd noises. You make them keep their attention riveted either on their own quiet task or on the main action of the scene. You turn them so they're facing generally upstage. You never let any one walk-on stay on stage for very long, or the audience starts expecting him to do something.

The surest way for a walk-on to get himself fired from a play is to become "creative"—to start fidgeting or doing some clever bit of stage business that distracts attention from the main action of the scene. Unless, of course, this is one of those rare occasions when the walk-on's new business is brilliantly funny—in which case, you might even pay him more and elevate the part.

You have the same options in fiction. If a character who isn't supposed to matter starts getting out of hand, distracting from the main thread of the story, you either cut her out entirely, or you figure out why you as a writer were so interested in her that you've spent more time on her than you meant to, and revise the story to make her matter more.

Most of the time, though, you want your walk-ons to disappear. You want them to fade back and be part of the scenery, part of the milieu. How do you do it in fiction?

## Stereotypes

We talked about stereotypes in Chapter 1, and I told you then that sometimes stereotyping would be exactly the tool of characterization you need.

This is the time.

A stereotype is a character who is a typical member of a group. He does exactly what the readers expect him to do. Therefore they take no notice of him—he disappears into the background.

As ordinary human beings, we may not *like* a particular stereotype if we happen to be the member of a group we think is viewed unfairly. But as writers, writing to our own community, we can't help but be aware of and use our community stereotypes in order to make placeholding characters behave exactly according to expectations.

If we think that a particular stereotype is unfair to the group it supposedly explains, then we're free to deliberately violate the stereotype. But the moment we do that, we have made the character strange, which will make him attract the readers' attention. He will no longer simply disappear—he isn't a walk-on anymore. He has stepped forward out of the milieu and joined the story.

## MINOR CHARACTERS

There's nothing wrong with a background character violating stereotype and attracting attention—as long as you realize that he isn't part of the background anymore. The readers will notice him, and they'll expect his strangeness to amount to something.

The audience still isn't supposed to care much about him; he isn't expected to play a continuing role in the story. He might be momentarily involved in the action, but then he'll disappear. Still, his individuality will set a mood, add humor, make the milieu more interesting or complete. The way to make such characters instantly memorable without leading the audience to expect them to do more is to make them eccentric, exaggerated, or obsessive.

## Eccentricity

Remember the movie *Beverly Hills Cop*? There were hundreds of place-holders in that film—thugs who shot at cops, cops who got shot at, people milling around in the hotel lobby, people at the hotel desk. They all acted exactly as you would expect them to act. They vanished. Unless you personally knew an actor who played one of the walk-ons, you don't remember any of them.

But I'll bet that as you walked out of the theater, you remembered Bronson Pinchot. Not by name, of course, not then. He was the desk attendant in the art gallery. You know, the one with the effeminate manner and the weird foreign accent. He had absolutely nothing to do with the story—if he had been a mere placeholder, you would never have noticed anything was missing. So why do you remember him?

It wasn't that he had a foreign accent. In southern California, a Spanish accent would merely have stereotyped him; he would have disappeared.

It wasn't his effeminacy. The audience would merely see him as a stereotypical homosexual. Again, he would disappear.

But the effeminacy and the accent were combined—the "foreigner" stereotype and the "effete homosexual" stereotype are rarely used together, and so the audience was surprised. What's more important, though, is that the accent was an *eccentric* one, completely unexpected. Pinchot based his accent on the speech of an Israeli he once knew; the accent was so rare that almost no one in the audience recognized it. It was a genuinely novel way to speak. He was not just a foreigner, he was a strange and effeminate foreigner. Furthermore, Pinchot's reactions to Eddie Murphy—the hint of annoyance, superiority, snottiness in his tone—made him even more eccentric. Eccentric enough to stick in our minds.

How memorable was he? From that bit part, he went directly into the TV series *Perfect Strangers*. Which goes to show that you can still parlay a bit part into a career.

And yet in *Beverly Hills Cop*, though we remembered him, we never expected his character to be important in the story. He existed only for a few laughs and to make Eddie Murphy's Detroit-cop character feel even more alien in L.A. Pinchot managed to steal the scene—to get his promotion from walk-on—without distorting the story. He was funny, but he made no great difference in the way the story went. He simply amused us for a moment.

Since he was a minor character, that was exactly what he needed to be. Likewise, in your stories you need to realize that your minor characters should *not* be deeply and carefully characterized. Like flashbulbs, they need to shine once, brightly, and then get tossed away.

## Exaggeration

Another way to make a minor character flash. You take a normal human trait, and make it just a little—or sometimes a lot—more extreme, like the character Sweet-Face in *Butch Cassidy and the Sundance Kid*. Butch and the Kid are in a whorehouse; the Pinkerton detectives ride up on the street below. There we see a pudgy-faced character who looks like the soul of innocence and believability. Butch tells Sundance a brief story about him—that with Sweet-Face covering for them, they're safe, because everybody believes him. His innocent look is an exaggeration, but sure enough, when Sweet-Face points out of town, as if to say "they went thataway," the Pinkertons take off in that direction.

A few moments later, the Pinkertons ride back, confront Sweet-Face again; Sweet-Face panics and points straight toward the room where Butch and the Kid are watching. His panic and betrayal are as exaggerated as his innocence was before. He sticks in the memory, and yet we never expected him to be important again in the plot.

## Obsessiveness

Let's go back to the example I gave before, of Nora's cabby, the one she paid a twenty for a five-dollar ride. The stereotypical reaction—"Hey, thanks, lady"—is so ordinary we can omit it entirely. But what if the cabdriver is obsessive?

"What is it, you trying to impress me? Trying to show me you're big time? Well, don't suck ego out of *me*, lady! I only take what I *earn!*"

Nora had no time for this. She hurried away from the cab. To her surprise, he jumped out and followed her, shouting at her with as much outrage as she'd expect if she hadn't paid him at all. "You can't do this to me in America!" he shouted. "I'm a Protestant, you never heard of the Protestant work ethic?"

Finally she stopped. He caught up with her, still scolding. "You can't do your rich-lady act with me, you hear me?"

"Shut up," she said. "Give me back the twenty." He did, and she gave him a five. "There," she said. "Satisfied?"

His mouth hung open; he looked at the five in utter disbelief. "What *is* this!" he said. "No tip?"

Now, that's a guy who won't let go. If you saw that scene in a movie or even read it in a novel, chances are you'd remember the cabdriver. Yet you wouldn't expect him to be important in the plot. If he showed up again it would be for more comic relief, not for anything important. For instance, when the story is all but over and Nora is coming home with Pete for a well-earned rest, it could be funny if they get in a cab and it turns out to be the same driver. The audience would remember him well enough for that. But they would be outraged if the cabdriver turned out to be an assassin or a long-lost cousin.

This would *not* be true, however, if this were the first scene in the story. At the beginning of the story, all the characters are equal—we don't know any of them at all. So if in fact you wanted to tell the story of how Nora got involved with this obsessive-compulsive cabdriver—or how the cabdriver managed to get Nora's attention so he could start dating her—this would be a pretty good beginning.

The other side of that coin is that if the cabdriver is in fact supposed to be minor, you could *not* begin the story with this scene. If these were the first five paragraphs of the story, we would naturally expect that the story was going to be *about* Nora and the cabby, and when Nora goes on through the story without ever seeing or even thinking of the cabdriver again, at some point many readers are going to ask, What was that business with the cabdriver all about?

This is because much of what makes the difference between major and minor characters is the amount of time you spend on them. And the amount of time is not absolute—it is relative to the total length of the story. In a 1,500-word story, this 150-word section would be 10 percent of the total—and that's a lot. In an 80,000-word novel, this 150-word section would be almost vanishingly brief. So the cabby would seem more important in a short story than in a novel.

However, if this scene comes at the *beginning* of a story, so that the reader doesn't know yet what the story is about, then the cabby is present in the entire 150 words of the story's first scene. At that point he seems to the reader to be almost as important as Nora—he is diminished only by the fact that he is not named and Nora is the point-of-view character. The reader has every reason to expect that the cabby will amount to something.

This is why it's a good idea to introduce at least a few major characters first, so that the first characters the reader meets—the characters who occupy 100 percent of the opening—really will turn out to matter to the story.

## MAJOR CHARACTERS

By now it should be obvious that the major characters are the ones who really matter, the ones the story is, to one degree or another, *about*. Their choices turn the story, their needs drive the story forward.

These are also the characters who most need to be characterized. Because they really matter to the story, you can devote as much time to them as strong characterization might require, and the rest of this book is devoted to showing you exactly how to do full characterization.

There are other cues you use to let the audience know which characters are major, besides the raw amount of time devoted to characterization:

### *Choices*

If a character is relatively powerful—powerful enough to make choices that change other characters' lives—the audience will remember her better and expect her to amount to something more in the story. If the other characters all regard a character as dangerous or powerful, the readers will, too.

## Focus

This leads to one of the most effective theatrical techniques for making the audience notice a character—have everyone on stage *look* at him, *listen* to him, or *talk about him* behind his back. If you do enough of this, you never have to bring the character on stage. We never see the title character in *Waiting for Godot*, for instance, and yet he is arguably the most important character in the play, and his failure to arrive is the most important "event."

You can use the same technique in fiction to focus the readers' attention on a character whether he's present or not. In *The Lord of the Rings*, the character of Sauron appears in person only once; beyond that, he personally intervenes in the story only a handful of times. Yet he is the engine driving almost every plot thread, the focus of everyone's attention far more often than any other character. The result is that readers "remember" Sauron as one of the most important characters in *The Lord of the Rings*—even though he almost never appears in the story at all.

## Frequency of Appearance

If a character keeps coming back, even if she's not all that exciting or powerful, we begin to expect her to do something important—or else why would the writer keep bringing her up? This is why, when movie stars are evaluating a script, they'll keep track of how many scenes their character will be in. If they aren't in enough scenes, they won't loom large enough in the audience's mind—and therefore the film won't be a "star vehicle."

Sometimes a character who should remain minor will keep coming back just because of her job—a bartender at the club where two major characters regularly meet, for instance. Then you need to reduce her importance—have her say very little, or have substitute bartenders show up on her night off, something to let the reader know that it doesn't matter much whether the bartender is there or not.

## Action

A character doesn't have to appear all that often, as long as every time he *does* appear, what he says and does has an important effect on the plot. On the other hand, a character who is often present but does almost nothing can quickly fade in the readers' memory. In the play *Romeo and Juliet*, Romeo spends a lot of time with his two friends, Benvolio and Mercutio. In fact, as I remember it Benvolio is present in more scenes than Mercutio, including the first scene in which we see Romeo himself. Yet Benvolio is completely forgettable, while Mercutio is one of the most memorable characters in the play. Why? Because Benvolio never does anything but listen to people and make a few bland comments, while Mercutio is flamboyant and provocative and funny and outrageous, and when he is onstage he either incites or is deeply involved in every action.

Rule of thumb: Passive characters will not seem as important as active characters.

## Sympathy

In another chapter I'll discuss techniques for making characters likable or sympathetic; for now, it's enough to say that the more endearing or charming a character is, the more the audience comes to like her as a human being, the more important that character will be to the audience, and the more they'll expect to see what becomes of her.

## Point of View

One of the most potent devices for making a character important to your readers is to use the character's point of view. The third part of this book is devoted to explaining point of view, so this will be only a brief reference. Rule of thumb: When a character in the story is used as the narrator or viewpoint character, his importance is greatly increased.

There are also some variables that are out of your control. A character might be extremely important to some readers because they think they resemble him, or because the character resembles someone they love or hate. Or a character you think of as important may seem unimportant to some readers because they have seen too many characters like him—to them, the character has become a cliche. In fact, if your story is very popular, it is likely to be imitated—and the fact that the market is flooded with imitations of your best character will soon make your character feel like an imitation, too, even though he's the original!

But since these things are generally out of your control, you can't very well use them to help you establish your hierarchy of characters. The techniques you *can* control are:

    Ordinariness vs. strangeness
    The amount of time devoted to the character
    The character's potential for making meaningful choices
    Other characters' focus on him
    The character's frequency of appearance
    The character's degree of involvement in the action
    Readers' sympathy for the character
    Narration from the character's point of view

As you use these techniques to varying degrees with the many characters in your story, an unconscious ranking of the characters will emerge in the readers' minds, starting with the least important background characters, moving up through the minor characters, to the major characters, and finally to two or three main characters or a single protagonist—the people or person the story is mostly about.

Chances are you won't be fully aware of the hierarchy of characters in your own story—it's almost impossible for a storyteller to have all these techniques completely under conscious control. But if you find that readers seem not to notice a character you think is important, or if a character starts "taking over" the story when you don't want him to, you can use these techniques to adjust the character's relative importance. And when these techniques *are* under your control, you can play your characters the way a harpist plays each string on the harp, a few at a time, for exactly the right balance and harmony.

# CHAPTER 7

# HOW TO RAISE THE EMOTIONAL STAKES

READING A STORY IS *NOT* A PASSIVE PROCESS. While a reader may seem to be sitting still, slowly turning pages, in his own mind he is going through a great many emotions. Underlying all of them is a strong tension. The stronger it is, the more the reader concentrates on finding out what happens next, the more attention he pays, the more intensely he feels all the emotions of the tale.

The amount of tension the reader feels depends partly on her emotional state, her imagination, her ability as a reader. But the strength of the story's tension also depends on choices *you* make. Some of these choices have to do with the story's structure—hinted at in Chapter 5—and others are simply outside the scope of this book. However, there are several things you can do with characters to raise the readers' emotional stake in the story, make them more emotionally involved in what's happening, make them care more about the outcome.

## SUFFERING

Pain is a sword with two edges. The character who suffers pain and the character who inflicts it are both made more memorable and more important.

Pain can be either physical or emotional. Great grief and great physical agony, well presented in the tale, can greatly increase the reader's emotional involvement. Remember, though, that you aren't using grief to make the reader grieve any more than you're using physical pain to make the reader bleed. Readers don't necessarily feel what the characters are feeling—when the villain cries out in his agony of defeat, the reader may be cheering inside. But the intensity of the characters' feeling, as long as it remains believable and bearable, will greatly intensify the reader's feelings—whatever they are.

Of course, not all pain is alike. A cut finger doesn't magnify a character very much. Ghastly physical torture can become unbearable to imagine, so that the reader refuses to remain engaged with the story and you lose him completely. The most powerful uses of physical and emotional pain are somewhere between the trivial and the unbearable.

In Stephen King's *The Dead Zone*, the main character suffers terribly: A traffic accident puts him in a coma for many years; he loses his career, the woman he loves, and many years of his life. Furthermore, when he finally recovers, he continues to suffer in body and soul. And with each twinge of pain and grief, the reader's emotional involvement in the story becomes more intense.

Notice that his pain is both physical and emotional. The loss of a loved one can weigh as heavily in the mind of the audience as the loss of a limb. However, *physical* pain is much easier to use because it doesn't have to be prepared for. If a character is tortured, as in King's novel *Misery*, the audience will wince in sympathetic agony even if they don't know the character very well—even if they have never seen the character before. Emotional loss does not come so easily. In *The Dead Zone*, King devoted several pages to creating a warm, valuable love relationship between the main character and the woman he loves. It is at a vital moment in their relationship that he has his terrible traffic accident. Now when he discovers that she married someone else during his coma, the readers know how much he loved her, and so the pain of losing her actually outweighs the physical pain he suffered.

Suffering loses effectiveness with repetition. The first time a character is hit in the head, the pain raises her importance; the third or fourth time, the character becomes comic, and her pain is a joke. Likewise, the first time you mention a character's grief, it raises his stature and makes the reader more emotionally involved. But if you keep harping on the character's suffering, the reader begins to feel that the character is whining, and the reader's emotional involvement decreases.

You can see this with audience reactions to slasher movies—those horror flicks in which the special effects department keeps coming up with cool new ways to dismember the characters. The hideous murders in these movies were originally devised to jack up the audience's emotions, higher and higher with each death. Rather sooner than they expected, however, many in the audience stopped being horrified and began to laugh. This is not really a sign of the audience's moral decay or inability to empathize; it's simply that an audience reaches a point when fictional pain is too difficult to bear. When pain or grief become unbearable in real life, human beings often develop fictions to cope with it—we call it insanity. When pain or grief become unbearable in fiction, readers simply disengage from the story, and either abandon the tale or laugh at it.

Does this mean that pain is a sharply limited character device? No— it is almost unlimited in its potential. But you must remember that you increase the power of suffering, not by describing the injury or loss in greater detail, but rather by showing more of its causes and effect. Blood and gore eventually make the audience gag; sobbing and moaning eventually earn the audience's laughter or contempt. On the other hand, if you make us understand how intensely the character loved before losing the loved one or trusted before being betrayed, then his grief will have far greater power, even if you show it with great economy. If you show a character coping with her pain or grief, refusing to succumb to it, then readers will wince or weep for her. Another rule of thumb: If your characters cry, your readers won't have to; if your characters have good reason to cry, and don't, your readers will do the weeping.

## SACRIFICE

Pain or grief also increase a reader's intensity in proportion to the character's degree of choice. Pete has broken his leg on a hike, and Nora has to set it for him. That scene will be painful, and will certainly magnify both characters as they cause and suffer pain. But Pete's pain will be far more powerful if he is alone and has to set the leg himself. As he ties a rope to his ankle, passes it around a tree trunk, braces his good leg and pulls on the end of the rope, the agony which he inflicts on himself will make the scene utterly unforgettable, even if we never see his face, even if his agony is never described at all. This works with emotional suffering as well. The climax of the movie *Broadcast News* comes when Holly Hunter's character is forced to choose between her desperate passion for William Hurt's charming but shallow character and her integrity as a journalist, which up to now has been the foundation of her whole life. When we see her give up her lover in order to preserve her integrity, our emotions are far more intense than they would have been if she had lost him under circumstances beyond her control. Self-chosen suffering for the sake of a greater good—sacrifice, in other words—is far more intense than pain alone.

When one character willingly inflicts pain on another, the torturer becomes as important, in our fear and loathing, as the victim becomes in our sympathy. This is the other side of the coin of sacrifice. If a character is driving a car and accidentally hits and injures a child, it has a powerful effect. But if a character deliberately chooses to cause someone else pain, the effect is even stronger. The audience may *hate* the character, but the intensity of feeling is much stronger than when the character caused pain without meaning to. It's no accident that the most memorable character in many stories is the sadistic villain; the hero often seems bland and forgettable by comparison.

## JEOPARDY

Jeopardy is anticipated pain or loss. As anyone who has been to a dentist knows, the anticipation of pain is often more potent than its actuality. When a character is threatened with something bad, the audience automatically focuses its attention on him. The more helpless the character and the more terrible the danger, the more importance the audience will attach to the character.

That is why children in danger are such powerful characters; so powerful, in fact, that some films become unbearable to watch. The film *Poltergeist* was strong stuff for that reason. Some horror-movie buffs pooh-poohed the film because "nothing really happened"; nobody got gruesomely killed. What they didn't realize is that a dozen creative slashings of teenage kids in a spatter movie won't equal the power of a single scene in which children are being dragged toward terrible death while their mother struggles vainly to try to reach them in time.

The films *Alien* and *Aliens* crossed the line for me. The jeopardy simply became unbearable. I had to leave the theater. I have since watched both films in their entirety—but never all at once. I could only watch them in sections, flipping cable channels now and then to break the tension caused by the unrelenting jeopardy.

The greater the jeopardy, the stronger the pain when the dreaded event actually occurs. In the TV movie *The Dollmaker*, I did not realize how powerfully the jeopardy had affected me until it was too late. Perhaps before I had children I could have borne it, but I have children now, and when the mother runs screaming to try to snatch up her little girl before her legs are run over by a moving train, the tension in me built to a point higher than I have ever experienced in a story. When the wheels finally reach the girl before her mother does, the girl's pain, combined with the climactic release of the exquisite jeopardy, pushed me over the edge. The first time I saw the film I had to turn off the television and weep. I couldn't get control of myself for fifteen minutes.

The writer had set up this jeopardy to be as powerful as it could possibly be. The little girl and the mother had already suffered so much emotional pain in the film that the audience already cared deeply about them both. And the reason the girl was off by herself was a painful emotional confrontation. So the audience's stake in these characters was already strong.

As the jeopardy develops, the girl is absolutely helpless—she has no idea the train is about to move. The mother is powerless to rescue her—how can she stop a train? How can she scream louder than the roaring of the engines? And the power of the train is like the fist of God, it is so irresistible, so uncompromising.

As a result, during the seconds—it feels like half an hour—when the mother is struggling to get into the train yard, racing to try to reach her daughter, the jeopardy made the characters more important to me, in those few moments, than any characters have ever been in my experience of reading and seeing stories. I could not bear to watch that scene again. I don't have to. I can relive every moment of it in my memory.

This particular example is more powerful than most jeopardy situations, of course, but it does show how jeopardy works. Jeopardy magnifies the stalker, the savior, and the prey, just as pain and sacrifice magnify sufferer and tormentor alike.

Pain and jeopardy work hand in hand, too. In Stephen King's *Misery*, the hero is already in great pain from an automobile accident, but he is in danger of even worse suffering from the insane woman who holds him incommunicado and drugged to the gills in her remote mountain home. The danger of greater pain is constant, as she regulates him by withholding drugs. But then comes the terrible moment when she actually maims him, cutting off first one part of his body, then another. It makes the jeopardy all the more terrible, to know absolutely that she means to carry out her threats.

It's important to remember that jeopardy only works to increase the audience's tension if the audience believes that the dreaded event might actually happen. In old-fashioned melodramas, the jeopardy was often grotesque—the hero was tied to a log heading into the sawmill; the heroine was bound to the railroad tracks as the train approached. But the audience eventually realized that there was no chance (in those days) that the storyteller would ever allow the hero to be cut to ribbons by the saw, or the heroine to be spattered along the tracks by the train. Contemporary standards of decorum simply did not allow such things to be shown in a story.

Writers of melodrama, aware that grotesque jeopardy had finally become unbelievable—and therefore laughable—switched tactics. Instead of trying to find ever-more-horrible threats, they used very simple threats, but they made them come true. The first time a writer had the villain jam a burning cigarette into the heroine's hand, the audience gasped and a threshold was crossed. The villain had proved that he not only *could* cause pain, he would. His next threat was credible again, and because the audience believed, jeopardy was again a powerful tool for creating tension.

# SEXUAL TENSION

Sexual tension is related to jeopardy. In fact, you could call it "jeopardy of sex," except that presumably your characters desire sex rather more than they desire pain. Sexual tension is so vital to so many stories that the term *romance* is now generally used to refer to stories that are *about* sexual tension. It crosses all cultural boundaries. When a man and woman meet in a story, we assume at least some degree of sexual possibility. If the two characters immediately become important to each other, the sexual tension increases—especially if they become important in a negative sense. Rivalry, contempt, anger—none of them make us doubt for a moment that the sexual possibility is real, and the more intense these negative feelings are, the more sexual tension there is.

However, for sexual tension to make two characters more important, the audience must recognize them as meeting the general social standards of sexual attractiveness. When Clark Gable and Claudette Colbert met in *It Happened One Night*, the audience instantly recognized them as suitable sex objects.

This does not mean that all participants in sexual tension have to be physically beautiful, though that is certainly the easiest way. If you have made an unbeautiful character important to us for other reasons, we will regard him as sexually attractive despite a lack of physical beauty, and sexual tension will work for him. John Merrick's devotion to the actress played by Anne Bancroft in *The Elephant Man* was charged with sexual energy, even though actor John Hurt's makeup was repulsive.

On a milder level, the television series *L. A. Law* brought off a similar effect between the characters played by Jill Eikenberry and Michael Tucker. Tucker is short and pudgy, with a receding hairline, playing meek tax lawyer Stuart Markowitz; Eikenberry is a tall, attractive, compelling woman playing high-powered trial lawyer Ann Kelsey. The audience did not see any sexual possibility between them. In fact, when a drunken Kelsey proposed a night of unwedded bliss to Markowitz at a party, it was comic because it was so unexpected—so odd. Gradually, however, the sexual tension grew as our sympathy with Markowitz grew. We recognized that he was a good man; we identified with him and his attraction to Kelsey; and finally we felt a strong desire to bring them together.

Sexual tension intensifies the audience's involvement with all characters involved. However, as several TV series have discovered to their sorrow, tension dissipates when characters come together in sexual harmony. It isn't like violence, which establishes the villain's credibility and makes the next round of jeopardy even more powerful. Instead, sexual fulfillment has the same effect on sexual tension that the death of the victim has on jeopardy. For that character, at least, the tension is over. The writers of *Cheers* quickly realized their mistake and split Sam and Diane; the writers of *Moonlighting* never gave David and Maddie a moment to enjoy sexual harmony before putting them back in hopeless, hilarious conflict—and the sexual tension remained high, at least for a while.

## SIGNS AND PORTENTS

Another way to increase the readers' intensity is to connect a character with the world around her, so that her fate is seen to have much wider consequences than her private loss or gain. King Lear's climactic moment is linked with a storm, and though we take his attempt to command the wind ("Blow, winds! Crack your cheeks!") as a sign of madness, the fact is that the wind *is* blowing, the storm *is* raging, and we receive the subliminal message that what happens to Lear has cosmic implications. His daughters' betrayal of their oaths to him, their plotted patricide, is more than a private tragedy—it is a disorder in the world, which must be resolved before the universe can again be at peace.

In tragedy and high romance, the connection between a character and the world around him can be quite open. The ark of the covenant in *Raiders of the Lost Ark* is more than a secret weapon—its opening represents the unleashing of the power of God. When the villain opens it, the storyteller makes sure we understand that it isn't a mere boobytrap that kills him. The ark isn't opened until it is brought to a special holy place, and when the lid comes off, we see spirits spiraling around, terrible winds and fire, finally culminating in a whirlwind that disturbs the very heavens. Likewise, Oedipus's sins cause a famine, which doesn't end until he pays the price; storms rage across the moors in *Wuthering Heights* exactly when the mood of the characters is most turbulent.

Even when you're trying for more subtlety, however, signs and portents are still vital tools in drawing your reader more intensely into the tale. You simply disguise the cosmic connections a little better. The great storm becomes a gentle drizzle; the flaming sky becomes a sweltering day;

the roll of thunder becomes a distant siren in the city; the famine becomes the wilting of a flower in the window. The connection between character and cosmos will still be there, and, often without consciously noticing the portents, the audience will become more intensely involved with what the character does.

You can't control everything the reader feels, and no two members of your audience will ever be emotionally involved in your story exactly to the same degree. Still, there are some things you *can* control, and if you use them deftly, without letting them get out of hand, you can lead most of your audience to intense emotional involvement with your characters. The audience won't necessarily *like* the characters, but they certainly won't be indifferent to them.

# CHAPTER 8

# WHAT SHOULD WE FEEL ABOUT THE CHARACTER?

ANY TIME YOU SHOW CONFLICT BETWEEN CHARACTERS, you want your audience to care about the outcome. Perhaps they'll have an intellectual interest, if the conflict is over some idea or principle they happen to care about—but their feelings will run far deeper if they have great sympathy for one or more of the characters in conflict.

Sometimes you'll want your readers to take sides—to be rooting for one character and hoping the other will fail. You'll want them to sympathize with the character who stands for what you believe in—the character you conceive of as representing Good.

In fact, your readers will respond this way even if you don't plan it. Let's say your main character is Howard Eastman, a much-decorated Vietnam veteran who has gone into government service. There he becomes deeply committed to the cause of a group of freedom fighters in a Central American country. When Congress votes to cut funding for these freedom fighters, Eastman determines to find ways to keep them alive and fighting. So at great risk—to himself and the administration—he circumvents Congress and finds various semi-legal ways of getting American money and weapons to his brave Central American friends.

If you have made Eastman sympathetic to your audience, they will assume that you approve of what he's doing, especially if you make his opponents unlikable. If you have created Eastman's character well and continue to make him sympathetic throughout the book, most readers will go along with you, liking Eastman and hoping he'll win. But what if you want them to disapprove of Eastman's corruption of government process for the sake of a cause? What if you want the audience to reach the conclusion that Eastman was *wrong*?

The easiest course is to make Eastman the villain from the beginning, so the audience never likes him. Then your hero will be the American government official who unmasks or defeats him, or perhaps the Central American commander opposing him on the field.

Considerably harder is to start out with a very likable, sympathetic Eastman, and then through the course of the book gradually and delicately bring the audience to lose sympathy with him. Again, however, this is much easier if you have another hero—perhaps one who seemed to be a "bad guy" at first—who can replace Eastman in the audience's sympathy.

The most daring course, yet the one most likely to transform your audience, is to keep Eastman sympathetic throughout, while facing him with an opponent who is *also* sympathetic throughout the story. The audience will like *both* characters—a lot—and as Eastman and his opponent come into deadly conflict, your readers will be emotionally torn.

This is *anguish*, perhaps the strongest of emotions you can make your audience experience directly (as opposed to sympathetically mirroring what your characters feel). Neither character is at all confused about what he wants to have happen, yet your audience, emotionally involved with both of them, cannot bear to have either character lose. The emotional stakes are raised to much greater intensity, and yet the moral issues will again be removed from a matter of mere sympathy; in having to choose between characters they love, the readers will be forced to decide on the basis of the moral issues between them. Who really *should* prevail?

This last strategy, of course, is far more dangerous, far less clear than the others. When you separate sympathy from moral decisions—exactly what a judge and jury must try to do in a trial—you can't be sure that your audience will reach the "right" conclusions; you can't be sure that they'll agree with you. But you *can* be sure that they'll *care* far more than they ever would from reading articles and essays on the issue.

In any event, all these strategies depend on the author's knowing how to get the audience to feel sympathy or antipathy toward a character.

There's another practical reason for knowing how to get your audience to like or dislike a character. Most readers of most types of fiction want to read about characters they like. And why shouldn't they? If you were going to take a three-day bus ride, wouldn't you hope to have a seatmate whose company you enjoyed? Your readers are investing considerable time in your story; if they dislike your main character, it's going to be a lot harder to persuade them to stay along for the whole ride.

At times, of course, you'll want to violate that general principle and tell a story whose main character is pretty repulsive. Even then, however, with almost no exceptions, the writer who brings off such a story successfully is really not making the main character completely unlikable. Instead, the character is given several major negative traits early in the story, and the traits remain prominent throughout, so that readers don't notice that the writer is using three dozen *other* techniques to create sympathy for the "unsympathetic" hero. The true "anti-hero" is rare in fiction. Most seeming anti-heroes are really heroes who need, metaphorically speaking, a bath.

One way or another, then, you're going to need to know how to arouse audience sympathy or antipathy toward a character. I've found in teaching writing classes that when beginning writers create an obnoxious main character, often it isn't because they had some notion of creating an anti-hero. Instead, these writers simply didn't realize that their hero was becoming obnoxious. They weren't in control.

# FIRST IMPRESSIONS

Characters, like people, make good or bad first impressions. When characters first show up in a story, we start to like them—or dislike them—right away.

## We Like What's Like Us

The word *like* has a lovely double meaning: The most important ingredient in how much we *like* a stranger when we first encounter him is how much he seems to be *like* us. With important exceptions, we tend to feel most comfortable with and personally attracted to people who belong to the communities that are important to us, and people who are like us in ways that we are proud of. All else being equal, we feel more at ease in approaching a stranger who is our age than one who is older or younger; the same applies to economic class, style of dress, and so on. Likewise, when we find out that someone belongs to the same church or plans to vote for the same candidate or has the same attitude toward the President or served in the same branch of the military or loves our favorite book or movie, our tension relaxes and we get some of that comfortable feeling of kinship—we "hit it off" from the start. It's as if we recognize them, even though we've never seen them before.

We tend to feel somewhat tense around people who don't seem very similar to us—people speaking a foreign language or wearing nonstandard costumes, or people who form a closed group to which we clearly don't belong. We know that we're not part of their community. And we get a definite *bad* impression of people who don't behave in ways that we have come to think of as "normal": people wearing the wrong clothes for the occasion, or talking too loudly, or using inappropriate language (too elevated or too low); people with bad personal hygiene; people who accost strangers on the street; people, in other words, who are not behaving in ways that *we* would behave. We tend to look past them, sidestep them, avoid them, shun them openly. They are not like us, and therefore we distrust or dislike them.

The things that make us instantly like or dislike people we meet in real life are pretty much the same things that make us instantly like or dislike the people we meet in fiction. We will immediately feel comfortable with a fictional character who reminds us of things we like about ourselves. We "recognize" the character. On the other hand, if we first see a character doing something physically gross or socially inept, or if we are shown a character who is foreign, alien, strange, then we tend to feel repelled, or at least not attracted.

Still, there's a kernel of truth in the adage "opposites attract." There are other, much stronger forces than mere similarity working to draw people together. We've all had the experience of learning to detest someone who seemed comfortably attractive at first; likewise, getting to know somebody better can help us overcome the immediate distance and suspicion that came from strangeness.

And that's a good thing for us as writers, because the one thing we can't possibly control in our fiction is how much our readers are going to feel themselves similar to our characters. Wouldn't it be horrible if the only readers who could possibly sympathize with a character were the ones who were just like him? How large an audience would there ever have been for *Amadeus*? There are so few of us who would qualify as a musical genius with an obnoxious mocking attitude. Or *One Flew Over the Cuckoo's Nest*—I've really never faced the choice of going to jail or being committed to a mental institution, have you? Both those plays (and films) depend absolutely on the audience developing enormous sympathy—no, *love*—for the main character. Yet in neither case did the author have the slightest hope of filling theaters with people who liked the character because he made a good first impression.

The liking that comes from a good first impression is immediate—and shallow. The dislike that comes from a bad first impression can be deeper; that's what makes bigotry such a powerful negative force. But both can be overcome by storytellers who have even stronger tools at hand.

## Editorial Resistance

Alas, you are certain to run into editors or producers who don't know that there are other ways to arouse sympathy. For instance, how many writers have been told, "The audience for books is mostly women, so you need a strong woman character in this book"? Too many—especially considering that it isn't completely true. What *is* true is that if you use a male protagonist in a book whose audience will be primarily women, you won't get instant identification. You have to work a lot harder to make the character sympathetic. You have to be a better writer.

You also have to have an editor who actually understands how storytelling works. These are relatively rare; most will reject your story or book because "women won't like it." And because stories with male protagonists probably won't get published for a female market (like romance novels or women's magazines), the editors can "prove" their maxim by saying, "Look—the only thing that sells is stories about women."

There are plenty of examples besides women's fiction. When a producer optioned the film rights to my novel *Ender's Game* back in 1986, the first thing he decided (*after* the contract was signed) was, "Of course, the character of Ender has got to be sixteen." Since the entire story depends on Ender being an innocent, trusting child, I balked. "Look," said the producer, "the only way to have a hit sci-fi movie is to get the teen audience. And to get the teen audience, you've got to have a teenage hero."

"What about *E.T.*?" said I. "What about *Poltergeist*? What about *Alien*? What about—"

"Those are exceptions," he said.

Hi-ho, as Kurt Vonnegut would say.

It took producer Michael Douglas years of work to get *One Flew Over the Cuckoo's Nest* produced; there was tremendous resistance, in large part due to the "unlikable" main character. Now that we know that the film was a masterpiece, now that it won all those Academy Awards, it's easy to criticize those who doubted the story would work. They were wrong—about that story.

But the general principle has a foundation in truth: Making a weird or unpleasant character likable is *very hard*. So we shouldn't be too critical of editors or producers who tell us that it can't be done—they've seen so many manuscripts and screenplays that tried to do it and failed miserably.

So if you know you're writing for an audience of women or teenagers or blue-collar workers or college graduates, it's a lot easier to win their sympathy if you make your main character, the one you want them to *like,* a woman or a teenager or a blue-collar worker or a college graduate. Unless there's a compelling reason in the story to do otherwise, why borrow trouble?

## Sympathy vs. Curiosity

While we tend to like characters that are like us, we also tend to be a little bored with them. It's strangeness, not familiarity, that excites our curiosity. It's hard to imagine a blander character than one who is exactly typical of a certain group. So even if you decide, for simplicity's sake, to use a main character—Nora—who is a member of the same community as your intended audience, you must also find ways to make Nora different and intriguing. Giving her a few attributes in common with the target audience starts you on the road toward sympathy—but doesn't get you very far along that road.

Since no two women or teenagers or blue-collar workers or college graduates are *exactly* alike, you couldn't possibly make Nora similar enough to everybody to attract the whole group anyway. The first impression that Nora gives the audience really has to accomplish no more than getting their attention. No matter whether the first impression was negative or positive, you will always end up relying on some of the other tools for creating lasting sympathy or antipathy.

# CHARACTERS WE LOVE

Here are the devices that will make an audience tend toward lasting sympathy with a character.

## Physical Attractiveness

One tool that makes actors into movie stars and ordinary films into smash hits simply isn't available to those of us who work in print, not with anything like the same power. A filmmaker has only to put Robert Redford or Kathleen Turner or Tom Cruise or Kelly McGillis or Harrison Ford on the screen (with good makeup, lighting and camera work, of course), and at least half the audience will have great sympathy for the characters they portray.

In print, we don't have that option. Oh, we can describe characters in terms that suggest physical attractiveness, we can show others being attracted to them—but we can never come close to the immediate impact of seeing an intriguing face or an attractive body on the screen or stage. We can never hear the exact timbre of the voice, can never catch that little smile or startled look that suggests a combination of humor and timidity and courage that is so endearing to the audience.

Don't you *have* to describe your character? Not necessarily. When I turned in the manuscript of my novel *Saints*, both my agent and my editor complained that I never described Dinah Kirkham, the main character.

"You never tell us her hair color," they said, "or the color of her eyes, or even how tall she is."

True enough, said I, but didn't you have a mental picture of her anyway? They both agreed that they had. Then, when I asked each of them what her image of Dinah was, you won't be surprised to learn that each described herself.

I had used other devices to create sympathy, and by avoiding physical description, I allowed my female readers to put themselves into Dinah's story far more deeply than if I had compelled them to see her another way. (If only I could have kept publishers from putting a painting of Dinah on the cover, the technique would have worked perfectly.)

You usually can't get away with neglecting to give *any* physical description of your main characters. My point is not that description of characters is bad—just that in print, at least, it isn't anywhere near as effective as other techniques for winning audience sympathy. Describe when you must, but don't imagine for a moment that saying your hero has "a firm jaw, a fine, straight nose, and a tumble of light brown hair over his forehead" will win the undying devotion of your readers.

It can actually make some readers resent your character. "Another incredibly good-looking woman," they'll sigh, hoping she eats five cheesecakes and gains six inches around the hips. "Another man who can press 300 pounds but still looks good in a suit," they'll murmur, while secretly hoping he gets pimples. Listing all the features that make a character look terrific is not the same thing as seeing a terrific-looking person on the screen or in person. When you see the real person, his or her beauty can overwhelm you; when you get only the list of beautiful features, you're more likely to see, not undeniable beauty, but all the people who got more dates than you in high school. Good-bye sympathy.

## Altruism: Victim, Savior, Sacrifice

Some of the devices we use to raise the emotional stakes—suffering, sacrifice, and jeopardy—also have a rather complicated role in creating sympathy.

### Victim

When Nora is the victim of suffering and jeopardy, the audience will pity her; they'll hope for her deliverance. But there's a price: Nora will seem *weak*, and along with pity there'll be at least a trace of contempt. (This is much of the reason why feminists object to having women in fiction always be rescued by men—even though the audience sympathizes with the female victim, they also disdain her.) You can compensate for this weakening of the victim by devoting some time to showing, in detail, that Nora had no choice but to put herself in the power of her tormentor. Or you can show how courageous Nora is for refusing to despair. This is actually easier to do when the suffering is physical; if Nora is the victim of emotional or psychological suffering, you have to work harder to make readers understand why she doesn't just *leave* the situation.

## Savior

The audience will like Pete when he acts as a rescuer, stepping in to stop Nora's suffering or save her from jeopardy. Pete's courage is admirable, of course, but even more the audience admires his sense of responsibility for other people. They'll admire Pete even if the rescue fails.

However, there's always a danger of having a rescuer look like a fool for plunging in without enough thought—what if Nora was dealing with the problem and Pete's "rescue" ends up making everything worse? Pete will still get credit for courage and responsibility, but he'll also get tagged as just a little on the dumb side.

When the victim's suffering is emotional or psychological, the rescuer runs a great risk of looking like a meddler. If Pete finds Nora lonely and suffering from the cruel domination of her parents, the audience won't approve if he immediately starts taking over, insisting on rescuing her. They'll wonder—correctly—if Pete is really saving Nora, or dominating her in place of her parents. If you want the audience to sympathize with Pete in his rescue attempt, you need to show his reluctance to intrude and the urgency of Nora's situation. It also helps if Nora gives some signal that she wants to be rescued.

## Sacrifice

When Nora chooses to sacrifice herself, it will feel important to the audience—but it won't necessarily win sympathy. There'll be pity for her suffering, of course, but before the audience will admire Nora for her sacrifice, they must feel that the cause she is willing to suffer or die for is important and right. They must also feel that Nora has no other decent choice or that her sacrifice will actually make a difference in helping other people.

Above all, the audience will have no sympathy for Nora if she chooses martyrdom for no good reason but the desire to have a noble and glorious death or to make other people like her more. If Nora has a decent alternative to being sacrificed, the audience will insist that she choose it, or the sacrifice will be seen as a stupid waste rather than a noble act.

# Plan and Purpose, Hunger and Dreams

Beginning writers often make the mistake of having their hero always *react* to the events of the story. The hero's reactions may all be perfectly reasonable, but the result is a character who seems to have no initiative—a puppet being pushed around on the end of a stick. You know the kind of story I mean:

> Nora was doing nothing in particular that morning—just enjoying the sunshine—when the car squealed around the corner and came to a halt in front of her. . . .

Yeah, right. How often are *you* outside doing nothing in particular? Nora would be much more interesting if she were outside for a reason, trying to accomplish something. Then when the events of the story change her life, we have a sense that she actually had a life to be changed! If Nora was hurrying to a meeting with her daughter's teacher, or rushing to the library to do research for a client, or worrying about possible results of the medical tests the doctor just gave her, she will still try to deal with her child's school problems or the client's deadline or the medical test results. It will increase the pressure on her—and increase the audience's sympathy for her.

Besides specific plans, your characters will have continuing needs, hungers, hopes, and dreams. If the audience has the same needs, then they'll sympathize with your character and hope those needs are satisfied. For instance, everybody understands the need for money—but you can make the audience sympathize with Nora even more by letting us know what she needs the money *for* and how long and hard she's been working to get it.

As a general rule, audience sympathy increases with the importance of the character's dream and the amount of effort the character has already expended to try to fulfill it.

You need to beware of cliches and over-sentimentality—only a naive reader is going to get worked up over a little boy who yearns for a puppy, unless you show why *this* kid needs a dog. Still, you can almost always get an audience to sympathize with your character's needs, even when they seem bizarre: Pete's obsession with owning as many expensive new cars as possible will make him seem strange and greedy—until we know that as he was growing up, his father had to struggle to keep their old, beat-up car in running order. The one time Pete's dad bought a new car, it ended up being repossessed under humiliating circumstances right after the layoffs at the plant. Now the audience will realize that Pete's obsession with cars is a response to his father's suffering. Instead of this hunger making him strange and unlikable, it will make him understandable and sympathetic.

When the story is *about* the character's plan—a quest or caper story—or when the story is *about* the character's need—as all character stories are—then this tool makes the character almost irresistibly sympathetic. That's why audiences find themselves rooting for heroes to succeed at the most appalling things—robberies, assassinations, marriage-wrecking love affairs. Once we're caught up in a character's plans and dreams, we're on her side *almost* without limit.

## Courage and Fair Play

The audience will like Nora better when they see her take physical, social, or financial risks to do what she believes is right or necessary. When Nora has the guts to risk losing her job rather than keep silent about a bribery scandal, we admire her—and fear for her.

Along with courage there must be a sense of fair play, however—when Nora finally wins and the boss is forced to pay her damages and back salary, she can never gloat. Nor can she ever do anything underhanded or sneaky to win—if she cheats, she loses sympathy. This is the same rule that made it so the good guy in a western always had to wait for the bad guy to draw first; the good guy in a swashbuckler always let the bad guy pick up his sword after disarming him; and the good girl in a romance never uses cheap sex to keep her man.

Times have changed, of course, and writers don't always hold their characters to those standards. What *hasn't* changed, however, is the fact that readers still respond warmly to a character who is brave and plays fair, and they lose sympathy for a character who is cowardly and cheats. This doesn't mean you can't or shouldn't write about characters who aren't always brave and gallant—but it does mean you will forfeit some audience sympathy.

## Attitude

A character's attitude toward other people, toward himself, and toward the events of the story can do a lot to win sympathy. When things go wrong, Pete doesn't whine or complain about it or blame everybody but himself—he takes responsibility for his own mistakes, refers to his problems with wry humor, and tries to solve them. Nora never brags about the good deeds she does—it embarrasses her when others praise her. When someone criticizes her, she never argues to defend herself. But when someone else is being criticized unfairly, Nora speaks up for him.

Pete always has sympathy for other people's suffering, always tries to see things from their point of view. Nora may get angry, but she'll always listen to the other person's explanations, and she's willing to trust people—even when they've proved before that they really aren't very trustworthy.

Other characters may fail to recognize what good people Pete and Nora are—but their very modesty and self-deprecating humor and refusal to defend themselves make the audience love them all the more.

## Draftee or Volunteer

If Nora is faced with a task that requires great courage, and it won't bring her much glory—no one will ever know she did it—the audience will sympathize with her most if she volunteers. It will diminish her if she has to be forced into acting. On the other hand, if the task at hand is one that will bring fame or fortune, then the audience will have much more sympathy for Nora if she doesn't put herself forward, but modestly waits to be called on.

It's this simple. If somebody says, "I've got a miserable, nasty job here that has to be done," then a character gains sympathy by volunteering. If somebody says, "If you succeed in this task, your name will be remembered for ten thousand years," then a character gains sympathy by modestly waiting to be drafted.

This is why Tolkien made sure that Frodo never volunteered to be the ringbearer in *The Lord of the Rings*; rather Frodo tried to give the ring to someone else until it became absolutely clear that he was the only one who could carry it. If Frodo had *wanted* to carry the ring, the audience wouldn't have felt anywhere near as much sympathy for him—all his troubles from then on would have been the result of his own hubris in thinking he could measure up to the task.

This is also why political candidates always prefer to have it appear that they are reluctant to run for office—their audience, too, has greater admiration for those who have greatness thrust upon them.

## Dependability

When a good guy says he'll do something, he keeps his word come hell or high water. If he breaks his word, he'd better have a good reason for it—and he'd better try to make up for it later.

I don't mean that sympathetic characters don't lie. A lie is a story told about the past, and dependability has to do with promises—stories the character tells about what she *will* do in the future.

How does this work? Pete stubbornly insists on trying to keep the family farm, even though it's losing money. We know he's going to fail, and if he sold it, he could pay for a college education for his younger brother, who hates the farm and hates Pete for making him stay there. The audience won't have much sympathy for stubborn, self-willed Pete.

But what if Pete is holding onto the farm because of a promise he made to his dying father? Now the audience will *like* him for his dependability. In fact, they'd lose sympathy for him if he *wasn't* stubborn. They'll hope something happens to let the younger brother get away and go to college; they might even hope that Pete loses the farm despite his best efforts, knowing that everybody's life will be better without the farm. But they won't want Pete to break his word, and if he finally does give in to these pressures, they'll expect him to feel deep remorse.

Don't underestimate the importance of a promise in fiction. The pledge, kept or broken, is one of the strongest motifs running through all of the world's storytelling. It's one of the deadliest accusations you can level against an enemy: He doesn't keep his word. And if your main character casually breaks a promise, it will leave such a sour taste in your reader's mouth that you'll never fully win back the reader's sympathy.

## Cleverness

Notice that I don't use the word *intelligence*. That's because in our society with its egalitarian ideals, any obvious display of intelligence or erudition suggests elitism, snobbery, arrogance.

Yet we love a character who is *clever* enough to think of solutions to knotty problems. Does this seem contradictory? It *is* contradictory. You have to walk a fine line, making Nora very clever without ever letting her be clever enough to *notice* how clever she is. Nora can have enormous self-confidence—but she can never think of herself as superior to someone else because she is smart and the other person is dumb. If she thinks of a brilliant plan and it *works*, it surprises her more than anybody.

A perfect example of this is Harrison Ford's character in *Raiders of the Lost Ark* and *Indiana Jones and the Temple of Doom*. Indiana Jones is a professor of archaeology—but we never watch him being intellectually incisive. The one time we see him in the classroom, lecturing, he is rather bumbling and confused—distracted by a coed who has written a come-on message on her eyelids.

Yet whenever things go wrong, Indiana Jones comes up with a brilliant—or dumb-lucky—solution. He's smart, but he isn't *intelligent*. The audience loves a character who solves problems and knows exactly the right facts when he needs them—but they don't like a character who flaunts his superior knowledge or acts as if he *knows* how clever he is.

## Endearing Imperfections: The Lovable Rogue

Now that we have a list of traits, actions, and attitudes that will persuade your audience to love a character, here's the rub: If Pete is *too* perfect, your audience will stop believing in him. We're back to that balancing act between caring and belief.

The answer to this problem is to give Pete some endearing imperfections. While using most of the sympathy tool kit to make the audience like him, deliberately give Pete some small, understandable foibles to make us believe in him.

Again, a Harrison Ford character is a perfect example. In the *Star Wars* movies, Han Solo keeps his word, comes to the rescue, is physically attractive, brave, and clever, and has a great sense of humor—but he is also boastful (Han Solo: "I think you just can't bear to let a gorgeous guy like me out of your sight." Princess Leia: "I don't know where you get your delusions, laser-brain." And later—Princess Leia: "I love you!" Han Solo: "I know.") and all his plans *seem* to be motivated by greed and self-interest. He also doesn't pay his bills.

The result? He's the best-liked character in one of the best-loved movies of all time.

Hercule Poirot's little vanities; Nero Wolfe's obsessive-compulsive behavior and his weight—a mere seventh of a ton; Sherlock Holmes's rudeness and his cocaine habit; Scarlett O'Hara's romantic delusions and brutally pragmatic actions; Rhett Butler's shady past and mocking attitude: All of these traits normally don't make us like people, but combined with all the traits that *do* arouse sympathy, the flaws only make us love the characters more.

# CHARACTERS WE HATE

Getting your audience to hate a character is much easier than trying to win their sympathy. Have a character do something wonderful, and it'll fade in our memory if he fails to measure up. Have a character do something loathesome, and we'll never forget.

## *Sadist or Bully*

To make us dislike somebody, simply show her deliberately causing someone else to suffer in body or mind. If she enjoys causing the pain, we'll hate her all the more. Remember the sadistic villain in William Goldman's *Marathon Man*, using a dentist's drill, without anesthetic, to torture the hero into telling information that he didn't have. Remember Elizabeth Barrett's father in *The Barretts of Wimpole Street*, whose whimsical and arbitrary commands made him impossible to please, so that everyone around him was constantly tortured by guilt or terrified of punishment. Remember the queen alien in *Aliens*, who did not kill her human victims, but instead kept them alive, cocooned and in hideous agony, so that her young could feed on them when they hatched. Remember Nurse Ratched in *One Flew Over the Cuckoo's Nest*, who kept up a cheerful, perky demeanor while deliberately subjecting her patients to degradation, making them less and less human. We hardly knew anything about these characters beyond their hunger for other people's suffering—yet it made each of them the most memorable character in the story. They became the embodiment of pure evil.

Predictably enough, the very power of this tool guarantees that it will be overused. How many times have you seen this scene: Good guy Pete is completely in villain Nora's power—only instead of taking a .357 Magnum and blowing him away, Nora spends ten minutes smearing him with flammable jelly, pouring gasoline over his head, and strapping butane lighters to his body—talking all the time about how she'll love watching him go off like a roman candle. At the end of those ten minutes, when the audience is so on edge they're starting to say, "So light the match already!" the police arrive in the nick of time and save Pete. If Nora hadn't been such a sadist, Pete would have been toast.

The James Bond movies made this cliche into an art form. Bond is forever getting captured, but instead of killing him, the bad guys always put him in a situation that will lead to certain death—and then walk away. Whereupon Bond cleverly escapes and lives to fight another day. Never mind that the sadistic villain has been overused and misused. You just have to be careful to make your villain's sadism believable.

It helps to keep in mind that the root of sadism is not the love of pain—it is the love of power, the sense of control over someone else's body, someone else's life. Thus it doesn't have to be physical torture. The effect is the same whenever one character forces his victim to recognize that the victim has no control over her own life. Nurse Ratched in *Cuckoo's Nest* and Mr. Barrett in *Wimpole Street* never resorted to physical torture; it made their sadism all the more horrible—and believable. They were bullies; they used their power to torment the little guy. That's the worst thing a character can do in fiction—the unpardonable sin.

## Assassin or Avenger?

By comparison, mere murder is nowhere near as powerful in making the audience dislike a character. Where bullying can never be justified enough to make the sadist sympathetic, murder and other crimes can. They are not surefire devices for creating antipathy. For instance, a character who is trying to assassinate Hitler or Stalin or Idi Amin is likely to have our sympathy right from the start—if the intended victim is made evil enough, the would-be assassin becomes a hero. The audience is never fully comfortable with the idea of cold, calculated murder—but the assassin can still be a hero.

When *The Godfather* first played in American theaters, the scenes of murder at the end of the movie brought cheers and applause from the audience. Why? Because every victim of Michael Corleone's hit men had earned our hatred by betraying a trust or by making a cynical, cowardly attack on a character we liked. But *The Godfather: Part II* carefully did just the opposite—it showed that the Corleones used murder, not for the sake of justice, but to increase their own power. When Michael orders the murder of his own brother, a weak, pathetic figure, we understand *why*, but it's still a monstrous act.

A rule of thumb: Murder and other crimes will only make a character into a villain if he commits the crime for selfish reasons, and if the crime harms people who don't deserve to be hurt. But if your character is committing a crime in order to save others from suffering, or if the victim of the crime richly deserves to suffer or die, then the crime will actually make your character sympathetic. In the classic caper movie *The Sting*, the characters played by Paul Newman and Robert Redford perpetrate an elaborate hoax in order to bilk the villain, played by Robert Shaw, out of a large amount of money. The motive for the con, however, was not the money—it was vengeance for the villain's casual murder of a friend of theirs. Shaw, on the other hand, was drawn into the con by his greed and by his desire to bring other people under his control.

The villain's crimes made us hate him. The heroes' crimes made us love them. Redford and Newman played crooks—but in this con their motives were unselfish, and compared to Shaw's character, they were saints. Motive makes all the difference in assigning a character's relative place within the moral spectrum a given work of fiction shows to be possible. A con man is an honest man, compared to a cold-blooded killer.

## Self-serving, Self-appointed

One of the nastiest things you can say about another person is that she is self-appointed. "I don't know why we need to pay any attention to self-appointed experts like Nora," says Pete—and unless Nora can show that she was in fact appointed by someone else, she has lost much of her credibility.

It's a strange thing about human nature, but we simultaneously disdain people who are dull and unambitious—and resent people who try to push their way up to a higher level. The younger brother trying to tag along when his older brother is out with his friends; the lower level coworker trying to tell you how to do your job; the buttinsky neighbor trying to give you advice on saving your marriage—don't these people know when they're not wanted?

So strong is our aversion to people trying to put themselves in a position where they weren't invited that it can overcome a great deal of sympathy. In *The Member of the Wedding*, Carson McCullers spends the bulk of the novel building up our sympathy for her main character, a lonely young girl who doesn't know where she belongs. This girl, Frankie, has come to believe in the delusion that she will be part of her older brother's wedding—that he and his new bride will welcome her along in their new life. "They are the 'we' of me," she says. Yet despite all our affection for Frankie, when she climbs into the back of the honeymoon car, we don't for a moment expect or even want the newlyweds to take her along. We grieve for Frankie, we ache for her disappointment, but we have no sympathy for her effort to include herself where she wasn't invited.

This is especially true with characters who try to take a high position they don't belong in. Usurpers get no sympathy in fiction. Shakespeare knew this: The audience would never have sympathized with the character Macbeth if he had simply appointed himself king and killed the present king out of pure ambition. Instead, Shakespeare went to elaborate lengths to show that Macbeth did *not* appoint himself. It was the three witches who first prophesied that he would be king; Macbeth did not take them seriously until the first part of their prophecy came true. Even then, he would have taken no action had his wife not urged him on to murder. Macbeth was a usurper, yes, but he did *not* appoint himself. That he was appointed by evil forces—the witches and his soon-to-be-mad wife—makes the audience agree that he must be deposed, but the fact that he was not self-appointed allows us to have some sympathy for him after all.

But by and large, a person who claims a position that he was not appointed to by an authority outside himself has utterly lost our sympathy. Former Secretary of State Alexander Haig was never able to live down that moment when, with President Reagan in surgery to remove a would-be assassin's bullet, Haig announced, "I'm in control here." He explained a thousand times that he meant only to inspire public confidence that the central government was not in disarray—but he could never overcome people's perception that he had tried to exercise power that simply did not belong to him.

A fictional example comes at the conclusion of the play *Inherit the*

*Wind*, by Jerome Lawrence and Robert E. Lee. Matthew Harrison Brady is completely discredited by the fact that he has appointed himself as attorney for the prosecution *and* as an expert on the Bible. His final collapse begins with his admission of the ultimate hubris. "God tells me to oppose the evil teachings of that man," he says, thereby confessing that he imagines that his words are God's words. It leads to his opponent, Henry Drummond, ridiculing him unmercifully. "The gospel according to Brady!" cries Drummond, and he bows down before his opponent in mockery, crying, "Brady, Brady, Brady almighty!" Ordinarily, Drummond's bullying of Brady would have lost Drummond all audience sympathy—but Brady's usurpation of authority is so audacious that Drummond's ridicule is not seen as bullying at all. It is the restoration of the just order of things—exposing Brady and bringing him down from the high position to which he appointed himself.

How long does our resentment of or annoyance with a self-appointed interloper last? Until he wins an invitation. Even after Pete has made us dislike him by forcing himself into a place where he wasn't wanted, our antipathy isn't permanent. If he later proves that he deserves his new place, if he earns the respect of others, then he ceases to be an interloper. He belongs. This is, in fact, the subject of countless stories—probably because at some time in our lives practically all of us have felt like interlopers, and we long for reassurance that we will eventually win acceptance in that new situation. The only thing that can save an interloper is vindication—but then he isn't an interloper at all.

## Oathbreaker

Nora grimly agrees to Pete's harsh terms. "All right," she says. "If you promise not to tell anyone about my involvement with Hiram Doakes, I'll tell you where he gets his funding. But my name can't come into it—it'll ruin my father's business and destroy my marriage."

"You have my word," says Pete. "I won't let this touch you at all."

Nora tells all, and leaves. Pete immediately picks up the phone and has his secretary place a call to the editor of the *Tribune*. "I've got the goods on Hiram Doakes," he says. "If you want the story, you've got it. My source? His lover for the past three years. Nora Simms. N-O-R-A, S-I-M-M-S. Her father owns Simms Construction. Of course you can use her name—just don't tell anybody you got it from me."

From that moment on, the audience knows that Pete is slime. When a character breaks a promise or betrays a trust, the audience takes that betrayal personally—Pete has achieved villain status, and readers will be longing for his downfall.

## Intellect

It's no accident that so many bad guys speak in very formal, precise language.

"Look, buddy, you can't get away with this," says the hero.

"Do you think not?" says the villain, raising an eyebrow. "Do you fancy you can terrify me with your absurd threats?"

"There's too many people already on to you," says the hero.

"Do you mean the police? Those pathetic bumblers?"

It isn't just the villain's vanity that makes us dislike him. It's the fact that he talks in an educated manner, using big words. You can almost hear him dropping r's as he speaks. No doubt he attended Harvard—if not Oxford.

This isn't true in every culture, but certainly the American audience resents any character who is smarter and better educated than other people. Robert Parker can only get away with having his detective, Spenser, quote poetry because he works so hard to establish Spenser as a tough guy. For every line of poetry, Spenser has to work out half an hour in the gym to win our forgiveness for his erudition. We're afraid of and resentful of people who know more than we do, and when they act as if they think it makes them superior to us, we hate them.

## Insanity

We are terrified of people who don't live in the same reality we do, who don't have the same definition of rational behavior. You can't talk to them, you can't reason with them; there is no common ground. However much mental health professionals might deplore it, the fact is that when the public is convinced someone is dangerously insane, all considerations go out the window except one: stopping this crazy person. Unless the storyteller works very hard to win sympathy for the insane character, the audience has no qualms about seeing him brutally subdued or killed. The world isn't safe as long as the madman has any chance of escaping. And if, like Charles Manson and his "family" or Adolf Hitler and the Nazi party, the madman has succeeded in convincing others that his version of reality is the truth, the audience's fear and loathing is all the greater.

In film and on stage, insanity is easy to depict—a wide-eyed stare or darting eyes, nervous tics. But the best actors don't resort to such easy tricks, and neither do the best writers. It is far more effective to convince the audience that a character is insane by letting us see her strange perceptions of reality—her paranoia or delusions.

"Do you think I don't know what you're doing?" asked Nora softly. "I know why you brought me here."

"Yeah," said Pete, a little confused. "I brought you here for dinner."

"You just want to impress all your friends," she said. "You just want them to see me with you. But it won't work. I'm in disguise. That's why I wore this red scarf. Nobody ever recognizes me when I wear this red scarf." She leaned forward and whispered a secret. "I took it from my mother's coffin before they buried her."

Oh good, thought Pete. Not only is this the most expensive blind date I've ever gone on, not only did Steve and Gracie back out at the last minute so I had to go alone, but also this Nora turns out to be crazy. If she isn't at least OK in bed, Steve will not live to see another day.

"Don't eat any of the shrimp sauce," Nora said. "It's poisoned."

There is no chance that the audience will be hoping for Pete and Nora to end up with a long-term relationship. They will have no sympathy for Nora's character—unless the author goes to extraordinary lengths to make her sympathetic, either by showing the cause of her insanity or by convincing us, somehow, that she isn't insane at all.

This is what was done in the brilliant film *A Woman Under the Influence*. The main character has just returned from a mental hospital, and her family treats her very gingerly; neither she nor they are fully convinced that she is cured. But as the film goes on, we gradually realize that while it was the main character who attempted suicide, she isn't crazy—it's her husband who's truly evil and insane, even though nobody else realizes it, and he makes her life so unbearable that suicide seems like the only possible escape. She is saved from her husband's pathological rage only by the heroic efforts of her little children. By the end of the film our sympathy with the woman is complete—but by then we also don't think of her as an insane person. It's her husband who's insane, and true to the rule, our only feeling for him then is loathing and fear.

The only time insanity can work *for* a character is when it's kept within safe bounds—minor eccentricities that can even be rather charming. And even then, an insane character is almost never viable as the main character in the story. The audience is rarely comfortable enough with insane characters to want to spend any length of time with them.

## Attitude

The bad guy's attitude toward himself and others is the mirror image of the good guy's. To make us dislike Pete, make him humorless, completely unable to laugh at himself. When things go wrong, have him whine and complain and blame everyone but himself. When things go right, have him take all the credit and boast about his accomplishment. Make sure Pete never shows regard for other people's feelings, judges people without listening to their explanations, and never trusts or believes anybody. Pete always treats rich and influential people better than he treats the poor and powerless, and he has no qualms about being a flaming hypocrite. In short, he treats other people as if they exist only to serve his purposes. You can be sure the audience will detest him.

## Redeeming Virtues: The Understandable Villain

While readers will eventually get sick of a hero who's too good to be true, they almost never refuse to believe in a villain. Unless you deliberately make the villain comic, there is almost no limit to the audience's willingness to hate and fear—the seemingly endless series of *Friday the 13th* sequels makes that plain enough.

That doesn't mean, however, that you *should* create completely evil villains. While many stories—perhaps most—draw clear distinctions between good guys and bad guys, there are also quite a few stories that don't.

At the beginning of this chapter I mentioned my fondness for stories in which *all* the characters are at least somewhat sympathetic, so that the audience is never given a clear list of people to love and people to hate.

Even if you don't go that far, however, you can still improve your story by making sure that your negative characters are as honestly depicted as your heroes.

What you must remember is that everybody is the hero of his own story. Even if a character is completely evil, he will no doubt have his own internal story that depicts him as noble. Perhaps he fancies himself a benefactor, an altruist. Perhaps he feels that his innate superiority gives him the right to exploit other people the way people exploit lower animals. Perhaps he feels that ill treatment he has suffered in the past justifies any harm he causes now. Perhaps he believes that everybody acts the way he acts—they just *pretend* to be nice. The bad guy doesn't necessarily believe his own version of events—or at least not all the time—but one way or another, the bad guy has found a way to justify his actions to himself, and if you're going to depict him honestly, you have to let your readers know his version of events.

You can soften your "bad guys" even further by partially justifying their actions. Just as you can make a hero more believable by giving him endearing imperfections, you can make a villain more believable by giving her compensating virtues. Show that there *is* someone she loves or respects; show that she does keep *some* promises; show that she really *was* deeply wronged at some time, so that her hate and rage is partially justified. You may never actually persuade your readers to *like* her, but you can win their respect. In fact, by giving your villain some ennobling qualities you actually make her a worthier opponent for your hero.

What you *can't* do, however, is make a sadist or a bully or a madman or a usurper into a completely sympathetic character. Any story that seems to do so always does it by showing the reader, at some point in the narrative, that in fact the character is *not* a sadist or a bully or a madman or a usurper, that when you thought he was, it was an illusion or a misperception; he was only pretending to be a bully in order to accomplish some noble purpose; he was under the influence of drugs or hypnosis and so it wasn't really "himself" doing all those bad things; his children were being held hostage and the person he killed with his package bomb really deserved to die anyway; his actions were fully justified if only people knew the true story; he really was the rightful heir to the throne and not a usurper at all; and so on.

The storyteller's strongest tools for provoking the readers' antipathy cannot be overwhelmed by the tools for arousing sympathy. As long as they remain true within the story—as long as you don't deny that Nora did the terrible things you showed her doing, as long as you don't deny that the things she did *were* terrible, and as long as you show that Nora is still the same person who did those bad things—then the audience will never be on Nora's side. The most you can do is soften their hatred for her, show that she is more to be pitied than to be hated or feared. Even if the readers come to feel great pity for Nora, at no point will they want her to emerge victorious.

Nobody wants Oedipus to stay married to his mother. Nobody is rooting for Macbeth to win.

# CHAPTER 9

# THE HERO AND THE COMMON MAN

WHEN THE ANCIENT GREEKS AND ROMANS told a serious story, the characters were kings and queens, great warriors and heroes, the sort of people who expected to receive visitations from the gods—heck, the gods were often their aunts and cousins anyway. But when the Greeks and Romans set out to tell a story about common, everyday people, the result was comedy, in which the characters were lewd and foolish and corrupt.

It was long believed that great poetry could never be written about low characters—magnificent art demanded magnificent subject matter. The rules have changed since then. The invention of the novel—with such landmarks in English as *Pamela, Tom Jones, Robinson Crusoe,* and *Tristram Shandy*—proved that wonderful stories could take common people seriously.

Oddly enough, however, storytelling keeps drifting toward extraordinary heroes, so that the common people have to be rediscovered every few decades or so. Noted critic Northrop Frye examined this pattern and came up with the idea that our preference in fictional heroes swings back and forth like a pendulum. Frye used the words *Realistic* and *Romantic* in a special way, as the two ends of a descriptive spectrum. Romantic, in this context, doesn't have anything to do with whether or not a character is in love. At first heroes become more and more Romantic (idealized, extraordinary, exotic, magnificent) until finally they become so overblown and so cliched that we cease to believe in or care about them. In reaction, the pendulum swings back the other way, and our fictional heroes become Realistic—common, plain people, living lives that are well within the experience of the readers. However, these Realistic heroes quickly become boring, because people who live lives no different from our own are not terribly interesting to read about—or to write about. So storytellers almost immediately begin making their heroes just a little out of the ordinary, so that readers will again be fascinated—until the Romantic hero is in the saddle again.

In creating characters, we don't have to worry about pendulums. What concerns us is that our main characters must be at once believable and interesting—simultaneously Realistic and Romantic. Each of us, however, finds a different balance between the two. How extraordinary or exotic or "elevated" do characters need to be for you to want to read or write about them? How much detail, how much commonness, how much familiarity must characters have before you believe in them? Your answer will be different from mine and from every other writer's; your audience will consist of readers who agree with your answer.

Look at the fiction market today, and you'll see what I mean. Do you want Romantic characters? Thrillers deal with people who are on the cutting edge of power in the world—spies, diplomats, heads of state—and their lives are never ordinary; even shopping for groceries, they have to watch out for the enemy. Historical romances deal with characters in exotic times and places, and usually people of high station in an era when class distinctions meant all the difference in the world. Glitter romances deal with the very rich, jetting between assignations in Rio, Paris, and Singapore. Mysteries offer us the detective as avenging angel, tracking down the guilty despite their best efforts to escape retribution. Fantasy, the true heir of the great Romantic tradition, still shows us kings and queens wielding the power of magic. Science fiction takes us to worlds that have never been, to show us new kinds of magic, new kinds of nobility, new kinds of humanity.

Yet every single one of these genres includes stories that rebel against Romantic excess, that insist on realism. John LeCarre's spy thrillers achieved great note in large part because his characters were *not* Romantic, James Bond-like heroes, but instead ordinary people who got sick, confused, tired, old; people who made mistakes and had to bear the consequences. Yet is George Smiley *really* ordinary? Of course not. He is only one of the "common people" by comparison with the extravagance that went before. We still look at George Smiley with admiration and awe; we still expect him to achieve great things. He still moves through an exotic world. He is still a true Hero, no matter how much shine has been taken off his armor.

The same pattern can be found among mystery novels. John Mortimer's wonderful hero Rumpole is an English barrister who will never achieve recognition, who isn't terribly successful and loses a lot of cases, and who certainly isn't rich. His home life is deplorable, as he endures a testy relationship with his shrewish wife whom he calls "She-who-must-be-obeyed." His very ordinariness is endearing—we read of him and feel that he is One Of Us. Yet Rumpole is really not ordinary at all, or we wouldn't like reading about him. After the realism has won our belief, we still see him solving cases through remarkable persistence and clever insights, and we come to believe that in fact he *deserves* great recognition and a place on the bench. Others may think he's ordinary, but *we* know he's a truly remarkable, admirable man. The same pattern is followed by other "ordinary" mystery heroes—Ruth Rendell's Inspector Wexford, Robert Parker's Spenser, and of course all the heroes of the American hard-boiled detective tradition.

Just when the fantasy genre seemed likely to lose its last connection with reality, Stephen R. Donaldson made a bitter-hearted leper named Thomas Covenant the reluctant hero of his stories; more recently, Megan

Lindholm's *Wizard of the Pigeons* found magic in a Vietnam veteran living among the street people of Seattle. A large part of Stephen King's appeal as a writer of horror, fantasy, and science fiction has been his insistence on using heroes from the American middle class, living in the familiar world of fast food, shopping malls, and television. Yet even as we recognize people and details from the real life around us, all these stories would have been pointless had their heroes not been extraordinary in one way or another, though their uniqueness was hidden even from themselves.

As I pointed out in Chapter 8, readers tend to like a character who is at least superficially like themselves. But they quickly lose interest unless this particular character is somehow out of the ordinary. The character may wear the mask of the common man, but underneath his true face must always be the face of the hero.

Why? Because we don't read stories to duplicate real life. In our own diaries and journals we tend to write down only what was out of the ordinary, skipping the dull parts of the day. Why should we read the dull parts in the life of a made-up character?

We read stories to get experiences we've never known firsthand, or to gain a clearer understanding of experiences we *have* had. In the process, we follow one or more characters the way we follow our "self" in our dreams; we assimilate the story as if what happened to the main characters had happened to us. We identify with heroes. As they move through the story, what happens to them happens to us.

In comedy, heroes go through all the terrible things that we fear or face in our own lives—but they teach us to look at disaster with enough distance that we can laugh at it. In non-comic fiction, the hero shows us what matters, what has value, what has meaning among the random and meaningless events of life. In all stories, the hero is our teacher-by-example, and if we are to be that hero's disciple for the duration of the tale, we must have *awe*: We must know that the hero has some insight, some knowledge that we ourselves do not understand, some value or power that we do not yet have.

This is true even in that great bastion of extreme realism, the academic/literary genre (those who refer to their genre as "serious literature"—as if the rest of us are just kidding). One reason why the academic/literary genre usually reaches such a small fragment of the reading public is because in their pursuit of seriousness, they have beaten down the Romantic impulse wherever it rears its head. But the Romantic impulse is still there. Even in the endless stories about college professors or advertising writers or housewives entering midlife crises and trying to make sense of their senseless lives, the heroes always seem to face some uncommon problems, always seem to be extraordinarily contemplative and perceptive, always seem to reach a moment of epiphany in which they pass along a key insight to the reader. Despite their seeming ordinariness, these heroes always turn out to be extraordinary, once we truly understand them.

Arthur Miller may have meant Willy Loman to be a non-heroic hero in *Death of a Salesman*—he was named "low man" to make sure we got the point—but by the end Miller has shown us that Loman dreamed of greatness for himself and his children and his failure to achieve it destroyed him. The fact that Loman reached such a point of despair that he killed himself moves him out of the ordinary—but what really makes Loman a figure of awe is that he *expected* himself and his sons to be great, that he measured himself against such high standards that, by trying to meet them, he became exactly the Romantic hero that Arthur Miller was trying to avoid. He was one of the knights of the round table who failed to find the Holy Grail—but he was nobly searching for it nonetheless.

The writers in the Realistic tradition—for instance, Updike, Bellow, and Fowles—still give their characters heroic proportion; only it's more restrained, used less boldly, better disguised. By the end of Bellow's novel *Humboldt's Gift*, Humboldt is definitely bigger than life; he is, in his own way, as romantically "enlarged" as Captain Blood or Rhett Butler. The difference is that Captain Blood was involved in jeopardy on page one and bigger than life by page thirty, while Humboldt didn't really become recognizably heroic in size until near the end of the book.

Without giving the audience some reason to feel awe toward the hero, there would be no story. Eliminate the usual sources of awe, the usual ways of making a character larger than life, and the storyteller will either find another or lose interest in the tale.

More recently, many academic/literary writers have striven to avoid "naive identification" by creating "aesthetic distance"—but these writers have merely replaced the character-hero with the author-as-hero, so that the admiration that used to be directed toward a character is now directed toward the artist who created the exquisite, extraordinary text.

If there is no awe, there is no audience. In every successful story—every story that is loved and admired by at least one reader who is not a close friend or blood relative of the author—the author has created characters who somehow inspire enough admiration, respect, or awe that readers are willing to identify with them, to become their disciples for the duration of the tale.

I'm not for a moment advocating that you artificially juice up your characters to make them more Romantic. That's no more likely to result in good characterization than overwhelming your heroes with humdrum details. You'll do much better if you trust your own instincts to choose the balance between Romance and Realism that's right for you and for your natural audience.

What you need is not a specific recipe but rather a general awareness: It's vital that along with making Nora seem exciting and wonderful, you also help your readers understand and believe in her, so they can connect her with their own lives. Along with making Pete seem understandable and believable, you should also show your readers why he is important enough and admirable enough to deserve a place in their memories, to be a worthy exemplar of the meanings of life.

Often when you find yourself blocked—when you can't bring yourself to start or continue a story—the reason is that you have forgotten or have not yet discovered what is extraordinary about your main character. Go back over your notes, over the part of the story you've already told, and ask yourself: What's so special about this woman that people should hear the story of her life? Or, more to the point, ask yourself: Why does her story matter to *me*?

You've got a story going. Pete's just an ordinary twenty-three-year-old man, just finishing college after a three-year stint in the army. Degree in business administration with good-enough but not spectacular grades, a few failed romances just like everybody else's failed romances. He's hired by a major corporation and put in charge of a department. After a year on the job, others are getting promoted—but not him. He just isn't doing all that good a job. He keeps getting distracted.

Then you don't know what to do. You sit down to write, and what you say doesn't seem to make any difference, it's all lousy. You're blocked. So you take a look at Pete's character. There's no reason to notice him, nothing obviously special about him. You realize that until you find—or invent—something extraordinary about him, you've got no story.

So you look for what it is that makes him not just different, but *better* or more admirable than the others. Why *isn't* he succeeding? What is it about the others that gets them promoted? You search through what you've written so far and you haven't answered that question. You did a great job of making him ordinary and common. But there *is* something different about him: He isn't getting promoted on the normal track. Why?

It's not that he's unambitious—he read *Iacocca* just like everybody else in the M.B.A. program, and he dreams of seven-figure salaries and million-dollar bonuses, of heading a company with a budget larger than Brazil's. So maybe his "lack" is that he can't bring himself to have the attitude toward his underlings that most other managers in his company seem to have. He doesn't regard them as machines that must run at maximum efficiency or be replaced; he can't bring himself to judge their worth according to the bottom line. Pete just can't stop caring about them as human beings.

If this is what makes Pete special, how does that affect your story? You've already got a character, an office manager named Nora. In the present draft you had Pete try to joke with her, but she took it as flirting and shut him down fast with a nasty little speech about sexual harassment. You never meant that relationship to go anywhere—you were just using Nora as a minor character to show Pete making an ordinary dumb mistake. But now that you have keyed in on Pete's extraordinary tendency to care about people even when it's bad for his company and his career, why not use Nora to develop that trait? Pete has good reason to think she's a jerk—if he could fire anybody, he could surely fire her, right?

So when Nora starts having problems, the solution is obvious: Get rid of her. She's inattentive. She makes mistakes. She isn't assigning work to her staff—one of her typists has even gone around *asking* for work because Nora hasn't assigned her anything in a week. Some of your other people are beginning to complain that Nora's office is slow in returning paperwork. Nora has been snapping at anyone who dares to ask about late or missing work, and morale in her office is awful.

But Pete can't just fire her. For one thing, he's afraid that she'll think he's firing her because she rejected his "sexual advances," even though *he* didn't think his joking had any sexual overtones. For another thing, she used to do terrific work—something must be wrong. So he calls her in and finds out that Nora is having a terrible time with her six-year-old in school and her three-year-old's day-care situation is awful; her ex-husband is trying to get custody, and the school and day-care problems play right into his hands. In other words, her life's a mess—and the very worst thing that could happen right now is to lose her job.

He talks about Nora to a friend from school who has a managerial job in the same city. The friend tells him to fire her—she isn't doing the work, and Pete doesn't have the right to turn the company into a charitable organization for people with screwed-up lives. He was hired as a manager, not a clergyman. But Pete can't bring himself to fire her. Instead he works late, going over Nora's workload and finding ways to redistribute it, to take up the slack—in essence, he ends up doing her job.

If this were a love story, you'd develop a romance between Pete and Nora. But that idea bores you. So you have Nora react nastily to Pete's "intrusions" into her office domain, not realizing that he's saving her bacon; she even complains about Pete to the people above *him*. He can't even tell them what he's doing—they'd be appalled if they knew he had done her job for her instead of staying in the role of a manager. After five months of Nora sniping at Pete while he covers for her, she finally gets her kids' problems straightened out, her husband off her back, and her life back in gear. Naturally, Pete reassigns to Nora all the work he had removed from her during her hard times. Nora, however, is outraged at a sudden doubling of her workload with no commensurate rise in salary. She quits—after writing nasty letters complaining about Pete to the people over him.

Maybe that's the end of your story; maybe it's just one incident along the way, with other plot threads weaving through the story. What matters is that it establishes that, while Pete is definitely a common man, there is also something uncommon about him—even heroic. He is able to empathize even with people who aren't nice to him. He is, in fact, a noble figure.

Sure, he gets so furious at Nora that he writes out her dismissal notice a half-dozen times before she finally quits. When she's gone, after doing real damage to his career when his only "crime" was helping hold her life together, he vows that he'll never be such a sucker again. These are all common, natural, ordinary reactions. But the audience knows that when it comes right down to it, Pete *will* do it again, over and over. He won't have a Lee Iacocca career—but the audience is in awe of him for a virtue he doesn't even value himself.

Searching for the extraordinary in your characters can help you write your story. More important, though, it will help your readers find what they're looking for in fiction. You won't please everybody. Some readers will reject your story because your hero isn't heroic enough for them to bother with; others because you made him too heroic for them to believe. That will always happen, and there's nothing you can do about it.

What you *can* do is search for what is "larger than life" in your characters and then make sure that your story reveals their nobility, their grandeur, however subtle and well-disguised it may be amid realistic and common details.

# CHAPTER 10

# THE COMIC CHARACTER: CONTROLLED DISBELIEF

LAST NIGHT I WATCHED REX REED'S REVIEW of Rob Reiner's film *The Princess Bride*. I usually disagree with everything Reed says, which is half the fun of watching him. One comment he made in this review was worth remembering. He said that Reiner's idea of creating a comic character was to give him a funny accent—and for Reed, that just wasn't enough. A wizard who talks like a New York Jew? Who can believe that?

Reed was right in principle. Using the wrong accent can destroy the believability of a character. I think immediately of the movie *Tess*, in which an otherwise powerful performance by Nastassia Kinski was deeply marred by an accent that made it impossible for me to believe her as a Wessex girl. In other films her accent hasn't been a problem, but *Tess* was an adaptation from Hardy's *Tess of the d'Urbervilles*, and in Hardy's works the Wessex milieu is so important that to be false to it is to be false to the story. To me it was a serious flaw in a movie that reached for greatness.

If Kinski's accent had been right for Wessex, I would not have noticed her speech at all. Because her accent was wrong, it weakened my belief and marred the movie. But in *The Princess Bride*, I thought Miracle Max's New York Jewish accent, dead wrong for the Romantic medieval milieu, was wonderfully funny.

What's the difference?

Comic characters cannot be believable in the same way that other characters are. They can't be *un*believable, either. But comedy almost always deals with pain, and comic characters almost always suffer. If we believed in them with the same intensity we bring to straight characters, their pain would be unbearable. Instead, the author gives the audience clues that the character is not to be taken seriously. Something is made deliberately "wrong" about the character, so that we know we aren't supposed to react with sympathy. Instead we're supposed to laugh.

That's what Miracle Max's accent helps to do. There's no way he could have a New York Jewish accent. We instantly recognize that he's wrong, out of place in the story. Yet he is exactly what we need: The hero of the story has just been killed, and we're hungry for relief. Max lifts up the hero's arm, lets it drop limply to the table, and says, in his impossible accent, "I've seen worse." We laugh because of the wrongness of his response.

At the same time, because this is a Romance, we hope that Miracle Max's name is for real. We want him to be able to resurrect the hero. Max's magical powers are *not* a joke—they are important, and within the context of the story, they are believable. Max's Jewish accent, being false, makes him comic; his magical power makes him important.

The problem is that the audience still has to believe in and care about comic characters. The goal of the comedy writer isn't doubt, but rather controlled disbelief. Characters must be believable enough that the audience will say, "Yes! Isn't that the truth! Isn't that what always happens! I've known people like that! That's exactly what always happens to me!" Yet the same characters must be unbelievable enough that the audience doesn't feel obliged to empathize with them. The characters must constantly give the audience permission to laugh at their misfortunes.

That's why comedy is so much harder to write well than straight fiction. The comedy writer always walks a delicate line between being too believable, and therefore not funny, and being too unbelievable, and therefore losing the audience's interest.

Remember that comic characters appear even in the most serious works, and that even the most serious characters have comic moments. And when you introduce a comic character into a story that must be utterly believable, the fragile balance of controlled disbelief becomes even more important.

Here are some of the devices we use to signal the audience that it's all right to laugh:

## DOING A "TAKE"

The simplest way of signaling comic unbelievability is to talk directly to the audience. In non-comic fiction it has long been out of fashion to write passages directly to the "dear reader," and in non-comic film and television, while we accept the convention of an occasional narrator who speaks to the audience, we don't expect a *character* to do so. Comedy, however, constantly breaks that convention. Woody Allen has his comic characters speak to the audience in film after film, using both voice-over narration and on-screen comments. On TV, Dobie Gillis spoke to the audience—but only when he was alone on screen. In the action comedy *Moonlighting*, every episode has at least one moment when one character reminds another of the fact that they're on a television show with an audience watching ("Why are we stopping here?" "It's time for a commercial.") For me, this device is too heavy-handed—it has crossed the line so far that it makes it hard for me to take the serious aspects of the show seriously; for many other viewers, however, it's the highlight of the show.

You can have direct contact with the audience without actually speaking to them. At one point in *Beverly Hills Cop*—an action movie that depends on our taking pain and jeopardy very seriously at times—there is a moment when Eddie Murphy is told something that strikes him as outrageous, whereupon he turns and looks straight into the camera with no expression at all on his face. He holds that connection for a single beat, not even a second, and then goes on. But the audience laughs in delight. Murphy's momentary awareness of the camera is not enough to destroy the audience's belief in the story, but it *is* a good comic signal not to take everything too seriously.

This is called a "take," a straight-to-the-audience reaction. The late comedian Jack Benny was the master of the take. Sometimes it seemed like he could stretch a take forever, earning laugh after laugh without saying a word. How did it work? Another character would say something outrageous, something that was either so dumb or so wrong or so rude that it would take a thousand words to answer. But Benny said nothing at all. Instead, he folded his arms and looked at the audience—a long, lingering look, with a disgusted expression on his face. Finally he turned back to look at the person who said the outrageous thing—but still couldn't answer. So again he would look at the audience. Sometimes, in despair, he would say, "Well." The audience would roar with laughter again and again during the take. I never saw it fail.

But Jack Benny was doing it in front of a live audience. How does a fiction writer do a take? One way is to insert comments to the reader. Kurt Vonnegut used to do it all the time. He'd pick a phrase like "so it goes" or "hi ho" and interject it repeatedly after something awful happened in the story. It provided exactly the same degree of controlled disbelief as Jack Benny folding his arms and looking at the audience or Eddie Murphy doing his deadpan take and then turning back to the action.

You can do it less flamboyantly than Vonnegut, of course. It can be done with a fillip of attitude:

> I yelled at the cat, kicked at it—finally it dropped the squirrel and took refuge on the neighbor's porch. The baby squirrel just lay there, trembling, but it didn't seem to be hurt. No blood, anyway, and as I reached down it took a few steps, so nothing was broken. I picked it up and carried it back to the tree, feeling like a hero for saving its life. Of course it bit my hand.

The paragraph ends with the narrator in pain. But the "of course" is a take—the narrator is looking at the audience with a mixture of disgust and resignation. You might as well give up on gratitude cause you ain't gonna get it, says that *of course*. It's a way of putting some distance between the audience and the pain.

We can do the same thing without a word.

> I yelled at the cat, kicked at it—finally it dropped the squirrel and took refuge on the neighbor's porch. The baby squirrel just lay there, trembling, but it didn't seem to be hurt. No blood, anyway, and as I reached down it took a few steps, so nothing was broken. I picked it up and carried it back to the tree, feeling like a hero for saving its life.
>     It bit my hand.

The paragraph break emphasizes the next sentence, calls attention to it, makes you pause just a beat to digest it. It's a take.

# EXAGGERATION

Let's continue the story:

> ... I picked it up and carried it back to the tree, feeling like a hero for saving its life. It bit my hand.
>
>   I put a bandage on the wound, but it got infected anyway. When my hand turned brown and got to the size of a boxing glove, I went to the doctor. He injected a quart of penicillin into my backside even though we both agreed that the problem was in my hand. As I left, he gave me several brochures about various brands of artificial arm. "You might want to look these over and decide which you like best," he said, "just in case you don't get lockjaw and die hideously."
>
>   I promised him that next time I'd take animal bites more seriously. I also made a firm resolution to look for every opportunity to feed baby squirrels to cats.

It *is* true that leaving an animal bite untreated could lead to gangrene, tetanus, or even rabies. But as you read this passage, you didn't for a moment believe that the narrator was really on the verge of losing his hand. Nor did you believe that his hand was really the size of a boxing glove, or that the narrator would actually catch baby squirrels and feed them to cats. The remark about squirrels was an exaggeration of his chagrin at how his kindness to animals turned out.

   Note, though, that in this version the narrator does not do a take, or give any other sign to the reader that he thinks this passage is funny. A vital principle of comic writing is not to laugh at your own humor—not to give a sign that either the author or the characters are amused at their own clever wit. It would have been deadly if the doctor's exaggerations, instead of being delivered deadpan, had been reported like this:

> "You might want to look these over and decide which you like best," he joked, "just in case you don't get lockjaw and die hideously." He giggled insanely as I left.

Now, I can't be sure that you thought the first version was particularly amusing, but I do know that this version is considerably *less* funny. This time the narrator tells us the doctor was joking, which spoils the fun of figuring out that the narrator is exaggerating. And the line about giggling insanely carries exaggeration too far. The writer is trying too hard, the disbelief is out of control, and both the humor and the story are dead in the water.

# DOWNPLAYING

The reverse of exaggeration is for a character to downplay the importance of her problems. Imagine a comic character being held at knifepoint by a vicious enemy—not usually a funny situation.

   If your strategy were exaggeration, you could have the heroine immediately begin to plead for her life in a comically exaggerated way. She would start to cry, fall to her knees, grovel, whine, and if you carry it just far enough, the audience will laugh.

But you could also have her downplay her fear. She could plead for her life with comic nonchalance: "I think we've got a little misunderstanding here. I don't know how you ever got the impression that I didn't like you. Actually I look up to you. I want to be just like you. Where did you buy that great knife?"

That same exaggerated nonchalance, that comic coolness, can show up in the narration.

> His ex-wife left him with so little that when his apartment got burglarized it took him an hour to notice it. He took a shower, fixed dinner, and read the paper; only when he went to turn on the TV did he realize it was gone.

A mild exaggeration; a mild amount of humor. But now we'll make it first person and exaggerate his nonchalant attitude a little more.

> I got home, saw the drawers dumped out, the couch ripped open, all the books off the shelves, and the TV missing. At first I figured my ex-wife had sent her lawyers over for another round. I only realized it was burglars when I saw that there wasn't a message in lipstick on the mirror. Usually she wrote things like "Die, capitalist pig" or "Helter-Skelter."

Not for a moment do you believe that the narrator thought any such thing. He's just being nonchalant about the burglary—and exaggerating his ex-wife's behavior, too. We aren't expected to believe his nonchalance. He is going through things that would make a normal person angry and afraid; but by downplaying his response to them, the narrator makes it amusing instead of infuriating.

# ODDNESS

When eccentricity is taken to extremes it becomes less believable, eventually leading to farce or melodrama. Oddness is the prime tool of the comic storyteller.

The use of a Jewish accent for Miracle Max is an example of simple oddness. The misplacement of a stereotype makes us laugh, makes us take all that the character does a bit less seriously. But stereotypes can only take you so far.

The same thing is often done with the way a character dresses. Costume is a stereotype—a construction worker dresses a certain way, a ballet dancer another. Putting a character in inappropriate dress can also make us laugh. That's why we have seen so many comedies with men in drag. Show a character wearing white socks with brown shoes and a blue suit, and we know he's a geek. Shakespeare makes Malvolio in *Twelfth Night* appear on stage comically dressed and cross-gartered as the result of a practical joke, and we laugh. It makes him funny—but it doesn't make us care.

Malvolio is made ridiculous by his absurd apparel; he is made important by the *reasons* for his strange clothing. The clothing, by itself, would be a trivial effect.

The trouble is that oddness is a tool you normally use for *minor* characters. Oddness, by itself, can't make a character major. It can even *diminish* a character.

If you have a major comic character, you'll use all the Romantic and Realistic techniques of characterization. So what makes him comic? It's a matter of timing. Very early in our acquaintance with the character, before the other techniques have had a chance to win the audience's firm belief, you undercut those other techniques by making the character just a little too odd or extreme to believe completely.

It's hard to imagine a serious play that couldn't be turned into a farce using this technique. *King Lear* could be hilarious with Bob Newhart in the lead. Imagine John Candy as Macbeth or Howie Mandel as Oedipus. If you recognize these comedians' names, you already know something about their eccentricities—Bob Newhart's resentful meekness, John Candy's cheerful but brutal insensitivity, Howie Mandel's manic indecision. If you saw them in these plays, their eccentricity would assert itself long before the other techniques of characterization came into play. Picture these moments:

Bob Newhart, looking slightly peeved and intoning, "Blow, winds! Crack your cheeks!"

Howie Mandel nervously rejecting several brooches until he finds just the right ones to jab out his eyes with.

John Candy's blustering confidence in himself as he tries to deal with the witches, while Gilda Radner, as Lady Macbeth, pushes him out of their room to go kill Duncan.

You would not *believe* any of these performers in the roles, not if they used their comic personas. But it is precisely their controlled disbelief that would make their performances hilariously funny.

Along these lines, it's worth pointing out that eccentricity, if carried to extremes in a major character, eventually becomes the *subject* of the comedy. Ben Jonson called it comedy of humors—comedy arising from a character being completely dominated by only one desire or temperament. Misers, hypochondriacs, hypocrites, cowards have traits that all humans share to some degree. Exaggerate the trait enough, and the characters are unbelievable enough to be funny. Exaggerate the trait out of all proportion, and they become either monstrous or utterly unbelievable. Comedy of humors carries exaggeration right to the edge of unbelievability or monstrosity. Your story can still be funny, but it also reduces your ability to move your audience. The Three Stooges and the Marx Brothers made people laugh, but they never really made people care.

# CHAPTER 11

# THE SERIOUS CHARACTER: MAKE US BELIEVE

DO YOU WANT YOUR READERS TO BELIEVE in your characters? The one thing you can never do is appeal to the facts. In a news story you quote sources; in history you cite documents. But in fiction you have no such recourse—the single worst defense of an unbelievable event or character is to say, "But that really happened once."

Fiction doesn't deal with what happened once. Fiction deals with what *happens*. Your job is not to create characters who exactly match reality. Your job is to create characters who *seem* real, who are plausible to the audience.

This chapter presents the tools of realism, the techniques that will earn your readers' trust. These methods won't make your story "truthful"—the truth of your tale arises from your unconscious choices, from your beliefs that are so ingrained that you may not even know you believe them, because it doesn't occur to you that they might not be true. What these tools provide is the *illusion* of truth.

Contradictory as that sounds, it's a vital part of storytelling. You must provide your audience with details that seem familiar and appropriate, so that they are constantly saying to themselves, "Yes, that's right, that's true, that's just the way it would be, people *do* that." With each "yes" the audience becomes more convinced that you are a storyteller who knows something.

They let down their barriers of skepticism and let you lead them through the world of your story, absorbing the people and events into their memories, identifying with your heroes, making their stories a part of themselves in a way that factual stories never can. Strike a false note, and barriers go back up; your readers pull out of the story a little, each time a little more, until you've lost them and your story has no more power over them.

I could make this chapter very short by telling you in a single word how to make your characters more believable: details. The more information about a character, the more the audience will believe in him.

It isn't really that simple, though. You don't want just any details, you want relevant, appropriate details. Nor do you want the details to stop the movement of the story any more than necessary. So the tools of realism are designed to present details about a character appropriately and effectively.

# ELABORATION OF MOTIVE

The most important tool that will help your audience believe in your characters is elaboration of motive. If you don't tell your audience what a character's motives are, the audience will assume the obvious motive: a simple, single motive, a naked archetype or a cliche. To make characters more believable, more real, we give them more complex, even contradictory motives, and we justify them better.

In the heroic fantasy film *Conan the Barbarian*, young Conan's mother is killed before his eyes. He spends the rest of the film searching for the murderer. It isn't hard for the audience to grasp the idea that he's looking for revenge.

Let's suppose that you wanted to start with the same situation, but you wanted Conan to be a more believable human being. His relentless obsession with revenge is not enough to sustain a realistic novel. The easiest step is to diversify—give him other motives, other interests, purposes, and loyalties. There would be many times when he did *not* think of revenge.

A more daring step is to make him even more complex: He is searching for the murderer, not to kill him, but to serve him. In Conan's mind the man's cruelty has been transformed into justice—he killed my mother, thinks Conan, because she was weak and small. I will be strong and large, and he will find me worthy.

This kind of motivation is borderline pathological—but it is also intriguing and believable, not at all the predictable revenge cliche.

Let's go back to Eddie Murphy's character in *Beverly Hills Cop*. Like Conan, he is given the simplest of motives—revenge for the death of a friend. Since it is an almost purely Romantic story, and a comic one at that, no more realism is needed; the audience found his character believable enough for the needs of the film.

But what if we wanted to make his character more real? We'd then have to invent a richer set of motives. What if his murdered friend was someone that Murphy had treated, not well, but badly, so that Murphy's desire for revenge is prompted not just by love but also by guilt. And let's say Murphy's tenacity in the case is not just because he's competitive and doesn't like to lose, but also because he's afraid that he's not very good as a cop, and if he doesn't succeed in this hard and dangerous case he won't be able to believe in himself. Add to this a bit of arrogance—there are times when he believes he *can't* fail, that he can't even die. And maybe he needs to show off a little, too.

One of the advantages of prose fiction is that you can bring all of a character's motives into the open. Because we can sometimes see into the characters' minds, their thoughts and feelings, their plans and reactions, we can also watch them shift from one motive to another. We can go one layer deeper, and discover motives that the characters don't even know they have.

Since motive is the character's purpose or intent when he takes an action, it is not something you can *add* to a character and then leave the rest of the story unchanged. The pursuit of ever-deeper motives is not a trivial game played on the surface of the story. Motive is at the story's heart. It is the most potent form of causal connection. So every revision of motive is a revision of the story.

Nora tells Pete that the man who was in her apartment was just a salesman. Pete reacts by saying cruel, vicious things to her, breaking a lamp, and storming out of her apartment. What does that scene *mean*?

At first glance, we might suppose Pete is insanely jealous. But what if we then learn that Pete knows the man—knows that he is a drug dealer and a former pimp? Now we understand that his rage doesn't come from a desire to control Nora, but rather from real concern for her welfare. Nora's lie is a silent witness to him that she is somehow involved with this man—in one way or another.

After a while, Nora confesses to Pete that the man in her apartment was her brother, but she hates him and doesn't want anyone she cares about to know that he has any connection with her. Now Pete understands her motive for lying. He's relieved.

Still later, the reader is shown a scene that makes it clear that the visitor was not her brother at all—he has been Nora's husband for ten years, and they have never been divorced. Now Nora's real motives are a mystery again.

Each new revelation of a main character's motive is not a simple matter of adding more information—it revises all the information that has gone before. Events that we thought meant one thing now mean another. The present constantly revises the meaning of the past. Revelation of the past constantly revises the meaning of the present. This is the primary device of detective fiction (and psychoanalysis), but all other genres use the technique as well.

There is a cost. The discovery of motive always requires examination of a character's thoughts, either through her dialogue with other characters, through direct telling of those thoughts, or by implication as new facts are revealed. All these examinations of motive come at the expense of action. A character who endlessly tries to understand her own motives eventually becomes a bore.

# ATTITUDE

One of the surest signs of an amateur story is when strange or important events happen around the narrator or point-of-view character, and he doesn't have an attitude toward them. Attitude is the other side of the coin of causation. Motive tells why he acts as he does; attitude is the way he reacts to outside events.

> Packer talked serious business on the phone, but when he walked into the restaurant I knew it was all bluff. His suit was shiny and too small, too short in the sleeves; his tie didn't come within six inches of his belt. I thought of asking him the name of his tailor, but he might be smart enough to know he was being insulted, and on the off chance he was an eccentric millionaire whose mother never taught him how to dress, I decided to hold off provoking him until after he paid for lunch.

This paragraph tells you something about Packer, of course—that he dresses awkwardly. You see Packer through the narrator's eyes, and this will always color your perception of him. The narrator feels contemptuous; so will you.

At the same time, his attitude also tells you about the narrator. He judges people by their clothing—whether they're worth taking seriously, whether he even thinks they're smart. Furthermore, he decides to treat this man civilly only because of a chance that he might actually have money.

This can be a complicated game. Push the narrator's contempt for Packer far enough, and we'll come to dislike the narrator and sympathize with Packer. If that's what you want, then it's working. But if you want the reader to like the narrator, you have to make sure his attitude doesn't get too flippant, that he never descends into meanness.

> Jacob was early for his appointment with Ryan's teacher; he stood by his car for a minute, looking at the place where Ryan spent his days. The Guilford Middle School looked bleak—long flat-roofed buildings of red brick, bare windows, lots of gravel and concrete. An institution.
>
> Going inside, Jacob hit his head on the door's low-hanging hinge assembly, a nasty bump that made him stop and close his eyes for a moment. When he opened them, it was as if the blow had made him color-blind. The corridor looked black and white. No, black and grey—nothing was clean enough to be called white. Bare fluorescent lights, blank walls interrupted only by doors with painted-over windows. Now Jacob understood why the only thing that ever seemed to go on at this place was discipline. It was a prison. The teacher was a warden, and poor Ryan had six months to go on his sentence.

Where does the attitude come from? At first only a few words: "bleak," "institution." But these words, which represent Jacob's attitude toward the school, are enough to set the tone. After that, the reader knows to interpret all the description as negative.

Without the attitude, though, there would be no point in describing the school. If Jacob weren't seeing it as a bleak institution, a dirty grey prison, the description would sound pretty much like every American school built since 1950. Might as well go straight to the scene with the teacher and not waste the reader's time visualizing the school at all.

Attitude can provide the tension in the scene. Here's the same scene twice, first without much attitude, then with more:

> An attractive-looking man came up to Nora's desk, glanced at her nameplate, and smiled at her. "Hi, Nora. Want some lunch?"

"No thanks," she answered. "I'll buy it somewhere else."

He looked confused.

"Aren't you the sandwich man? The last place I worked, they had a man who came around taking sandwich orders."

Now let's try the same opening, *with* attitude, and then go on, seeing how the scene develops.

He had a sharp, clean look about him, he was thin and wore clothes well, but Nora didn't like the confident way he looked down at her. As if he had a right to decide things for her. She had had bosses with that look, and they always ended up talking about her clothing and how she ought to brighten up the office by wearing something a little lower in the neckline.

His gaze dropped to the nameplate on her desk, just for a moment. Then he looked her in the eye again. "Hi, Nora. Want some lunch?" he said.

That's right, don't ask if I want lunch with *you*, just ask if I want lunch. If I say no, does that mean I have to sit at my desk and go hungry? "No thanks," she answered. "I'll buy it somewhere else."

He looked confused. She enjoyed that.

"Aren't you the sandwich man?" she asked. "The last place I worked, they had a man who came around taking sandwich orders."

He wasn't stupid—he knew he was being put down. "I was too cocky, right?"

"Not at all. I think you were just cocky enough."

That was a mistake. She was bantering with him now, and he was the kind who thought banter was a come-on. He started into some silly story about how a guy gets nervous when he sees a beautiful woman, his genes take over and he starts to swagger and preen.

"Preen?"

"Like peacocks and grouses. Put on a display. But that's not me. I'm really a sensitive guy. I make Phil Donahue look like a truck driver."

Time to put a stop to this. "You don't want to have lunch with me. I have seven children at home and three different social diseases. I also lead men on and then yell rape when they get too close. I am every nightmare you ever had about a domineering career woman. I think a man like you would call a woman like me a castrating bitch."

He didn't answer right away. Just looked at her, his smile gone cold. "No," he finally said. "That's what my mother would call you." He stood up. "You're new here. I asked you to lunch. My mistake, sorry." He walked on past her desk and out the door.

That's right, act hurt. You were just being friendly, and I jumped all over you. But I know better than that. I've seen that smile on too many faces not to know what lies behind it and where it leads. The man I'll go to lunch with is the one who doesn't speak to me until the normal course of work brings us together, and he won't ask me to lunch until he knows my name without looking at the nameplate on my desk.

Notice how the scene shifts, increasing the tension every time. At first, Nora's attitude disposes us to see the man as an overconfident womanizer. She stereotypes him, and we share her perception. The moment he admits the stereotype, though, by saying, "Too cocky?" our sympathy changes a little. We begin to think he might be decent after all—at least he's smart enough to know he's being put down. Then, when she doesn't pay attention to the next thing he says (we know she didn't pay attention because his dialogue isn't given in full), we begin to wonder if she isn't losing a romantic opportunity. (In reading fiction, we're always looking for romantic opportunities, and there *is* sexual tension in this scene, beginning from the moment she noticed that he was sharp-looking, thin, and wore clothes well.) Her speech about seven children and three social diseases is way too strong—we really lose sympathy with her.

In writing this, my first off-the-shelf follow-up was to have her reflect the audience perception at that point, and feel regret for having treated him so badly. Since that was my first response, though, I questioned it, and instead let her recognize the effect that his "hurt" attitude was designed to have, and then counter it by reflecting on what she *would* respond favorably to. This put her attitude in perspective, and instead of our thinking that the man wasn't so bad after all, we are now measuring him against her standard. We are fully on her side again, and though a romantic relationship with this guy is still a story possibility, we won't be disappointed if she finds somebody else.

Also, it was because I was giving her attitude that I came up with the conflict in the first place. If I had written the whole scene the way the first version began, I would never have invented the relationship that emerged. She would have had no reason to turn him down. She would still have been a stranger to me, and so she would remain a stranger to the audience.

Wasn't it because of her attitude that you took interest in her at all?

Notice that it is primarily through attitudes that we establish the meaning of relationships between people. Attitude tells us what people *notice* about each other, and what value they assign to what they see. Look at these brief scenes, all from Pete's point of view, all giving his attitude:

"What a day," she said.
     Yeah, right. Poor dear, couldn't she find a single dress that fit right?

"What a day," she said.
     She could say anything right now, and it would be music. He didn't realize how much he missed her until she came back.

"What a day," she said.
     She would tell him about it. They'd have dinner, watch TV, go to bed; if she didn't talk about how tired she was, they'd have sex. It was Tuesday. *Moonlighting*. So they'd definitely have sex, unless it was a rerun.

"What a day," she said.
     He looked at her sharply. Did she guess where he had been today? What he had done? No. She was too dull for that. An intelligent idea, even if one came along, would never get past her faded blue housedress.

You get the idea. The particular way your character responds to events lets the reader know who he is. It also helps *you* discover your character, since each bit of attitude you come up with will help you decide what your character will do next. Attitude and motive thus become inextricably intertwined. The character's response to event X will provide his motive for doing Y and Z.

# THE REMEMBERED PAST

One of the things I noticed as I started working with science fiction was that so many of the main characters seemed to come out of nowhere. They had no families; they all seemed to be loners and drifters who had no roots. This is fine, within the romantic tradition; does Dirty Harry have a mother? Does Aragorn? Darcy? Natty Bumppo? Rhett Butler? There's not much evidence for it. But it doesn't matter, in romance, because the story *becomes* the character's past. That is, by the end of the story, you know all the things the character did earlier in the story, so that now he does have connections with other people.

To fully realize a character, however, you must give him a whole life. He has a past, an elaborate set of meaningful connections to other people: family, friends, enemies, teachers, employers.

The most obvious way to tell a character's whole life is, of course, to begin the story with her birth. This is, however, the romantic tradition again. After all, no matter whether you're writing romance or realism, you have to begin the story at exactly the point where the main character becomes interesting and unique. If you start at her birth, then she must be bigger than life from the cradle. John Irving made the title character of *The World According to Garp* extraordinary from the moment of conception, when his very odd mother, a nurse in a hospital, impregnated herself using the body of a serviceman with terminal brain damage. But you can't always begin your stories with such bizarre events.

Instead, you will probably begin your story when your main characters are already nearly adults, with a wealth of experience behind them. How can you give a sense of the past?

## *Flashback*

The most obvious technique—and the least effective and most overused—is the flashback. The present action stops for a while as the character (or, worse yet, the narrator) remembers some key event from days of yore. The problem with this technique is exactly that: The action *stops* for the flashback. Time after time I have seen student stories or stories submitted to me as an editor that began like this:

> Nora peered through her windshield, trying to see through the heavy snowfall. "I can't be late," she murmured. It took all her concentration just to stay at forty miles per hour. Yet the events of the last few weeks kept intruding, taking her mind off the road. She thought back to her last quarrel with Pete.
>     [Here we get a fifteen-paragraph summary of all the stuff that happened up to yesterday.]

Her mind returned to the snowy road before her. There was her house. She pulled into the driveway and went inside. She ate dinner and watched TV, unable to concentrate, waiting for Pete's phone call. When he hadn't called by midnight, she went to bed.

The next morning . . .

Cringe along with me, please. Whatever is in that flashback wouldn't really give Nora a past, because she has no *present*. The flashback won't provide us with *additional* information about the character—it will provide us with our *only* information. Nothing happens on that snowy road *except* the flashback. The character has not yet been made important in the present moment—she is merely a stereotyped image, and a singularly dull one at that: a woman driving in the snow. By the time the flashback is over, the reader will have forgotten about the snow—there's nothing to remember anyway. We have no anchor in the present moment, so we are soon hopelessly adrift in memory.

A rule of thumb: If you feel a need to have a flashback on the first or second page of your story, either your story should begin with the events of the flashback, or you should get us involved with some compelling present characters and events before flashing back.

I usually prefer the former choice—beginning the story with the first events that matter. However, sometimes, many pages into a story, there's a real need for the character to remember some key event. If we're well rooted in the story, if we know enough and care enough about the character for the flashback to be important to us, then it can work very well. But it still has a serious cost. It stops the present action. The longer the flashback takes, the harder it is for the audience to remember what was happening just before the flashback began. So flashbacks should be rare, they should be brief, and they should take place only after you have anchored the story in the present action.

## Memory as a Present Event

Slightly more effective is having one character tell another a story out of the past. If you set it up properly, the telling of the story, besides conveying past information, can also *be* present action. Take, for example, the hiding-behind-tapestries scene in James Goldman's *The Lion in Winter*. Each of King Henry's three sons has come to King Philip of France, trying to make a deal with him to destroy all the others. Now Henry himself comes, and his sons hide behind tapestries as the two kings confront each other.

Provoked beyond endurance, Philip tells Henry a story about his childhood. But the story he tells does not stop the action—it *is* the action. Philip tells how he was homosexually seduced by Henry's son Richard, and how he went along with the act, though he loathed it, in order to be able to tell Henry about it now.

With the pain that this revelation causes Henry—not to mention Richard, behind the curtain—the story is doing double duty. It gives us some of the past of Richard and Philip, fleshing them out as characters; it also causes terrible emotional pain in the present, which strengthens Henry and Richard as victims and Philip as tormentor.

Notice, though, that the story is not just any story. It is about pain in the past, Philip's pain. It isn't enough just to tell random stories from a character's past. They have to be stories that are important.

Flashbacks can also follow this rule, and become part of a present event. If, for instance, a character's memory of a past event causes him to make a key decision, or take an action he would otherwise not have taken, then the memory is part of the present action, not really an interruption at all.

However, convenient memories can strain the reader's credulity. If it's a memory the character could have called to mind at any point, having her think of it just in time to make a key decision may seem like an implausible coincidence, as if the author is controlling events too tightly. If the memory is going to prompt a present decision, then the memory in turn must have been prompted by a recent event. Better yet, it should be a memory of something that the character never understood; new information or a new experience has changed the meaning of that event in her mind, so she isn't just remembering, she's also revising. Then the memory isn't passive, it's an active part of the story.

## Quick References

It's possible to drop in memories with only a slight pause in the forward movement of the story:

> I stood on the edge and saw how far down the bay was and suddenly remembered the cat I threw off the roof when I was a kid, how it twisted and snapped and clawed at the air. Never did find anything to hold onto till it hit the ground, and after that it didn't snap or claw or twist or breathe or anything. Took me fifteen minutes to crawl down the ladder off the roof after watching the cat fall. I was sure wishing for a ladder now.

> She pretended to be interested in his stories, but he knew that glazed look she got, her eyes not quite focused as she murmured occasionally to make him think she was listening. He used to murmur just like that during all those excruciating breakfasts when Nora insisted on telling him her dreams from the night before. It always felt to him like her dreams lasted longer than she slept. But it had never occurred to him that he could bore somebody else that badly.

If these quick references to the past are pertinent to the present events in the story, they won't feel like they're much of a break in the action, even if they don't make a significant change in the events of the story.

A rule of thumb: The shorter the memory, the less important it needs to be in order to justify stopping the story for it. If memories are short enough, they can be completely irrelevant:

> I don't recommend the restaurant. Worst food I ever had since I ate six live crickets on a two-dollar bet.

The six live crickets have nothing to do with the story. And it doesn't really tell you much specific information about the character. You certainly don't expect this information to make a difference in the story. But this brief memory still enriches the audience's concept of the character by implying some strangeness in his past; the audience will assume that there are plenty of other stories he could tell if he had the time. Without saying very much, you give the audience the impression that they know this character very well.

# THE IMPLIED PAST

It's possible to add to your character's past without stopping the action or even overtly mentioning her past at all, by giving her an *implied past*. You give readers a sense that the character has already lived a full life without telling them exactly what that past *was*.

## Expectation

What a character *expects* will happen in the present tells us instantly what has happened before in his past.

Suppose Pete steps toward a young girl, smiling, and extends his hand to give her a doughnut. To his surprise, she cringes away as if afraid she'll be struck. The audience knows at once—without the narrator having to say it—that the child has been beaten often enough that she *expects* a beating. Without slowing down the action at all, you have given a sense of the character's past and told us something of her pain.

Each of the following passages implies things about a character's past:

> The clerk repeated, "Cash or charge?" Nora looked helplessly at Pete. He spread his hands as if to show he wasn't holding a Gold Card. "You're the one doing the shopping," he said. "*I* can't afford this stuff." Still she made no move to pay. Finally he gave up and opened her purse for her. It was stuffed full of cash. He peeled two hundreds off an inch-thick stack and gave them to the clerk. Then he put the change and the receipt into the purse and snapped it shut.
>
> "You ought to use some of that to hire a bodyguard," he said. "The junkie who mugs you could o.d. and die, and then his family would sue you."
>
> She smiled and shrugged a little.
>
> As they left, Pete heard the clerk telling somebody, "And it was all hundreds! The whole purse!"

> Pete watched for a gap in the speeding cars and stepped out into the road. Immediately drivers began swerving and slamming on their brakes. If everybody had kept going smoothly, he would have made it across the road easily; as it was, he barely made it back to the curb alive. How can people ever cross streets in America, he thought, if drivers go crazy every time they see a pedestrian?

As soon as Pete got in the door Nora began to cry. "I didn't mean to do it," she said over and over again. "I'm sorry, I'm sorry." It took fifteen minutes before she'd believe him when he said it was no big deal. "But it's completely smashed," she said. Hadn't she ever heard of insurance?

Pete noticed that Nora kept sliding the bills between her thumb and fingers. Finally he realized she was counting them, again and again, as if she had to make sure they were all there.

Nora was finally calm enough that she could talk to Pete again, but when she went into the living room, there he was, straightening the magazines, dusting, arranging the pillows, trying to make her feel guilty for being such a slob. It made her so angry that there was no way she could take part in a reasonable discussion.

She rushed out of the apartment, ignoring him when he called her name. "Nora! Nora!" His wheedling tone reminded her of the way bratty children say *mommy*. "Maw-mee! Naw-rah!"

As she waited for the elevator, she imagined Pete calling out to his mother in just the same tone he had used with her. Then she remembered her mother-in-law's immaculate house, and realized that Pete's housecleaning routine was probably what he had done as a child to placate the old bitch when she was angry at him.

After these bitter, terrible arguments, did you really think that cleaning the house would make everything all right again? I'll never kill you, Pete, no matter how angry you make me—but I might just kill your mother.

Every one of these vignettes reveals a character's expectations, implying a story from his or her past. Yet not one of them slows the action very much. They add depth to the characterization without subtracting momentum from the forward movement of the story.

## Habits

Everyone alive has habits, some of them meaningless, but many of them the result of the patterns of our lives. If a character paces or drums his fingers on the table, you know that he's tense and this is the way he shows it. But your characters should also have specific habits that tell something about their lives:

"Where are you going?" Pete asked. "I didn't say to turn there."

"I'm sorry," Nora said, flustered. "This is the way I always take Ryan to school. I wasn't thinking."

Pete was back in an hour with the groceries and the change. He counted it out backward into her hand. "Seventeen sixty-two, sixty-five, seventy-five, eighteen, nineteen, and twenty."

Nora laughed.

Only then did he realize what he had done. He laughed ruefully. "Twenty years since I worked in Dad's store, and I'm still counting change like a clerk."

Nora looked carefully to the left and stepped out into the street. A taxi slammed on its brakes and swerved to avoid hitting her—from the right. Oh yes, thought Nora. They drive on the wrong side of the road here. My pedestrian survival training from New York won't be much help in London.

Pete left a 6:30 wake-up order with the hotel operator, turned off the television, and climbed into bed. He slept on the left side, of course, even though Nora hadn't been there to sleep on the right side since they separated four years before.

Nora noticed that every time Pete wrote a check, he drew three horizontal lines in every space between the words and numbers. "Do you really think the grocery store people are going to alter your check to say one million and thirty-three dollars and forty-four cents?"

"It's like fastening your seatbelt or locking your car," said Pete. "Do it even when it doesn't matter, and you won't forget to do it when it does."

Too many habits, of course, and your characters will seem obsessive-compulsive. But anybody who's been alive for any length of time has *some* habits, and it helps us believe in and understand your characters when we see what their habits are.

## Networks

Anyone who has been alive for any length of time has also made many connections with other people. Unless a character has been torn from his or her normal milieu, those connections are going to show up.

Pete noticed the way people in the store looked at Nora. Quick, furtive glances. He couldn't see anything wrong with her—no run in her stocking, no underwear showing. He didn't catch on until he realized that the store detective was shadowing them. Apparently Nora was known here, and not as a big spender.

Nora knew that Pete was not the man of her dreams when the motel clerk took his check without asking for ID. She thought it might be classy to be recognized at the Hilton, but not at a motel that rents a room for ten dollars an hour. Still, a man who pays by check is probably telling the truth when he says he isn't married.

Everybody Pete and Nora ran into did the same thing. Just as they were about to ask her a question, they'd glance at Pete and then smile and say something noncommittal. Nora and Pete stopped for lunch at a diner called the White Trash Saloon. It took a few minutes before Nora realized that the used-up looking waitress was Suzy Parker from high school. The last ten years hadn't been good to her.

Suzy recognized Nora too and finally asked the question the others had sidestepped: "How's Joe Bob?"

Nora smiled icily back. "He's home taking care of our seven children while Pete and I have a madcap, whirlwind affair."

The waitress thought about this for a moment. "You don't have no seven children," she finally said. "Too damn thin."

Nora couldn't help noticing that all the unopened letters on the kitchen table had transparent windows, and a lot of them said FINAL NOTICE. Even through the closed door, she could hear Pete shouting into the telephone. "I'll make payments on that piece of junk any month that it runs! And if you send somebody to pick it up, I'll blast their head off!" A minute later he came back in, grinning. "An old girlfriend," he said.

Sometimes the relationships that your character has with other people around him will be important to the story, but often they'll be there merely to give a sense that he has a full life, or to add an occasional comic touch. No matter how you use these mini-relationships in your story, though, the main benefit is that your characters won't seem to be puppets, alive only when they're on stage and someone is pulling the strings. They'll seem to have a real life outside the story as well, a network of relationships reaching far and wide. Though only a small part of that network is explored in your story, the reader senses that the rest of the network is there.

# JUSTIFICATION

There is nothing so outré, so off-the-wall, so impossible or bizarre or outrageous that you *cannot* make it believable within a story. It all depends on how hard you want to work at justifying it.

Nora stood on the roof. She was only nine stories up, but it might as well be nine miles. There was no escape. Pete came toward her, the long knife glimmering in the moonlight. Nora trembled, but she knew what she had to do. So she reached out, slapped the knife out of his hand, picked him up over her head and threw him off the roof. All those years of lifting weights and taking judo classes had paid off at last.

If that last sentence is the first time Nora's weight lifting has ever been mentioned in the story, the audience will be outraged by this scene. Here they've been so worried about Pete and his knife, and all along Nora was apparently built like an orangutan.

Does that mean you can't have Nora throw Pete off the roof? Of course not. All you have to do is tell us about her weight lifting and judo classes much earlier in the story, so we already know that she's strong and well trained long before she gives Pete the heave-ho. Furthermore, you have to make Nora the kind of woman who would defy sexual stereotypes and go into heavy weight lifting. Why would she do that? Is it to get a muscular, healthy body? To be stronger than the man who once raped her? A reaction to her fear of her breast cancer recurring? Or did a close friend get her involved in body building just for sociability, and she discovered she liked it? Whatever reason you invent, she will have to become a different person in order to justify her being able to pick Pete up and throw him off the roof.

Of course, if we knew all that about her, we wouldn't have the same sense of jeopardy as Pete chased her—we'd know that Nora was a woman who could take care of herself. But that doesn't mean the scene would be without tension. There are several strategies available:

1. Give Pete a gun, so we'll fear that her strength will be useless against him. Then you'll have to figure out a way to deal with the gun—but you'll have the tension of jeopardy back again.

2. Change the source of the tension. Instead of fearing that Pete will kill her, she (and the audience) fears that she will have to kill Pete, and she could not bear to do so. She warns him, but he behaves as if he wants to die. Merely hurting him has not stopped him in the past. If she kills him, terrible things will happen. The audience fears that she might *not* kill him, yet knows that she will also suffer terribly if she does.

3. Make her feat less outlandish. Instead of having her slap away the knife, pick him up, and throw him off the building, have her sidestep the knife and use Pete's momentum to push him off. That doesn't require her to be anywhere near as strong; you could have her just beginning her judo lessons and can skip the whole weight lifting idea altogether. This still requires some preparation, and it requires more detail during the fight on the roof, but it will work.

4. Make the conclusion a believable accident. Pete actually stabs her. She nearly faints from the pain, stumbles, lurches into Pete. He loses his balance; she falls, but grabs at his legs, pleading with him not to stab her again. With her holding his feet, he can't recover his balance. He falls off the building. If you show this process in great detail, it will be believable; best of all, it requires no preparation at all, since it's well within a normal person's ability.

If you decide to spend a lot of time making Nora believable as a weight lifter, you have to be careful not to get carried away. If the weight lifting only affects the story by allowing Nora to throw Pete off the roof, then you should introduce the weight lifting early, but not keep harping on it, not show her doing nothing *but* weight lifting. If it becomes too dominant in the story, the reader will expect it to amount to much more than just a way for her to save her life. "Nora goes through all that weight lifting," the reader will say, "just so she can toss this guy? Will she stop weight lifting now?" The amount of justification must be in proportion to the event being justified, or it leads the reader to expect things that you aren't going to deliver.

As a general rule, the more bizarre and unbelievable the character's behavior and the more important it is to the story, the earlier in the story you have to begin justifying it and the more time you'll need to spend to make it believable.

# TRANSFORMATIONS

REAL PEOPLE SEEM TO CHANGE. There are physical changes: The little kid next door is suddenly great-looking—or a hoodlum. Your friends from youth get old; your fat friend suddenly loses weight; your husband grows a mustache; your wife changes her hair style and starts wearing a whole new style of clothes.

There are changes in people's roles: The rich man goes bankrupt; the farmer sells his land and opens a fast food outlet in another state; the intense young girl becomes a wife and mother; the wife and mother stays a mother but no longer is a wife; new management comes in and the forty-eight-year-old executive is suddenly unemployed.

All these changes can be pretty surprising, even jarring. But what really disturbs us is when people's basic nature seems to change. Somebody you trusted doesn't keep his word and doesn't even act sorry about it. Somebody you loved is suddenly cruel to you, and you can't think why, what you did to deserve it. Someone who was always boring suddenly becomes fascinating. Someone who never did anything well, who seemed like a complete failure, unexpectedly does something admirable and fine.

## WHY PEOPLE CHANGE

In real life we never fully understand why people do these things. We have names for some of the changes—*mid-life crisis, growing up, going through a phase, nervous breakdown, finding herself, a selfish streak, showing his true colors, born again, going off the deep end*—but these labels are at best an attempt to reassure ourselves. Because there's already a name for the way we see somebody changing, we don't have to be quite so frightened by the change. But we still know nothing, or almost nothing, about the cause. We still know nothing, really, about what's going on inside other people's heads.

We try to bind people into their roles so that we can be sure of them. Slavery, serfdom, fealty, oaths of office, contracts, unions, corporations, laws, marriage, going steady, flattery, hypocrisy—all are strategies for controlling and predicting what the people around us are going to do. Yet still these people surprise us with escape, revolution, betrayal, lawsuits, strikes, sellouts, crime, divorce, faithlessness, gossip, confession, and we have to revise again our understanding of the world.

One of the reasons fiction exists at all is to deal with that fear of inexplicable change, that uncertain dread that lurks in the background of all our human relationships. Because fiction lets us see people's motives, the causes of their behavior, these stories about made-up people help us guess at the motives and causes of real people's behavior.

This doesn't mean that your fictional characters have to change. One of the common themes in fiction is that people's fundamental natures *don't* change, no matter how much you wish they might. Macbeth's desire to rise to high office seduces him into believing the witches' prophecy and agreeing to his wife's plan; that hunger for a lofty station is still with him at the end, making him seek death rather than endure the humiliation of public display in his defeat. The message of such stories is that once you truly know people, you can count on them staying the same. If they ever seem to change, it's because you didn't really understand them in the first place.

## You Can't Change

Your fiction can develop this theme in three ways:

1. You can tell stories in which characters are who they are from beginning to end, working out their destinies along the same relentless lines. Some might criticize your stories because your characters never change, but many readers will be grateful to live in your fictional world, where some people, at least, can be counted on to stand firm. In *Wuthering Heights*, Heathcliff and Cathy try to resist their passionate childhood attachment to each other, but all the changes are futile, for they keep returning to be their true selves, wild children living like beautiful animals among the moors.

2. You can tell stories about people who seem to change, but then reveal that this was their true nature all along. They were only pretending to be what you thought they were; or perhaps they simply hadn't had the power or opportunity to reveal themselves. It wasn't until Macbeth had a victory under his belt, a new title after his name, and King Duncan asleep in a bedroom in his castle that he was able to reveal his true character as a murderer—but maybe he was a murderer all along. Another example: Oedipus was born to kill his mother and father. His parents can't stop him from fulfilling his nature even by trying to kill him; he can't stop himself from being himself even by fleeing what he thinks is his homeland. He was born to commit patricide and incest, and all his attempts to pretend to be another kind of man come to nothing.

3. Tell stories about people who want to change, but can't until they discover their own true nature; then, when they change the outward pattern of their lives, they are only becoming true to their newfound self. Ayn

Rand's sympathetic characters in *The Fountainhead* and *Atlas Shrugged* do not make themselves into geniuses, they don't develop greatness. Only when they break free of the shackles of society and discard the myths about what they ought to be do they discover the greatness that lay within them all along, and finally rise to fulfill their heroic role.

In all these stories, the characters are not transformed, they are unmasked.

## Other Things Change You

Another great theme in fiction is that people *do* change, but for causes beyond their control:

1. The cause of change in people might be the drives and hungers born in their genes. D.H. Lawrence told stories—*The Rainbow, Lady Chatterly's Lover*—in which characters did not really act because of their motives at all. They might think they had a particular purpose in mind, but in fact their choices always came down to the needs of their bodies. This view of people as animals pretending to be human shows up as often in the bleak hard-boiled detective novels of Raymond Chandler and Ross Macdonald as in the tragicomic Irish novels of James Joyce. This is not a message of despair—these writers all show a kind of nobility in their characters' struggle to transcend their nature.

2. The cause of change in people might be the way they're treated by others. George Bernard Shaw's *Pygmalion* asserts the idea that a flower girl can become a lady, in soul as well as appearance, if only she is trained and educated properly. Robert Parker's Spenser novels often show people shaped by the pressures of the world around them; if the person is not too far gone, then by changing the environment, you can change the person. In one of his best novels, Parker has Spenser take a troubled young boy up to an isolated cabin in the woods, and through hard work and a whole new set of expectations, the boy becomes a new person and has a life completely different from the one he seemed destined to live out.

## You Change Yourself

A third fictional theme dealing with human change is that we can change our own nature by an act of will. Never mind the argument that the will to change must have been part of a person's nature all along, so that by changing he is in fact remaining the same—that's a quibble compared to the important notion of becoming what you *want* rather than what you were born to be or what others force you to become. George Bernard Shaw's assertions and theories notwithstanding, before Eliza Dolittle in *Pygmalion* begins the training and education that transform her from a flower girl to a lady, she has the hunger to change—it's because of the force of her own will that she persuades Henry Higgins to teach her, and by the force of her own will that she succeeds. Shaw talked a lot about how people are shaped by their environment, but in play after play, a strong-willed hero chooses to transcend heredity and environment alike, and succeeds in becoming someone new; that's the theme his stories demonstrate, whether he meant it that way or not. No matter what theories of human behavior you think you believe, the causes you show for your character's change will reveal what you *really* believe. But you must show some cause for the transformation.

## JUSTIFYING CHANGES

When your characters undergo physical changes or changes of role, you wouldn't dream of letting the change pass without explanation. A character who was male for ten chapters can't suddenly turn up as a female without some kind of explanation—or your reader would throw your book against the wall in disgust. And if a character goes through a change of social role, you always show both the causes and the results of the change. It would be unthinkable to have characters change jobs, marital status, or relative wealth without some explanation and some change in the patterns of their lives.

The same is true of your characters' patterns of behavior. If Pete is a quiet, shy fellow, reluctant to put himself forward, he doesn't suddenly walk up to a gorgeous model and hit her up for a date—not unless you show us that *this* model is different from all other women, or show us that Pete has been taking assertiveness training to cure his shyness, or let us see that the recent death of Pete's father has loosed some of Pete's inner restraint—or some other plausible cause for his change.

You don't necessarily have to show us the cause of his change *before* he changes, or even at the same time. But if you *don't* show the cause, you need to signal your reader that you're aware that Pete is behaving strangely, so that the reader knows that the cause of his change is a mystery that will be resolved sometime before the end of the story. For instance, you might have one of Pete's friends with him when he walks up to the model and asks her out; the friend could then react with the same astonishment that the reader would feel, a clear signal to the reader that the author hasn't gone crazy and can be trusted to explain Pete's change.

There is no "right" way to justify changes in character, but you should keep in mind that the more important the character and the greater the change, the more time you will have to devote to explaining the transformation. If Nora stops smoking in the process of your story, the motivation for the change won't need much justification—most smokers say they want to stop, and most reasons for stopping are well known. But if Nora is a major character who's involved in a lot of the continuing action of the story, you'll have to deal with why she chose to stop *now*, and show how her behavior changes during the struggle.

Make sure you know what the change in the character really is. If Nora has tried to give up smoking dozens of times before and always failed after a single day, you'll have to explain what was different about *this* time, why she found the strength to succeed. Maybe she got pregnant; maybe she is involved with a man who hates cigarettes; maybe her company has gone smoke-free; maybe she had a cancer scare during her latest checkup. Because her pattern of behavior was to try to give up smoking and then fail, what you have to justify is not the desire to give up smoking, but the fact that this time she succeeded. The real change is that she is now *able* to quit, not that she is willing to make the attempt.

There is an exception to the rule that you must explain why characters change. A fourth fictional theme is that changes in human beings are random, absurd, uncaused; that all stories about why people do what they do are pure fiction. In this view, people do things because they do them, for no reason at all. Only when someone else notices what they're doing is there any attempt to explain, and all the explanations are pleasant lies. And if, perhaps, there is some real cause for human change, these stories assert that we'll never know the cause, so there might as well not be one. The works of existential writers like Franz Kafka and Jean-Paul Sartre and the absurdist plays of Samuel Beckett and Harold Pinter develop this idea.

If absurdism is your bent, however, don't imagine that this means you can then change your characters however and whenever you want, without explanation. So deeply ingrained is the human need to find causes for human change that if a story denies that there is any kind of discoverable cause, that denial becomes the most important issue in the story. Usually, you must establish from the beginning that people will change randomly, without explanation, so that your readers realize they're visiting an absurd universe and stop expecting explanation. If, on the other hand, your story seems to be set in a "normal" universe in which there's always a reason when people change, then when a character goes through a shocking, inexplicable change, your story will have to be *about* the very inexplicability of that character's transformation.

Oh, you *can* have a major inexplicable change and have no one in the story remark on it, but you can't blame your readers for concluding that you're an incompetent writer and that the unjustified change was a mistake.

Worse still, your readers might conclude that the unjustified change was a practical joke you were playing on the them, as if you were saying, "Oh, were you starting to care about these characters? Were you starting to take this story seriously? Well, here, I'll show you that it's all silly and I can do *anything*." Of course you can do anything. But your implicit contract with your readers says you *won't* do just anything—that your story will mean something, even if the meaning is that there is no meaning. The great absurdist writers keep that contract.

Even comedy is not an exception. However, when a character changes in a comedy, the justification for the change can be somewhat less believable than in non-comic fiction. The zanier the farce, the sillier the reason you can offer for a character's change—but there must still be some reason, or you lose the audience's trust.

# PART III
# PERFORMING CHARACTERS

# CHAPTER 13

# VOICES

WHO IS TELLING YOUR STORY?

You are, of course. You choose what story to tell, which incidents matter, which scenes to show, which events to tell about. It is out of your mind that all the invention comes, all the characters, all the background details, all the ideas.

But when it comes time to speak the words of the story, whose voice will the reader hear?

It is never exactly your own voice. The very fact that you're writing down the words rather than speaking them will make the style more formal. The fact that you write more slowly than you speak, that you can see your words as you put them down, changes the way you produce and control your language. It's another voice.

Also, the fact that you can't see the audience's response requires you to be more precise and calculating in your written language—in speech, when you can look at your audience and judge whether or not they understand you, such precision isn't necessary. Even if you "write" by dictating into a tape recorder, it will not be your normal speech patterns, but rather your more regulated "dictation dialect." You've made this distinction many times—you instantly recognize the difference between natural extemporaneous speech, memorized speech, and speech that is being read.

It isn't just the difference between writing and speaking, though. You have many voices. You have one voice you use with your parents; another you use with your siblings. You might have a company voice. Most people have a separate telephone voice—professional secretaries and receptionists almost always do. If you have children, you doubtless have not one but two, probably three voices—the stern reproving voice, the affectionate approving voice, and the baby talk you used when they were little, which still drifts back when they're hurt and you're comforting them. You have a voice for service people and clerks, and another voice for public speaking.

Of course, your larynx produces the sound for all these oral voices. But the sound is only a small part of a "voice"—at least the kind of voice I'm talking about. Each of your voices has its own vocabulary. They overlap, but less than you might suppose. Each has its own sentence structure, its own level of diction. One might be slangy, another formal, another relaxed; in one voice you might have some blue language available, while another voice never produces those words.

This came home to me when I was a teenager. One summer I worked as an actor in a summer theater, where the language among the company could have made sailors blush; I was as colorful as any of them. Yet I lived at home, where such language simply wasn't used. So clear was the difference in the two voices that I didn't even have to think about not using certain words where my parents could hear them. I never caught myself about to use the wrong words at home, because those words just weren't available in my "home" voice.

Does that sound like a split personality? Perhaps the function of our brain that lets us develop these different "voices" is the very function that drives multiple personalities—it seems likely enough. But the truth is that normal people all have at least a few different voices they can turn on at will. Most of the time you aren't aware of the difference—you use these voices by habit. When others change voices, you probably hear only the sound differences—a whining child, perhaps, or a friend trying to sweet-talk you, or a would-be date turning you down gently. At such times it's hard to be analytical—but if you don't already know what I mean by "voices," listen to other people move from relationship to relationship during the day, and notice how their vocabulary and syntax change for different tasks. They become slightly different in most cases, radically different in some.

You don't *think* about these differences when you use a different voice. You just change mindset—usually unconsciously—and slip into the pattern of speech habitual for that relationship.

I grew up out west, but now live in the South—in the Piedmont region of North Carolina, where the southern accent is fairly mild. Still, when I'm with southerners with good, solid accents, I catch myself talking the way they do—not just making my vowels like theirs, but also using their figures of speech, even making up southern-style metaphors and similes from time to time. "I'm as depressed as a chipmunk in a cat's mouth." "He went home so fast he slammed the door before he opened it." "It was raining so hard that if you looked up with a smile, you'd drown." I don't think about it—I get busy talking and my brain just kicks in with the right voice.

When it comes to telling a story, far more choices open up to you. You can use voices in writing that you never use in speech. I'm not just talking about regional dialects, either, though the cadences of Brooklyn, Boston, Philadelphia, Chicago, Houston, New Orleans, or the San Fernando Valley can bring color and life to the telling of a story. There's also attitude—cynical, flippant, wondering, cold, nostalgic. And level—crude, slangy, informal, formal, elevated, magisterial.

In fact, there are so many possibilities that I find that when I'm at the keyboard telling a story, it's almost as if I'm acting. I'm "in character," improvising the performance of my story using words and syntax that one of the characters in my tale might use.

This makes sense when I'm using a first-person narrator. The narrative voice *has* to sound like the first-person narrator; if it doesn't, it's a flaw in the author's technique.

But I find myself writing "in character" even when I'm using third person, even when the narrator isn't a specific person at all. I usually write in a voice similar to the voice of the viewpoint character, even though that character is not the narrator. In reading other writers' work, I find that, as often as not, they do the same thing.

The only clear exceptions are those authors who have a pronounced habitual style, so they use the same voice in all their stories. To a degree, of course, every author will have stylistic patterns that show up in every tale. The characters will always have some overtones of the author's own style of speech. We can't escape completely from our own underlying voices even when we try. But usually the narrative voice is not exactly identical to the author's natural speech—we always put on a voice of one sort or another when we tell a tale.

The underlying voice that repeats from one story to the next is your natural style. This book isn't about style. So I'm only going to deal with aspects of voice that change from character to character, from book to book.

When you actually set out to write down your story, you have a lot of choices to make—narrator, point-of-view character, tense, level of penetration, rhetorical stance. In the next few chapters I'll deal with the strengths and weaknesses of all these choices, so you can decide which one is best for each story you write, and how to carry out the choice you made.

# PERSON

So now we come back to the question: Whose voice will the reader hear?

You probably already know the difference between first person and third person, but just in case you got shortchanged in high school, I'm going to review all the "persons" here with a simple chart:

|  | Singular | Plural |
|---|---|---|
| **First Person** | I go | We go |
| **Second Person** | You go (thou goest) | You go (y'all go) |
| **Third Person** | He goes, she goes | They go |

If this feels like a grammar lesson, that's because it is.

However, most stories you read—almost all of them, in fact, including news stories, history, and science—will be written in either first person or third person.

First person is used for the eyewitness account, the story in which I tell you what I saw and did, what happened to me:

I gave up trying to figure out what Deena was up to and concentrated on getting drunk. Deep drunk, as fast as possible. After all, I had a long drive home, and if I wasn't drunk I'd probably get so bored I'd fall asleep at the wheel. But somewhere along in there the bartender got my car keys and the next morning I woke up in my apartment with a hangover, a note telling me where my keys were, and nobody in bed beside me.

Third person is when the narrator was not present as a character; instead, the narrator tells you what happened to other people:

Pete finally gave up trying to figure out what Deena was up to and concentrated on getting drunk. Deep drunk, as fast as possible. The way he figured, he had a long drive home, and if he wasn't drunk he'd probably get so bored he'd fall asleep at the wheel. But the bartender was earning his money that night. He got Pete's car keys, took a twenty out of his wallet, and sent him home in a cab. In exchange for the twenty, the driver hauled Pete up the stairs and left him a note on his pillow to tell him which bar his car keys were in. Pete woke up next morning with his arm reaching out for Deena. He found the note instead.

Notice that the two paragraphs both tell essentially the same story. But as I got into writing the second version, a simple translation of the first-person account just wouldn't do the job. In first person you can only write what the narrator saw when he was there; in Pete's case, that means when he was there *and conscious*. In the third-person narration, the narrator could go on observing even when Pete wasn't too alert. Also, I allowed the third-person narrator to express an attitude: "The bartender was earning his money that night." Now, you might take that as expressing Pete's attitude, or you might not. But in the first-person narration, Pete's is the only possible attitude.

Your decision whether to use first person or third person is not so much a grammatical choice as a narrative strategy. If you want the narrator to be a character who takes part in the events of the story, you'll use first person. If you either want the narrator to be a character who did *not* take part in the events, or want the narrator not to be identified as a character at all, you'll use third person.

Even though you've chosen one overall "person" for the tale, you'll still have bits in many other "persons." For instance, in a third-person narration, one character might tell a story to another, and that tale-within-a-tale could be in first person:

"I just went to the store," she said. "At night. Late. I was juggling the car keys and the grocery bag and this guy came up. Really weird. He didn't *do* anything, but he scared me to death."

Or, in a first-person narration, the narrator might tell about something that someone else did:

She told me the story, but I couldn't figure out why she was still so upset. She said she went to the store that night and this stranger got to her as she was fumbling with the car keys and a heavy bag of groceries. Didn't do anything to her, but he was weird, and she was scared to death. But why was it still bothering her a week later?

In each case, someone within your tale is telling *another* story, and that story does not have to be in the same "person" as the overall tale, as long as it's a "person" that makes sense.

What about second person, or third-person plural, or other possible narrative voices? Well, there's nothing to stop you from trying. A student of mine once wrote a very effective short-short story in third-person plural, in which the members of a group of soldiers were never individuated, and only group feelings and responses were explained. It was strange but powerful; but then, the story was *about* the fact that the group was so tightly bonded they might as well have been a single individual.

Second-person singular is used only occasionally in fiction—but in other settings, you've read it a lot. Every recipe you ever followed was written in second person, using imperative mood, in which the word *you* is understood but not said: "(You) fold two eggs into batter, beat for two minutes or 200 strokes. . . ." Second person also shows up in a few other places, like the Ten Commandments: "Thou shalt not kill." These both tell normative stories—stories that you are intended to act out in order to bring them to life.

Remember, though, that the "person" of a story is the consistent pattern of the narration, the way that the main characters are referred to by the narrator. Just because the author addresses his readers as "you" doesn't make the story a second-person narrative. As long as the reader is treated as the reader, and not as a character in the story, direct address to the reader has nothing to do with the narrative voice:

> You think you know all about crime, don't you? You feel smug, you say "I'd be calm" or "I'd beat the crap out of him"—but it all falls apart, I promise you. When I felt the gun barrel in my back, all I could think was Please don't kill me I'm not done with living yet. In other words, I started to whine inside. I started to wish I had more money to give him, thousands of dollars, just to reward him for letting me live.

That passage was a first-person narrative. The direct address to the reader told a little hypothetical second-person tale about the reader's supposed attitudes, but the story itself was a first-person account.

Most of the time, though, you'll use either first person or third person, and those are the only two narrative voices we'll examine at length.

# TENSE

Almost every story you'll ever read or hear is in past tense. Newspapers, broadcast news, history, science, gossip, and fiction—the overwhelming majority of these storytelling forms use the past tense. It's what most audiences expect when they pick up a work of fiction.

There are occasions when present tense is the natural mode. For instance, most of this book is in present tense. I'm not writing fiction, of course; instead I'm trying to tell you something about the way fiction works, the ongoing process. I'm not telling you what happened *once*, I'm telling you what happens repeatedly, and so present tense is mandatory. How-to books, philosophy, and scientific theories (as opposed to scientific reports on experimental results) are written in the present. All dramatic literature is written in present tense.

There are also fictional uses for present tense. In the academic/literary genre, present tense narrative has passed from being a daring experiment to being the preferred tense for short stories—or at least the most common.

There are other, much stranger possibilities. I can imagine a story in imperative mood, for instance, as if the readers were receiving directions from someone speaking through radio receivers implanted in their ears. (Note that, as with a recipe, the imperative mood in a story requires the second person):

> Go up the stairs. Pay no attention to the child shivering in the dark corner on the first landing. Step over the vomit and don't put any weight on the railing. Your key fits half the doors in this building; the other half don't lock. Open the door with the number 77 on it. Don't bother reading the obscenity scrawled under the number—it isn't in English anyway, and you didn't do very well in high school Spanish. You don't even remember Spanish well enough to tell if the graffito *is* in Spanish. There are a lot of Haitians around here; it might be French.
>
> Open the door and go inside. Breathe through your mouth. This guy's been dead for a few days, and these rooms get kind of stuffy in the summer. Open a window. No, forget that—they're probably stuck shut, and you don't have much time. You're not the maid here, anyway. Let the police clean it up, after you call them. But not yet. You've got a wallet to look for. Hold your breath and try not to look at what's happening to his skin. Don't try to figure out what he looked like before he got all bloated up. It doesn't make any difference if you ever saw this guy alive or not. Just go through the pockets, that's right. Put your hands into the pockets, deep, all the way in, even though the fabric of the pocket lining is so thin, even though his skin under the pocket is soft and taut, like leftover corn meal mush in the fridge, jiggly, holding together but ready to fall apart if you push too hard.
>
> Take everything out of the pockets, every pocket. You can wash later. You can shower again and again. You can scrub your hands until they bleed before you finally feel clean enough to sleep tonight.
>
> Got it all? Then get out of there.

Weird but interesting, right? Still, I don't think I could put up with a very long story written this way, and for me, at least, there'd have to be some reason within the story for it to be written in imperative mood. Maybe the story is an accusation or a speculation; maybe the story is a running monologue, the narrator talking to himself. There'd have to be *some* justification within the story, some reason why this strange approach was needed, or I'd feel as if the author put me to a lot of extra work just so he could dazzle me with a linguistic special effect.

As long as we're doing special effects, what about future tense? A story told by a fortune-teller:

> You will meet a tall handsome stranger. Oh? You think that's a cliche? Too vague for you? Too anonymous? Then let's see how you like the detailed version. A tall handsome stranger, but you will pay no attention to him. He will keep following you around. You will wonder if he plans some sexual or violent act. He will give you no sign of it. I will not tell you, either. If you want him to go away, you will have to give him the small red folder. You don't have that folder yet—it will be given to you by someone you thought was dead. Perhaps it will be given to you by someone who really is dead. If you give him that folder, he will go away. Or at least I think he'll go away. The vision isn't clear.

Again, it's easy to imagine writing in an odd tense, but very hard work to do it—and hard work to read it, too. In reading these two examples, you were constantly aware that there was something strange about the narration. Strangeness always attracts the audience's attention, in the story or in its performance; but strangeness in the writing calls attention away from the events of the story. That alone is usually enough to make a storyteller reject a strange tense.

I gave you these examples just to point out that there really are a lot of options—but almost every time, your story and your audience will be best served by the tense that is so universally used that audiences don't notice it: the past. Because past tense and first or third person are the conventional choices, they are invisible. The audience doesn't notice them. Therefore they become a channel between the story and the audience. If the audience *does* notice the tense or "person," it *is* a barrier.

There are many young writers, particularly those with training in college literature classes, who believe that good writing must be unconventional, challenging, strange. This is a natural misconception. In literature courses we study many stories that were written for another time and place. The language has changed, as have the literary conventions and expectations of the audience. Also, the most common method of literature classes is dissection—cutting a story to bits to analyze symbols and discover sources. We also hear some writers praised because they were revolutionary or experimental, violating the conventions and expectations of their time. So it's no surprise if many young storytellers reach the conclusion that great writing is writing that has to be studied, decoded, and analyzed, that if a story can be clearly and easily understood, it must be somehow childish, inconsequential, or trite.

This is far from the truth. Most great writers followed all but a few of the conventions of their time. Most wrote very clearly, in the common language of their time; their goal was to be understood. Indeed, Dante and Chaucer were each the starting point of a national literature precisely because they refused to write in an arcane language that nobody understood, and instead wrote in the vernacular, so that people could receive their stories and poetry in words they used every day.

In a way, every story you tell is experimental—you have never told that story before, and your audience has never heard you tell it. There are plenty of challenges for the audience in the process of getting used to your voice, to the kind of events and characters you write about. Even when you write as clearly as you can, many readers will misunderstand you or reject your vision of the world. So why would you want to make the story even *more* difficult, so that even readers who would otherwise understand and believe in and care about your story are driven away?

Of course, if your purpose in writing is to be admired, to impress people with your cleverness or skill, then the story itself is only a secondary concern to you, and your writing will be designed to dazzle your readers more than to enlighten them. But if your purpose in writing is to transform your audience, to give them a clear memory and understanding of truthful and important tales, your writing will be not an end in itself, but a tool. Sometimes, to tell the tale as it must be told, you will have to violate conventions or try out new techniques; sometimes this will make your story more difficult or challenging to read. But I believe the great writers will always be the ones who have passionate, truthful stories to tell, and who do all they can to help their readers receive them.

A rule of thumb: Choose the simplest, clearest, least noticeable technique that will still accomplish what the story requires.

# CHAPTER 14

# PRESENTATION VS. REPRESENTATION

THERE ARE TWO WAYS OF RELATING to the audience during the performance of a story. The difference is clearest in theater. In a representational play, the actors all act as if there were a fourth wall between them and the audience. If they look in the direction of the audience, they give no sign of seeing that anyone is out there looking at them. Instead, they pretend that they're seeing only what would be there if the play were real—another wall of the drawing room, or the rest of the Forest of Arden. This technique helps the audience maintain the illusion of reality (or, as it is commonly called, the willing suspension of disbelief). Though of course the audience knows they are watching a play, the actors do as little as possible to remind them of it.

Of course, no play is ever perfectly representational. For instance, if the actors sit down at dinner, the major characters—or at least the taller ones—tend to group themselves on the upstage side of the table, the side farther from the audience, so they will *face* the audience. Furthermore, the script generally has people speaking in coherent language, often with complete sentences, which real people rarely do. If you know what to look for, you'll see the actors, the director, the lighting technician, the makeup artist, the playwright, and everybody else working very hard to sustain the illusion of reality.

All this is in the effort to deal with the audience's constant query: "Oh yeah?" And despite the players' best effort to be "real" (David Belasco, a naturalistic producer at the turn of the century, once transplanted an actual apartment, stained wallpaper and all, to the stage), the fact is that even the most representational theater is still being presented to an audience, with reality distorted in a thousand ways in order to help the audience receive it.

Presentational theater, on the other hand, tears down that imaginary fourth wall. The actors don't just admit the audience is there, they make constant contact with the audience. This style is at its extreme in the art of stand-up comedy, where the actor even talks to the audience about the audience's response. (Comedians *are* actors playing a role, of course— you don't think Johnny Carson or Rodney Dangerfield or Howie Mandel or Elayne Boosler are *really* like their comedic personas, do you?) The actors and the audience are engaged in continuous conversation.

Somewhere between the two extremes are the plays where the actors don't usually speak right to the audience, but still don't attempt to recreate reality in full. Shakespeare's plays were originally performed on a nearly bare stage. If you needed the Forest of Arden, an actor would say, in effect, "Here we are in the Forest of Arden." If they were at a castle, somebody would say, "For three days we have waited here at Caernarvon Castle," and this told the audience all they needed to know; their imagination would supply the trees.

We aren't talking about the difference between romance and realism here. We're talking about the storytellers' relationship with the audience. In fiction, the representational writer *never* addresses her audience. The narrator never expresses a personal opinion. All the focus is on the events, and everything is expressed through the point of view of a character in the story. In a representational first-person account, the narrator has clearly in mind who it is she's talking to, and it isn't the reading audience. Think of John Hersey's *The Wall,* where he carefully maintains the illusion that the novel is actually a journal written by a participant in the uprising of the Warsaw Ghetto during World War II. When I read the book at the naive age of seventeen, I was completely taken in; it took several days of baffling searches through the library for more information before I finally realized that the book was fiction. I remember very well the depth of the illusion and how much more power it lent to the story; when I later wrote my historical novel *Saints,* I very carefully framed it as an absolutely representational document, complete with a "historian" as the narrator and phony acknowledgments to people who are either disguised or never existed at all.

On the other hand, fiction can be highly presentational. Kurt Vonnegut is a prime example. He speaks directly to the audience; he refers to himself; the author's hand is so obvious in the story that the reader never forgets that he is reading fiction.

Sometimes the boundary between representational and presentational becomes hopelessly muddied. William Goldman's classic *The Princess Bride* is both at once. The romance itself is plainly presentational—the supposed author, "Morgenstern," makes comments and asides to his audience. But Morgenstern's story is "framed" by a present-day story narrated by a sort of pseudo-William Goldman as a modern screenwriter who is rediscovering the Morgenstern classic he adored as a child. The present-day "Goldman" constantly interrupts the flow of the romance to comment on Morgenstern or on his own reaction to the story. Yet the frame story itself, about Goldman's experiences as a screenwriter in Hollywood, is absolutely representational. Goldman sustains the illusion that, while the romance by Morgenstern is fiction, it really is by Morgenstern. It is, in other words, a presentational story within a representational one, and if that sounds hopelessly confusing to you, I assure you that it isn't. Goldman manipulates the complex structure so flawlessly that I used the book as a basic text in my freshman composition and literature class the year I taught at Notre Dame. After understanding the structure of *The Princess*

*Bride,* my students were quite ready to deal with something as relatively simple as *King Lear*.

What does this have to do with you? You must decide where your story will be on the continuum between presentational and representational storytelling. Either approach has its drawbacks and its advantages. You must decide what your story needs—and what you're good at—and then use that approach consistently.

Whichever way you choose to write, you must let the audience know *immediately* what to expect. Nothing is more cruelly jarring than to get fifty pages into a representational novel and have the narrator suddenly spring a "dear reader" on us.

Not that it isn't possible to switch from one to another in midstream. I wrote a novel which seemed to be representational except, perhaps, for a certain archness of tone—a "toldness" about the tale—and only gradually dropped hints that the book was being written by one of the characters in the book, who was writing it in order to persuade another character not to kill the protagonist. My editor and I finally agreed, though, that I had been too subtle. I ended up going back and making it plain from the beginning that the book was being written *to* one of the characters in order to persuade him to a course of action. The only puzzle I left in place was that I didn't reveal until the end of the book which character was writing it. I *could* have left it the other way, but it wasn't worth the cost to the audience. The gradual shift in the first version brought no great benefit, and stood a good chance of seriously diminishing the readers' emotional involvement in the book.

Here are a couple of story openings, just to show you the difference. The first is extremely representational—it is meant to feel like a real document a character might have produced. The second is extremely presentational—it is meant to sound like a writer who is keenly aware of his contemporary audience. Yet, oddly enough, they both are narrated by a self-conscious narrator, who is sensitive to the fact that he is writing something he means someone to read:

My name is Macon Anderson and I pray God will guide my pen. I also pray he'll find some way to keep these scraps of paper from getting found and going up in flames or down the toilet along with my hope of freedom; I also pray that he'll find some way to get it out of here and into someone else's hands. But what are my prayers? Why should you care? You with your house payments and day-care costs, you with your chance of a promotion and your plans for a vacation at Disney World, what do you ever pray for, if you pray at all? To hell with you, anyway. Paper is too precious, this pencil is too short for me to waste more of it on you. You aren't real, anyway. Real people are the ones whose stink I smell in the morning, whose hands snag on the rough bark of trees and mingle their blood with mine, whose eyes look longingly at my scrap of bread and then study my body, wondering how my strength is holding up, and whether I'm weak enough now that it's safe to start trying to steal food from me. I'm still too strong for them—this is how I know that God lives and answers prayers.

Listen tight, boys and girls, this is what you stayed up so late to read. Your mommy and daddy have gone to bed, you've got the flashlight on under the covers, and now I'm going to tell you the story of Mike and Betty Meekly, who got fed up and shot their parents in the head one day. Your folks don't want you to read this book because they're afraid you'll get ideas. Hell, they got nothing to worry about. After years of watching television, you wouldn't know an idea if it came up and spit in your face.

Remember that I made up this story. It's all lies. So even if you happen to have heard some news story about some girl who figured her daddy had poked around in her underwear—for the last time—or about some boy who figured his folks had hit him with a garden tool—for the last time—even if you saw pictures of that kid getting out of court on a six-month suspended sentence, I don't want you to start getting the idea that this story is *true*. OK? Because I don't want some fruitcake suing me for having led him into killing his parents because my novel told him it was a justifiable kind of homicide. I want to go on record right now as saying that even if your parents are the most unconscionable swine who ever produced accidental, unwanted, and mistreated offspring, I don't think you should kill them. I officially encourage you to avoid even *thinking* about murder. I'm just a fiction writer, telling entertaining fibs for people who haven't got enough imagination to invent their own daydreams of bloody vengeance.

Both narrators address their audience directly. But the first story is meant to be received as an actual journal scribbled by a prisoner on scraps of paper, chronicling his life in a concentration camp, while the second one is meant to be received as a work of fiction, constantly making the reader aware of the author's not-so-hidden agenda. So the first story's direct address to the "audience" is representational—it enhances the illusion that the story being told is true. While the second story is presentational—it makes it impossible to forget that the story is fiction.

Two more examples, now, both in third person:

Martin volunteered to do the shopping just so he could get out of the house. The house was too small these days, too crowded now that he had no job to get to, now that he could sleep as late as he wanted. He could hear every noise that Deanne made, mucking around in the kitchen; and she could hear every sound the television made, as he dozed through his daily pilgrimage through *Jeopardy!*, *Wheel of Fortune*, *Superior Court*, and *The Love Connection*. Martin knew that every theme song was a reminder to Deanne that he wasn't out looking for work. Every time she spoke to him it felt to him like a reproof, even though he knew that her words were innocent, that she was walking on eggshells trying to keep him from getting mad at her again. So he went and did the shopping, even though it always made him feel even worse because he ran out of money so much sooner than he ran out of grocery list.

Sary's job at *The Daily Record* was to go through all the reporters' stories and put in typographical errors. Now that the paper was set directly from the computer files that the reporters typed in, there was no typesetting stage in which errors could be created. Papers might actually start coming out *error-free*. Management was deeply worried about this during the lockout when they got rid of the damned typesetters union once and for all. Typos were a part of newspaper life. If they didn't get a hundred letters a week complaining about bad grammar or misspellings, how would they know anybody was paying attention? If they never had a dumb headline or a screwed-up classified ad, how could they ever get a mention in those little end-of-column clippings in *The New Yorker*? So they created the position of typographical editor, hired Sary, and set her to work turning *from* into *form*, *there* into *their*, taking single lines of text out of one column and putting them in another, and occasionally getting creative and inserting meaningless things like "XxxxxX75 Petunia. There they gSSSgp" into the middle of an article on some poor geek's presidential campaign. Sary was good at her job, and took pride in it. The paper got two quotes in *The New Yorker* the first year she was on the job, had to make seven "Our Mistake" corrections because of public complaints, and all in all she was worth her weight in gold. If it weren't for hemorrhoids her life would be perfect. Not that *she* had hemorrhoids—she didn't even have a semi-cancerous polyp or anything. Her boss's hemorrhoids, that's what made life less than perfect for Sary.

Why is the first example representational, and the second example presentational? In the first story, everything is seen from Martin's point of view. There is no sense of the narrator intruding with his own evaluation of things, or even of the narrator supplying any information that Martin couldn't know. Even Deanne's attitudes are obviously Martin's *assumption* of what her attitude must be. The narrator is almost invisible.

In the second example, however, Sary is being talked *about*. We aren't getting her perceptions of anything. Instead, we're getting the narrator's snide tone and whimsical invention. The reader can't even be sure yet whether Sary's job really is what the narrator says it is, or if in fact she's a copyeditor who happens to get attention only when a typo slips past her, in which case she gets blamed as if she had deliberately put it there. No matter what turns out to be true, the narrator has inserted himself between the audience and Sary. We're going to see her from a distance, through the narrator's skewed and somewhat wry perceptions.

It is much easier for readers to get emotionally involved in a representational story. With their "oh yeah?" response constantly dealt with, they can forget they're reading fiction and become completely absorbed in what happens. But the representational writer denies himself the chance to engage his reader directly; the technique of representational writing forbids the writer to point things out directly, or to make comments on the scenes he shows. Instead, if the writer insists on making those points, he must work out a way for a character to say the things he wants said, or see things the way he wants them seen, and there's nothing to stop the reader from missing the point entirely.

On the other hand, it is much easier to present clear ideas in a presentational story; satire and comedy, because they require less emotional involvement, suffer least from the disruptions caused by presentational writing. In fact, you might be able to make a good case for the idea that presentational writing can *only* be funny these days. A genteel "dear reader" interruption is simply not among the current protocols of serious storytelling, whereas gonzo comic writing almost demands that the narrator remind her audience constantly that fiction is what's going on here. As long as your story is not one that depends on your audience feeling a deep emotional involvement with the characters, you can use a presentational voice with little risk.

One thing must be understood. The more you rely on the narrator's voice to carry the story instead of the events themselves, the better your writing has to be. Because when the audience's attention is drawn away from the story, it goes *somewhere*. They're staring at your style close up, and if your voice happens not to be very entertaining, you've lost them.

Another way of putting it is this: In a good representational story, the audience will forgive a certain clumsiness of writing because they care so much about the characters and events. In a good presentational story, the audience will forgive a certain shallowness of story because they so enjoy the writer's style and attitude. So you not only have to know what's good for your story, you also have to know what type of story your particular talents are best suited for.

# CHAPTER 15

# DRAMATIC VS. NARRATIVE

YOU'VE NO DOUBT HEARD THE SLOGAN "Show, don't tell." Under some circumstances, that advice is good; under others, it's exactly wrong. Storytellers constantly have to choose between showing, telling, and ignoring.

Of these, showing is what you do least often; but since showing is also what takes up the most space, it deceives many critics into saying "The good writers show much more than they tell." Critics say this because they examine only the text; we writers know better, because we deal with the story.

The very terms are misleading. How can you *show* anything in fiction? The story always has a narrator. On the other hand, in theater and movies you show almost *everything*. That's because plays and films are dramatic in form. The action unfolds in "real time" while the audience watches. Fiction has a narrator, a storyteller. Instead of the audience seeing events directly, they are unavoidably filtered through the perceptions of the narrator.

Yet film is *not* completely dramatic—it only seems that way to the audience. In fact the screenwriter carefully chooses which information to present as a scene, and which information to have someone on-screen tell about, as an off-screen event. If you think about it, films would be deadly if they showed everything.

Take *Three Days of the Condor*, a Robert Redford vehicle in the 1970s. (The book was *Six Days of the Condor*—they started compressing right from the start.) If the filmmakers actually showed us everything, it would take three days to see the film. They left out a lot of stuff. We didn't need to see every bite he ate, every time he went to the bathroom, every step he took. To suggest a journey, they only had to show him starting out and then arriving. To suggest a night's sleep, they only had to show him going to bed in darkness. If we then see him walking around in daylight, we assume it's the next day. We fill in the trivial information. We don't need to be told it, because it has nothing important to do with the story. This is the stuff that gets ignored—and fiction writers make the same kinds of choices all the time.

A lot of information that *is* important to the story is still not important enough to be worth a whole scene. For instance, if characters are searching for vital information, and it takes a day of poring over files and books, we need only a montage of short clips of mountains of books, armloads of files, weary-looking actors getting bleary-eyed from reading—thirty seconds of film time. This is the filmic equivalent of "telling." In fiction, you would have covered the events of the search even more economically, by saying, "They went through nineteen file drawers, paper by paper. They cracked open books that had ten years of dust on them. Even after all that searching, they almost missed the answer when they found it." There it is—a day compressed into three sentences.

It would be ridiculous to show all that searching instead of telling it. While the fact that they worked hard to get the information is important to the story, it isn't important that the reader actually experience it. Instead, the storyteller gives them enough information to let them know that the search happened, that it wasn't easy. Then the storyteller relies on the audience's memory of similar hard research in their lives, or their imagination of how hard it must be or how boring it would be to do all that reading. In this case the right advice is "Tell, don't show." That is the *narrative* technique, to tell what happened without taking much time.

The important scenes, the ones that must be presented dramatically, are relatively rare—but they end up taking the bulk of the screen or stage time because "showing" is so terribly time-consuming. What you show as a scene will stick in the audience's memory far more than things that are only told about. To the audience, what seems to happen in a film is all the neat scenes, all the tense moments. But the storyteller knows that most things that happen in a film are only told about, hinted at, glossed over, just as most things that happen in fiction are given in brief narrative form.

What is the difference between dramatic and narrative, between showing and telling in fiction?

For sixteen years I put up with his constant whining. His students were stupid. He was never given any good courses to teach. They always assigned him the most worthless graduate students to advise. He was sure they would never renew his contract. When they renewed it, he was equally sure they'd never give him tenure. By the time the decision was made, I was praying he was right.

Unfortunately, he got tenure—and a raise every year, his own personal computer, and several good convention trips a year, and all the time I had to listen to his whining in faculty meetings, the faculty lounge, the corridors; even in my office I could hear him whining clear down the hall. It was too much to hope that another university would hire him, though I praised him to every department chairman I met, hoping they'd try to lure him away.

I began to dream of ways he might die. A fall in the snow. Getting run over by a truck. His bookshelves tumbling over on him. Accidentally taking an overdose of Serutan. I imagined him arriving at the emergency room, whimpering at the doctors and saying, "I know you're just going to let me die." I imagined the doctors saying, "Damn straight."

But I didn't kill him.

He came into my office without knocking, something even my wife doesn't do. "I don't know why I put up with this," he said.

Oddly enough, exactly the same sentence was running through my mind.

"This new rule about doing our own photocopying is obviously aimed at me," he said. "They're trying to harass me into leaving."

"If you'd have your students buy textbooks instead of copying entire books for them—"

"There is no single book that is suited to my classes. But I should have guessed you'd act like this. You probably suggested that they cut off my photo-copying privileges."

"There's a cutback. We lost two student aides. It has nothing to do with you."

"So you're one of them. Fine. I don't need you. I can get a job anywhere."

If I had thought there was a chance he'd actually quit his job, I would have said something snide. However, I knew perfectly well that his whining would eventually lead the chairman or the dean or somebody to assign a student aide to him personally, just to do his photocopying—and if I said anything nasty to him in the process, he'd whine about that, too, and I'd end up sitting through meetings with the dean about my inability to be supportive of other faculty members.

So I didn't say anything. I just looked him in the eye and smiled, hoping all the while that he would die. It was a deep, sincere desire, one that I had often felt before. But I didn't kill him.

The same two characters; pretty much the same information. We learn that there is tension between them, and the narrator believes that the conflict arises entirely from the other teacher's whining. But the first version is merely told, not shown.

What difference does it make? Notice that the second version, the scene, takes longer, though it gets through far less overall information and covers far less time than the narrative version.

At the same time, the pure narrative seems like a mere prelude. It is leading up to the story. We expect it to be followed by a scene. After reading the narrative paragraph, we still feel that nothing has yet happened. But at the end of the scene, we feel that something *has* happened.

The scene makes the tension between characters more immediate and real. But the narrative makes it seem as if it has gone on longer, so that the annoyance isn't triggered by a single incident, but rather by a cumulative list of offenses.

Which one of these is the "right" choice? Either one could be right; either could be wrong. Factors like rhythm, pace, and tone come into play—these are outside the scope of this book. However, if the author wanted the reader to get a feel for the murder victim, to remember him as a character instead of simply getting the narrator's attitude toward him, this or some other scene would be essential. Characters are made more real through scenes than through narrative.

# CHAPTER 16

# FIRST-PERSON NARRATIVE

WHEN YOU USE A FIRST-PERSON NARRATOR, you are almost required to tell the story in someone else's voice—the voice of the character telling the tale. A careless writer will have all her first-person narrators talk amazingly like herself, but if you take characterization seriously, the use of first person will lead you to discover a new voice for each story told by a different narrator.

One mistake many writers have made—particularly nineteenth-century humorists like Artemis Ward—is to make the first-person narrator's voice so eccentric or heavily accented that the story becomes almost unreadable. In fairness, I should point out that in Ward's own time, stories tended to be read aloud; the heavily accented writing did not slow down the pace, since reading aloud is already slow; and it also provided the reader with a guide to pronouncing the comical accents.

But by and large you should attempt to create the narrator's voice through his attitude and implied past, letting the speech reflect his educational level and regional accent only in syntax and word choice, not in odd spellings or endless pronunciation guides. Nothing is more deadly than trying to read sentence after sentence written like this: "Ah niver did figgah out whah in hivven's name a good ol' boah lahk 'at wen' crazy an' stahted in killin' folks." Furthermore, the narrator doesn't hear his own accent anyway, and so would never write it that way. The narrator would write: "I never did figure out why in heaven's name a good old boy like that went crazy and started in killing folks." That's what he *thinks* he said, and it's only because *you* have a different accent that you think his words should be spelled another way.

Cheapest of all is when writers try to show someone is uneducated by using apostrophes willy-nilly: "I'm goin' t' th' store, Nell. We're runnin' out o' beer." In the first place, *most* people, even educated people, drop letters in normal, informal speech. Anyone who *never* does is a hopeless prig. In the second place, the dropped g in *ing* endings is actually older than the pronounced g, and therefore is arguably more correct; certainly it is a natural survival of the ancient spoken tongue, and doesn't really denote an uneducated person—except to someone who is uneducated. It almost invariably comes across as a way for the author to show that he sneers at the person who speaks that way, and only rarely is this the conclusion you'll want the audience to reach about your first-person narrator.

# WHICH PERSON IS FIRST?

The main limitation on the first-person narrative is that your narrator has to be present at the key scenes. A first-person narrator who merely hears about the major events of the story is no good to you at all. So you have to work your narrator into the action so tightly that he is present whenever you need him to observe something.

The easiest way is to make the narrator the protagonist (or vice versa—make your protagonist the narrator). The trouble here is that the protagonist is the character with whom the audience sympathizes. She is likely to do interesting and important things during the course of the story, or suffer terrible loss or pain; how well will her voice serve to tell about these things?

For instance, if one of the key events is the death of the protagonist's beloved child, how coherently is she going to be able to write about the events leading up to it? If she is too emotional, it will become melodramatic; if too graphic, it will become unbearably intense. Yet if you retreat, and her narration becomes clear and cool, you run the risk of having the audience regard her as cold and heartless. This is not to say it can't be done—it just requires a careful balance.

The timid writer, of course, will decide not to show that key event at all, or will use telling rather than showing:

> We finally got Johnny into a decent school, Bill's job was settling down, and I could forget about those people and their terrible phone calls for hours at a time. I thought everything was going to be all right, until I heard someone screaming and pounding on my door one day. I knew at once that those people hadn't forgotten me, that they had done something terrible, just like they said. I opened the door. It was my neighbor, Rainie. "He just drove off!" she cried. "Matt's calling the ambulance—"
> There's no point in me telling you about the next few days. If you have a child of your own, you already know; if you don't, you can't possibly understand. They didn't try to contact me until we got home from Johnny's burial. Maybe it was a sense of decency—presumably they have children, too. More likely they were waiting until they thought I was calmed down enough to be rational. To listen.
> I listened. I still had a husband and two other children.

The narrator isn't out on the street watching when her child is killed. No horrifying moment as she realizes that the truck is going to jump the sidewalk and hit her son. No descriptions of a crumpled body on the street. For a first-person narrator to describe such things at all might seem ghoulish. To adequately express the emotions might be impossible. To describe it all coldly would be too clinical. Yet to skip over the events, as in the example, is rather coy.

Choose one. Maybe coyness is in character; maybe the character is clinical. Maybe you're a good enough writer to tell the immediate feelings of a mother who watched her child die—without getting maudlin or grotesque. These choices are all available.

But there are several other choices to keep in mind. You can decide to use a different narrator. Why not the neighbor woman, Rainie? Make her the protagonist's close confidante, so she can be closely involved in this woman's struggle. She can actually see the accident with the less passionate horror of a bystander, avoiding the much stronger emotions of a parent. She has enough distance to be a clear, direct narrator; enough closeness to witness everything.

Or you can use a third-person narrator—with all the drawbacks and benefits that entails. We'll discuss those later.

Arthur Conan Doyle chose well in deciding not to have Sherlock Holmes narrate his own stories. Using Watson as narrator allowed Doyle to withhold information from the audience without being unfair. Holmes knew certain information, but Watson didn't, so Watson could tell us all that he knew in the order he found it out, without spoiling the surprise. Since Watson never knows as much as Holmes, neither do we.

There is another benefit, though. Imagine if we had to listen to Holmes's intellectual, arrogant tone through every word of the story. Instead of admiring his godlike mind from below, we would find him insufferably conceited. He might even be ridiculous. This is the choice Agatha Christie made with Hercule Poirot—but Poirot was never worshipped as audiences have worshipped Sherlock Holmes.

The narrator's voice is your greatest asset—and your greatest drawback. Your first-person narrator can't be a bore, or your story will be boring. She can't describe herself performing noble acts, or she will seem vain for having told the tale at all.

Yet you can tell us much about your narrator by showing him do a brave, heroic act without him giving us a sign that he realizes the act was heroic at all. Or he can do something terrible, all the while explaining exactly why his crime was not a crime at all, but a necessary act—while we listen in horror.

She wouldn't be quiet, even when I tried to tell her how important it was for her not to say those things. There's some things a man just doesn't have to put up with from a woman. You listen to them blab on all the time about their girl friends and going shopping and what the kids did, and you figure that's just what women's heads are full of. But when she starts getting down on a man for doing what men do, well, that's over the line, that's more than a man has to put up with. What she's really doing, she's just trying to get you to prove to her that you really *are* a man, maybe sometimes just because you've been too tired sometimes, or too nice about it in bed, so you hear her talking like that, you don't put your hands in your pockets. You knock her around, you let her know that you still got the power in your arm, you still got the strength to be the man she needs you to be. It hurts her, of course, but it hurts her sweet, that's what my dad always said, she gets a bloody lip but it tastes sweet to her because she knows she's got a real man. Only this time she just wouldn't quiet down, she just kept yelling at me and saying crap that I don't have to put up with, and then she kept trying to go out onto the street and spread all our family business all over the neighborhood, and I couldn't let her do that, could I? You wouldn't either, man, and don't tell me you never hit your woman a little bit harder than you meant to, what with her mouthing off.

We may not *love* this character, but we know him better from hearing his version of his actions than we ever would by hearing them described by someone else. This passage ostensibly defends the narrator's mistreatment of his wife, but in fact it reveals very clearly his monstrous misconception of the way other people think and feel. That's one of the best reasons to use first person—to let us live for a while in a strange or twisted world, to see the world as someone else sees it. Yet because the narrator is not the author, but rather a character, the readers know that the author doesn't necessarily agree with the narrator. In fact, in this passage, if I handled the irony properly, it should be clear to a late-twentieth-century reader that the author is completely *out* of sympathy with the narrator.

# NO FOURTH WALL

A third-person narrator flits like an invisible bird from place to place—readers don't usually spend much time worrying about how she happens to know all this stuff, or why she's writing it down. The narrator is a storyteller, plain and simple; we ignore her, and listen to the tale.

But the first-person narrator is physically taking part in the story. Therefore, he must have some reason for telling the story. By implication, he must also have some idea of who his audience is. Even though you, the author, may be maintaining a fourth wall between your characters and your readers, he, the narrator, is *not* keeping that fourth wall between himself and the audience *he* thinks he's telling the story to.

The most common way of dealing with this problem has always been the frame story. Several people gather, conversing; one thing leads to another, until one begins to entertain or inform all the others by telling the main story. No one expects anything significant to happen in the frame—it's just an excuse for the first-person narrator to tell his story to an audience that is *not* the reader of the book. The frame is told in third person; only the tale-within-a-tale is told in first person.

You know of many examples, I'm sure. Rudyard Kipling used the device often; H. G. Wells's *The Time Machine* has a frame story, as do countless tales-told-in-a-bar. One drawback is that such stories are oral, and so you deny yourself the use of formal written language. Another problem is that since the story opens with the frame, if the frame is dull the audience may never get to the story you really care about.

The frame is not the only way to deal with the fact that the character is narrating a story. Some first-person stories are told as epistolaries, letters from one person to another (*The Color Purple*, for instance). Some are cast as speeches, diary entries, essays, explanations to a judge, confessions to an analyst (remember the punchline at the end of *Portnoy's Complaint*?). The narrator's purpose in writing may be to tell a curious tale, to persuade the presumed audience to a course of action, to excuse the narrator for some crime. Or the narrator may be explaining why he admires his friend, who is the protagonist of the story—which is presumably the reason why Watson set down his tales of Sherlock Holmes and Archie Goodwin told us of the exploits of Nero Wolfe.

In choosing a first-person narrator you should have in mind what his reason is for telling the tale; tale-telling is part of his character. Whether you explain her purpose or not, knowing it yourself will help you shape and control the presentation of the story; it will help establish which events the character would tell and which she would leave out, which she would lie about and which she would tell straight.

## UNRELIABLE NARRATORS

What? Your first-person narrator might lie? Of course. But if you mean him to be a liar, you must find ways to let your audience know that he is unreliable.

The easiest way is to have him get caught in one lie and admit it—the audience immediately begins to suspect him of lying about other things, too. Even then, your audience has a right to expect that you, the author, will let them know *which* of the narrator's statements to believe and which are lies.

One way to clue in the audience is to establish another character, *not* the narrator, whose word we trust, and let her corroborate the key events that really happened. Usually this corroboration takes place in scenes within the story, but some storytellers go to the extreme of letting this more reliable narrator take over the first-person narration part of the way through.

Switching first-person narrators in mid-story is usually ineffective and always difficult, because it violates the illusion that the character is "really" telling the tale. But if you find you must change narrators, it helps to give your readers some clue. For instance, if the first eight chapters are narrated by Nora, you might put in a division page that says, "Part I: Nora." When Pete takes over as narrator, again you put in a page that is blank except for the words "Part II: Pete." Or you could establish multiple narrators in a frame—both characters are present in the bar or the courtroom, and we expect both to tell their parts of the story.

More difficult than changing to a more-reliable narrator is the technique of letting us know the truth of the story by implication. The narrator is lying about the things that matter to him; you must therefore carefully let us know his *motive* for lying so that we'll know which parts of his story would need to be faked to accomplish his purpose. Is he concealing the facts about his own crimes? Then you can lead us to doubt his words concerning his own alibi or his own reaction to the crime. Is the story a letter in which the narrator is trying to persuade another character of his faithful love for her? Then obviously we will doubt his story about what actually went on when he was alone in the room with her rival.

The use of an unreliable narrator can add a delicious element of uncertainty to a story, with occasional revisions of the readers' understanding of all that went before. But used badly, or to excess, the unreliable narrator leaves the reader wondering why he's bothering to read the story, or furious that the author never let him know what "really" happened. It's a dangerous thing to attempt, and only occasionally worth doing.

One exception, just to show you what it's like when it's done well, is Thomas Gavin's brilliant novel *The Last Film of Emile Vico*. The first-person narrator is a 1930s movie cameraman, writing the book as a memoir of his relationship with Vico, who has recently disappeared under mysterious circumstances. But we soon realize that the narrator, Griswold Farley, suspects himself of murdering Vico—or rather suspects the other personality that occasionally dominates him, a figure he calls Spyhawk. He suspects Spyhawk because Spyhawk seems to know more about the events surrounding Vico's disappearance than Farley himself knows. However, Farley can't be sure—in the past, Spyhawk has caused Farley to feel guilt for wrongs that he didn't commit. Thus Farley himself knows that his own memories are not reliable; nor can he trust the feelings Spyhawk gives him. The result is that the entire novel is structured as an idea story—Farley and the reader are trying to discover the truth about the mystery of Vico's disappearance and Farley's involvement in it.

Another reason to study Gavin's book is that he handles the first-person point of view so expertly. The narrator constantly *sees* everything from a camera's-eye view, as if he observes even his own life through a lens; indeed, his alternate personality is exactly the kind of "spy" that a cameraman represents. This motif shows up throughout the narrative, so that it's part of the narrator's self; after a short time, the reader is no longer consciously aware of it, yet continues to see the story as if framed in a camera's shot.

At the beginning of chapter eight, as Farley launches into a flashback, he switches to present tense, because he is writing this part of his memoir as if it were a movie script. Instead of being an odd, inappropriate choice, present tense has purpose and meaning within the story; it is exactly appropriate for what narrator Farley and author Gavin are trying to accomplish.

# DISTANCE IN TIME

One thing Gavin is wrestling with in *The Last Film of Emile Vico* is a problem that comes with all first-person narrators: the problem of time. The narrator, as a participant in the events, is telling about what happened in the *past*. He is looking backward. He is distant in time from the story itself.

Contrast this with the third-person narrator. Even though most third-person accounts are told in past tense, they feel quite immediate. There is not necessarily any sense of the narrator *remembering* the events. They are recounted as they are experienced. There is no distance in time.

However, with third person there *is* distance in space. That is, the narrator, though she can dip into one or more minds, is never a person who is actually there. She is always an invisible observer, always at some distance.

So first person is distant in time, third person in space. Consciously or not, storytellers struggle to break down both barriers and achieve immediacy. The use of present tense and stream of consciousness were attempts to bridge the first-person time barrier—with little success, I might add, since both techniques tend to drive away the vast majority of the potential audience. The use of deep penetration in the limited third person is an attempt to break down the barrier of space in that narrative voice, and it works very well; thus it has become the most widely used narrative approach. (I'll explain "deep penetration" when I deal with third person in Chapter 17.)

One way to minimize the distance in time is to have the first-person narrator tell the story in chunks, writing it as the story goes along. Gavin does this in *Emile Vico*. The memoir is begun in a hotel room, where the narrator is in hiding, afraid that a relentless-seeming police detective is going to find evidence linking him to Vico's disappearance. At the time the early chapters are written, the narrator himself does not know how things will come out. He does not know the end from the beginning, because the first part, at least, is written before the story has ended—solving another problem with first-person narration that I'll deal with more in a moment.

Another example of solving the time-distance problem is Gene Wolfe's historical novel *Soldier of the Mist*. The narrator is a former soldier, apparently a survivor of the invading Persian army at the time of Thermopylae. A wound—or a curse from the gods—has stolen from him his ability to retain long-term memory. He wakes up each morning remembering nothing from the night before. So the novel is written as the journal he keeps to remind himself of his entire life—the book becomes his memory. Each day he begins by reading all of the book to date, until it becomes too long; his friends or fellow travelers even have to remind him to read the book, because he forgets that he has written it. Therefore there are gaps during the times when he forgot the book existed, and what happened during those lost sections can never be recovered except for the few scraps of information that others can give him about himself.

Certainly this book has defeated the first-person time-distance problem—but, alas, at a high price, since we are forced to put up with some of the repetitions and irrelevancies that such an artless character would include in a book he is writing, not to entertain, but to inform himself. In short, the very truthfulness of the characterization makes it harder to maintain the intensity of emotional involvement, since reading itself becomes hard work under that circumstance. In the art of storytelling, every good thing has its price. In the case of Wolfe's and Gavin's books, the price is well worth paying—in my opinion. Other readers, though, may not agree. Each author has treated his first-person narrator more realistically, which opens his book to one group of readers; but in the process, the book has also been closed to another potential audience. That's what happens with every choice you make.

# WITHHOLDING INFORMATION

One technical problem with most first-person stories, arising out of distance in time, is that the narrator knows the end of the story. There's really nothing to stop him from announcing it from the start. Imagine a book that begins this way:

> In the Case of the Vanishing Hitchhiker, we found out by the end that the hitchhiker was really the long-lost daughter of the man who picked her up, traveling in disguise, and he never knew it until long after he killed her and threw her body into the newly poured cement foundation of his new office building.

After that sentence, there isn't much of the mystery left to wonder about through the rest of the book. Yet potentially the first-person narrator could give us such information at the beginning of most stories.

Telling the end at the beginning is a fatal error only with idea stories; many a character or milieu or event story thrives on the dramatic irony that comes from knowing the end from the beginning. Still, the fact that the first-person narrator *doesn't* tell us the ending is a constant, unconscious reminder of artifice. She is deliberately leaving us in suspense. So unless the narrator is supposed to *be* a mystery writer, leaving us in suspense is probably out of character for her.

This is not the problem it might be, because the contemporary community of writers and readers has developed a convention for dealing fairly with the reader in first-person stories. Readers allow the first-person narrator to withhold the ending, as long as he tells us at each stage in the story all that the character knew at that point in time.

If the narrator is a detective, he tells us everything that the barmaid told him after he gave her a sawbuck tip. He doesn't say, "She told me more, too, but I didn't realize how important it was till later," and then hold back the information until the end of the story—if he does more than a few times, we start to get annoyed, and properly so. The author is diddling with us. She is creating more distance between us and the story by making the narrator an artificer, our enemy in the quest for information instead of our ally. The author who does this usually thinks she's increasing the suspense. In fact, she's weakening the suspense by decreasing the readers' involvement with and trust in the narrator.

That was only a mild example. You've seen worse—and if you'll think back to your response at the time, you'll realize how annoying it was, how very ineffective and distancing. For instance, instead of saying "She told me more, too" at the time of the interview, some authors don't even say that much—they just have the character remember at some key moment later on, "I thought back and remembered something else the barmaid said, something that didn't seem important to me at the time." Now, if what he remembers is something he *told* us she said at the time, that's perfectly fair; but if this is new information to the reader, we have a right to feel that we've been improperly deceived.

The worst case is when the first-person narrator refuses to tell us something that *he himself did*. Some of the best writers have done this, of course, but that doesn't make it any less faulty. Here's a passage near the end of a mystery novel:

> Everything was clear in my mind now. Only a few things remained to be done, to set things up properly. I called Jim and asked him to make a couple of phone calls, and I stopped at the Seven-Eleven to buy a simple household article. Then I drove to Maynard's mansion and rang the doorbell. Everyone would be there that night, I knew.

Until now the narrator has been telling us everything he did at the time he did it. Now, though, he is deliberately withholding information about what he did—who it was that he asked Jim to call and what simple household article he bought. Now, if it has been established that the narrator is consciously writing a mystery story (as with Archie Goodwin in Rex Stout's mysteries), then the character is perfectly justified in violating the convention of telling what the narrator knew at the time he knew it. But if the narrator has *not* been established as a mystery writer, this technique will violate his character and introduce falseness into the tale.

The fact that the narrator is telling the story at all makes it obvious that whatever risks she went through in the course of the story, she lived through it, so putting the narrator in jeopardy of death won't be terribly convincing. There are other kinds of jeopardy, though, that can still work fine. While the first-person narrator can't die, that doesn't mean that terrible, irrevocable things can't happen to her. In Stephen King's *Misery*, one of the horrors of the book is that the narrator, though he obviously survived, still lost limbs and other appendages to his mad captor's blade. When his captor threatened to do awful things to him, we knew that those awful things could actually happen; the jeopardy was quite convincing.

# LAPSES

All these drawbacks to first-person narrative are problems that arise when you handle first person *well*. Alack, I'm forced to tell you the sad truth that first person is very difficult. Though first person is usually the first choice of the novice storyteller, since it seems so simple and natural, it is considerably harder to handle well than third person, so that the novice usually betrays himself.

Where do the mistakes come? Most commonly, the novice writer inadvertently confesses in the first page that the first-person narrator is a fraud, that he is merely a mask behind which an incompetent writer is trying to hide:

> I watched Nora from across the room, the way her hands danced in the air like mad ballerinas, graceful and yet far too busy. She was upset, worried about the upcoming deal. The people who tried to converse with her were all so boring, their talk so petty; yet she tried to act as if she were interested, even excited

about the subject at hand, so that they would never guess how tense she was. She thought back to how things began, back in Rotterdam in the last years before she met Pete and her life dissolved in ruins . . .

I don't need to go on, do I? There is no way in the world that the first-person narrator can possibly know what is worrying Nora, or her motives as she converses with other people. Still, he *might* be merely guessing at her thoughts or motives—until we get to the last sentence, where he gets inside her head for a flashback. This is simply impossible—it is a technique of third-person narrative, one which is completely unavailable to first-person narrators unless they happen to have supernatural powers. Yet you would be amazed how many young writers make this mistake.

The first-person flaws in this next example are more subtle:

I awoke with a brutal headache. My hand brushed a paper off my pillow as I reached across the bed. I opened my eyes and winced against the pain of the sunlight streaming through the window. I was overcome with a sense of terrible loss; grief streamed through me again. I got up and staggered to the bathroom, each step like a knife through my head. I took the aspirin bottle off the shelf, turned it upside down. I turned on the water and got into the shower. It beat down on my head, streamed down my face, rivulets pouring down my body, cleansing me. I toweled myself roughly, then dressed in the same clothes I had dropped on the bathroom floor. Grief was all I could think of, grief so deep I felt nauseated. There was nothing to eat in the kitchen except peanut butter, graham crackers, and baking soda. I put a teaspoon full of baking soda in a glass of water and drank it down.

The flaw here isn't that the passage is cold and melodramatic by turns—though of course it is. The flaw is that the first-person narrator is watching himself as if from a distance, not seeing inside his own head at all. He sees *what* he does, but never *why*. We watch him as if through a camera—but since he is the narrator, he wouldn't *watch* himself do these things, he would remember them from the inside.

He didn't *observe* these actions when they were going on, he performed them. Yet we are given no clue about what any of his actions mean. He might be hung over, but he might also be sick. And why are we told so much about the shower? What does the shower *mean*? Why does it matter? It seems like any other shower. We all get wet in the shower. We all have the water beat on our heads and stream down our faces; the whole point of showers is for them to cleanse us. There is no reason for us to be shown this particular shower, because it is no different from any other shower, and the narrator has given us no reason to think it means more than usual.

In fact, if a friend of yours were telling you a story, and he got off onto a tangent about his shower—"the water felt so good beating down on my head, streaming down my body, cleansing me"—wouldn't you tell him to forget about the stupid shower and get on with the *story*? Of course you would. So why should the reader, who is *not* your friend (and unlikely to become one, if you write like this), put up with such irrelevant nonsense?

The only seeming exceptions are the two melodramatic sentences about strong emotion: "I was overcome . . ." and "Grief was all I could think of . . ." Yet even here, we are not told *what* he is grieving about. So this barely qualifies as being inside the narrator's head. Instead we are given abstract *labels* for emotions, not the *experience* of those emotions, or the reasons why the narrator feels them.

If there is any point to using a first-person narrator, it is in order to experience everything through his perceptions, colored by his attitudes, driven by his motives—yet we got nothing of that in this sample. This supposedly first-person account is as impersonal as a phone book. It is also exactly what a majority of novices do when writing first-person accounts.

Here is the same passage told more as a real person might tell of it:

> I woke that morning with a brutal headache. I reached out for Nora, as usual, but the bed was empty. Just a piece of paper, which I brushed off my pillow, not caring to know what the note said. It wasn't from her. She hadn't been here for days. Months. When would I stop reaching for her? On my deathbed would I expect to find her there, and once again be disappointed? No, maybe on my deathbed she'd be there, watching me so she could enjoy the process, the bitch.
>
> I opened my eyes and regretted it at once—sunlight streaming through the window is never kind to a man with a hangover like the one I had. I got up and staggered to the bathroom, each step like a knife through my head. The shower was too cold, then too hot, and they don't make a brand of soap that could have made me feel clean. The aspirin bottle was empty, of course, but it didn't matter—there weren't enough aspirin in the world to deal with a headache like mine.
>
> I toweled myself roughly, punishing myself for being the kind of jerk who has to wake up alone. Then I got dressed. I wasn't completely uncivilized—I *thought* of putting on clean clothes. But it wasn't worth the effort. I put on the same clothes I had dropped on the bathroom floor.
>
> There was nothing to eat in the kitchen except peanut butter, graham crackers, and baking soda. The peanut butter and graham crackers made me want to puke. I put a teaspoon full of baking soda in a glass of water and drank it down. Turned out even worse than I expected. I went back into the bathroom and threw up. Oh what a beautiful morning.

This version, while it still doesn't tell us why Nora left, at least gives us more reason to care about what's going on. We aren't seeing the narrator from the outside, we're watching him from the inside—which is exactly what first-person narration is supposed to do.

Note that we get characterization this time, which was almost entirely missing from the first version of this passage. We know *why* his hand brushes the pillow; we know why he doesn't pick up the note. We know how he feels about Nora—not just nebulous and melodramatic feelings of grief, but clear, specific attitudes and emotions. He doesn't describe the shower, he responds to it—an attitude, not a photograph. We know *why* he decides to wear the dirty clothes from the day before.

Your first-person narrator might be the kind of person who doesn't easily confess his motives or his feelings. Of course, in that case one wonders why he would write the story at all, or why the author would be so self-destructive as to attempt to write a first-person story told by a taciturn character. If for some reason you do want to write a story told by such a character, even *he* would not write the first version of this passage. If he is not in the mood for confession, he would not describe his morning. In particular, he would not confess to such things as putting on dirty clothes; nor would he describe something as private as a shower.

If the first-person narrator doesn't want to confess anything personal, that is also an attitude, and will show up in his writing:

> Everything that happened to me this morning? All right, I woke up hung over and there wasn't any aspirin in the cabinet. I tried to settle my stomach with baking soda and ended up puking. I put on dirty clothes and went outside and spent the rest of the morning yelling obscenities at passing drivers and kicking dogs and little children. I ate lunch at McDonald's and didn't throw away my trash or stack my tray. That took me up till noon. Is that what you wanted to know?

First-person narration *must* reveal the narrator's character or it isn't worth doing. The narrator must be the kind of person who would tell the tale, and her motives and attitudes must show up in the story. If you find that you can't do this, then you have three choices: You can admit that first-person narrative isn't going to work in this story, and switch to third person; invent your first-person character and create her voice by discovering her attitudes, motives, expectations, and past; or experiment with other first-person narrators until you find one whose character you *can* create.

# CHAPTER ·17

# THIRD PERSON

MOST WRITERS DON'T ACTUALLY THINK OF THEMSELVES as God. We are much too humble for that. But within the world of our story, we do have nearly absolute power. Our characters live and die by our decisions; their families and friendships, location and livelihood depend on our whims. They go through the most terrible suffering because we thought it would be more interesting if they did, and just when they finally settle down to live a normal life again, we close the book and snuff them out.

Unfortunately, all that godlike power is usually used in private. We may be manipulating our characters like tormented puppets through the landscape of our own demented minds, but we conceal all that from our readers. All our artistry as performers of fiction is designed to give the audience the illusion that our characters do what they do for their own reasons, that our story is a natural, believable series of events.

The only time we can act out our godlike role in front of the audience is when we write using the third-person omniscient point of view.

## OMNISCIENT VS. LIMITED POINT OF VIEW

As an omniscient narrator, you float over the landscape wherever you want, moving from place to place in the twinkling of an eye. You pull the reader along with you like Superman taking Lois Lane out for a flight, and whenever you see something interesting, you explain to the reader exactly what's going on. You can show the reader every character's thoughts, dreams, memories, and desires; you can let the reader see any moment of the past or future.

The limited third-person narrator, on the other hand, doesn't fly freely over the landscape. Instead, the limited narrator is led through the story by one character, seeing only what that character sees; aware of what that character (the "viewpoint character") thinks and wants and remembers, but unable to do more than guess at any other character's inner life. You *can* switch viewpoint characters from time to time, but trading viewpoints requires a clear division—a chapter break or a line space. The limited third-person narrator can never change viewpoints in mid-scene.

## What Omniscient Narrators Do Best

Only the omniscient narrator can write passages like this:

> It took Pete two months to work up the courage to ask Nora out. She was so delicate-looking, so frail-boned, her skin translucent, her straw-brown hair wisping off into golden sparks around her face. How could a beer-and-football guy like Pete ever impress Nora Danzer? So he studied the kinds of things that fragile beauties are impressed with—the current exhibit at the Metropolitan Museum, the art of cinema; he drew the line at opera. When he was ready at last, he wrote his invitation on a whimsical Sandra Boynton card and left it on her desk with a single daffodil.
>
> He didn't leave his office, didn't dare to pass her desk until eleven o'clock. The single flower was in a slender vase. She looked up at him and smiled that gentle smile and said, "I've never been asked so sweetly. Of course I'll go."
>
> Taking her out was like taking a final exam. Pete knew he was failing, but he couldn't figure out why. He kept bumbling along, trying to impress Nora with his sensitivity, never guessing that Nora was much more comfortable with beer-and-football types. She had grown up with brothers who thought that "fun" was any outdoor game that left scabs. She had often told her friends that all but six of her delicate, fragile bones had been broken during childhood—at least she could hardly remember a time when she didn't have a cast on some part of her body. She liked rowdiness, laughter, crude humor and general silliness; she had thought Pete was like that, from the way he bantered and joked with the others at the office.
>
> So all Pete's talk about the relative merits of the comic visions of Woody Allen and Groucho Marx only confused and intimidated her. She was sure that if she tried to change the subject to things *she* cared about—the 'Skins' chances of getting a third Super Bowl victory in the 80s, for instance—he would gaze at her with surprise and contempt, and take her home. She didn't want to go home. She wanted to be at an easy, comfortable bar somewhere, getting slightly drunk and laughing with Pete's buddies.
>
> So did Pete. After all, Pete was the guy who had run the length of the bar at Hokey's, naked, because Walter Payton didn't score a touchdown in Super Bowl XX. Why did he think he belonged with someone as refined as Nora? He was sure she saw through his disguise and knew he was just another former high school jock—that's why her eyes were glazing over while he talked.
>
> They sipped their tasteless Perrier, ate as if three asparagus spears and a dime-sized medallion of flounder made a meal, and pretended they were deeply interested in Polanski's post-American movies. If only each had known that the other slept through most of *Tess*.

In this story fragment, I tried to show the omniscient point of view at its best. Because the narrator can see into both Pete's and Nora's minds, switching back and forth at will, we know things that neither character knows; the pleasure of this scene is that neither character's point of view is accurate, but ours is.

No other point of view but omniscient would allow a narrator to say that last sentence: "If only each had known that the other slept through most of *Tess*."

If either Pete or Nora were a first-person narrator, we would have seen that scene from only one point of view. We would have shared in that character's misunderstanding of the other. Later, of course, there could be a scene in which they confess the truth to each other; at that point we would think back to their horrible first date and realize that it was all a ridiculous mistake. But we would not have the pleasure or the tension of knowing it was a mistake while the scene was actually happening. (Unless, of course, the first-person narrator violated the time-flow of the story and closed the scene by saying, "Later I found out that Nora had slept through most of *Tess*. It was one more thing we had in common." But such a reminder that all these events happened long ago would usually be a gross mistake in a first-person account because it would distance the reader from the immediacy of the story.) A limited third-person narrator would also be forced to show us the scene from only one character's point of view at a time. But limited third-person offers a few more options than first person. We could still have that later confession scene—in fact, a scene of unmasking is mandatory in a story that hinges on characters misunderstanding each other's true nature.

## Changing Viewpoint Characters

The limited narrator can also change viewpoint characters. Not in mid-scene or even mid-paragraph, as the omniscient narrator does, but from one scene to another, as long as there is a clear transitional break. The most obvious transitional break, and therefore the one that works best, is the chapter break. If chapter one is from Pete's point of view—with his worries about asking Nora out for a date, his preparation for the "final exam," and so on—then chapter two can be from Nora's point of view. We'll remember how anxious Pete was to keep "delicate" Nora from guessing that he was really a beer-drinking jock, so as we see the date from Nora's point of view, with her memories of her brothers playing roughly in the yard, her longing to talk football and drink beer in a bar, we'll get most of the delicious irony of knowing the truth about two characters who are deceiving each other too well.

But what if you want to write a short story, not a book? Can't you switch viewpoint characters without having to resort to a chapter structure?

Yes. The next-clearest transitional device in fiction is the "line space"—a double-double space if you work on a typewriter, two hard carriage returns if you work on a word processor. It looks like this:

In your manuscript, however, you must mark a line space so the typesetting and layout will know that it's a deliberate space that should appear in the finished book. Usually a line space is marked in manuscript with three asterisks, like this:

\*     \*     \*

The asterisks will usually appear in the finished book or magazine only if the line space falls at a page break. The rest of the time they'll be deleted, leaving only a blank line.

The first part of our story, using Pete as the viewpoint character, ends with the line space. Readers are trained to recognize a line space as a signal that a major change is taking place in the story—a change of location, a long passage of time, or a change in viewpoint character. However, you must be careful that you establish what the change is *immediately* after the line space. The first sentence should use Nora's name and make it clear that the narrator is now following her point of view. The first paragraph should also let us know, directly or by implication, where she is and how long it has been since the events just before the line space.

A change of viewpoint character is the most difficult transition for readers to make. (All right, a jump of 900 years and a change of planet might be harder, but usually time and place changes are a matter of a few days and a few miles.) It's a lot easier for readers to adapt to the viewpoint change if they have already met the new viewpoint character, and it's even easier if the new viewpoint character is already very important in the story. In this case, because the section from Pete's viewpoint is focused on his feelings and plans for Nora, we won't have any confusion at all when the section immediately after the line space begins:

> Nora had never seen nouvelle cuisine before. To her the half-empty plate looked like someone in the kitchen had decided to put her on a diet. Had Pete called ahead to tell them she was too fat or something?

Since the section before focused on Pete's upcoming date with Nora, readers will remember easily who Nora is, and will have little trouble guessing from this opening that Nora is now out on the date with Pete.

Just as important is the fact that this paragraph immediately establishes Nora's point of view. In the last section, we would have become used to seeing everything from Pete's perspective, getting his thoughts and attitudes and memories. The first sentence after the line break gives us information about Nora that Pete would not know—her unfamiliarity with nouvelle cuisine. His point of view has been clearly violated; hers is being clearly established. The second sentence gives her attitude—her humorously paranoid guess about the chef's motive for putting such a small amount of food on a plate. And to complete the viewpoint shift, the third sentence starts showing us Pete, our previous viewpoint character, only this time from her point of view—her uncertainty about how he is judging her. Since Pete's viewpoint section would have shown us how he practically worshipped Nora and thought she was the most fragile, beautiful woman he'd ever known, having Nora speculate that Pete might think she was too fat lets us know that Nora's self-image is wildly different from Pete's image of her. The viewpoint shift is complete in three sentences, and readers will settle in comfortably with Nora's point of view.

Because we've had experience with Pete's point of view, the limited third-person version of the dinner scene would have most of the irony we had in the omniscient version. Presumably the previous section, from Pete's point of view, would have told us about his buck-naked run along the bar at Hokey's after losing a football bet, so when Nora starts wishing she could talk about football during dinner, we'll remember Pete's football fanaticism and realize that if Pete would just stop pretending to be what he thinks Nora is, the real Nora would certainly enjoy the real Pete. The irony is working. We don't have to wait for a later confession scene, as we would in first person. By changing viewpoint characters, a limited third-person narrator can get most of the same kind of narrative effects as an omniscient narrator.

What the limited third-person narrator can't do is match the omniscient narrator's brevity. The omniscient passage was six paragraphs long. The limited third-person version would have to be far longer. Pete's viewpoint section, to feel complete, would have to be far longer than the two-and-a-half paragraphs he gets in the omniscient passage. To develop his point of view effectively, we'd have to go into much more detail about his preparations for asking Nora out. Perhaps we'd establish his network of relationships at work, show him trying to find out more about her, show him trying to change his image to fit what he thinks she'll want. By the time we are ready to change viewpoint characters, we have to know Pete well enough that his view of the world—and especially of himself and Nora—will stay in our memory throughout the section from Nora's point of view.

The omniscient narrator can tell more story and reveal more character in less time than it takes the limited third-person narrator. That's the greatest advantage of the omniscient narrator.

## The Limited Narrator's Advantage

If the limited narrator takes so much longer to do the same job as the omniscient narrator, why do we need the limited third-person narrator at all? Why, for heaven's sake, is limited third-person the overwhelmingly dominant narrative voice in American fiction today?

It's a matter of distance. As the omniscient narrator slips in and out of different characters' minds, he keeps the reader from fully engaging with any of the characters. The omniscient passage quoted above is far more presentational than representational—we're constantly being reminded that the narrator is telling us a story about Pete and Nora. We never get deeply enough involved with either of them to fully identify with them, to begin to feel what they're feeling. Instead of sharing Nora's frustration or Pete's bafflement, we are forced to take a distant, ironic, amused stance, watching what they do but not experiencing it.

The limited third-person strategy is to trade time for distance. Sure, we spend more time getting through the same amount of story, but in return we get a much deeper, more intense involvement with the lives of the viewpoint characters. The omniscient narrator is always there, tugging at our hands, pulling us from place to place. We see everything and everybody as the *narrator* sees them, not as the characters see them. We are always outside looking in.

For instance, whose point of view are we getting in this sentence? "He kept bumbling along, trying to impress Nora with his sensitivity, never guessing that Nora was much more comfortable with beer-and-football types." Perhaps Pete sees himself as "bumbling along," and certainly we are seeing inside his head as we see him "trying to impress Nora with his sensitivity"—but would he actually use those words to describe himself? Is he really so cynical that he thinks of himself as *faking* sensitivity? Or does he think that he's actually trying to *become*, not "sensitive," but worthy of her? We're getting an attitude here, but it isn't really Pete's attitude—it's the narrator's. The narrator sees Pete as bumbling and trying to fake sensitivity.

Likewise, when we are told that Nora "had often told her friends that all but six of her delicate, fragile bones had been broken during childhood," who is actually using the words "delicate" and "fragile"? Not Pete—he doesn't know what Nora has told her friends. And not Nora— she doesn't see herself as delicate and fragile, it's Pete who does. The phrase "delicate, fragile bones" is a direct echo of Pete's assessment of Nora as "delicate-looking, frail-boned" in the first paragraph, yet it is inserted ironically into Nora's memory of her own childhood. Again, the narrator is openly intruding into the story, nudging the reader into seeing the humor of the situation.

"She liked rowdiness, laughter, crude humor, and general silliness," says the narrator. But that isn't the way Nora would think of it. If that sentence were written from her point of view, it would be more like this:

> She liked guys who knew how to have a good time, get a little rowdy, have some laughs. She thought of telling him the joke about Mickey Mouse and Minnie Mouse getting a divorce, but she knew a guy like Pete would never appreciate a punchline with the $f$-word in it.

To let us know, from *Nora's* point of view, that she likes crude humor, we have to see a sample of the humor she likes—if she is not the over-literate type Pete thinks she is, she is also unlikely to think of her own taste in humor as "crude."

These two sentences from Nora's viewpoint take longer than the omniscient narrator's nine-word clause—but they also get us more deeply involved in Nora's character, give us a much clearer and more powerful view of the world as she sees it. The omniscient narrator sees the world through the wrong end of the binoculars—readers can see everything, but it all looks very small and far away. The limited third-person narrator can't let readers see as many different things in as short a period of time, but what the readers do see, they see "up close and personal."

Think of the limited third-person narrator as a combination of the most important *representational* features of the omniscient and first-person narrators. The limited narrator gets much closer to the viewpoint characters than the omniscient narrator can, giving readers the experience of living in the character's world—much the way the first-person narrator gives readers an intimate look at the world through the narrator's eyes. At the same time, with limited third-person narration the viewpoint character isn't actually telling the story, constantly reminding us that he is showing us himself, that he's looking back on these events from some point in the story's future.

Look at the way first-person and limited third-person narrators would deal with the event contained in this sentence from the omniscient narration: "When he was ready at last, he wrote his invitation on a whimsical Sandra Boynton card and left it on her desk with a single daffodil." Here's a possible limited third-person version:

> Pete got to work at seven-fifteen so he could leave the flower and the card for Nora without anybody watching. He filled the bud vase with water from the drinking fountain, put the daffodil in it, set the vase on Nora's desk, and leaned the envelope against it. It looked too formal, like a proposal of marriage or an apology or something. So he took the card out of the envelope. That was better. But the vase still bothered him—it would put too much pressure on her. If she turned him down, she could just throw away a flower, but she might feel like she had to return the vase. So he took the daffodil out of the vase and laid it on her desk. It got water all over her blotter. He grabbed a handful of her tissues and dabbed up the water and dried the stem of the flower. He laid down the card so it mostly covered the water spots and put the daffodil at an angle across the card. Then he wrapped the vase in the wet tissues, carried it to his office, and put it in the wastebasket.

We're getting an experience here that the omniscient version didn't provide—we're living through Pete's indecision and nervousness step by step, moment by moment. Even though it's in past tense, it feels like the present. We're identifying with Pete as we live through all the agonizing, trivial, yet vital strategic decisions in his campaign to give Nora exactly the right impression.

Would this work as well in first person? Try it and see:

> I got to work at seven-fifteen so I could leave the flower and the card for Nora without anybody watching. I filled the bud vase with water from the drinking fountain, put the daffodil in it, set the vase on Nora's desk, and leaned the envelope against it. It looked too formal, like a proposal of marriage or an apology or something. So I took the card out of the envelope. That was better. But the vase still bothered me—it would put too much pressure on her. If she turned me down, she could just throw away a flower, but she might feel like she had to return the vase. So I took the daffodil out of the vase and laid it on her desk. It got water all over her blotter. I grabbed a handful of her tissues and dabbed up the water and dried the stem of the flower. I laid down the card so it mostly covered the water spots and put the daffodil at an angle across the card. Then I wrapped the vase in the wet tissues, carried it to my office, and put it in the wastebasket.

At first glance, it might seem to be exactly the same. But the effect is different in at least one important way. The limited third-person version is told straight. You are clearly meant to empathize with Pete's indecision, to worry about whether Nora will accept the invitation, to care about what she thinks. You are living through the experience with Pete *as he lives it*.

But in the first-person version, there is an unconscious assumption about *why* Pete-the-narrator is telling this event in such detail. Even though the narrator makes no comments like "I was such a fool in those days," the time-distance effect is still operating. Pete-the-narrator obviously does not *still* feel the same uncertainty and anxiety that Pete-in-the-story felt, yet for some reason Pete-the-narrator has chosen to tell this incident. Since it shows Pete-in-the-story in such a vulnerable position, it would be unthinkable for Pete-the-narrator to recount it unless he thought it was amusing, unless he had clearly wised up somehow since then and could look back on his old self with comic distance. Without being conscious of it, readers will still adjust to this comic distance.

Furthermore, in a first-person narrative we would know that Nora must have some long-term importance to Pete, because he's telling about it; we know the first date must have worked out well or else her turndown was so spectacular it scarred Pete for life. In the limited third-person version, it's possible that the incident with Nora may end up being completely trivial to Pete—but vitally important to Nora. The third-person limited narration allows more story line options.

Of course, the differences between first-person and limited third-person narrators may seem very subtle in this example, because the two versions are identical except for changing "he" and "him" to "I" and "me." If I had actually been writing this incident in first person from the start, the differences would have been much greater, because the writing would have been shaped by Pete's own voice.

## MAKING UP YOUR MIND

Which type of narrator should you use? By now it should be clear that none is intrinsically, absolutely "better" than the others. All have been used by excellent writers to tell wonderful tales. But it still matters very much which one you choose. Here are some things to keep in mind.

1. First-person and omniscient narrations are by nature more presentational than limited third-person—readers will notice the narrator more. If your goal is to get your readers emotionally involved with your main characters, with minimal distraction from their belief in the story, then the limited third-person narrator is your best choice.

2. If you're writing humor, however, first-person or omniscient narration can help you create comic distance. These intrusive narrators can make wry comments or write with the kind of wit that calls attention to itself, without jarring or surprising a reader who is deeply involved with the characters.

3. If you want brevity, covering great spans of time and space or many characters without writing hundreds or thousands of pages to do it, the omniscient narrator may be your best choice.

4. If you want the sense of truth that comes from an eyewitness account, first person usually feels less fictional, more factual.

5. If you're uncertain of your ability as a *writer*, while you're quite confident of the strength of the *story*, the limited third-person narration invites a clean, unobtrusive writing style—a plain tale plainly told. You can still write beautifully using the limited third person, but your writing is

more likely to be ignored—thus covering a multitude of sins. However, if you know you can write dazzling prose but the story itself is often your weakness, the omniscient and the first person invite you to play with language even if it distracts a bit from the tale itself. In limited third person you can't have those lovely digressions that make Vonnegut, for instance, such a delight to read.

It's no accident that the overwhelming majority of fiction published today uses the limited third-person narrator. Most readers read for the sake of the story. They want to immerse themselves in the lives of the characters, and for that purpose, the limited third person is the best. It combines the flexibility of omniscience with the intensity of the first person. It's also an easier choice for a beginning writer, partly because it doesn't require the same level of mastery of the language, and partly because it will simply be more familiar and therefore feel more "natural" to writers who have grown up in a literary community where limited third-person predominates. (This is also the best reason for avoiding present tense; except for the academic/literary genre, present tense is very uncommon and so feels surprising, distracting, and "unnatural"; the more common past tense feels natural and invisible. Ironically, this makes past tense feel more immediate while present tense feels more distant; most readers are more likely to feel that a past-tense story is happening "now" than a present-tense story.)

Even though limited third person is currently the more common and ' natural" narrative choice, if the story you're telling needs omniscience or the first person, don't hesitate a moment to use the narrative strategy that's right for the story. Both omniscience and first person are still common enough that your audience won't be startled or put off by the choice (though first person is far more common than omniscience). If you use them, readers won't think you're showing off as they would if you were to write in some bizarre narrative voice, like second-person imperative mood or third-person plural future tense.

Just be aware of the limitations of each narrative strategy, so you can compensate for them. I've already mentioned Thomas Gavin's *The Last Film of Emile Vico*, which uses first person to brilliant effect. Likewise, Michael Bishop's *Unicorn Mountain* uses the omniscient viewpoint to excellent effect. Both writers pay a price for their choice, but it would be hard to imagine *Emile Vico* without the unique vision that comes from having a cinematographer as a narrator, and the marvelous feeling of tribal unity that comes at the end of *Unicorn Mountain* would be impossible if we had not seen almost every moment of the story from the viewpoint of practically every major character who was present.

# LEVELS OF PENETRATION

Once you've decided to write a limited third-person narration, you still have a choice to make: how deeply to penetrate the viewpoint character's mind.

Look at Figure 1, which represents the omniscient point of view. The camera is looking down on the scene—it can see everything. The dotted lines represent the narrator's ability to also show us everything going on inside every character's head—but we always see the scene as a whole from the *narrator's* point of view, and the narrator is not in the scene. We are never inside the scene; we are always watching from a distance.

Figure 2 represents the first-person narration. Now we see inside only one character's head, the narrator-in-the-story, and we see only what the narrator saw, experiencing the world as he experienced it—but we still watch from a distance, because it is all told from the perspective of the

**Figure 1**
*The omniscient narrator*

**Figure 2**
*The first-person narrator*

present narrator recounting events in his past. Even though the present narrator and the narrator-in-the-story are the "same" person, there is still a gulf between them.

The limited third-person narration is like first person in that we see only the scenes that the viewpoint character is in, and see only the viewpoint character's mind; it's like omniscience in that we see the action of the story unfolding now instead of remembering it later. We are not far separated from the action in either space or time.

But how deeply have we penetrated the viewpoint character's mind? Figure 3 is light penetration; we can see inside the viewpoint character's mind, we observe only scenes where the viewpoint character is present— but we don't actually experience the scenes as if we were seeing them through the viewpoint character's eyes. The narrator tells what happens

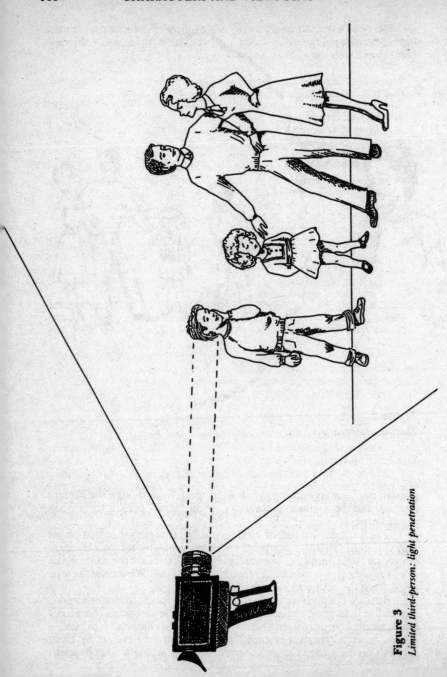

**Figure 3**
*Limited third-person: light penetration*

in the scene in a neutral voice, only giving us the viewpoint character's attitudes when the narrator turns away from the scene and dips into the viewpoint character's mind:

> Pete waited fifteen minutes before Nora showed up wearing a vivid blue dress that Pete had never seen before. "Do you like it?" asked Nora.
> It looks outrageous, thought Pete, like neon woven into cloth. "Terrific," he said, smiling.
> Nora studied Pete's face for a moment, then glared. "You always want me to be frowsy and boring," she said.

Figure 4 shows deep penetration, in which we *do* experience the scenes as if we were seeing them through the viewpoint character's eyes. We don't see things as they really happen, we see them only as Pete thinks they happen. We are so closely involved with the viewpoint character's thoughts that we don't have to dip into his mind; we never really leave:

> Pete wasn't surprised that Nora was fifteen minutes late, and of course she showed up wearing a new dress. A blue dress. No, not just blue. *Vivid* blue, like neon woven into cloth.
> "Do you like it?" asked Nora.
> Pete forced himself to smile. "Terrific."
> As usual, she could read his mind despite his best efforts to be a cheerful, easy-to-get-along-with hypocrite. She glared at him. "You always want me to be frowsy and boring."

In the deep-penetration version, we never need a tag like "Pete thought," because we're getting his thoughts all along. The phrase "of course" in the first sentence is not the narrator's comment, it's Pete's. The passage "A blue dress. No, not just blue. *Vivid* blue . . ." is not the narrator commenting on the dress—it's Pete who's judging what Nora wears.

When Pete says "terrific" and smiles, the light-penetration version sees his smile from the outside; the deep-penetration version is more like first person, telling us something about the motivation behind the smile: Pete has to force himself to smile.

Where the light-penetration version tells us that Nora studied Pete's face before she realized he was lying, the deep-penetration passage says that Nora could read Pete's mind. We know, of course, that Nora can't *really* read Pete's mind; that's just the way it feels to Pete. With deep penetration, the viewpoint character's attitude colors everything that happens. Unlike first person, however, we're getting the viewpoint character's attitude *at the time of the events*, not his memory of that attitude or his attitude as he looks back on the event.

Figure 5 shows another alternative: the cinematic point of view. In this version of limited third person, we only see what the viewpoint character is present to see—but we *never* see inside his or anyone else's head. It is as if the narrator were a movie camera looking over the viewpoint character's shoulder, going where he goes, turning when he turns, noticing what he notices—but never showing anything but what the eye can see, never hearing anything but what the ear can hear:

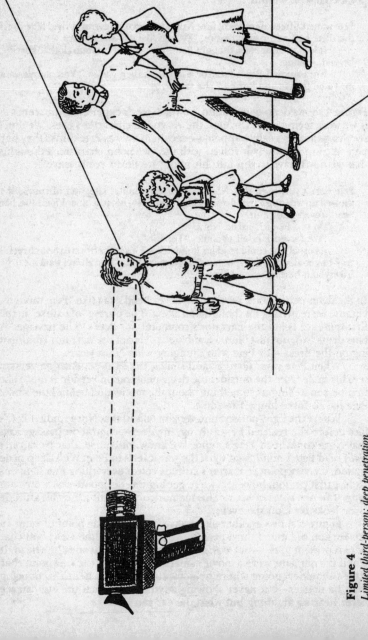

**Figure 4**
*Limited third-person: deep penetration*

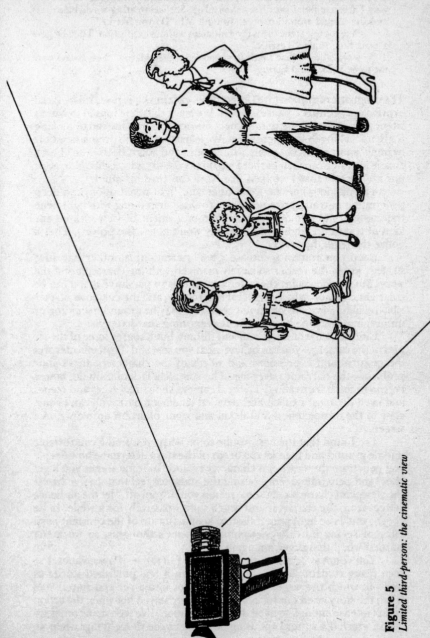

**Figure 5**
*Limited third-person: the cinematic view*

When Pete arrived, Nora wasn't there. He sighed and immediately sat down to wait. Fifteen minutes later Nora showed up. She was wearing a vivid blue dress, and she turned around once, showing it off. "Do you like it?"

Pete looked at the dress for a moment without expression. Then he gave a weak little smile. "Terrific."

Nora studied Pete's face for a moment, then glared. "You always want me to be frowsy and boring."

The cinematic narration gives *no* attitude, except as it is revealed by facial expressions, gestures, pauses, words. We learn that Pete is used to Nora's lateness only because he immediately sits down to wait instead of looking for her or calling to see where she is. We learn that Nora's dress is new only by implication, when she turns around once and asks if he likes it. The cinematic narrator can't tell us that Pete thinks the dress looks like blue neon, nor are we told that Pete feels like Nora can read his mind.

The dividing lines between cinematic, light-penetration, and deep-penetration narratives are not firm. You can drift along with light penetration, then slip into deep penetration or a cinematic view without any kind of transition, and readers usually won't notice the process. They'll notice the *result*, however.

Deep penetration is intense, "hot" narration; no other narrative strategy keeps the reader so closely involved with the character and the story. But the viewpoint character's attitude is so pervasive that it can become annoying or exhausting if carried too far, and the narrative isn't terribly reliable, since the viewpoint character may be misunderstanding or misjudging everyone he meets and everything that happens.

Cinematic narration is cool and distant, but it shares some of the virtues of the camera—you can believe what you see, and if you misinterpret the gestures and expressions and words of the characters, that's your problem—the narrator never lies. The complete lack of attitude, however, can become frustrating. The real camera shows real faces and scenes, and even the most explicit and detailed cinematic narration can't come close to the completeness and detail and vigor of action unfolding on a screen.

I've found that the best results come when you find a comfortable middle ground and then let the needs of the story determine how deeply you penetrate the viewpoint character's mind. In some scenes you'll get "hot" and penetrate deeply, letting the audience feel that they've *become* the viewpoint character. In some scenes you'll "cool off," let the audience retreat from the character and watch things passively for a while. In between, you'll use light penetration to keep us aware of the constant possibility of seeing into the viewpoint character's thoughts, so we aren't startled when things get hot again.

You've got to be aware, though, of the full range of possibilities. I've seen many student stories—and more than a few published stories as well—in which the writer unconsciously got into a rut and stayed cool when the story cried out for her to get hot, or stayed hot when the action wasn't intense enough to need deep penetration. I've seen many other stories in which the writer kept using he-thought/she-thought tags when we were so deeply into the character that even such tiny intrusions by the narrator were distracting and unnecessary.

No one level of penetration is likely to be right for a whole story. The use of cinematic narration as a consistent strategy for entire stories has been in vogue in recent years, in the mistaken notion that fiction can be improved by imitating film. The resulting fiction is almost always lame, since there isn't a writer alive whose prose is so good it can replace a camera at what a camera does best: taking in an entire moment at a glance. It takes a writer too many words to try to create that moment—after three paragraphs it isn't a moment anymore. The ironic thing is that cinematographers and film directors have struggled for years to try to make up for their inability to do what fiction does so easily: tell us what's going on inside a character's mind. How they struggle with camera angles and shadows! How the actors struggle with words and pauses, with the gentlest changes in expression, the slightest of gestures—all to convey to the audience what the fiction writer can express easily in a sentence or a phrase of deep penetration into the viewpoint character's mind.

I suspect, however, that one reason some writers resort—often inadvertently—to the cinematic viewpoint is that they don't *know* their viewpoint character well enough to show his attitude toward anything. They start writing without first inventing their characters, and instead of inventing and exploring them as they go along, they avoid their characters entirely, showing us only the most superficial of gestures, telling us only the words the characters say. The result is writing like this:

> She sat down beside him. "I'm so nervous," she said.
>
> "Nothing to be nervous about," he answered soothingly. "You'll do fine. You've been rehearsing your dance routines for months, and in just a few more minutes you'll go on stage and do just what I know you can do. Didn't I teach you everything I know?" he said jokingly.
>
> "It's easy for *you* to be confident, sitting down here," she said, gulping nervously at her drink.
>
> He laid his hand on her arm. "Steady, girl," he said. "You don't want the alcohol to get up and dance for you."
>
> She jerked her arm away. "I've been sober for months!" she snapped. "I can have a little drink to steady my nerves if I want! You don't have to be my nursemaid anymore."

Talk talk talk. The dialogue is being used for narrative purposes—to tell us that she's a dancer who's going on stage for an important performance after months of rehearsal, and that she has had a drinking problem in the past and he had some kind of caretaker role in her recovery from previous bouts of drunkenness. Attitude is being shown through the dialogue, too, by having the characters blurt out all their feelings—and in case we don't get it, the author adds words like *soothingly* and *jokingly* and *snapped*. The result? Melodrama. We're being forced to watch two complete strangers showing powerful emotions and talking about personal affairs that mean nothing to us. It would be embarrassing to watch in real life, and it's embarrassing and off-putting to read.

But with penetration somewhere between light and deep, we get a much more restrained, believable scene, and we end up knowing the characters far better:

> Pete could tell Nora was nervous even before she sat down beside him—she was jittery and her smile disappeared almost instantly. She stared off into space for a moment. Pete wondered if she was going over her routine again—she had done that a lot during the last few months, doing the steps and turns and kicks and leaps over and over in her mind, terrified that she'd forget something, make some mistake and get lost and stand there looking like an idiot the way she did two years ago in Phoenix. No matter how many times Pete reassured her that it was the alcohol that made her forget, she always answered by saying, "All the dead brain cells are still dead." Hell, maybe she was right. Maybe her memory wasn't what it used to be. But she still had the moves, she still had the body, and when she got on stage the musicians might as well pack up and go home, nobody would notice what they played, nobody would care, it was Nora in that pool of light on stage, doing things so daring and so dangerous and so sweet that you couldn't breathe for watching her.
>
> She reached out and put her hand around Pete's drink. He laid his hand gently on her arm.
>
> "I just wanted to see what you were drinking," she said.
>
> "Whiskey."
>
> He didn't move his hand. She shrugged in annoyance and pulled her arm away.
>
> Go ahead and be pissed off at me, kid, but no way is alcohol going up on that stage with you to dance.

In this version there are only two lines of spoken dialogue and nobody gets embarrassingly angry in public. Furthermore, you know both Pete and Nora far better than before, because you've seen Pete's memories of Nora's struggle with alcohol filtered through his own strong love for her—or at least for her dancing. We also know more about Nora's attitude toward herself; the "dead brain cells" line tells us that she thinks of herself as permanently damaged, so that she is terrified of dancing again.

The scene still isn't perfect, but it's a lot better now because we were able to get inside Pete's mind and see Nora through his eyes, with his attitude toward her, his knowledge of their shared past.

Yet the second scene wasn't all deep penetration. While Pete's memories were deep and hot, the incident with the drink is cinematic and cool. We aren't told why Pete lays his hand gently on her arm—we already know about her drinking problem and we can guess. Nor do we need to be told that she's lying when she says "I just wanted to see what you were drinking," or what he's feeling when he answers with a single word and refuses to move his hand. We already know enough about their relationship that we supply our own heat for the scene. And yet we can drop back into deep penetration with the last paragraph, without even needing "he thought" to tell us we're back inside Pete's head.

Mastery of different levels of penetration is a vital part of bringing your characters to life. This is where you have the most control over your readers' experience, where you have the best chance to determine how well readers will know your characters and how much they'll care.

# CHAPTER 18

# A PRIVATE POPULATION EXPLOSION

WE'VE COME A LONG WAY THROUGH THIS BOOK, from invention of your characters to analysis of their role in the story, from making your characters sympathetic to letting your readers see inside your characters' minds.

Good characterization isn't a simple recipe to follow—there are too many possibilities, too many variables for any writer ever to put down a story and say, "There. The characterization is finished."

As long as your mind is alert to possibilities, your characters will grow and develop and deepen and change with every outline you make and every draft you write.

And as you become more aware of what's possible in characterization, the more experience you get in storytelling as a whole, the better the decisions you'll make and the fuller and more believable your characters will be.

If you're serious about storytelling, you'll write many stories and people them with hundreds of different characters. Even though all the characters are created by your own imagination, you still come to know them just as your readers do, except that you'll know them better and care about them even more.

Sometimes, looking back on something you wrote years before, you'll find one of your characters doing or saying something that will astonish you. How did I know she'd say that? you'll wonder. How did I ever know that *that* was who she was?

You'll realize then what your readers already know: that the people in your fictional world are worth knowing. Because you took the time and trouble to discover them, develop them, and present them skillfully, your readers will know those fictional people of yours far better than they'll ever understand the people of flesh and blood around them.

If your fictional vision was a good and truthful one, your characters will help your readers understand their families, their friends, their enemies, and the countless mysterious and dangerous strangers who will touch their lives, powerfully and irresistibly. And you, looking back, will join them in saying a resounding Yes to the people in your tales.

Yes. I know you, I believe in you, you're important to me. Yes.

# INDEX

## A

Abilities, 12
Absurdism, 123
Academic-literary fiction, 38, 48, 50, 52, 95, 96, 131, 163
Accent, 10, 99; Israeli, 62; New York Jewish, 99, 100, 103; regional, 143; southern, 127
Account: eyewitness, 128, 162; first person, 153, 157; third person, 148, 149
Action, 65, 107
Active characters, 66
"Aesthetic distance," 96
Agent Orange, 38
Agony: of defeat, 68; physical, 68
Alice (in Wonderland), 56
*Alien*, 71, 78, 86
*Aliens*, 71
Allegory, 42, 52
Allen, Woody, 12, 100, 156
Alternate personality, 148
Altruism, 80
*Amadeus*, 78
Amateur, 43, 107
Analogy, 30
Anderson, Macon, 136
Anguish, 76
Antipathy, 36, 76, 79, 87, 89, 92
Archetypal, 22, 106
Art of storytelling, 149
Artifice, 159
Asterisks, 157
*Atlas Shrugged*, 121
Attitude(s), 7, 10, 27, 29, 30, 31, 38, 42, 44, 49, 50, 78, 83, 85, 86, 91, 97, 101, 107-111, 127, 130, 138, 142, 153, 154, 158, 160, 167, 170
Audience: first, 15; natural, 57, 59
Author-as-hero, 96
Awe, 96, 98

## B

Baby squirrel, 101, 102
Babysitting, 17-22
Background, 1, 27, 61, 66
"Bad guys," 37, 76, 86, 91, 92

Balance, 48, 55, 67, 93, 144
Balancing act, 85
*Barretts of Wimpole Street*, 86, 87
Barrier, 132, 149
Behavior: causes of, 129; changes of, 122; misinterpreting, 7; patterns of, 122, 123
Bellow, Saul, 96
Benny, Jack, 101
Betrayal, 6, 28, 53, 54, 63, 69, 87, 89, 151
*Beverly Hills Cop*, 62, 100, 106
*Bible*, 44, 45, 89
Bishop, Michael, 30, 163
Blind (color/gender), 7
Body, 13
Bond, James, 86, 94
Boredom, 42, 50, 145
Break: chapter, 157; line, 158; page, 157; transitional, 157
*Broadcast News*, 70
Bully, 86, 87, 89, 92
Bumstead, Dagwood, 13
*Butch Cassidy & the Sundance Kid*, 63
Butler, Rhett, 86, 96, 111

## C

Cabdriver, 60, 63, 64
Caernarvon Castle, 135
Camera's eye-view, 148
Candy, John, 104
Caper stories, 51, 52, 82
Captain Blood, 96
Caricature, 22
Causal questions, 17-21, 24, 32
Cause: beyond control, 121; of change, 121-123; and result, 17, 27
Chandler, Raymond, 121
Change, 119, 120, 122, 129; attitude, 29; cause of, 121-123; characters, 23, 51, 157, 159; environment, 121; inexplicable, 120; justifying, 122, 123; permanent, 52; viewpoints, 155, 158
Chapter break, 157
Character(s), 48, 52, 53, 56; active, 66; "anti-hero," 76; assassin, 5, 63,

87, 88; avenger, 87; "bad guy,"
76, 91, 92; balanced, 38;
behavior, 4, 6; bring to life, 172;
bully, 86, 89; comic, 99, 100,
102, 104; common man, 93, 95,
98; dangerous, 65; flesh out, 38;
frequency of appearance, 65;
from nowhere, 39, 111; getting
to know, 4-8; habits, 11; hero, 5,
12, 35, 70-72, 76, 86, 87, 91, 92,
94, 95, 98, 102; hierarchy of,
66; ideas for, 17, 25;
interrogating, 17-21; lovable
rogue, 85; madman, 90, 92;
main, 23, 26, 35, 39, 49, 51, 52,
62, 63, 66, 69, 75, 76, 78, 79,
88, 91, 95, 96, 107, 111, 130,
162; major, 14, 15, 35, 50, 59,
60, 64, 65, 66, 104, 122, 163;
memorable, 65, 70; minor, 14,
35, 59-62, 64-66, 97, 104;
negative, 92; oathbreaker, 89;
one-to-a-race, 57; point of view,
66, 67; powerful, 70; questions
to ask of, 16; ranking of, 66;
sadist, 86, 87; savior, 71, 80, 81;
self-appointed, 88, 89;
self-serving, 88, 89;
split-personality, 127; standing
for ideas, 52; story, 52, 53;
suggested by story, 34;
sympathetic, 66, 173; title, 39,
65; unbelievable, 105;
unfamiliar, 8; we hate, 86; we
love, 79; what he means to do,
6; viewpoint, 128, 155, 158, 160,
167, 170, 171; you really know,
28
Characterization, 2, 5, 13, 48, 51, 52,
53, 54, 57, 58, 61, 63, 104, 115,
149, 153; full, 52, 53, 64;
richer-than-normal, 52;
stereotypes, 10
Charity, act of, 16
*Cheers,* 73
*China Syndrome, The,* 37
Choice, degree of, 70
*Chronicles of Thomas Covenant the*

*Unbeliever,* 54
Cinematic: narration, 170-172; point
of view, 167; view, 170, 171
Cinematographer, 1, 163, 171
Classifying, 7, 8
Cleverness, 85
Cliché, 2, 22, 23, 32, 45, 66, 82, 93,
106, 132
Climax, 55, 70
Clinical, 144, 145
Clues, 99
Colonna, Jerry, 55
*Color Purple, The,* 146
Comedians, 104, 134
Comedic personas, 135
Comedy, 93, 99, 104, 123; of humors,
104; stand-up, 134; writer, 100
Comic, 91, 100, 103, 104, 106, 156;
characters, 69, 99; coolness,
103; distance, 162; sidekick, 55;
situation, 26; writing, 102
Common: man, 93, 95; people, 93
Compare, 7, 30
Complications, 1, 21, 35, 56
Compulsive, 64, 85, 116
*Conan the Barbarian,* 106
Confession scene, 159
Conflict, 35, 75, 76
Confusion, 15, 42, 43
"Connecting the Unconnected," 39
Connections. *See* Relationships
Consistency, maintain, 45
Contract with the reader, 54, 55
Contradiction, 8
Control, 67, 74, 76, 102, 126, 172
Controlled disbelief, 99, 100, 104
Conventional choices, 132
Conventions, literary, 132, 133, 151
Cool (Cinematic), 170, 172
"Cool off," 170
Corroborate, 147
Cosmic connections, 73
Costume, 1, 103
*Count of Monte Cristo, The,* 54
Courage, 83
Cowards, 104
Crazy. *See* Insanity
Crime, 87

Culture, 49, 50, 56, 72
Curiosity, 8, 11, 79

**D**

Daffodil, 156, 161
*Dead Zone, The,* 69
"Dear Reader," 136, 138
*Death of a Salesman,* 95
Deceive, 10, 150, 157
Decisions, 41, 44, 45, 48; present, 113;
    to change, 53
Deep penetration, 149, 167, 170-172
Degree of choice, 70
Dependability, 84
Description. *See* Physical
Details, 1, 27, 28, 29, 44, 105, 106
Detective, 51, 94, 116, 149, 150
Detective novels, 51, 107
Device(s), 11
Dialect: dictation, 126; regional, 127
Dialogue, record, 26
Digression(s), 55, 57
Dilemma, 56, 59, 60
Direct address, 130, 135
Director(s), 1, 55, 60, 171
Dirty Harry, 111
Disbelief, suspension of, 134
Discover characters, 45
Discrimination, racial, 10
Disguise, 28, 135
Disorder, 54, 73
Dissection, 132
Distance, 159: comic, 162; in space,
    148, 149; in time, 148-150;
    time-distance effect, 161; watch
    from a, 164
Distracting, 42, 45, 50, 60, 61, 162,
    171
Doing a "Take," 100, 101, 102
*Dollmaker, The,* 71
Donaldson, Stephen R., 94
Downplaying, 102, 103
Doyle, Arthur Conan, 145
Draftee, 83
Drag, men in, 103
Dramatic, 140, 141; irony, 150;
    literature, 131; vs. narrative,
    140
Dream(s), 39, 82, 95, 97

**E**

*E.T.,* 78
Eccentricities, 51, 52, 62, 104
Eccentricity, 62, 103, 104
Editorial resistance, 78
Educated, 143
Educational fiction, 38
*Elephant Man,* 72
Elven-folk, 25, 56

Emotion(s), 29, 68, 69, 70, 76, 144,
    145, 153, 171
Emotional, 144; involvement, 16, 38,
    59, 74, 76, 138, 149, 162; pain,
    68, 69, 81; stakes, 68
Empathize, 69, 100
*Ender's Game,* 39, 78
Enlighten, dazzle vs., 133
Environment, 121, 122
Epiphany, 95
Epistolaries, 146
Ethnic traits, 19
Events(s), 48, 49, 53, 54, 56, 107, 110,
    113, 126, 129, 135, 139, 140,
    141, 147, 148, 155; important,
    65; key, 111; major, 144; past,
    28; recent, 113; story, 53;
    unbelievable, 105
Evil: force, 54; pure, 86
Exaggeration, 22-24, 27, 32, 40, 62,
    63, 65, 102-104
Examination, 107
Existential writers, 123
Exotic, 94
Expectation(s), 7, 9, 49, 50, 114, 115,
    121, 132, 154
Experimental, 132
Explain, why characters change, 123
Extreme(s), 12, 95, 134, 135
Eyewitness account, 128, 162

**F**

Fair: being, 37; play, courage and, 83
"Faith, hope and clarity," 16
False, 99
Falseness, 17
Familiar, 8
Family role, 9, 10
Fantasy, 12, 22, 25, 26, 42, 50, 94, 95,
    106
*Far From the Madding Crowd,* 12
Farce, 103, 123
Fiction, 130; bad, 27; historical, 38, 50;
    non-comic, 100; prose, 106;
    science, 12, 38, 48, 50, 52, 94,
    111; straight, 100
Fictional character, 14
Film, 100, 106
First impressions, 77
First person, 103, 130, 132, 146, 161;
    character, 154, 160; narrative,
    130, 143, 154, 162, 164;
    narrator, 103, 128, 144,
    146-149, 152, 154, 156, 160,
    163; story, 150, 153, 161
Flashback, 111-113, 148
*Fletch,* 51, 52
*Fletch, Too,* 51
*Fletch Won,* 51
Focus, 15, 23, 30, 37, 45, 49, 50, 54,

65, 66, 135, 158
Forest of Arden, 134, 135
*Fountainhead*, 121
Fourth wall, 134, 146
Fowles, John, 96
Frame story, 135, 146, 147
*Friday the 13th*, 91
Frequency of appearance, 65, 66
Frye, Northrop, 93
Future tense, 131

**G**

Gavin, Thomas, 148, 149, 163
General rule, 15, 82, 118
Genre(s), 94, 95, 107, 131;
    academic-literary fiction, 38, 48,
    50, 52, 95, 131, 163; caper
    stories, 51, 52, 82; comedy, 93,
    99, 104, 123; detective novels,
    94; fantasy, 94, 95; glitter
    romances, 94; historical fiction,
    38, 48, 50; horror, 69, 70, 95,
    151; mysteries, 48, 51, 94, 151;
    publishing, 48; romances, 93;
    Russian novels, 43; science
    fiction, 12, 38, 48, 50, 52, 95;
    slasher, 67, 71; thrillers, 48, 50,
    54, 94; westerns, 48, 50
Getting to know a character, 4-8
Ghoulish, 144
Gillis, Dobie, 100
Glitter romances, 94
*Godfather, The*, 87
*Godfather: Part II, The*, 87
Godot, 65
Goldman, James, 112
Goldman, William, 86, 135
"Good guys," 37, 86, 91
Goodwin, Archie, 147, 151
Gossip, 7, 130
Greeks, ancient, 93
Grief, 68-70, 153
Grotesque, 144
*Gulliver's Travels*, 49
Gut-level response, 16

**H**

Habits, 11, 13, 56, 115, 116, 127
Haig, Alexander, 88
Half-twist, 26
Hardy, Thomas, 99
Harmony, 16, 67, 73
Hatchet job, 27
*Havelok the Dane*, 54
Herbert, Frank, 50
Hero, 5, 12, 70, 71, 72, 86, 87, 91, 94,
    95, 98, 102; anti-hero, 76;
    author-as-hero, 96; and
    common man, 93; "good guys,"
    86, 91, 92; identify with, 95,
    105; non-heroic, 95; realistic,
    93; reluctant, 94; romantic, 93,
    96; savior, 71, 80, 81
Heroic, 145; proportion, 96; role, 121
Hersey, John, 135
Historical fiction, 38, 48, 50, 94
History, 10, 39, 128, 130
Holmes, Sherlock, 85, 145, 147
Horror, 69, 70, 95, 151
Hot narration, 170
How-to books, 131
"Huh?," 15, 24
*Humboldt's Gift*, 96
Humor, 55, 56, 62, 102, 156, 160
Hypochondriacs, 104
Hypocrite, 5, 104
Hypocrisy, 10
Hypothetical, 130

**I**

Idea(s), 17, 21, 37-39, 45, 48, 51, 52,
    57; by chance, 39; for
    characters, 25; from life, 25;
    from story, 34-36; from
    unrelated source, 39;
    interrogating an, 22, 23, 25; net,
    25, 32, 39, 40; servants of,
    36-39; story, 51, 52, 53, 54, 55,
    56, 150
Identity, 7, 12, 42
*Iliad*, 26
Illusion, 6, 135; of truth, 105, 155; of
    reality, 134
Imagination 2, 16, 29
Immediacy, 149
Imperative mood, 130, 131
Imperfections, endearing, 85
Implausible coincidence, 113
Implication(s), 147, 158
"In character," 127, 128
*Indiana Jones and the Temple of Doom*, 85
Individuality, 62
*Inherit the Wind*, 88, 89
Insanity, 69, 90, 91
Intellect, 89
Interrogating; the character, 17, 33;
    an idea, 22, 23, 25
Interview, 28, 29
Intrusive narrators, 162, 171
Invent, 1, 2, 27, 32, 39, 48; character,
    48, 54, 154
Invention, 2, 45, 46, 171; of
    character(s), 1, 28, 29, 173
Involvement, emotional, 68, 69, 138,
    159, 162
Irony, 6, 157-159, 160, 163, 191;
    dramatic, 150
Irving, John, 111
Isolde, 54
*It Happened One Night*, 72

**J**

Jeopardy, 70-72, 80, 96, 100, 117, 118, 151
Jobs, 9
Jonson, Ben, 104
Journal, 135, 137, 149
Journey, 140
Joyce, James, 121
Judgments, 8
Justification, 16, 27, 55, 117, 118, 122, 131
Justify, 53, 92, 122, 123, 151
Justifying, 27, 117

**K**

Kafka, Franz, 123
Key: decision, 113; events, 111, 112, 144, 147; moment, 150; scenes, 141, 144
*King Lear*, 73, 104, 136
King, Stephen, 69, 71, 95, 151
Kinski, Nastassia, 99

**L**

*L.A. Law*, 72, 73
Label(s), 41, 42, 153
*Lady Chatterly's Lover*, 121
Lancelot, 54
Landers, Ann, 39
Language 1, 126, 132, 146, 163; arcane, 132; calculating, 126; precise, 126
Lapses, 151-154
Larger than life, 98
*Last Film of Emile Vico, The*, 148, 149, 163
Lawrence, D. H., 121
Lawrence, Jerome, 89
LeCarre, John, 94
Lee, Robert E., 89
Letters, 39, 146
Level of penetration, 128, 163, 164, 172
Liar, 5, 147
Lie(s), 17, 37, 84, 123, 147
Light penetration, 167, 170, 171
Limited point-of-view, 159-161
Limited third person, 149, 155, 157, 158, 161-163, 165, 167
Lindholm, Megan, 94, 95
Line break, 158
Line space, 157, 158
Linguistic special effects, 131
*Lion in Winter, The*, 12, 112
Literary conventions, 132
Literature, dramatic, 131
*Lord of the Rings, The*, 50, 54, 56, 57, 65, 84, 111
*Love and Death*, 12
*Love Connection, The*, 137

**M**

Macbeth, 54, 88, 92, 104, 120
Macdonald, Ross, 121
Magic, 95
Magical powers, 100
Mandel, Howie, 104, 134
*Marathon Man*, 86
Marx Brothers, 104
Marx, Groucho, 156
Mask, 95
Maudlin, 144
McCullers, Carson, 88
Mcdonald, Gregory, 51
Melodrama(s), 34, 72, 103, 152, 171
Melodramatic, 21, 144, 153
*Member of the Wedding, The* 88
Memoir, 148, 149
Memories, 28, 31-33, 157, 158, 172
Memory, 2, 6, 16, 17, 27, 31, 32, 36, 63, 105, 112-114, 133, 141, 149, 160, 167
Metaphors, 127
MICE quotient, 48, 57
Milieu, 48, 49, 50, 53, 55-57, 60-62, 99
Miller, Arthur, 95, 96
Mimesis, 25
Mind: making up your, 162; net for ideas, 25; sorting process, 8; viewpoint character, 165, 171
Miracle Max, 99, 100, 103
Misconception, 132
Miser, 104
*Misery*, 69, 71, 151
Models, 27-29
Monologue, 2, 131
Monosyllable, 42
Mood, 62, 130
*Moonlighting*, 73, 100
Moral: issues, 76, value, 5
Morgenstern, 135
Motive(s), 5, 10, 13, 17, 21, 28, 29, 51, 87, 106, 107, 111, 120, 121, 147, 154
Mouse, Mickey and Minnie, 160
Mozart, Wolfgang Amadeus, 2
Mr. Arella, 32-34
Murder, 87
Murphy, Eddie, 62, 100, 101, 106
Musical names, 43, 44
Mysteries, 48, 94; classic English, 51; locked room, 51; murder, 51; puzzle, 51; Rex Stout, 151
Mystery, 52, 54, 94, 150; characters, 12, 42, 52, 56; novel, 151; writer, 150, 151

**N**

Naive identification, 96
Names, 41-43; musical, 43, 44
Narration, 66, 103, 132, 144, 149;

cinematic, 170, 171; first person, 129, 147; "hot," 170; patterns, 130

Narrative, 141, 142, 148, 171; dramatic vs. narrative, 140, 141; first person, 130, 143; present tense, 131; second person, 130; strategy, 129; voice(s), 130, 149

Narrator, 43, 66, 100, 101, 102, 107, 111, 114, 128, 129, 131, 135, 138, 139, 140, 142, 144, 145, 156, 159, 163-165; first person, 128, 143, 144, 146-148, 150, 151, 162; in-the-story, 164, 165; limited third person, 155, 162, 163; omniscient, 155, 162, 163; Pete-the-narrator, 161, 162; self-conscious, 136; third person, 145, 146

Narrators, 162; intrusive, 162, 171; multiple, 147; reliable, 147; unreliable, 147, 148

Narrator's eyes, 108

*National Geographic*, 40

Natural, 119-121, 163; audience, 57, 96; style, 128

Nature, true, 157

Network(s), 10, 116, 117; of relationships, 52, 117, 159

Neutral voice, 167

"New" memories, 32

News: broadcast, 130; papers, 130; stories, 39, 128

Niven, Larry, 2

Nobility, 98

Nonchalance, 103

Non-comic fiction, 100

Normative stories, 130

### O

Oathbreaker, 89

Objective(s), 17. 29

Observation(s), 9, 26

Obsessiveness, 12, 62-64, 85, 116

Oddness, 103, 104

Oedipus, 54, 73, 92, 104, 120

"Oh Yeah?," 14, 24, 134

Omniscient: vs. limited point-of-view, 155, 156; narrator, 155-163, 165; third person point-of-view, 155

*One Flew Over the Cuckoo's Nest*, 78, 79, 86, 87

Opinions, 7

Ordinariness, 66

Ordinary, 25, 66

Oversentimentality, 82

### P

Pace, 142, 143

Page break, 157

Pain, 68-70, 99, 101, 114, 118, 144; emotional, 68, 69; physical, 68

*Pamela*, 93

Parker, Robert, 12, 42, 52, 90, 94, 121

Passionate stories, 133

Passive: character, 66; memory, 113; process, 68

Past, 6, 13, 58, 111, 148; discovering, 154; implied, 114, 115; remembered, 111; revelation of, 107; tense, 130, 161, 163

Patronymic, 43

Patterns, 11, 42, 43, 53, 55, 94; of behavior, 122, 123; of lives, 115, 120, 122; of narration, 130; of speech, 126, 127

Pendulum, 93

Penetrated, 165

Penetration: deep, 149, 167, 171, 172; level of, 128, 163, 164, 171, 172; light, 167, 171

People: common, 94; everyday, 93; you know, 27

Person, 128-130, 132; first, 128-130, 132, 135, 146, 148, 150, 167; first . . . narrative, 143; first . . . narrator, 129, 143, 144, 146, 147, 152; limited third . . . narrator, 159; second, 128, 130, 131, 163; second . . . singular, 130; third, 128-130, 132, 137, 146, 149, 151, 161-163; third . . . narrator, 129, 130, 145, 146, 148, 152, 160; third . . . omniscient point-of-view, 155, 156, 164; third . . . plural, 130

Personal: opinion, 135; problems, 27

Personality: alternate, 148; different facets of, 11; split, 127

Persuasive fiction, 38

Philosophy, 131

Physical: appearance, 13; attractiveness, 79, 80, 85; beauty, 13, 72; changes, 119; description, 13, 80; handicaps, 13; locations, 49; pain, 68, 69; problems, 13; strength, 13; suffering, 81; torture, 68, 86, 87

Pinchot, Bronson, 62

Pinter, Harold, 123

Placeholders, 59, 60, 62

Plausible, 27

Play, 1, 65, 73, 122, 134

Plays, 12, 54, 65, 66, 73, 89, 121-123, 135, 140

Plot, 1, 2, 49, 52, 59, 63, 65

Point-of-view, 1, 2, 38, 66, 83, 138, 148, 155-157, 159, 160; cinematic, 167; character, 107, 128, 135, 156, 157; third person

omniscient, 163
Poirot, Hercule, 85, 145
Polemic, 36, 37, 39
Pollution, 36, 37, 39
*Poltergeist*, 70, 78
*Portnoy's Complaint*, 146
Preference(s), 12
Prejudice, 78
Present: action, 112, 113; anchor in the, 112; event, 112, 113; meaning of, 107; tense, 148, 149, 161, 163
Presentation, 134-137, 147, 159; vs. representation, 134-137, 159
Presentational, 138, 139, 162; theatre, 134
*Prince and the Pauper, The*, 54
*Princess Bride, The*, 99, 135, 136
Promise, 84, 89, 92
Proportion, heroic, 96
Prose fiction, 106
Protagonist, 53, 56, 136, 144, 145, 147
Psychological suffering, 81
Puppets, 117, 155
*Pygmalion*, 121

**Q**

Questions: and answers, 17-20; ask characters, 16; motive, 21; readers ask, 14; recent, 21

**R**

Racial, 10, 41
Radner, Gilda, 104
*Raiders of the Lost Ark*, 4, 73, 85
*Rainbow, The*, 121
Rand, Ayn, 121
Reader(s), 8, 12, 13, 14-16; contract with, 54-58
Reagan, Ronald, 88
Real-life, 5, 29, 69, 95, 119, 171; characters, 27; incidents, 27
"Realtime," 140
Realism, 95, 106, 111, 135
Realistic, 93, 98, 104; tradition, 96
Reality, 17, 44, 135
Redeeming virtues, 91
Redford, Robert, 79, 87, 140
Reed, Rex, 99
Regional traits, 10
Relationship(s), 1, 10, 13, 31, 33, 34, 36, 52, 53, 69, 91, 117, 127, 135, 148; among characters, 2, 11, 110, 120; author-character, 28; change, 33; connections, 10, 116; different, 10; mini-, 117
Remembered past, 111
Rendell, Ruth, 94
Representation, 134
Representational, 134-139, 150, 159,

160; play, 134; theatre, 134; write, 135, 138
Reputation, 6, 7, 13
Respect, 96
Response, gut-level, 16
Result(s), 17-21; question, 20, 21, 22, 23
Reveal self, 16
Revelation, 107
Revise(s), 2, 6, 107, 120
Revolutionary, 132
Rhetorical stance, 128
Rhythm, 142
*Road to Rio*, 55
*Robinson Crusoe*, 93
Role(s), 1, 38, 52, 53, 55, 60, 62, 80, 173; changes in, 119, 122; heroic, 121; major, 35; story, 34
Romance, 72, 73, 111, 135
Romans, ancient, 93
Romantic, 93, 94, 104; characters, 94; excess, 94; hero, 96; impulse, 95; opportunity, 110; tradition, 54, 94, 111
*Romeo and Juliet*, 65
Rule of thumb, 43, 55, 59, 66, 70, 87, 112, 113, 133
Rumpole, 94
Russian novel, 43
Rut, 42

**S**

Sacrifice, 70, 80
Sadism, 86
Sadist, 86, 87, 92
*Saints*, 80, 135
Sartre, Jean-Paul, 123
Savior, 71, 80, 81
Scene, confession, 159
Scenes, key, 141, 144
Science, 128, 130
Science fiction, 12, 38, 48, 50, 52
Scientific theories, 131
Screen, on and off, 140
Screenwriter, 135, 140
Second person, 128, 130, 131
Second person imperative mood, 163
Self: -alienation, 31; -appointed, 88, 89; -psychoanalysis, 32; -serving, 88
Sense of past, 111
Serendipity, 39
Serious character, 105
"Serious literature," 95
Setting, 1, 9, 11, 23, 34, 49, 50, 60
Seventh grade, 32, 33
Sex, 9, 30, 38, 72
Sexual: attractiveness, 30, 38, 72; harmony, 73; stereotypes, 9, 117; tension, 72, 73

Shakespeare, William, 88, 103, 135
Shallow, 5, 21, 23, 70, 139
Shaw, George Bernard, 121
Shaw, Robert, 87
Show, 140-142
Sidhe, 25, 26
Signal: comic, 101; your reader, 122, 158
Signs and portents, 73, 74
Similes, 127
Simplicity vs. complexity, 21
*Six Days of the Condor*, 140
Slasher movies, 69, 71
Smiley, George, 94
"So What?," 14, 24
*Soldier of the Mist*, 149
Sorting process, 8
Southerners, 10, 127
Space, 165; barrier of, 149; deliberate, 157; distance in, 148, 149; line space, 157, 158
Speak, to the audience, 135
*Speaker for the Dead*, 39
Speaking vs. writing, 126
Special effects, linguistic, 131
Speculation, 39, 40, 131
Speech, 126, 143; style of, 128
Spenser, Edmund, 12, 42, 52, 90, 94, 121
Split personality, 127
Stalker, 71
Stand-up comedy, 134
*Star Wars* series, 85
Starting point, 28, 29, 32, 38
Stereotype(s), 7-11, 23, 50, 52, 61, 62, 63, 109, 112; age, 9; community, 64; conscious use of, 10; costume, 103; ethnic, 10; exceptions to, 10; family role, 9, 10; foreigners, 10; identifying according to, 7; job, 9; northerners, 10; Oriental-Americans, 10; physical, 10, 13; power of, 9; racial, 9, 10, 57; sex, 9; sexual, 117; southerners, 10; westerners, 10
Stereotyping, 7, 8, 9, 61
*Sting, The*, 87
Story, 14-16, 21, 23, 34, 51-57, 112, 113, 128, 130, 132, 133, 139, 150, 157; character, 52, 53, 57, 150; choice, 16; event, 54, 150; detective, 51, 107; history, 128; idea, 51; ideas from, 34-36; milieu, 54, 150; news, 128; normative, 130; passionate and truthful, 133; possibilities, 11, 12, 21, 24, 33; powerful, 21; presentational, 139;

representational, 139; science, 128; short, 14, 157; wonderful, 40
Storyline, 50-52, 54-57, 162
Storyteller, 1, 2, 7, 8, 15, 37, 57, 93, 96, 103, 141, 149
Storytelling, 17, 45, 46, 57, 67, 72, 73, 136, 138, 149
Stout, Rex, 12, 151
Straight fiction, 100
Strange, strangeness, 8, 25, 31, 37, 50, 62, 66, 77, 107, 114, 122, 132, 173
Stranger(s), 8, 25, 31, 37, 173
Strong-willed, 149
Structure, 49-55, 57, 68, 135
Style: natural, 128; of speech, 128; writer's, 139
Stylistic patterns, 128
Subliminal clues, 9, 42
Subplot, 55, 56
Suffer, 99, 144
Suffering, 68-70, 80, 81, 83
*Superior Court*, 137
Superman, 12, 155
Suspense, 8, 15, 150
Suspension of disbelief, 134
Symbol(s), 38, 132
Symbolic, 42, 52
Symbolism, 52
Sympathize, 28, 53, 75, 81, 82, 108, 144
Sympathy, 66, 70, 75, 76, 78-80, 82, 83-88, 90-92, 99, 109, 110, 144, 146; vs. curiosity, 79
Syntax, 127

**T**

Tagged, 42
Taglines, 44
Tags, 43, 170
Tale-within-a-tale, 129, 130, 146
Talents, 12, 13
Tales-told-in-a-bar, 146
Tastes, 12, 13, 28
Teacher-by-example, 95
"Tell, Don't Show," 141, 142
Ten commandments, 130
Tense, 128, 130, 132; future, 131; past, 130, 132, 163; present, 130, 131, 148, 149, 163; strange, 132
Tension, 55, 68, 72, 73, 108, 142, 157; forms early stages of fear, 8; jeopardy, 118; sexual, 72, 73, 110
*Tess*, 99, 156, 157
*Tess of the d'Urbervilles*, 99
Theme(s), fictional, 31, 38, 120-123
Third person, 128-130, 132, 137, 146,

149, 151, 152, 155; limited . . .
narrator, 158, 159, 161;
narrator, 145, 148; omniscient
point-of-view, 155, 156, 164;
plural future tense, 163
"Thousand Ideas in an Hour, A,"
17-23
*Three Days of the Condor,* 140
Three Stooges, The, 104
Thrillers, 48, 50, 54, 94
Time, 148, 159, 165; barrier, 149;
-distance effect, 161; distance in,
148-150; film, 151; flow, 157;
passage of, 158; real, 140
*Time Machine,* 146
Timing, 104
Tir-Nan-Og, 25
"Toldness," 136
*Tom Jones,* 93
Tone, 1, 142
Tormentor, 71
Tragedy, 73
Tragi-comic, 121
Traits, 10, 76, 85, 97, 104; ethnic, 10;
regional, 10
Transform, 28, 121, 133
Transformation(s), 52, 119, 121-123;
character, 52
Transition, 158, 170
Transitional: break, 157; device, 157
Tristan, 54
*Tristram Shandy,* 93
Truth, illusion of, 105
Truthful stories, 133
*Twelfth Night,* 103
Twist(s), 1, 14, 22-24, 32, 38, 40, 51
Type(s), 50

**U**

Unbelievable, 105
Uncertainties, 15
Uncertainty, 8
Unconscious level, 8
Unconventional, 132
Underlying voice, 128
Understandability, 16
Uneducated, 143
Unfamiliar, 8, 50
*Unicorn Mountain,* 30, 163
Uniqueness, 95
Unmasked, 121
Unmasking, 157
Unreliable narrators, 147, 148
Updike, John, 96
Usurper(s), 54, 88, 89, 92
*Utopia,* 49

**V**

Vernacular, 132

Vico, Emile, 148
Victim, 70, 80, 81, 86, 87
Vietnam, 38, 75, 95
Viewpoint character, 66, 128, 155,
158-160, 165, 167, 170, 171
Viewpoints, trading, 155
Villain(s), 28, 34, 68, 70, 73, 86, 87,
89; understandable, 91, 92
Vindication, 89
Violence, 29
Vision: of hope, 17; of the world, 133
Vocabulary, 126, 127
Voice(s), 126-28, 132, 139, 143, 145,
149; narrative, 130; natural
style, 128; neutral, 167;
presentational, 138; underlying,
128
Volunteer, 83, 84
Vonnegut, Kurt, 78, 101, 135, 163

**W**

*Waiting for Godot,* 65
Walk-ons, 59-62
*Wall, The,* 135
Ward, Artemis, 143
Watergate, 54
Wells, H. G., 146
Westerns, 48, 50
Wexford, Inspector, 94
"What If?," 39
*Wheel of Fortune,* 137
"Whole Life," 111
*Who's Afraid of Virginia Woolf?,* 12
Wiggin, Ender, 78
Will: act of, 121; own, 121; to change,
121
Willing suspension of disbelief, 134
Witches, 88, 104, 120
Withholding information, 150
*Wizard of the Pigeons,* 95
Wolfe, Gene, 22, 149
Wolfe, Nero, 12, 85, 147
*Woman Under the Influence, A,* 91
"Wonderful Stories," 40
Wondering, 39, 40
*World According to Garp, The,* 111
Writer(s): attitude, 139; competence
of, 15; earn the title of, 1;
mystery, 150; objective of, 17;
representational, 135, 138;
screen, 135, 140; style, 139
Writing: good, 132; persuasive, 37;
presentational, 138, 139;
representational, 138, 139
*Wuthering Heights,* 54, 73, 120

**XYZ**

Yourself, ideas from, 29